S0-ANN-020

WITHDRAWN

Rethinking International Development Series
Series Editors: **Andy Sumner,** Fellow of the Vulnerability and Poverty Research Team, Institute of Development Studies, UK.
Ray Kiely, Professor of International Politics, Queen Mary University of London, UK.

Palgrave Macmillan is delighted to announce a new series dedicated to publishing cutting-edge titles that focus on the broad area of 'development'.
The core aims of the series are to present critical work that:

is cross disciplinary;
challenges orthodoxies;
reconciles theoretical depth with empirical research;
explores the frontiers of development studies in terms of 'development' in both North and South and global inter-connectedness;
reflects on claims to knowledge and intervening in other people's lives.

Titles include:

Simon Feeny and Matthew Clarke
THE MILLENNIUM DEVELOPMENT GOALS AND BEYOND
International Assistance to the Asia-Pacific

Niamh Gaynor
TRANSFORMING PARTICIPATION?
The Politics of Development in Malawi and Ireland

Xiaoming Huang, Alex C. Tan and Sekhar Bandyopadhyay (*editors*)
CHINA AND INDIA, AND THE END OF DEVELOPMENT MODELS

Sue Kenny and Matthew Clarke (*editors*)
CHALLENGING CAPACITY BUILDING
Comparative Perspectives

Sara C. Motta and Alf Gunvald Nilsen (*editors*)
SOCIAL MOVEMENTS IN THE GLOBAL SOUTH
Dispossession, Development and Resistance

Eric Rugraff, Diego Sánchez-Ancochea, Andy Sumner (*editors*)
TRANSNATIONAL CORPORATIONS AND DEVELOPMENT POLICY
Critical Perspectives

Rachel Sabates-Wheeler and Rayah Feldman (*editors*)
MIGRATION AND SOCIAL PROTECTION
Claiming Social Rights Beyond Borders

Jens Stilhoff Sörensen (*editor*)
CHALLENGING THE AID PARADIGM
Western Currents and Asian Alternatives

Andy Sumner and Meera Tiwari
AFTER 2015: INTERNATIONAL DEVELOPMENT POLICY AT A CROSSROADS

Rethinking International Development Series
Series Standing Order ISBN 978–0–230–53751–4 (hardback)

You can receive future titles in this series as they are published by placing a standing order. Please contact your bookseller or, in case of difficulty, write to us at the address below with your name and address, the title of the series and the ISBN quoted above.

Customer Services Department, Macmillan Distribution Ltd, Houndmills, Basingstoke, Hampshire RG21 6XS, England

---

China, India and the End of Development Models

Edited by

Xiaoming Huang
Professor of International Relations, Victoria University of Wellington, New Zealand

Alex C. Tan
Associate Professor of Political Science, University of Canterbury, New Zealand

and

Sekhar Bandyopadhyay
Professor of Asian History, Victoria University of Wellington, New Zealand

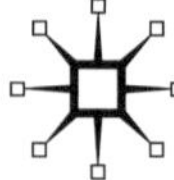

First published 2012 by
PALGRAVE MACMILLAN

Palgrave Macmillan in the UK is an imprint of Macmillan Publishers Limited, registered in England, company number 785998, of Houndmills, Basingstoke, Hampshire RG21 6XS.

Palgrave Macmillan in the US is a division of St Martin's Press LLC, 175 Fifth Avenue, New York, NY 10010.

Palgrave Macmillan is the global academic imprint of the above companies and has companies and representatives throughout the world.

Palgrave® and Macmillan® are registered trademarks in the United States, the United Kingdom, Europe and other countries.

ISBN 978–0–230–30158–0

This book is printed on paper suitable for recycling and made from fully managed and sustained forest sources. Logging, pulping and manufacturing processes are expected to conform to the environmental regulations of the country of origin.

A catalogue record for this book is available from the British Library.

A catalog record for this book is available from the Library of Congress.

10 9 8 7 6 5 4 3 2 1
21 20 19 18 17 16 15 14 13 12

Printed and bound in the United Stataes of America

Contents

List of Tables

List of Figures

List of Abbreviations

ABD	Asian Development Bank
ACHR	Asian Centre for Human Rights
AMC	asset management corporation
ASEAN	Association of Southeast Asian Nations
AWSJ	*Asian Wall Street Journal*
BIS	Bank of International Settlements
BUP	Bhumi Uchched Pratirodh Committee (Committee to Prevent Eviction from the Land)
CAR	capital adequacy ratio
CPC	Communist Party of China
CPI (M)	Communist Party of India (Marxist)
EFA	Education-for-All
EDI	Education-for-All Development Index
EFW	Economic Freedom of the World
EIU	Economist Intelligence Unit
EME	emerging market economy
EPI	Environmental Performance Index
FDI	foreign direct investment
FIE	foreign invested enterprise
FTA	free trade agreement
GATT	General Agreement on Tariffs and Trade
GCRI	Global Climate Risk Index
GDP	gross domestic product
HDI	Human Development Index
ICOR	incremental capital-output ratio
ICT	information and communication technology
IIT	Indian Institutes of Technology
IIM	Indian Institute of Management

ILO	International Labor Organization
IPR	intellectual property rights
JUH	Jamait-e-Ulema Hind
MFN	most-favored-nation
NHS	National Household Surveys
NPE	National Policy on Education
NPL	nonperforming loan
OECD	Organization for Economic Cooperation and Development
PWI	Proportional Environmental Impact
PPP	purchasing power parity
PRC	People's Republic of China
PWT	Penn World Tables
RMB	*renminbi*
SAARC	South Asian Association for Regional Cooperation
S&T	Science and Technology
SCE	state-controlled enterprise
SEZ	special economic zone
SIC	former Soviet Union, India and China
SOB	state-owned bank
SOE	state owned enterprise
TAA	Trade Adjustment Assistance
TFP	total factor productivity
TNC	transnational corporation
UNDP	United Nations Development Program
UNESCO	United Nations Economic, Scientific, and Cultural Organization
WEO	World Economic Outlook
WGI	Worldwide Governance Indicators
WTO	World Trade Organization

Notes on Contributors

Sekhar Bandyopadhyay is Professor of Asian History at Victoria University of Wellington. His primary research interest is in nationalism and the minorities in colonial and post-colonial India. He is also interested in the history of Indian migration and the Indian diaspora. Professor Bandyopadhyay is the author of *Decolonization in South Asia: Meanings of Freedom in Post-independence West Bengal* (Routledge 2009).

Zhiyue Bo is Senior Research Fellow at the East Asian Institute of the National University of Singapore. He obtained his Bachelor of Law and Master of Law in International Politics from Peking University and PhD in Political Science from the University of Chicago. Dr Bo has taught at Peking University, Roosevelt University, the University of Chicago, American University, St John Fisher College, Tarleton State University, and the Chinese University of Hong Kong. He is a recipient of the Trustees' Distinguished Scholar Award at St John Fisher College and the inaugural holder of the Joe and Theresa Long Endowed Chair in Social Sciences at Tarleton State University. Dr Bo's research interests include China's elite politics, Chinese provincial leaders, central-local relations, cross-strait relations, Sino-US relations, international relations theories, and global governance. He is the author of a trilogy on China's elite politics: *Chinese Provincial Leaders: Economic Performance and Political Mobility since 1949* (Sharpe 2002), *China's Elite Politics: Political Transition and Power Balancing* (World Scientific 2007), and *China's Elite Politics: Governance and Democratization* (World Scientific 2010).

Srikanta Chatterjee is an Emeritus Professor of Economics and Finance at Massey University. Professor Chatterjee holds a PhD from the London School of Economics. Professor Chatterjee's teaching areas include international trade, international finance, international business, the Asia-Pacific economies, and the development experiences of China and India. He has researched and published in all of these areas, and in the areas of income distribution and inequality, applied demand modeling, and computable general equilibrium modeling of trade policies. He has authored, co-authored, and edited six books, and published articles in *The Journal of Public Economics, The Economic Record, The Australian and New Zealand Journal of Statistics, The Journal of International Trade* and

The Journal of International Development. He has been involved in consultancy work at local, national, and international levels.

Zhenglai Deng is Distinguished Professor of Jurisprudence and Political Theory at Fudan University. Professor Deng is editor-in-chief of *Fudan China Studies* and *China Social Sciences Quarterly*. He is an adjunct professor, guest professor, or honorary professor at many Chinese universities including Jilin University, Zhejiang University, Nanjing University, Renmin University of China, Southwest University of Political Science and Law, Northwest University of Political Science and Law, Jiangxi University of Finance and Economics, Hubei University of Economics and Business, Nanjing Normal University, Hua Zhong Normal University, and University of Macau. Professor Deng's research has focused on legal philosophy, political philosophy, and various social science cross-disciplinary areas. He has published nearly 20 sole-authored books, around 20 translated books, and numerous edited books, including *State and Society: China's Civil Society*; *Research and Reflections: Autonomy of China's Social Sciences*; *Freedom and Order: Hayekian Social Theories*; *Hayekian Legal Philosophy*; *Rules, Order, and Ignorance: Hayekian Liberalism*, and *China's Legal Science: Where is it headed?*

Dilip K. Das is Professor of International Economics and International Finance and Director of the Institute of Asian Business, SolBridge International School of Business, Woosong University, South Korea. Prior to that, he has worked at INSEAD, France; and Graduate School of Business, Sydney University; and International Management Institute, India. Professor Das received BA and MA (Economics) from St John's College, Agra, India; and MPhil, and PhD in international economics from the University of Geneva, Switzerland. Professor Das's research interests focus on international finance and banking, international trade and WTO-related issues, international business and strategy, and the Asian economy, including Chinese and Japanese economies. His most recent interest is globalization and the global business environment. He is the author, co-author, and editor of 27 books, with the latest being *The Chinese Economic Renaissance: Apocalypse or Cornucopia* (Palgrave Macmillan 2008).

Xiaoming Huang is Professor of International Relations at Victoria University of Wellington, and Director of the Contemporary China Research Centre. Professor Huang received his PhD in international relations from University of Southern California, Los Angeles, and MA and BA in international relations from Peking University. Professor

Huang teaches East Asian politics, international relations of East Asia, and China's politics and international relations at Victoria University of Wellington. Professor Huang's research falls in the area of East Asia's political economy, the modern development of China, and the international relations of East Asia. His publications have appeared in *International Studies Quarterly, The Journal of International Relations and Development, The Journal of the Asia-Pacific Economy*, and elsewhere. He is the author of *The Rise and Fall of the East Asian Growth System: Institutional Competitiveness and Rapid Economic Growth* (Routledge 2005), *Politics in Pacific Asia* (Palgrave Macmillan 2009), and *The Institutional Dynamics of China's Great Transformation* (Routledge 2010).

Jun Fu is Professor of Political Economy and Executive Dean of the School of Government at Peking University. Professor Fu holds a BA from Beijing Foreign Studies University, an LLB from the Foreign Affairs College, and an MA and PhD, both from Harvard University. Professor Fu's teaching and research focuses on the interplay between hierarchies and markets. He is the author of *Institutions and Investments: Foreign Direct Investment in China during an Era of Reforms* (University of Michigan Press 2000), *Antitrust and Competition Policy: Economic Theory, International Experience, and Implications for China* (Peking University Press 2004), and *The Dao of the Wealth of Nations* (Peking University Press 2009).

Bruce Gilley is Assistant Professor of Political Science at the Hatfield School of Governance of Portland State University, USA. He earned his BA in International Relations at the University of Toronto. He went on to finish his MPhil in Economics at the University of Oxford and his PhD in Politics at Princeton University. Dr Gilley's research centers on democracy, legitimacy, and global politics. He is a specialist on the comparative politics of China and Asia. Dr Gilley is the author of four university-press books, including *China's Democratic Future* (2004) and *The Right to Rule: How States Win and Lose Legitimacy* (2009), in addition to several co-edited volumes. His articles have appeared in *Foreign Affairs, Comparative Political Studies*, and *The European Journal of Political Research*.

Lei Guang is Professor of Political Science and Director of the Center for Asian and Pacific Studies at San Diego State University, San Diego. Professor Guang joined the political science department at San Diego State University after receiving his PhD from the University of Minnesota in 1999. He has an MA in political science from the Johns

Hopkins University, and majored in English and American Studies in his college and postgraduate studies in China. Professor Guang's research has focused on the everyday politics of ordinary citizens, most notably in China, but also in other developing countries such as India. He has studied migrants, peasants, protesters, urban job seekers, and informal-sector workers, as well as the grandiose political discourses surrounding them. His scholarly publications have appeared in numerous edited volumes and in academic journals such as *Politics & Society, International Migration Review, Critical Asian Studies, Pacific Review, Journal of Contemporary China, China Quarterly, Modern China, Harvard China Review, International Review*, and *Dushu*.

Krishna Kumar is a Senior Economist at RAND, and directs the Program of Research and Policy in International Development. He is also a Professor at the Pardee RAND Graduate School of Public Policy, where he leads the Rosenfeld Program on Asian Development. Dr Kumar received his PhD in Economics from the University of Chicago. His research focuses on economic growth and development, particularly on the role of education and human capital. He has studied the strengths and weaknesses of the Chinese and Indian education systems, education policies for sub-Saharan African economies, the role of economic openness on education and growth, the role of general and skill-specific education in explaining US-Europe productivity differences, optimal subsidy for higher education in the US, and the role of social capital in economic development, among other topics. His research has been published in leading journals on economic growth and development and macroeconomics.

Ying Liu is a Visiting Professor at the School of Public and Environmental Affairs at Indiana University, and an Adjunct Researcher at the RAND Corporation in Santa Monica, California. Dr Liu received her PhD in Public Policy Analysis from Pardee RAND Graduate School; and a BA in economics and an MA in Political Science from Peking University. Her research interests include a wide range of public policy issues related to international development, particularly in the area of international education and health. She has examined education policies in countries such as Qatar, China, India, and the United States through various research projects at RAND and at the Harvard Center for Education Research.

Alex C. Tan is Associate Professor of Political Science at the University of Canterbury. He is also Senior Fellow at the John Goodwin Tower

Center for Political Studies at Southern Methodist University in Dallas, USA, and Research Associate of the National Cheng Chi University Election Study Center in Taipei. A former banker with HSBC in Taipei and a research fellow with Taiwan Institute of Economic Research, Dr Tan held academic appointments at the University of North Texas and at Southern Methodist University in United States and visiting professorships at Texas A&M University and Nihon University (Japan). Alex received his BA in Economics from the Ateneo de Manila University, MA in Economics from the University of California at Santa Barbara, and PhD in Political Science at Texas A&M University. Dr Tan's research focuses on comparative political parties, comparative political economy, and comparative politics of Taiwan, East Asia, and Western Europe.

Wing Thye Woo is Professor at University of California at Davis, Yangtze River Scholar at the Central University of Finance and Economics in Beijing, Director of the East Asia Program within The Earth Institute at Columbia University, and Non-resident Senior Fellow at the Brookings Institution. Professor Woo holds a BA (High Honours) in Economics and a BS in Engineering from Swarthmore College in 1976, and received an MA in Economics from Yale in 1978, and an MA and a PhD in Economics from Harvard in 1982. Professor Woo's current research focuses on the economic issues of East Asia (particularly, China, Indonesia, and Malaysia), international financial architecture, comparative economic growth, state enterprise restructuring, fiscal management, and exchange rate economics. He is the author of *Fiscal Management and Economic Reform in the People's Republic of China* (Oxford University Press 1995).

Jason Young is Lecturer in Political Science at Victoria University of Wellington. His most recent project focuses on labor markets, internal migration, and reform of the *huji* institution in China. He is a research associate of the Contemporary China Research Centre, member of the New Zealand Asian Studies Society and holder of the Victoria University of Wellington PhD Scholarship. His research interests include Chinese political development, the international relations of East Asia, and New Zealand–China trade.

1
Introduction: Development Experiences and Development Models

Xiaoming Huang

This book intends to achieve two objectives through a cross-disciplinary, comparative examination of the growth and development experiences of China and India in recent decades: to establish whether China and India exhibit a significant pattern or patterns of economic growth and development and share a set of factors that have been enabling their growth and development; and to understand how such a pattern and set of factors relate to the world's experiences of modern economic growth and development before them, as often conceptualized and debated in development models.

The first task is a challenge. In the past ten years or so, comparing China and India has become a real enterprise of its own.[1] Over the past 30 years, their impressive growth performances and development experiences have caused a new wave of global anxiety about the rise of power and wealth outside the developed world.[2] Much of the attention has been focused on the impact of the rising China and India on the global economic system, wealth distribution, and geopolitical relations. More pointedly, scholarly interests and debates have focused largely on how the rising China and India would change the international political and economic structure, how China and India share and differ on key economic indicators, and whether India or China would outperform the other in the long run. What is missing amidst the anxieties and fanfare about the two new "giants" is a genuine scholarly interest in an understanding of the conditions and dynamics of the economic growth and social transformation in these two unique countries of diverse economic, political, social, cultural, international, and historical conditions, and what the growth and development experiences of China and India mean for the world experiences of modern economic growth and development.

This latter interest above – that is, how the growth and development experiences of China and India fit into the large picture of the rise and expansion of the world modern economy, and perhaps increasingly the capitalist market economy – leads to the second aspect of our interest in this project. The record-breaking high-speed growth and expansion of the Chinese and Indian economies immediately reminds people of the miracle economies of East Asia in the second half of the twentieth century. Starting in the 1950s and 1960s with Japan, then the "four little dragons" in the 1960s and 1970s, then the extension of the "East Asian miracle" to the rest of the Pacific Asia in the 1980s and 1990s, and now China and India, scholars must have enough empirical evidence to revisit some of the perennial issues in post-war development research and debate: Is the developmental state essential for economic growth? Is export concentration inevitable? Are corporate groupings necessary? Do regime types matter? What role does law play in economic development? How do cultural and social relations contribute to economic and social development?

However, in contrast to the great fanfare of the impact of rising China and India, there is little interest in the growing body of literature on China and India to link this latest wave of rapid growth to the early waves of the rapid growth in Asia, and understand the broad implications of the growth and development experiences for the modern world economic system. The reasons for this are complicated indeed. Most observers and commentators have taken on the issue with an underlying assumption that China and India are different. Evidence from China and India offers seemingly opposite answers to almost every question above: China is seen as a classic example of the developmental state, while India is not. While India is a country of pluralist politics, China is not. China's growth has been dominated by exports, while India's is not. China is a society of Confucian tradition, while India is far away from Confucianism, culturally and socially. If China and India are so different and given China is so close to the Asian model of economic growth, it would seem to be an impossible mission to connect China and India together to the East Asian growth experiences just for the sake of constituting a "model."

If, however, our intentions here were not to use the latest Chinese and Indian experiences to vindicate the East Asian model, but rather to take the Chinese and Indian cases to revisit some of the key issues in the debates over the East Asian model, we would gain some new knowledge as to how modern economic growth and development work. Perhaps much of the earlier debates over the East Asian model experiences have been largely misled by limited historical experiences and empirical evidence. China and India may be able to fill in the empirical as well as theoretical gaps.

Beyond the East Asian model of economic growth, however, there seem to be even more interesting insights to gain from the significant experiences of China and India. The East Asian economic "miracle," along with the successes and failures in many other parts of the developing world, are often treated as instances of "unusual" experiences of economic start-off and catch-up, and a transition from a pre-modern, often subsistent, to a modern economy. There is a further and more telling disconnection between development economics on economies of developing countries and growth economics that focuses more on mature and advanced economies. The early "Atlantic miracle" from the seventeenth to nineteenth centuries (Polanyi 1944) laid the foundation for systematic inquiry and understanding of how the economy works under modern conditions, with labor, capital, and the market at its core. The Great Depression of the 1930s and the post-war miracles of Germany and Japan generated great interest and research into different ways of managing the market and different types of state-market relations, and thus different forms of capitalism (Albert 1993; Hall and Soskice 2001; Hollingsworth and Boyer 1997; Miller 2005; Shonfield 1965; and Streeck and Yamamura 2001).

The continual validity, dynamism, and diversity of modern capitalism, however, do not usually extend beyond the Atlantic miracle, with the unusual exception of Japan. The East Asian model economies, however impressive, have always been looked upon with suspicion and caution.[3] They are not real modern economies, or more precisely, modern capitalist market economies. They are twisted, distorted, crony, corrupt, or authoritarian forms of capitalism. In this conjuncture, the growth performance and development experiences of China and India are more interesting and timely because they provide rare contrasting cases of the success of modern economic growth. They will allow us to consider the underlying logic of the historical waves of the emergence and expansion of the modern economy, and in turn better understand the significance of the Chinese and Indian experiences.

For such an understanding of the broad implications, we will need to have a better understanding of the growth and development experiences themselves first. Are China and India wholly market economies now? Do China and India bring in new insights as to how the market economy works, how the state should relate to the market, and whether social order and economic dynamism can both be important values for an economy? Is there anything more fundamental for the working of the market economy that early-developed economies have not experienced or were unable to deal with? Is there a discernable pattern or "model" of growth generation and development enablement in China and/or India that distinguishes themselves from their predecessors?

This introductory chapter lays out in more detail the analytical framework that informs the work in this volume. This is a framework that places the development experiences of China and India in the context of the larger debate about different experiences and models of modern economic growth and development, from the Anglo-Saxon model in the early modern times and the Rhine model of the post War Germany, Sweden, Japan, and so on, and from the original modern capitalism in the more developed world to the East Asian model economies in post-war East Asia.

This chapter will first look at the empirical evidence of the patterns of economic growth in China and India on major economic and non-economic indicators as relevant to our discussion. While individual chapters will further explore and compare particular aspects of the empirical evidence, we provide here at the beginning a more general description of the economic growth of the two countries and a measurement of key variables considered to be critical for modern economic growth in the existing literature and previous debates. This will provide a valid basis for comparison of China and India, and allow them to be related to the broader experiences of modern economic growth and development.

We will then examine two sets of debates, or two significant fields of inquiry about modern economic growth and development, which surprisingly do not communicate to each other as much as they should have. The first one is mainstream growth economics, and comparative capitalism in particular, which focuses primarily on modern capitalist development in advanced economies; the second is development economics, which explores how modern economic growth and development is possible in the developing world, and uses largely different theoretical concepts and frameworks. The Anglo-Saxon model and the Rhine model are two dominant theoretical constructs of the first; the Latin American model and East Asian model are two of the latter. Finally, we will explore how China and India might fit into the world of the diverse experiences of modern economic growth, and provide organizing questions and hypotheses for the contributors for chapters in this volume.

1 Growth performance, pattern, and accounting

The history of modern economic development in China and India can both be traced back to the late 1940s when India became an independent sovereign state in 1947 and a unified China with an effective central government was established in 1949.[4] Interestingly, the subsequent early post-war decades witnessed very similar growth performances and patterns in these two countries, even though the two countries deferred significantly in their political systems and social structures. Under the strong influence of the nationalist ideology and the inspirations of economic catch up and modernization, found popular among newly independent new states in the early post-war Asia, Latin America, and Africa, similar economic development patterns evolved in China and India that featured centralized, bureaucratic, and nationalistic control of the planning and management of their economies. Indeed, the two economies shared a significant number of "socialist" features.[5] This period of the Chinese economy ran until the late 1970s when the Deng Xiaoping-led reform and opening-up started, while in India the socialist model continued until the early 1990s, when reforms and economic liberalization in 1991 were initiated by the Rao government.

The similar economic models were accompanied by a stable pattern of growth performance in these two countries. As Figure 1.1[6] shows, from 1950 to 1978, India's real GDP per capita was consistently twice of the level of China. The average rate of real GDP per capita growth (Figure 1.2) for India from 1950 to 1991 was 2.11 percent, while that for China in its respective socialist period from 1952 to 1976 was similarly 2.78 percent.

China started to close the gap with India in real GDP per capita from the 1980s and passed over India in 1991, the very same year India started its reform and liberalization. Since then, China has rapidly increased its lead. For the period of 1978–2009, China's annual growth rate in real GDP per capita is 8.63 percent, while for its own new economic period from 1991 to 2009; India's average growth rate is 4.94 percent. In 2009, China's real GDP per capita is 2.36 times higher than India's.

The growth patterns and performances of China and India in the past 60 years, as reflected in real GDP per capita change in Figure 1.1 and Figure 1.2, allow several observations. First, the post-war growth experiences are surprisingly similar: from the first period of "socialist" economy to the second period of reform, economic opening and liberalization, and transition to a capitalist market economy. Given the

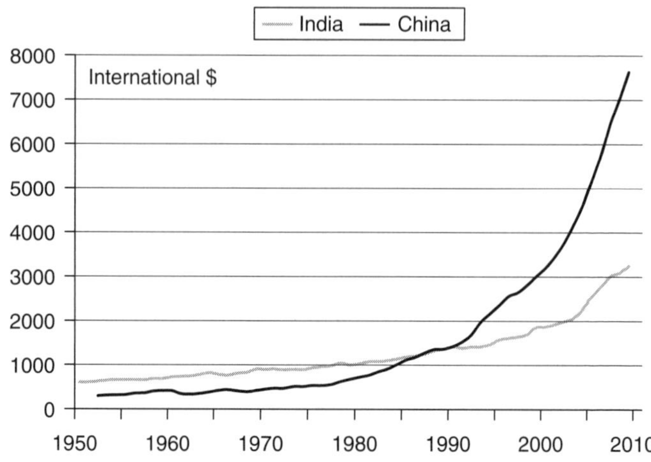

Figure 1.1 Real GDP per capita: India and China (1950–2007)
Source: Heston, Summers and Atens 2011.

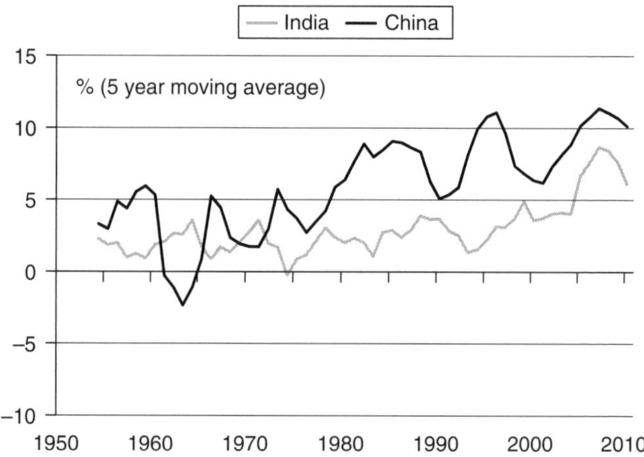

Figure 1.2 Annual change in real GDP per capita: India and China (1950–2007)
Source: Heston, Summers and Atens 2011.

contrasting growth performances between the two periods, one must accept that economic reform, liberalization, and opening in both countries seem to be critical in making possible the dynamic and successful economic performances in the second period. Second, China's growth performance in the second period has been significantly better than India's – not only in the extent of the change in real GDP per capita, but also in the speed of the change and the duration of the high speed growth.

These two observations lead to two further considerations that require more than just pure observation. The first one follows on the first observation. If economic reform, liberalization, and opening are instrumental in generating new economic dynamics and consequently impressive growth performance, what does precisely this reform, liberalization, and opening entail in each country? While their economies are both labeled by many as "socialist" in the first period, it is apparent that their socialisms were significantly different in terms of the ownership and organization of economic activity, and associated legal and political institutions, and social structure.[7] In the second period of reform, liberalization, and opening, the two economies have indeed converged on the principles, values, and institutions of the market economy and become new instances of the capitalist market economy? To help consider these questions, we bring a set of data on the extent of economic "freedom" of the two economies.

The Economic Freedom of the World index provides an overall measurement of how "free" an economy is (from 0 to 10, with 10 being the most liberal) on the basis of the size of government expenditure, taxes, and enterprises; legal structure and security of property rights; access to sound money; freedom to trade internationally; and regulation of credit, labor, and business (Gwartney and Lawson 2009) – key ingredients of the liberal reform and market economy movement of the 1990s, and arguably the principal measures of the marketization levels of an economy. As Figure 1.3[8] shows, India's level of economic freedom has been generally higher than China's – only to converge in recent years – and the level of economic freedom has been moving up in both countries. From 1990 to 2008, India's level of economic freedom increased by 1.35, while China's increased 2.21 from 1980 to 2008. The actual level (average 5.93 for India and 5.66 for China) has been a little bit above the world average.

To add to the mixed picture, India is more "liberal" in government size (Figure 1.4), legal structure and property rights (Figure 1.5), and regulation (Figure 1.8), and China is more "liberal" in access to sound money (Figure 1.6) and freedom to trade internationally (Figure 1.7).

Evidence from India and China is mixed, to say the least, and there is no clear and meaningful pattern of correlation with their economic performances. To the extent that their levels are increased and higher than

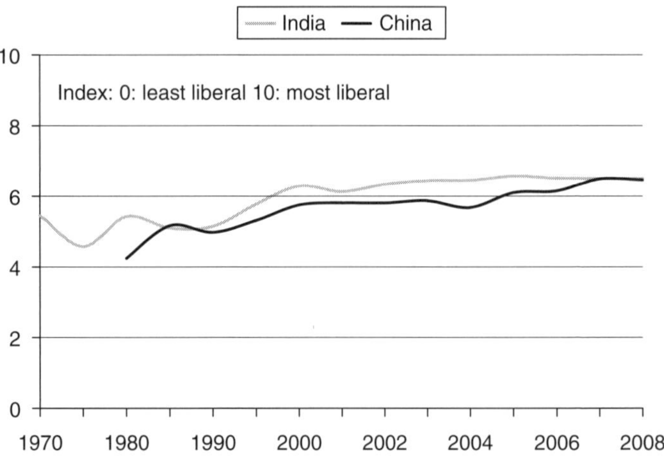

Figure 1.3 Economic freedom – China and India (1970–2009)
Source: Gwartney and Lawson 2009.

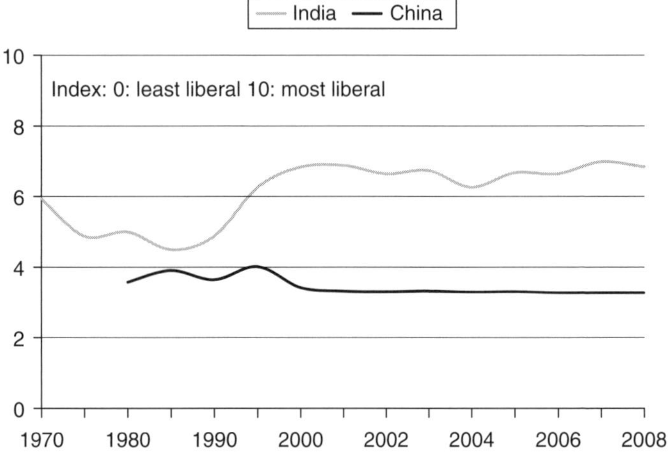

Figure 1.4 Economic freedom – Size of government: Expenditure, taxes, and enterprises (1970–2009)
Source: Gwartney and Lawson 2009.

before, there is an improvement. But their levels are in the middle range in global comparisons. Clearly, if marketization and liberal reforms are suspected to be a – if not the – driving force of the growth performance, more serious theorizing and empirical support would be needed.

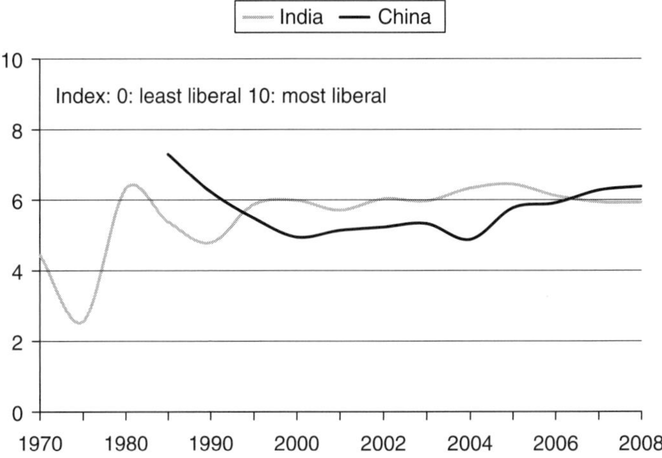

Figure 1.5 Economic freedom – legal structure and security of property rights (1970–2009)
Source: Gwartney and Lawson 2009.

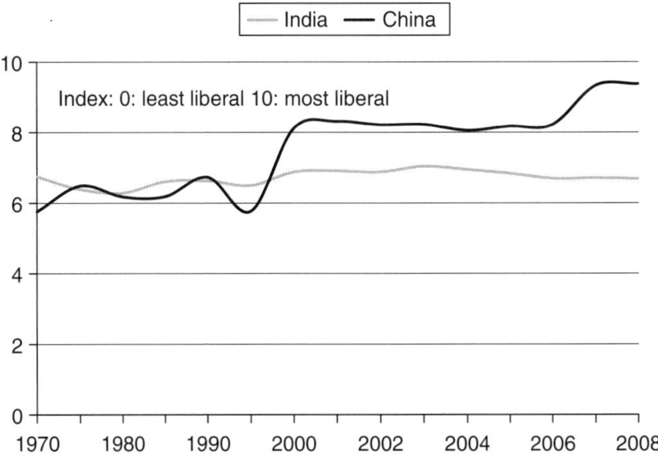

Figure 1.6 Economic freedom – Access to sound money (1970–2009)
Source: Gwartney and Lawson 2009.

The second consideration concerns the other observation. If China has indeed performed better than India and the evidence on marketization and liberation from the first consideration is not capable of providing a definitive explanation for this, we might need to look beyond

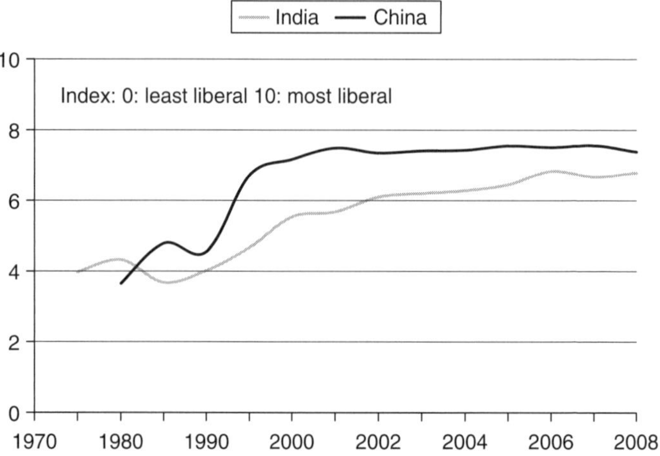

Figure 1.7 Economic freedom – Freedom to trade internationally (1970–2009)
Source: Gwartney and Lawson 2009.

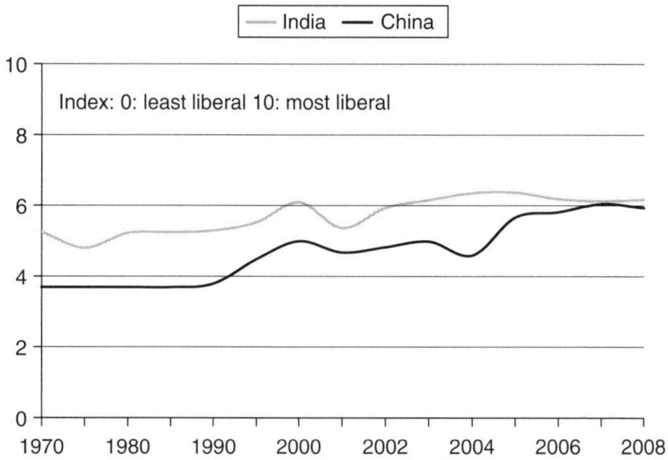

Figure 1.8 Economic freedom – Regulation of credit, labor, and business (1970–2009)
Source: Gwartney and Lawson 2009.

pure GDP-based performance indicators to see why this is the case. This is not only necessary as a way of explaining the growth performance in the two countries. It also links China and India to the broad literature on growth and development studies. Explanations of economic growth performance often come in two categories. Those in the first category, usually referred to as growth accounting, intend to establish patterns or structures of factor inputs to growth outcomes through statistical models. These factors often conventionally include land, capital, labor, and total factor productivity (TFP). A much larger range of different studies in the second category are interested in "non-economic" factors, forces, and arrangements that enable or shape the structure of the factor inputs and thus growth outcomes.

To facilitate discussion, we again bring in two sets of data. The first set of data on the scope and change of factors in the first category, and the other set on those non-economic factors, forces, and arrangements in the second categories. On the first data set, we include capital investment, labor productivity, and industrial structure, and economic openness as indicators of the general growth pattern and factor structure, and as a background for further and more detailed discussion in Chapters 2 and 3. Figures 1.9[9] and 1.10 show gross fixed capital formation and real GDP per person employed for the 50 years from 1960 to 2010. Figures 1.11, 1.12, and 1.13 are contributions of the three sectors to real GDP, agriculture, industry and services, also from 1960 to 2010. Finally, Figure 1.14 shows trade as a percentage of GDP, measuring economic openness for the two countries from 1950 to 2009.

Factors, forces, and arrangements in the second category are the usual suspects in broad growth analysis and attribution for the cause of economic growth. They featured prominently in the last round of debates on the East Asian model. When it comes to China and India, the first, and most often cited factor is the political system or type of government. India is the world's largest democracy and China is the world's largest party-state. As Figure 1.15[10] shows, India and China differ substantially on the extent of citizens' rights and participation and the political accountability of government. China is in the middle of the negative range, while India is a bit above the neutral. This runs against the backdrop of the growth performances we discussed above in which China has performed better than India.

Challenging the popular theorizing above, claims are put forward to argue that political stability, certainty, and predictability are instrumental for economic growth, particularly for countries in the early stage of their modern transformation (Huntington 1968, and much of the East Asian model debate). Here the evidence (Figure 1.16) shows that both India and China are in the negative territory with regard to political stability, while China has higher government stability than India, perhaps confirming their respective growth performances.

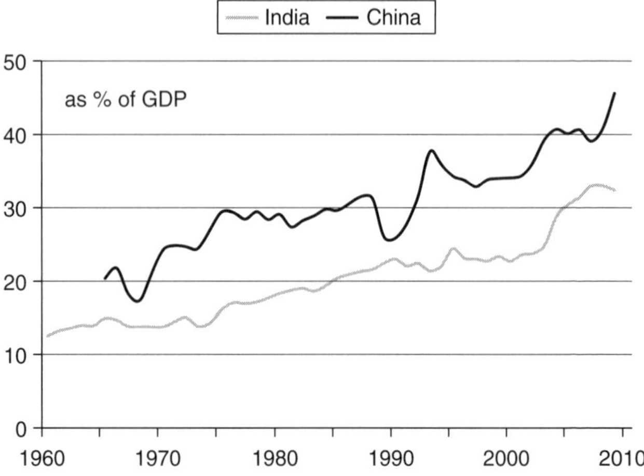

Figure 1.9 Gross fixed capital formation (1960–2010)
Source: World Bank 2011.

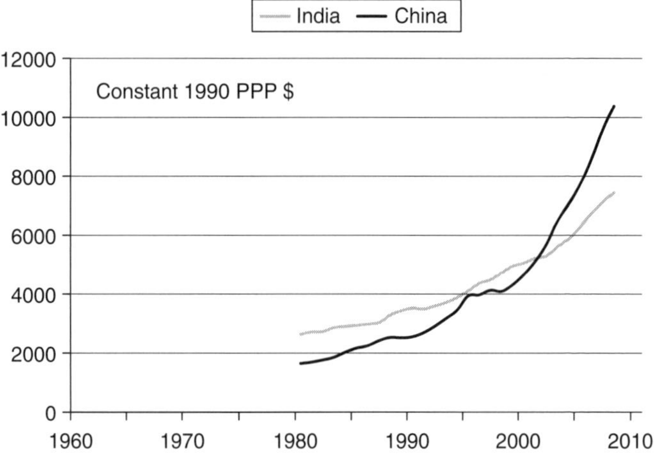

Figure 1.10 GDP per person employed (1960–2010)
Source: World Bank 2011.

Further down the list of Huntington/Pye's modern state requirements[11] is the problem of governability: government effectiveness. The third dimension of the WGI data measures the quality of public policies and services. Figure 1.17 shows, contrary to popular beliefs, that China

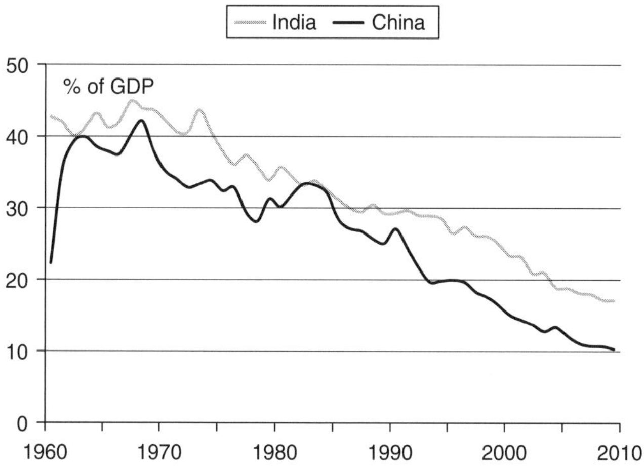

Figure 1.11 Agriculture, value added (1960–2010)
Source: World Bank 2011.

Figure 1.12 Industry, value added (1960–2010)
Source: World Bank 2011.

and India share a similar level of government effectiveness that revolves around the median level of the world. This similar pattern is observed also in regulatory qualities that measure government's ability to shape its relationship with the private sector (Figure 1.18).

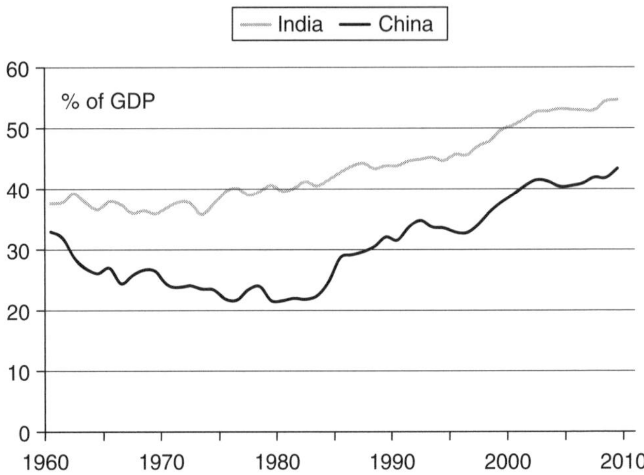

Figure 1.13 Services, value added (1960–2010)
Source: World Bank 2011.

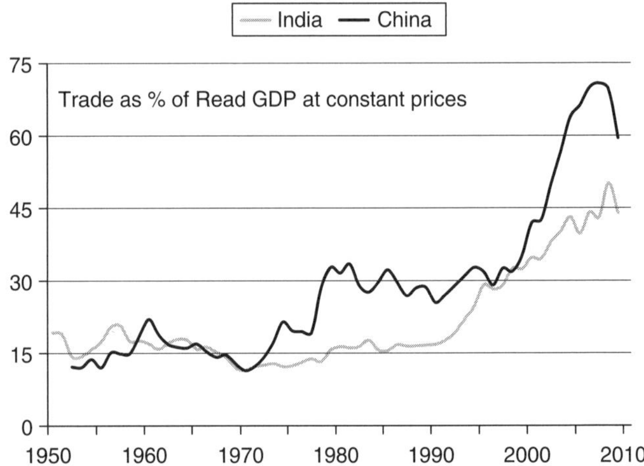

Figure 1.14 Openness (1950–2009)
Source: Heston, Summers and Atens 2011.

Rule of law is another popular area of debate and theorizing about modern economic growth. The rule of law provides a necessary level of trust and certainty required for modern economic activities. In debates over the East Asian model, however, no definitive new knowledge

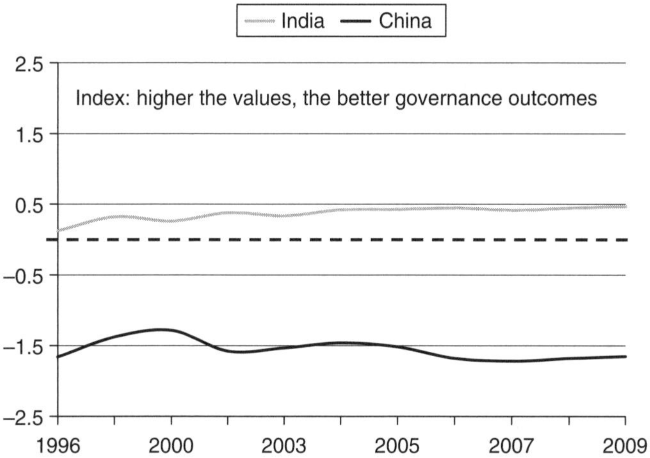

Figure 1.15 Voice and accountability: China and India (1996–2009)
Source: Kaufmann, Kraay and Mastruzzi 2010.

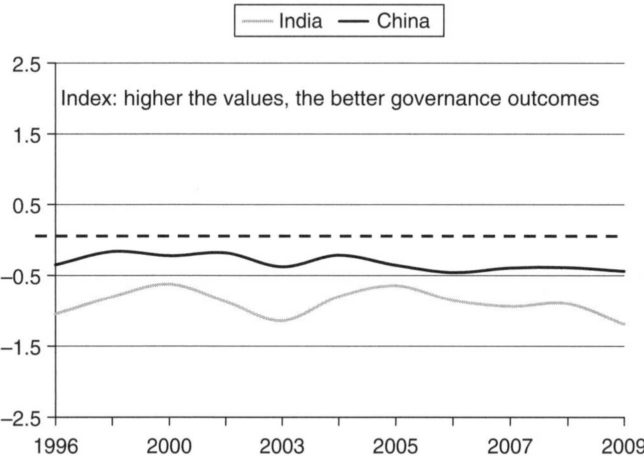

Figure 1.16 Political stability and no violence: India and China (1996–2009)
Source: Kaufmann, Kraay and Mastruzzi 2010.

was gained as to whether this has been the case in relation with the effective economic performance – much the same as debates on the first dimension concerning regime types (Brown and Gutterman 1998; Ginsburg 2000; Jayasuriya 1999; Peerenboom 2004; Pistor and Wellons 1999; and Rosett, Cheng and Woo 2002). The data on China and India

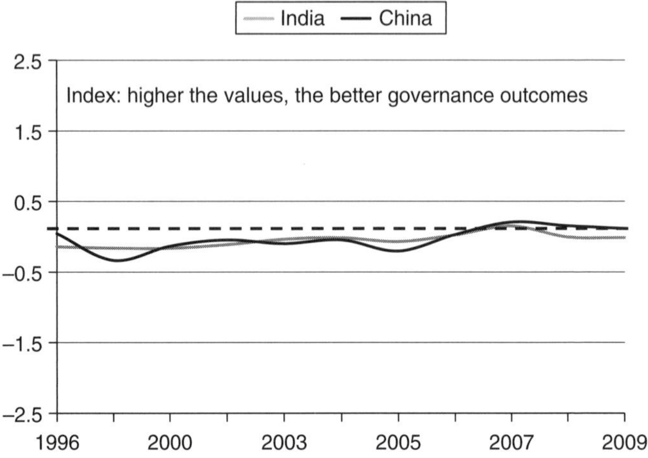

Figure 1.17 Government effectiveness – India and China (1996–2009)
Source: Kaufmann, Kraay and Mastruzzi 2010.

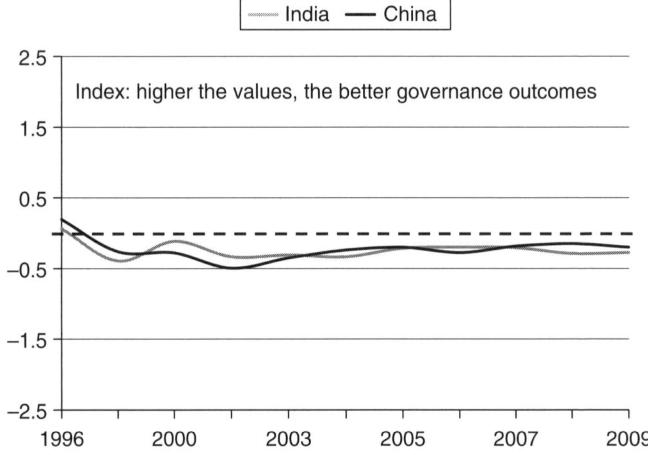

Figure 1.18 Regulatory quality: India and China (1996–2009)
Source: Kaufmann, Kraay and Mastruzzi 2010.

here is sure to add more confusion. We see in Figure 1.19 that India is one step higher than China in rule of law consistently over the period.

Lastly, there is significant literature on the relationship between corruption and economic growth (Kang 2002; Kidd and Richter 2003;

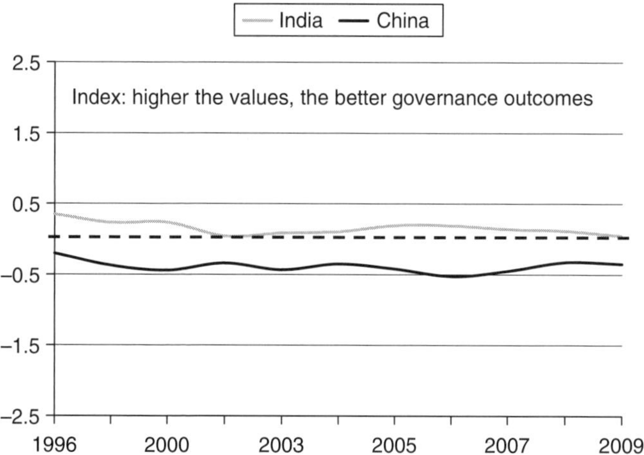

Figure 1.19 Rule of law: India and China (1996–2009)
Source: Kaufmann, Kraay and Mastruzzi 2010.

Lindsey and Dick 2002). One group argue that corruption distorts the normal function of the market, business confidence, and government-business relations (Bello and Rosenfeld 1992; Clifford 1994; Hutchfroft 1991; Lingle 1998; Tanzi and Davoodi 1998). The other group, arising from institutional economics and cultural studies, believe "corruption" reflects inefficiency and ineffectiveness of the formal institutional setting for sound economic activities, and indeed provides a remedying alternative to the institutional deficiency so that economic activity can move forward and allocation of resources and capacity can take place (Mauro 1997). Looking at the indicators of control of corruption in China and India (Figure 1.20), both seem to be largely on the same level, below the world average, although India has in later years been better than China.

Clearly, the data on these regular growth enabling/arresting factors do not confirm any existing theories, considering the actual performance of the two countries. This is not really surprising. The data also fails to provide convincing evidence for a pattern in their growth experiences that would allow us to contemplate new theories of economic miracles.

2 Are we all capitalists now?

Distinct experiences and patterns of successful modern economic growth have long been a subject of intensive scholarly interest. Such

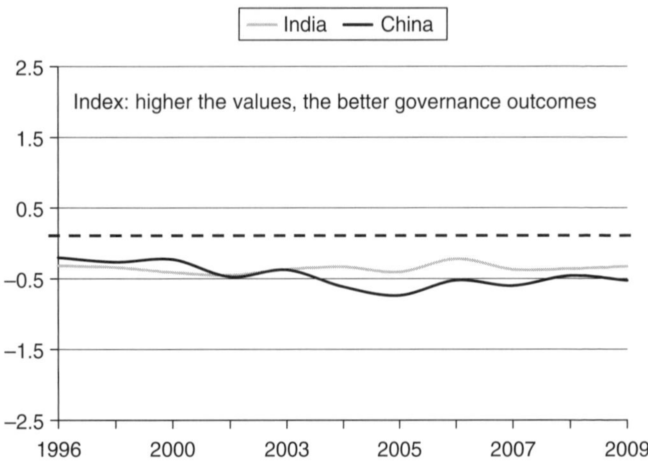

Figure 1.20 Control of corruption: India and China (1996–2009)
Source: Kaufmann, Kraay and Mastruzzi 2010.

strong scholarly interest arose in response to the rise and expansion of modern capitalism in Western Europe, North America, and beyond, and to the desire to understand how the modern economic system works in individual nation-states, the nature of the world economic system, and the rise and fall of particular national economies.

While there can be further differences and variations between any two "capitalist" economies.[12] scholars generally accept that there are two significantly different "models" of modern capitalism. When Michel Albert talked about the problems of the American model and the economic and social "superiority" of the Rhine model, capitalism was confined to the "two capitalisms" (Albert 1993: ix). Much earlier in Andrew Shonfield's work in 1965 on modern capitalism, which led to a whole new field of scholarship on comparative capitalism, capitalism was also mainly referred to Europe and the United States (Shonfield 1965). In both cases, the key that separates the two capitalisms are how the state relates to the market and the approach to planning. In Albert's three stages of capitalism, for example, it was "capitalism [the market] against the state" in the eighteenth and nineteenth centuries, "capitalism disciplined by the state" in the first half of the twentieth century, and "capitalism instead of the market" in the later part of the twentieth century.

Accordingly, the Anglo-Saxon model is built upon the primacy of efficiency of the market and profitability. It is primarily the market prices that determine the allocation of resources and deployment of productive factors. Individual preferences, secure and private ownership, and fair competition are the keys for the market to function. The market in turn allows an optimal equilibrium to form among resources and factors. Economic activities are accountable primarily to shareholders. Maximum profitability is a principal incentive for economic activities. The Anglo-Saxon model delivers high investment returns, rapid economic growth, and strong finance and service sectors, but also great income gaps and regular business circles.

The second model, the Rhine model, usually includes Germany, Nordic countries, and, ambiguously, Japan. This model brings broader public interests to bear on economic activities. Economic activities are accountable to stakeholders beyond owners and shareholders. Social fairness in addition to efficiency, and social order in addition to individual preferences and competition, become relevant and important values in economic activities. Income gaps are relatively narrower. The state manages economic activities on behalf of the broad public interest.

These two models reflect the national conditions of the respective countries. They can also be seen as reflecting different stages in the historical evolution of world capitalism. Early work on modern economic growth, often referred to as neo-classical growth model, reflects very much the dominant form of the Anglo-Saxon growth experiences, from the early works of Adam Smith, to Roy F. Harrod and Evsey Domar, Robert Solow, and Robert E. Lucas in more recent times, scholarly concern has been to understand market equilibriums and explain growth accordingly. Total factor productivity (TFP), and then efficiency, profitability, and market equilibrium dominated the discourse of growth economics. The Anglo-Saxon model experienced a world-impacting break of the "general equilibrium" in the 1930s. The Great Depression was fundamentally a function of the Anglo-Saxon model wherein individual business cycles accumulated into one of the greatest in scale and intensity, exacerbated only by uncertainties over national and international developments of the time.

Corrective responses in both economic theory and business practice came in different colors and substances. Within the Anglo-Saxon economies, Keynesianism looked for the aid of the state in the provision of factors for the overall stability of market equilibrium. While the New Deal is seen as reactive, corrective, and temporal, Keynesian theory and practice left a great impact on the Anglo-Saxon model.

Post-war developments in both economic theory and practice in continental Europe formed a different but more fundamental response to the Anglo-Saxon problem. Walter Eucken and Franz Böhm, later referred to as leading thinkers of the Freiburg school, developed a more subtle view of how to make the market work for society. Economic order, according to them, is necessary for the market to work. Such economic order caters to the broader interests of society. Together societal interests and the economic order form the basis of an overall economic and social system in which the market economy operates. The state is a natural "agent" for ensuring this order through law, regulative management, and fair market competition. The successful post-war economic recovery and growth in Germany and many other European countries has been attributed to this more balanced model of economic growth. Hence, the "social market economy" is seen as a distinct model of modern economic growth. Japan's great growth performance after World War II is also seen as an instance of this model.

Along these two models, and indeed, in contrast with the capitalist market economy in general, there was another dominant model of economic growth that competed for primacy in many parts of the world. The socialist economic model emerged and spread across a large number of countries, from the Soviet Union to China and from countries in Asian to those in Europe. India, for all purposes, was in many ways "more socialist" than the socialist countries. The socialist model stood on the other end of the spectrum of prices versus planning, efficiency versus fairness, market versus regulation, individual preferences versus collective interests, and ownership versus stakeholders. The model was intended to achieve greater fairness and equality through public ownership and centralized planning, control, and management. Adding to these general principles of the socialist economy was the unique economic theory that shaped economic policy and practice in the Soviet Union and China in particular: a significant emphasis on the heavy industrial sector at the expense of the agricultural sector.

The socialist economy failed in the Soviet Union, China, East Europe, East Asia, India, and, indeed, everywhere. At the same time, the Anglo-Saxon model rolled back in the 1980s in the United Kingdom and the United States, and throughout the world in the 1990s and beyond. Economic reform, opening, and liberalization started initially in China and then in India. It seems natural to suspect that the emergent economies of China and India are the latest instances of the conversion to global capitalism via Anglo-Saxon capitalism (Dore 2000a). The question we presented to the authors in this volume is whether the growth experiences of China and India are indeed instances of the capitalist market economy and what contributions these growth experiences make to our understanding of the working of modern economic growth.

3 How "Asian" is the economic growth of China and India?

While there is a great deal to learn from putting the growth experiences of China and India into the historical and comparative context of the modern capitalist economy, China and India do not usually feature well in the literature of growth economics, and indeed that of comparative capitalism. Partially, as we suggested earlier, there is some uncertainty about the precise nature of these two emergent economies.[13] More profoundly, though, scholarship on economic growth has long been evolving along two separate lines. For careful readers and writers, "economic growth" and "economic development" can mean different things, not necessarily because economic "development" entails a broader set of dynamics, indicators, or values. Rather, for many, "economic growth is usually distinguished from economic development, the latter term being restricted to economies that are close to the subsistence level. The term economic growth is applied to economies already experiencing rising per capital incomes" (Cornwall 2010). In plain language, from the perspective of mainstream growth economics, economic growth is for advanced economies and economic development for developing economies.

This is one of the reasons why waves of rapid economic growth in post-war East Asia have largely been treated as a separate category of economic activity. From Japan in the 1950s and 1960s to the "four little dragons" (Singapore, South Korea, Taiwan, and Hong Kong) and the Southeast Asian tigers (Malaysia, Indonesia, Thailand) in the 1960s to 1990s, scholarly interests have focused greatly on the role of government in economic activities;[14] whether Confucianism is compatible with the modern economy; whether the military should be part of the governing force for organizing economic activities; whether democracy is a necessary condition or consequence of economic growth; and whether labor conditions, corruption, and resources depletion are worthy costs of economic development.

There are two distinct groups of experiences in this category that have generated significant scholarly interest and debate. These experiences and the rich literature drawing on them are largely outside the literature of comparative capitalism. The first is the largely "unsuccessful" drive for rapid economic growth in Latin America in the 1960s and 1970s. The failure of the Latin American experiences was generally attributed to the problem of the global capitalist structure. More precisely, the dependency theorists[15] argue that the structure of the world capitalist economy is such that the growth of Latin American economy is dependent on the function of the world economic system, and as Latin American countries are located in the periphery of the system, their economies are reduced to a supporting role to the global capitalist core and are mainly functioning to provide raw material and primary products to the world economic system under the terms of the global capital. Under such a structure, what actually "develops" is the underdevelopment of the Latin American countries in the periphery and their dependency on the core.

In contrast, countries in East and Southeast Asia, mostly from "the periphery" of the world economic system as well, produced a very different economic growth performance under almost the same structural conditions, and, in doing so, raised many critical questions to some of the general theories and hypotheses developed from the Latin American experiences. The East Asian experiences confirmed with dependency theories that unconstrained global flows of capital, products, and materials can lead to growth in one place and harvest in another, and in the end to the perpetuation of the peripheral position of the "peripheral" economies. The East Asian experiences challenge, however, the underlying assumption of the dependency theories that the world economic system can reproduce the core-peripheral structure in perpetuity, and the position of peripheral countries in the periphery is structurally determined. The East Asian experiences have demonstrated that the internal conditions and methods to these countries themselves can make a significant difference, and countries can move from the periphery to the core. Japan is an early example.

More specifically, these conditions and methods concern first and foremost an effective state that is able to mobilize and organize resources and materials at the national level; make political decisions on public policy priorities, resource allocation, and benefits distribution; and function as a controller for resources, materials, and interaction and flow across national boundaries. Second, there is an institutional framework that the state can utilize to separate domestic and international spheres of economic activity, and develop industrial policy to promote industries that are competitive for international markets. Third, the overall political environment and social structure can tolerate state-led campaigns for this specific form of rapid economic growth, development, and social transformation.

Then there is China's high-speed growth performance from the early 1980s and India from the early 1990s. The growth experiences of the East Asian model economies are useful as a strong point of reference for a comparative examination of China and India. There has been interesting debate over whether China should even be seen as an instance of the East Asian model (Baek 2005; Boltho and Weber 2009). Apart from the legacy of its Communist political system and socialist economy, China matched the East Asian model economy on most counts: export concentration in a dual market (domestic and international) economic environment, national organization of economic activities by government with its claimed national interests and industrial policy, close relationships with the business community, control of distributional demands, support of a centripetal and corporatist society, and benefits from international capital, market, and economic institutions (see Huang 2005).

If whether China is an instance of the East Asian model is still debatable, the case that India's growth is not the working of an East Asian model economy seems to be self-evident. India is not an East Asian model economy on most counts. India has an effective multi-party parliamentary democracy, while most Asian model economies achieved their post-war rapid economic growth under some form of a non-pluralist political system. While India is culturally and religiously rich, it has not much to do with Confucianism or the Asian values as Lee Kwan Yew defines. While most East Asian model economies relied heavily on export markets for their sustained growth, India's growth was not primarily from exports, at least not from manufacturing and agriculture. While East Asian model economies had some their comparative advantage built upon control and management of distributional demands such as those from labor, interests groups, environment groups, and so on, India has a strong pluralist, and even populist civic culture.

China and India may or may not resemble East Asian model economies. Their positions, however, in the overall world economic structure and the upward movement as a consequence of their rapid economic growth are similar to those of East Asian model economies. It is the transition from a pre-modern or even subsistent economy that put them in the category of emerging, developing, and transitional economies. The growth experiences and development performances of the Asian model economies, with the only exception perhaps of Japan, are generally taken as historically unique with unclear value for general economic theory, and are difficult to be acknowledged as a legitimate form of modern economy, not even in a broad embrace of comparative capitalism.

If the growth experiences of China and India were seen as further instances of the East Asian model in action, then it would be more than "statistically significant" to claim that the Asian model is a working model of modern economy, or of the modern capitalist market economy, to be precise. The questions we presented to our authors in this volume were these: using the East Asian model economies as a point of reference, how much are the growth experiences of China and India of the East Asian model economy? What can a comparative analysis of China and India contribute to the debate on the East Asian model of economic growth? And, indeed, how can a comparative analysis of China and India help us better to understand the East Asian model, and/or perhaps to see whether the claim of the East Asian model of economic growth and development is legitimate and meaningful?

4 Plan of the book

The growth experiences and performances of China and India present a unique opportunity for us to test some of the long-held theories and claims about modern economic growth and development, and to build a bridge between the two seemingly separate strands of literature and scholarly interest. Indeed, what do the growth experiences of China and India mean for the real world of the modern economy and for the world economic system? What contributions can they make to the existing literature on the conditions and consequences of modern economic growth and development, and to the debates about the nature of the modern economy – its forms, substance, and manifestations?

Different models of growth experiences are often approached from different disciplinary and theoretical perspectives. At the core of growth economics are conventional growth accounting models that explain growth outcomes according to key economic factors such as capital, land, labor, and productivity. Beyond these growth-accounting models are institutional models, such as those of new institutionalism, built on institutional factors and arrangements that facilitate the economic factors. Further beyond are "East Asian model factors" that either provide additional sources of competitiveness and productivity or, as institutional factors, facilitate positive input of the economic factors. Finally, there are paradigmatic and philosophical models that build on fundamentally different purposes and the nature of modern economic activities where growth and development are either less paramount values or explicable beyond rational social science analytical frameworks.

The chapters in this volume are organized around this series of concentric circles of models or frameworks. More specifically, we want to see whether scholarly debate and anxiety about different models of economic growth and development may have seen the end of the utility of these various models. Development models are valuable for providing interesting *descriptions* of the patterns and dynamics of modern economic growth and development. Their *explanations* of how those patterns have been shaped are less effective. Even more problematic is that these models are often intended or regarded as a guide for future economic growth and development, mostly in other national and social settings. East Asian model economies have grown and developed in spite of the popular prescriptive models. China and India have gained their economic performance today regardless of the widely-held expectations and advice of the past. And it seems to be difficult to deny that they are all forms of modern capitalist market economy.

The discussion and debate on the Rhine model (versus the Anglo-Saxon model), the capitalist market model (versus the socialist model), and the East Asian model (versus, again, the Anglo-Saxon model) has opened up greater intellectual space for us to accept and accommodate various forms of modern economy of a more pluralist nature on a much larger scale then conventionally perceived, but have not been able to settle definitely many of the issues debated in growth and development economics. China and India, with their growth and development unfolding in front of us, may allow us to move one step closer to that. We want to see if such a case can be made in this volume.

The first two chapters provide conventional accounts of the growth experiences, largely using the growth accounting framework and methodology. This growth accounting is most often used by mainstream economists. We provide explanations of the growth experiences using this framework to see how mainstream economic models fit with the growth experiences. As this growth accounting is intended as a general model for modern economic growth, we can see, in applying this framework, how far China and India's economies have transformed or "converged." Dilip Das uses a modified framework of the original growth accounting to examine the growth performances and the associated patterns of enabling factors. It compares India and China according to principal economic variables such as capital accumulation, labor productivity, and total factor productivity, as well as two key sectors: external sector with trade and FDI, and regional and global integration measured through the gravity model. Srikanta Chatterjee in Chapter 3 frames the growth factors relationship in a supply–demand model, and uses that model to explain the growth patterns of China and India. Both chapters intend to ascertain and establish the patterns of economic growth of China and India as framed in the conventional models of growth accounting and analysis.

Jun Fu presents a classical institutional model of economic growth, and in a significant way relates the growth experiences of China, and, by extension, India, to broad world experiences of the modern (capitalist market) economy. Drawing on new institutional economics in his chapter, Fu wants to demonstrate what is the fundamental logic that drives modern economic activities, how China's experience is an instance of the working of such institutional logic, and, therefore, how China's experience is very much covered, anticipated, and can be explained by classical economic theories such as Adam Smith, Joseph Schumpeter, and Robert Lucas. All three of these chapters aim to demonstrate how the emergent Chinese and Indian economies relate to modern (capitalist market) economies and how the instruments we employ to explain the growth experiences relate to standard economic theories and models.

The next four chapters develop their accounts of the growth experiences on a single factor or dynamic in a framework of growth system (Huang 2005). This growth system model is often used in explaining the East Asian model of growth and development, and looks largely at non-economic factors as part of the enabling environment and mechanisms for an explanation of competitiveness and productivity. Studies often identify a significant factor believed to make growth and development possible and build a theoretical model on such a factor (e.g., Confucian culture and society, industrial policy, developmental state, corporatism, *kereitsu/chaebol*, etc.). The four chapters deploy such a model to China and India, looking at the role of state–society relations, political regimes and institutions, education, and population management systems.

The first two chapters in this group engage issues featured prominently in early debates on the East Asian model – one involving state-society relations and political parties, the other regime types and political change – and examine how state regime types relate to economic development and how behaviors of the state and citizens are actually shaped in development activities. Lei Guang uses a modified state–society model to explain a shared pattern of government and citizens' behavior in development-related social conflicts. There is a significant literature on the rule of law and the role of regime types in economic development and how distributional demands are shaped in growth process. Guang's chapter shows precisely how politics and political institutions operate with economic development, and how political institutions are both the causes of development driven social conflicts and a solution to them. Guang goes beyond the simplistic framework of democratic vs. authoritarian regime types and sees a more complex relationship between political institutions and economic development. The chapter makes a case that explains whether a seemingly similar pattern of social consequences of market economic growth would suggest a similar growth model and a pattern of growth generation.

Regime types and economic development has been a central issue in the debate over the East Asian model of economic growth. This is a particularly interesting issue for China and India because of their contrasting political systems but shared successful development story. Zhiyue Bo takes on this issue in his chapter. Chapter 6 draws on an extensive empirical investigation undertaken in China and India. It focuses particularly on economic growth and political change at the state/provincial level to see how change in local political leadership affects local economic performance, and further whether regime types matter in economic development of these two countries.

The next two chapters examine the role of education and labor migration. Chapter 7 by Krishna Kumar and Ying Liu investigates and compares the role education has played in economic growth and development in China and India. Education influences and is also influenced by economic development, an issue that has been well recognized in the debate over the East Asian model of economic growth. The chapter examines education attainment patterns in India and China, as reflected in sectoral composition, employment structure, and trade composition in the two countries, and how these patterns relate to the patterns of economic growth. The authors want to see whether there is an underlying pattern between China and India in this education–development relationship.

Jason Young's Chapter 8 brings together institutions and labor, two significant factors in the East Asian model economies, and examines the role of labor market and regulation in economic growth in China and India by looking at how institutions have shaped labor movement in the two countries, how this has in turn affected their growth and development patterns, and how their different patterns of labor migration led to their different experiences ofthe Lewis transition as anticipated in mainstream theories or models on developing economies.

The economic rise of China and India provides a unique opportunity to compare the role of internal labor flows in the development of two nations with agricultural populations of unprecedented scale. Young puts forward a comparison of the formal institutional arrangements of China's *hukou* institution and the predominantly informal arrangements that shape labor migration and segmentation in India, and questions the assumption that development entails free rural to urban migration in the classic Lewisian sense. In doing so, he also puts the developmental state model to the test.

The last three chapters bring the problem of development models to a profoundly different level. According to many, models of growth economics, new institutional theories, and East Asian model explanations are informed by the same set of premises and imperatives of modern capitalist market economy: rapid economic growth and how to make this happen. There are scholarly interests, however, that go beyond the dominant paradigm of the modern capitalist economy. These interests question not so much the causality and technical details of the forces, factors, and relations that enable economic development but, rather, the purpose and values of rapid economic growth and development, often defined in terms of GDP growth or per capita income. These scholarly interests provide broader analytical frameworks for us to understand growth and development, often with a model of their own defining the future directions and purposes of development, as well as strategies for a better kind of growth and development.

Wing Thye Woo, with his extensive expertise in the research and analysis of the Chinese economy, lays out the foundations for the Chinese economy to move forward. In his view, the conditions for the 1978–2005 policy framework, which has made rapid economic growth in China possible for the past 30 years, are long gone. Woo's chapter proposes to examine the system of China's economic growth and development in three critical but fundamental areas – economic mechanisms, governance institutions, and resources supply – and to see whether the current system would be able to provide the necessary conditions for sustainable development and even survival, and for the emergence of a mature modern economy. Without necessarily challenging the purposes and values of economic growth and development, Woo seeks to understand the fundamental improvements that are required for the system to work in the years to come, and the best strategy to achieve them.

Bruce Gilley in Chapter 10 goes one step further and takes issue with the problem of "development." In his view, there are two different models of the modern economy: the outgrown, catch up "development" models, and sustainability models. The two models involve not only two different visions about the values and purpose of modern society, but also two different strategies of resource allocation and prioritization.

In this chapter, Gilley develops a "model" for measuring sustainability and uses this to assess the growth experiences of China and India. Looking at the conditions for sustainable development gives us a broad understanding of the growth experiences of China and India and provides insight as to whether further growth and development in the two countries will lead to a "matured" economy.

Finally, the precise nature of China's development experience and how it relates to broad human development experiences is taken up by Zhenglai Deng. Deng tackles the challenge at two different levels. The first is the precise nature of the Chinese development experience. There is a long tradition in both India and China within which alternative forms and purpose of economic activities were entertained.[16] Deng's chapter portraits China's growth experience as an example of different values, purposes and enabling mechanisms in modern economy, and explains Chinese development experience through his concept of living wisdom. At another level, Deng urges scholars to allow more intellectual space for appreciating development experiences. Such a shift in thinking and understanding development experiences requires a fundamentally different analytical framework and methodology.

Notes

1. There has been a surge of publications on China and India in the past five years. A quick glance gives one a clear indication of the scale and magnitude of such an enterprise. Many are general comparisons of these two countries on broad range of indicators: Friedman and Gilley (2005) and Bardhan (2010) on the two giants; Ramesh (2005) and Sheth (2008) on "Chindia"; Mohanty (2007) on grass-roots democracy; Meredith (2007) and Smith (2007) on elephant and dragon; and Kalist (2006), Cheru and Obi (2010), and Lam and Lim (2009). Some are general economic analyses of China and India: Ahya and Xie (2004), Das (2006a). There are a few on growth structure, reform, development strategy, and sustainability: Chaudhuri and Ravallion (2006), Aziz, Dunaway, and Prasad (2006), Chai and Roy (2006), Laszlo (2011), and Li and Zhang (2008). How China and India affect global distribution of wealth and power and the world economic system is a key issue for many: Srinivasan (2006), Winters and Yusuf (2007), Mahtaney (2007), Thirlwell (2007), Enderwick (2007), and Rowthorn (2006). There is a long list of studies on factors and sectors of economic growth: Bowles and Harris (2010) and Cooper (2006) on labor; Kowalski (2008) on trade; Lee et al. (2007) on manufacturing; Ohara and Kimura (2009) on industrial development; Prater, Swafford, and Yellepeddi (2009) on operational issues; Bosworth and Collins (2008) on factor inputs; Rao, Cheng, and Narain (2003) on education; Valli and Saccone (2009) on structural change; and Merrill, Taylor, and Poole (2010) on industrial capacity.

2. Fascination about the awakening dragon and elephant, and the emergent giants, is clearly driving the discourse. Some ask the carefully phrased question – whether the "developed world" or "advanced economies," can cope with the rise of China and India (Thirlwell 2007; and Rowthorn 2006).
3. Under careful scrutiny, East Asian growth and development is often associated with, if not attributed to, corruption, crony capitalism, unfair trade policies and practices, unconventional production organization, and institutional competitiveness, plus lawless, deplorable labor conditions, and environmental depletion, led by dictatorial, military, or authoritarian regimes.
4. Of course, there are views that trace "modern" economic development in these two countries to much earlier times. We will not engage with this debate here.
5. See chapters in this volume, particularly Chapter 2 for further discussion on this.
6. This set of pattern descriptions for Figure 1.1 to Figure 1.2 is based on data from Penn World Table 7.0 (Heston, Summers and Aten 2011).
7. See Chai and Roy (2006) for a systematic treatment of this issue. Also Bardhan (2010) and Das (2006a).
8. This set of pattern descriptions for Figure 1.3 to Figure 1.8 is based on data from *The Economic Freedom of the World Index* (Gwartney and Lawson 2009).
9. This set of pattern descriptions for Figure 1.9 to Figure 1.14 is based on data from The World Bank's *World Development Indicators* (WDI, World Bank 2011).
10. This set of pattern descriptions in Figures 1.15 to 1.20 is based on data from the World Bank's *Worldwide Governance Indicators* (WGI, Kaufmann, Kraay, and Mastruzzi 2010).
11. For both Huntington (1968) and Pye (1966), accountability and governability are two distinct and equally important values for the modern state. As Huntington puts it, for developing societies in their early stage of modern state building the problem of governability is more urgent.
12. There is for example a large literature on the variety of capitalism that examines differences among capitalist economies in corporate structure, financial systems, industrial relations, role of the state, including Andrew Shonfield's US-Europe contrasts (Shonfield 1965: 15–18), Michel Albert's American model vs. the Rhine model (1993), liberal market economy vs. coordinated market economy (Miller 2005: 18), as well as Ronald Dore's stock market capitalism and welfare capitalism (Dore 2000), nonliberal capitalism (Streeck and Yamamura 1995, and institutional capitalism in various forms (Crouch and Streeck 1997).
13. For China, one debate is about the level of marketization and the extent of economic liberalization. Yasheng Huang, for example, argues (2008) that the past 30 years have not seen a progressive movement towards the capitalist market economy. The reform programs in the 1980s were the most liberal. There has been a mixture of market and state in recent developments. There is still the risk that statist capitalism can dominate China; see also Andreas (2008). Another debate concerns the ambiguous nature of the Chinese economy because of dual track transition, ambiguous arrangements, and the transitional nature of the economy (See Fan 1996, Lau, Qian, and Ronald 2000, and Li 1996).

14. The whole debate about the developmental state makes great sense with East Asian growth itself. But as scholars of comparative capitalism have already demonstrated in their discussion of the Rhine model, East Asian countries are not the only or even first countries to have sought a greater role for the state in managing the market and ensuring social order under market conditions.
15. Among them are Paul Baran, Theotônio Dos Santos, ECLA, Andre Gunder Frank, and Fernando Henrique Cardoso.
16. Village, communal, self reliant economic activities in India, and Mao's idealist economic system in China, for example.

2

Growth Paradigms of China and India: A Conventional Framework of Growth Analysis

Dilip K. Das

China and India were noted for their economic prowess and prosperity in the remote past, albeit the recent history of one is replete with distressful colonization and of the other with feudal incompetence, leading to economic turmoil. In the mid-twentieth century, they were widely regarded as demographic behemoths and economic weaklings. Until the early 1980s, the two labor-abundant economies were impoverished, with income levels at the bottom of the world scale. India's per capita income was approximately equal to the World Bank's 1980 average for the low-income countries and China's about two thirds that of India. During the last decade of the twentieth century the mindset of academicians, policy-makers in the public policy arena, business professionals, and opinion-leaders underwent an insightful transformation regarding the two economies.

This chapter uses a modified framework of the original growth accounting, as developed in the works of Robert Solow in the 1950s (Solow 1956), for a comparative description of the growth paradigms of China and India. My concept of growth paradigm[1] includes the historical pattern by which the two economies have come through to where they are now, the overall growth performance over time as defined in GDP and GDP per capita growth, and the weighing structure of factors that are believed to contribute to economic growth, such as capital accumulation, labor productivity, and total factor productivity (TFP). Moreover, for their economic growth under contemporary world economic conditions, the performance of the external sector and the levels of regional and global economic integration of the two economies are essential parts of the growth paradigm.

The growth accounting framework is modified for two reasons. First, this research analyzes and assesses the contributing factors but does not compute the actual contributions as would be in the case of the work of Solow and many other conventional growth accounting scholars. Computing of the actual contributions would be required for a precise measurement of the causal relations between these factors and growth. This is outside the scope of this chapter. Second, some of the elements in the growth paradigm here go beyond the conventional growth accounting framework. It is no longer enough to cite only saving and labor to account for economic growth under contemporary conditions, particularly for growth at such a large scale.

This chapter starts with an examination of how the two economies transformed themselves and prepared conditions for rapid economic growth. It will then provide a brief description of the growth performances, not so much the overall patterns already laid out in the introduction chapter, but more highlighting key aspects interesting to our discussion. The main part of the chapter will focus on factors and total factor productivity as core parts of the growth paradigm, followed by a discussion of the performance of the external sector and the level of regional and global integration. The chapter hopes to provide a comparative description of the scope and nature of economic growth in the language of mainstream growth economics and macroeconomic analysis, which will allow us to have a better understanding of the growth experience in a broad context of modern economic development.

1 Growth in historical perspective

If a long-term historical perspective is taken, China and India were, until the early-nineteenth century, among the largest economies on the planet. Angus Maddison, a noted economic historian, calculated that during the pre-industrial revolution era, particularly in the beginning of the eighteenth century, China and India were two dominant world economies (Maddison 1998). In purchasing power parity (PPP) terms, they together accounted for 45.7 percent of global GDP. Their GDPs were almost equal in size, and the GDP of the whole of Europe was approximately of the same size as that of China and India individually. Thus, at this juncture in economic history, these two economies were two of the world's largest.

The two economies took comparable turns over the twentieth century. For a long period, they remained a little ahead or behind each other in terms of per capita income and the total size of GDP. Angus Maddison (2001) has computed their per capita incomes in constant 1990 international dollars[2] for different periods. The two countries started the twentieth century at a low-income level. The share of world income for each one was much smaller than their share of world population. In 1913, China's share of world GDP was 8.9 percent, while its share of population was 26.4 percent. For India, its share of world GDP was 7.5 percent, while its share of world population was 17 percent. By 1950, these ratios had deteriorated further, reflecting worsening poverty in the two countries.

This scenario underwent a dramatic transformation. China turned in a stellar economic performance during the closing decades of the twentieth century. Rapid acceleration in GDP growth in real terms attracted global attention and inspired widespread accolades. The best macroeconomic performance in the preceding three decades was recorded during the 2002–7 period, when the economy grew at an average growth rate of 10.5 percent and the inflation rate was kept under 2 percent. In the beginning of the twenty-first century, China was being seen by many analysts as an economic superpower of the future. It emerged as a low-cost manufacturing juggernaut invading global markets in a sizeable array of products, with a high and rapidly rising level of merchandise exports and imports. Gradually, China moved up the technology ladder and began exporting high-technology products at an increasing pace. By 2006, it surpassed the EU and the US as the largest exporter of high-technology products in the global economy. China's share of high-technology exports was 16.9 percent of the total, while that of the EU 15 percent and the US 16.8 percent (Meri 2009). The downside, however, was that resolute export promotion rendered the economy export-dependent.

Although both economies launched macroeconomic reforms and restructuring, they were markedly different in their approaches and processes. Indian reforms started in an *ad hoc* manner, in an extremely tentative and overly cautious way in the mid-1980s. However, following a severe balance-of-payments crisis, a well-designed reform program was launched in 1991. In contrast, the Chinese reforms, which were launched in late 1978, did not comprise a detailed outline of macroeconomic transformation but were essentially based on gradual, incremental, and somewhat experimental changes in the macroeconomic structure. Several bold steps were taken in quick succession. Deng Xiaoping's dictums of "doing what works," "seeking truth from facts," and "crossing the river by groping for stepping stones underneath" were carefully followed by those who implemented reforms. They were essentially guided by principles of pragmatism. Yet confident reform measures were frequently taken. In addition, China's WTO accession began in the mid-1980s, which quickened the pace of its reforms of the external sector. Establishing special economic zones (SEZs) also had the same impact on the economy.

China implemented its macroeconomic reforms aggressively and at a brisk pace. Its implementation of economic reform was purposive and sure-footed. Conversely, the implementation of the Indian reform program was lackadaisical and poor at best. There were periods of backtracking in important reform areas. In terms of liberalizing the external sector the two economies adopted radically different stances and progressed at different paces. China opened its economy to trade and financial flows earlier and far more than did India. The latter had a history of stringent protectionism, to which it remained wedded even after launching its reform program. Trade and financial barriers in India were brought down in an exceedingly sluggish fashion.

Reforms *inter alia* were instrumental in GDP growth and initiated structural transformation in the two economies. However, as industrialization progressed, India benefitted much less than China from economies of scale and from the "fordist model of growth" (Valli and Saccone 2009: 101). This model of growth is associated with a stage of strong, interlinked growth of industrial and services sectors in which scale economies and network economies assume enormous importance and become significant contributors to growth. In China, towards the end of the 1980s, the strategic sectors of the fordist growth model were electrical domestic appliances and their interlinked sectors, which included steel, plastics, power generation, and so on. With the passage of time, other sectors were added to this list. They were microelectronics, telecommunications, and energy. After 2000 more industrial sectors gained strength and joined in as dynamic sectors that promoted fordist growth. Principal among them were industrial vehicles, motorcycles, and automobiles.

Likewise, in India, the key dynamic sectors in the early 1990s were machinery, household electrical appliances, steel, and pharmaceuticals. Recent additions to this list are software services, telecommunications, motorcycles, and automobiles. Structural transformation in China passed through two phases of fordist growth. The first phase lasted between 1978 and the mid-1990s. This phase was largely based on the growth of the domestic markets. The second phase spanned from the late 1990s to the beginning of the global financial crisis and recession in the late 1990s. This phase was supported and accelerated by both rapid export growth and massive inflows of foreign direct investment (FDI). Industrialization in India, since the mid-1980s, did progress but it was discernibly less rapid and widespread than in China. However, during this period the services sector in India was a larger part of the economy than in China and grew at a relatively rapid pace.

In the early 2010s, China's structural reforms appear to have deepened far more than those belatedly initiated in India. The post-reform economic transformation achieved by China is far greater than that achieved by India. Despite elements of experimentation during the initial period, China's growth strategy turned out to be methodical, deliberate, and pragmatic. Conversely, although India started with a properly laid out macroeconomic reform program, its growth strategy seemed to be impromptu, opportunistic, and often chaotic. Major macroeconomic decisions in India could not be taken without inordinate delays because of its multi-party, pluralist politics. The one-party system in China facilitated and accelerated its macroeconomic decision-making process. This fact is amply demonstrated by the rapid pace of economic reform implementation in China in comparison to its disconcertingly slow pace in India.

Notwithstanding the stop-go pace of reforms, in the early and mid-2000s, the pace of Indian economic growth transformed further. India seemed to be joining China in the category of the world's fastest growing economies. During the period of the Tenth Five Year Plan (2002–7), the average annual GDP growth rate reached 7.8 percent. During this period, 2005 and 2006 were the years of highest rates of GDP growth – 9.4 and 9.6 percent, respectively. This growth rate was not far behind China's double-digit growth. To some analysts, this heady pace seemed unsustainable (Das 2009a).

2 Growth performance and impact

Differences in growth experiences have had a distinct impact on economic growth and standards of living in the two countries. Over the years, a large gap has emerged in per capita income and therefore in the quality of life between the two countries. According to 2008 statistics, per capita national income at market prices and exchange rates in China was US $2940. The corresponding figure for India was US$1070, approximately a third that of China. Thus, the Chinese live significantly better than the Indians do.

If per capita incomes are compared using the PPP figures, the comparison appears somewhat better for India. The per capita national income of China in PPP terms was $6020 and that of India $2960 (World Bank 2011). According to this indicator, living standards in

China are approximately twice of those of India. In addition, the Human Development Index (HDI, UNDP 2009), computed by the United Nations Development Program (UNDP), shows that China stood at 92nd position out of 194 countries that were included in the index and India at 134th. Recent economic transformation has led to the emergence of a middle class of substantive size in both countries. This includes an upwardly mobile group of well-trained professionals. This has profound implications for the shifting of consumption patterns in the two countries (Das 2009b).

At the end of the 2000s, as the economic circumstances of the two economies had markedly improved, so did their status in the global economy. China and India grew into the first and third largest economies of Asia. According to the 2010 statistics, at market prices and exchange rates, China was the second largest economy in the world, with a GDP of $5.88 trillion. Indian GDP was $1.54 trillion and it ranked 12th. If the two countries' GDP is measured in terms of PPP, their status improves further. China ($10.01 trillion) was the 2nd largest economy in the world and India ($4.06 trillion) the 4th (IMF 2011). Given their remote history of economic strength, their current rapid growth could justly be regarded as their economic renaissance. Their re-emergence is something akin to a "second Asian economic miracle." Two Goldman Sachs studies (2003 and 2004) projected the countries' future growth trajectories and assigned them higher status in the global economy over the next of two decades. Their newly acquired status in the global economy will involve them in key roles in several areas of global economic and financial policy debates.

The two economies achieved markedly differing degrees of success in alleviating the mass poverty from which they suffered during their pre-reform eras. China had one of the highest proportions of population in poverty in the world in 1980. At that time, only four countries (Burkina Faso, Cambodia, Mali, and Uganda) had higher poverty levels than China. Poverty measures are usually based on National Household Surveys (NHS). In China, they measure household incomes while in India they measure household expenditure. Using a common poverty line set at $1.25 a day and taking PPP exchange rates for consumption in 2005, Ravallion (2009) compared the rate of poverty alleviation in the two economies. NHS statistics reveal that poverty means for China were 84.0 percent in 1981, 53.7 percent in 1993, and 16.3 percent in 2005. This was a high pace of change in an upward direction.

In comparison, poverty means for India were 59.8 percent in 1981, 49.4 percent in 1993, and 41.6 percent in 2005. The growth elasticity of poverty reduction, that is, proportional change in poverty per unit of GDP per capita growth, was –0.8 for China and –0.4 for India. These are large differences in the impact of a given rate of GDP growth on poverty reduction. Initial conditions and macroeconomic and socio-economic policies lie behind these large differences in the elasticity of poverty reduction in the two economies. In addition, China's growth-promoting pro-poor reforms were reflected well in the impact they had on poverty.

In the decades during the post-independence period, India had remained a moribund, underperforming economy. It paid high economic and social costs for socialist economic policies and a heavy emphasis on the development of the public sector. Remnants of its old import-substituting industrialization strategy continued to be part of its macroeconomic strategy until recent years. Protectionist barriers widely pervaded, and they were reduced at an extremely slow pace. GDP growth rate began picking up in the mid-1980s. India's per capita income has doubled since 1980. During the same period, China's per capita income rose seven-fold. During the contemporary post-reform era, Indian GDP growth remained much slower than that of China.

Yet economic transformation in India was still substantive. Indian economic performance positively recorded improvements when compared to that of its past, although it did not match the dynamic growth of China. Despite improvement and upturn, India fell behind China in every indicator of economic and social well-being. Likewise, in spite of recent improvements in export performance, India's exports remained far lower than those of China. In 2009, China surpassed Germany as the largest exporting economy in the world. India still does not have a place of prestige on the league table of major global exporters annually published by the World Trade Organization (WTO).

Due to their rapid growth, growing financial influence, and new-found sense of assertiveness, China and India are already making their presence felt on the global economic landscape of the early twenty-first century. As leading emerging market economies (EMEs), they are having a say in shaping the contours of the evolving international monetary system. In the aftermath of the global economic and financial crisis of 2007–09, the international monetary system is sure to change away from the US-dominated system, towards a multi-polar one. The shift in the economic power structure of the global economy warrants and justifies a move towards multi-polarity. The evolving system is likely to be more inclusive and region based, in which the large EMEs are sure to have a say. In a multi-polar world, which economies or groups thereof would play a crucial role in shaping the future global economic and financial architecture? Three economic poles obviously stand out, namely the US, the Euro area, and the large EMEs, represented by China and India, or perhaps the BRIC economies. All three poles share common interests and goals in creating and operating an efficiently performing global economic and financial system (Dailami and Masson 2009).

Notwithstanding the fact that they are still lower-middle income economies,[3] their sheer size and remarkable GDP growth rate have turned China and India into substantive contributors to the global economy. Around the turn of the twenty-first century, they began to have an impact on the growth of the global economy. In the recent past, the US economy has ceased to be the singular locomotive of global growth. China and India, along with the other large EMEs, have become meaningful global entities in their own right. Since the late 1990s, China's contribution to global growth became significant. It contributed to global GDP growth far more than India. However, during the mid-2000s, the gap between the two economies began to narrow; Indian GDP growth rate picked up further after 2003. This was a structural increase in growth rather than a mere cyclical upturn (Poddar and Yi 2007). Productivity growth drove nearly one-half of this growth, which was sustained during the 2003–7 period. This in turn increased India's contribution to global growth.

While the global economic and financial crisis of 2007–9 affected them adversely, China and India were two out of three economies that did not slip into negative GDP growth during 2009. Notwithstanding a deceleration in their GDP growth rates, China, India and Indonesia were the three economies that escaped economic contraction and a severe recession. Both China and India remained resilient despite the headwinds created by a severe global recession. With their large and growing domestic markets, they weathered the storm better than the advanced industrial economies. Notwithstanding the crisis and recession, both of them were projected to turn in impressive performances. Due to their economic resilience, the global economic crisis did not entail a turn for worse. In addition, the two Asian giants led the rebound of the global economy.

The vulnerability of the Chinese economy to the global financial crisis and recession was higher because, like the other East Asian model economies, it is highly open, albeit this does not apply to its financial sector. The export sector was hit hard by the crisis and recession. In the last quarter of 2008, a significant proportion of exporting firms slashed production and their labor forces in half. This caused a sharp drop in industrial production. That being said, in early 2010 it was widely felt among economists who study the Chinese economy that China had had a "good" crisis. It responded swiftly and decisively. Its monetary and fiscal stimulus was one of the largest and transmitted into the real economy with a relatively short time lag. As planned, it successfully lifted domestic demand.

One of the reasons why the Indian economy was less vulnerable was because it is much less open and export-dependent than China and the East Asian-model economies. Secondly, while reforms and their implementation did not progress at a satisfactory pace, whatever reforms did take place made the Indian economy resistant to external shocks. Financial and banking sector reforms played a definitive role in rendering the economy shock-resistant. The timely and coordinated monetary and fiscal stimulus packages devised by all the major advanced industrial economies and several large EMEs steadied the global financial markets earlier than most expectations, which benefitted the Indian economy. These stimulus packages also helped sustain global demand, which worked towards making the Indian economy resilient.

3 Factors and total factor productivity analysis

The determinants of rapid growth and their sustainability are valuable research and policy issues. Mainstream growth accounting identifies the accumulation of physical capital, demographic factors, and technological advancement as factors behind growth outcomes. Capital accumulation determines the capital-to-labor ratio in the steady state and influences the GDP growth rate. The inventory of determinants does not end here. There are myriad other determinants of growth for an economy. For instance, TFP growth is an important source of growth. It is a measure of gains in the efficiency with which the factor inputs are utilized. The external sector, which made a substantive contribution to the rapid growth of the so-called miracle economies of East Asia, is another one. Governance and macroeconomic management, labor legislation, educational standard and policy (or human capital) are some of the other vital factors that impinge upon growth.

In this section, we will analyze and determine the pattern or structure of inputs to growth outcomes in China and India of the factors that are generally regarded as essential for economic growth in conventional growth accounting frameworks, such as capital accumulation, labor supply, and total factor productivity; and other economic factors that are uniquely importantly for economic growth under contemporary conditions in countries such China and India: the contributions of exports and global and regional economic integration.

a Capital accumulation

Using standard growth accounting technique, Bosworth and Collins (2008) estimated that two of the most important factors that contributed to rapid growth in the two economies over the 1978–2004 period were capital accumulation and TFP, or efficiency gains. Contributions made by these two factors were approximately equal in the two economies. IMF (2006) and Kalish (2006) came up with broadly comparable conclusions.

Acceleration in the pace of capital formation in China took place first in 1978 when the macroeconomic reforms were launched, and again in the early 1990s when the economy was further liberalized to foreign competition. In India, capital stock building did not start until the early 1990s, as the industrial investment licensing system was ending. When rates of capital formation and TFP growth in the two economies are compared, China was found to have performed far better than India. It achieved its growth "through both substantial increases in capital per worker and rates of total factor productivity growth more than double those for India" (Bosworth and Collins 2008: 54). Comparison of the rate of capital formation made by Herd and Dougherty (2007) put China ahead by 4 percent to 5 percent over the 1978–2008 period. In more recent years, this difference increased to abound 7 percent. It evidently translated into similar differentials of capital per worker. A more rapid growth in capital stock in China was translated into higher capital intensity of production processes.

Rates of savings and investment in China and India are more revealing and buttress the above observation. The saving rate in the Chinese economy was high. In recent years, it became much higher and hovered around 45 percent of GDP. There were years when it crossed 50 percent of GDP. Such a commendable saving performance helped China sustain a high investment rate. Therefore, the rate of capital formation in China was also high, reaching close to 45 percent of GDP (Table 2.2). Yu (2009) asserted that China over-invested, which, *inter alia*, caused a high dependency on exports.[4]

In contrast, India's saving rate hovered around 20 percent of GDP, but this has increased to 35 percent in recent years. Still, the investment rate was appreciably lower than that in China. Capital formation remained around 25 percent of the GDP, that is, around 20 percentage points lower than that of China (Table 2.1). Ominously, large public sector deficits have remained a perennial and detrimental shortcoming of Indian macroeconomic management. Fiscal profligacy has remained

Table 2.1 Saving and capital formation

	1987	1997	2006
	Gross Capital Formation		
China	37.3	37.9	44.4
India	22.0	23.9	36.0
	Gross National Savings		
China	37.3	41.8	53.8
India	20.9	24.7	35.3

Unit: Percentage of GDP.
Source: World Bank 2011.

Table 2.2 Labor productivity growth

	1980–89	1990–99	2000–05
China	7.51	8.66	7.67
India	2.78	4.36	3.76

Unit: Percentage of annual change.
Source: Herd and Dougherty (2007).

a historic weakness of the Indian economy. It chronically marred the saving performance of the economy and absorbed a large part of household savings. This is an area of Indian economic policy and management that has been for decades, and continues to be, in pressing need of mending (Das 2010).

b Labor productivity and labor market practices

Growth accounting analyses also show that labor productivity growth played a decisive role in improving labor quality and TFP in both economies, once economic reforms were launched (Herd and Dougherty 2007). India had an additional advantage in this respect because its working age population grew faster than the total population. However, as discussed earlier, the rate of capital accumulation in India was markedly lower than that in China. Therefore, labor productivity growth in India was responsible for a larger contribution to TFP growth than in China. That said, labor productivity growth in India was found to be much slower than that in China (Table 2.2). Lee and colleagues (Lee, Rao, and Shepherd 2007) came to a similar conclusion regarding labor productivity in the manufacturing sector in the two economies. An important factor that buttressed labor productivity growth in China was labor movement from low-productivity agriculture to high-productivity industry and services sectors.

The glaring contrast between labor market practices and legislation in the two countries is notable. The labor market in India continued to be an albatross around the neck of the economy because of the endurance of archaic and irrational labor legislation. Despite high costs to the economy, India did not abandon employment protection policies and legislation that it had adopted during its socialist past. Judged from the norms of the advanced industrial economies, they are draconian. Enterprises in India cannot retrench labor without problems. They cannot change the job description of workers, which would be regarded as labor exploitation. Herd and Dougherty (2007: 81) noted that Indian states with "higher degrees of restrictive labor legislation have been found to have higher poverty levels." Restrictiveness of employment protection has remained one of the factors holding back the growth of Indian GDP. Conversely, China swiftly reduced restrictiveness in its employment protection since the mid-1990s as its SOE (state-owned enterprise) sector was being wound down. At the same time, employment generation in the private sector gained momentum, offsetting the retrenchment in SOEs. This policy move had a positive effect on China's labor productivity and TFP growth, which in turn favorably influenced GDP growth.

c Growth in total factor productivity

Macroeconomic reforms, capital accumulation, and increases in labor productivity in the two economies indeed favorably impacted their TFP growth in general. Hesitant reforms and their tardy implementation in India caused slow pick up in the TFP growth and *pari passu* slow increase in the saving and investment performance. In contrast, in China, the pace of reforms and their implementation was strong and it stayed the course. Converting SOEs into private enterprises provided a strong impetus to TFP growth. Herd and Dougherty (2007: 77) concluded, "from a purely accounting perspective, over the last 25 years, about 40 percent of the difference in labor productivity growth in China and India has come from lower TFP growth."

The trends of TFP increase in the three principal sectors of the economy in the two countries differ. Growth of agricultural output per worker and agricultural productivity in China outstripped that in India. One notable trait of the Indian agricultural sector was that growth in employment in agriculture continued to increase after 1993; it occurred essentially due to inadequate expansion of the other two sectors, namely industry and services.

One basic difference between the economic structures of the two countries is the size of the industrial sector, which includes manufacturing. As seen in Table 2.3, the size of the industrial sector remained strikingly larger in China than that in India. While in China it accounted for almost half of GDP, in India its contribution remained less than a third.

This sector grew in both the economies since the early 1980s and capital per worker increased. However, Bosworth and Collins (2008) show that China recorded much faster TFP gains in the industrial sector than India did. Spectacular growth in output per worker since 1993 in China is attributed to both an increase in capital per worker and TFP improvements. Large empirical exercises reported higher productivity in the manufacturing sector in China than in India. For instance, Lee et al. (2007) concluded that for the 1980–2002 period, productivity in Chinese manufacturing output was much higher than that in India. Performance of the manufacturing sector was directly influenced by the nature and pace of economic reforms and the tenacity with which they were pursued. Hsieh and Klenow (2009) also reported higher manufacturing TFP in China than in India.

The services sector expanded briskly in both economies. It was relatively larger in India and its rapid pace of expansion in recent years attracted global attention (Table 2.4). China's services sector output grew steadily at the rate of 5 percent per year during 1978–2004, and since 1993 it has also recorded increases in capital per worker in the

Table 2.3 Size of the industrial sector

	1987	1997	2006
China	43.9	47.5	48.1
India	26.3	26.8	29.3

Unit: Percentage of GDP.
Source: World Bank 2011.

Table 2.4 Size of the services sector

	1987	1997	2006
China	29.3	34.4	40.0
India	44.3	47.1	52.4

Unit: Percentage of GDP.
Source: World Bank 2011.

services sector. India's services sector not only matched China's commendable performance but also its growth accelerated after 1993 and its output per worker exceeded 5 percent per year. What was remarkable about this achievement was that capital per worker in the services sector in India increased only modestly. A large part of the increase in output is attributed to the increase in TFP. It was possible due to the expansion of relatively modern sub-sectors, such as finance and business services. Such sub-sectors become highly productive when supported by information and communication technology (ICT). However, it needs to be noted that the largest sub-sectors in India were wholesale and retail trade, and transport.[5]

The rapid TFP growth in China and India during their recent growth spurt period sets them apart from the East Asian miracle economies. Their rapid growth during the 1970s and 1980s was largely based on factor input accumulation.

4 External sector, and regional and global integration

Both the economies benefitted from the recent wave of economic globalization. It enabled them to make a short cut to economic modernization. Ongoing global integration facilitated a leap from traditional sectors to those incorporating modern and advanced technologies in both economies. In particular, China's strategy of creating SEZs made it an exceptional success in attracting FDI, both from the Chinese diaspora in the surrounding Asian economies and from around the world. In no time it became, and continued to remain, the most attractive EME for investment by the transnational corporations (TNCs). In contrast, India only recently tried to develop SEZs and was not able to create successful ones like those in China. It also did not develop into a large recipient of FDI because of excessive government interference and bureaucratic rigmarole. That said, in recent years FDI inflows to India have shown improvement. Overall, economic and financial integration with the global economy benefitted China far more than it benefitted India.

Multilateral trade in goods and services and regional and global integration were areas in which the China turned in an outstanding performance, while India remained a slow mover or a downright laggard. That said, India's export performance has remarkably improved in comparison to its past. In addition, it recorded marked improvements since 2005 in the area of trade. However, sub-regional, regional, and global integration continue to be areas where India made little progress.

a External sector performance

Both the economies were near autarkies in the past. They were marginal traders in the early 1980s and accounted for a minuscule share of world trade in goods and services. The Chinese economy was even more autarkic than that of India, which had a history of exceedingly high protectionism. China's foreign trade (imports + exports) in 1978 was paltry, at $21 billion (Das 2008).

In the multilateral trade arena, the two economies started from a low base. However, China, over the last three decades, and India, over the last two decades, liberalized their respective external sectors. They adopted and implemented outward-oriented economic policies at a markedly different pace. China also adopted a multipronged approach to develop, invigorate, and promote the external sector.[6] Policy officials in China took a leaf from the book of the East Asian model economies and purposefully promoted exports of manufactured goods. The ultimate objective was to strengthen this sector so that it turned into an engine of economic growth. This strategy succeeded and Chinese economy has emerged as a manufacturing juggernaut of impressive proportions.

According to the 2008 WTO statistics, China's exports were $1.42 trillion and its share in total world exports was 8.9 percent. This made China the second largest exporting economy in the world after Germany. Comparable Indian exports were $177.5 billion, or 1.1 percent of the total world exports. This gave India the 27th position on the WTO league table of large exporting economies (WTO 2009). These trends partly reflect the trends in output growth in the two countries. According to *The Wall Street Journal* (2010: January 7), based on statistics released by China's customs agency, China surpassed Germany in 2009 to become the largest exporter in the world.[7] Thus the Chinese economy travelled the distance from near autarky to the largest exporting economy in an amazingly short time span. The external sector of the Chinese economy is functioning in a dynamic manner and this is demonstrated by the fact that China's share in world merchandise trade is higher than that in world output, while the reverse holds for India. China's share in multilateral trade passed its share in global output in 2002.

In the exports of commercial services, China's exports were $146.4 billion in 2008. Its share in total world commercial services trade was 3.9 percent and it was the fifth largest exporter of commercial services. In comparison, India's exports were $102.6 billon. Its share in total world commercial services trade was 2.7 percent and it was the ninth largest exporter (WTO 2009). Thus in this one area India is not far behind China. It is essentially because of India's notable success in information and communication technology (ICT) sector. This is one sector of the economy that fortuitously developed without government interference and therefore bureaucratic inefficiency, corruption, and malfeasance could not obstruct its growth. India's ten-million strong bureaucracy has massive economic and social costs.

During the contemporary period, China has maintained a current account surplus ranging between 8 and 11.5 percent of its GDP. Conversely, India has had a tradition of a current account deficit, usually ranging between 2 and 3 percent of its GDP. The crisis and recession are likely to widen India's deficit. At the end of 2009, China's foreign exchange reserves were $2.4 trillion, the highest in the world. China held 23.3 percent of the world's total reserves. The comparable figure for India was $287 billion; it was the sixth largest holder of foreign exchange reserves in the world.

b Regional and global integration

Over the last three decades, China has cultivated close regional and global trade ties. India failed to do so. The trading pattern that China has developed is to import from other emerging-market economies and developing economies, and export to the EU and the US. No comparable pattern has emerged for India. The two economies have gradually increased their mutual trade and investment, and have been discussing forming a bilateral free trade agreement (FTA).

As estimated in trade intensities as computed by Bhattacharaya and Bhattacharyay using the gravity model (2007), China and India have considerable bilateral trade potential. As for benefits, in the short run India's potential gains from an FTA were found to be lower than those of China because of high tariffs. However, in the long-run, when the tariff levels were brought down, India's gains from an FTA increased and grew larger than those for China. Their bilateral trade exceeded $50 billion in 2009. China is the second largest trade partner of India; in contrast India is not an important trading partner of China.

The gravity model is highly suitable and beneficial in estimating trade linkages and trade intensities of economies. It helps reach revealing conclusions. Estimates of trade intensities for the two economies show that China is "highly integrated relative to fundamentals," whereas India is "poorly integrated in global trade relative to fundamentals" (Bussiere and Mehl 2008: 17). In terms of bilateral trade linkages, estimates demonstrated the same results; that is, they were stronger for China in relation to its fundamentals, while in the case of India bilateral trade linkages were found to be weak in relation to its fundamentals. China was also found to be well integrated with the large commodity exporters, such as Australia, Canada, and India. Additionally, it was found to have been highly integrated with the other Asian EMEs relative to what its economic size, location, and other relevant fundamentals would justify.

One reason behind this was the well-developed Asian production networks, of which China is an integral part. These networks have succeeded in producing a myriad of manufactured products, and high-technology goods in particular. They are highly active in ICT hardware production and exports. The production networks contributed significantly to the export performance of China and other Asian economies. These production chains enabled China to make ideal utilization of its comparative advantage in a low-wage labor force.

The results of the same gravity model exercise showed India to be far less integrated with its neighboring Asian economies than suggested by its fundamentals. This weakness began with its weaker trade links with the other South Asian countries, even though the South Asian Association for Regional Cooperation (SAARC) has existed for almost two decades. It has so far proved to be an insubstantial entity, essentially due to historical and political reasons. India also did not make much progress in integrating with the Southeast Asian or East Asian economies. Conversely, China integrated well and at a rapid rate with these two groups of Asian economies.

5 Beyond the conventional framework

Two populous giants of Asia that were a domineering part of the global economy in the remote past had become two of the most impoverished economies in the world. During the closing decades of the twentieth century their economies began to transform and they began to grow rapidly again. In the first decade of the twenty-first century, they began making a discernible global economic impact. Their re-emergence into global economic prominence is regarded as one of the most important economic events of the contemporary period.

During their present growth spurt, while the two economies grew at a commendable pace and succeeded in alleviating poverty in their respective societies, their individual growth performances had a great deal of disparity. There were marked differences in their growth paradigms. A comparison of principal economic variables and sectors demonstrates that the Chinese economy performed far superior to the Indian. We have compared and contrasted the rapid growth in the two economies and point to the reasons behind the better-performed growth trajectory of the Chinese economy. In particular, the analysis in this chapter has examined the principal economic factors behind the disparity in the growth paradigms of the two economies. Differences in growth paradigms had a distinct impact on economic growth and the relative standards of living and poverty alleviation in the two economies.

The macroeconomic reforms and restructuring in China were implemented at a far more rapid pace than in India. In particular, the external sector was liberalized more aggressively in China than in India. It was instrumental in more greatly benefitting China from the ongoing globalization than India. Slow and incomplete reforms in India resulted in a large cost to the economy. The growth accounting framework revealed that although both the economies accelerated capital accumulation, acceleration in the pace of capital accumulation started in China earlier. Various comparisons of TFP growth reveal that China performed far better than India, while India also recorded marked improvements. Hesitant macroeconomic reforms were one of the reasons behind slow improvement in TFP in India. In particular, China did far better in TFP growth in the manufacturing sector. Differences in rates of saving and investment in both economies are also revealing. They confirm the same conclusion that China performed much better than India.

Our growth accounting analysis also revealed that an increase in labor productivity favorably affected TFP growth in the two economies. Labor productivity growth in India was high, but remained low in comparison to China. This conclusion applies emphatically to the manufacturing sector. There are glaring differences in the labor market practices and legislation. Unlike China's, the Indian economy continued with its archaic and irrational labor legislation. Restrictive employment protection has remained one of the factors holding Indian GDP growth back.

In the twin areas of multilateral trade in goods and services and regional and global economic integration, China turned in an extraordinary performance. India remained a slow mover. Yet India's external sector has been performing far superior to its past languid performance. Gravity model estimates of trade intensities for the two economies show that China is highly integrated relative to its fundamentals, while India is poorly integrated into global trade. China's regional and global trade and financial ties, as well as those with the other EMEs, have also grown strong, while India has made scant progress. Like China, India also did not develop into a successful FDI recipient until recently.

Thus viewed, the two populous Asian giants have performed ebulliently over the recent decades, but it is obvious that the Chinese economy outperformed the Indian economy by a wide margin. That China is emerging as a global economic powerhouse is a foregone conclusion. It is also clear that India's economic present is far better than its past but, based on its recent performance, it cannot be counted on to grow into a China-like economic powerhouse of global dimension.

In conclusion, this chapter is intended to provide a comparative description of the growth paradigm of China and India. The purpose here is much less ambitious than classical growth accounting, where the contributions of standard inputs such as land, capital, and labor to growth outcomes are precisely computed through sophisticated mathematic models. The paradigm we describe here establishes patterns of growth performance of the two economies over time and patterns of factor inputs to the growth outcomes of these economies. Clearly, given the historical conditions of transition in the economic system and the contemporary world economic conditions of global and regional integration, the narrow, conventional factor input analysis is not sufficient to reflect the growth paradigm. In these two cases, macroeconomic reform policy and external sector and global and regional integration are significant enabling and structuring factors. The analysis and evidence presented in this chapter has demonstrated that there is no clear pattern of growth in these two well-performing economies. While they both have performed impressively, they also performed differently. Growth accounting may be able to describe variations in their factor input structure and growth outcomes; however, a convincing explanation would require more than just a growth accounting description.

Notes

1. Or, growth pattern or model, as many others might prefer.
2. International dollar is used to measure GDP in PPP terms.
3. According to the World Bank classification, lower-middle income group of countries have per capita income ranging between US$976 and US $3855 per annum.
4. In 2007, China's export to GDP ratio was 35 percent. In 2008, exports declined.
5. The source of statistics regarding TFP here is Bosworth and Collins (2008).
6. See Das (2008) for more detailed discussion on this.
7. According to China's customs agency, China's exports in 2009 were $1.2 trillion. This was ahead of the $1.17 trillion forecast for Germany by its foreign trade organization.

3

A Supply–Demand Analysis of Economic Growth of China and India

Srikanta Chatterjee

After a long period of slow growth and policy-induced relative isolation from the world economy, both China and India initiated market-oriented reform programs in the late 1970s and early 1990s respectively. The changes that have come in their train have begun to change the face of not just the two giant economies, but of the world as a whole. Understanding the underlying forces that have contributed to this remarkable transformation is therefore a worthwhile exercise in itself. It may also provide rich empirical evidence for us to understand the working of the modern capitalist economy and the world economic system.

The economic transformation of China and India has, quite understandably, attracted great attention in both the academic literature and the general media (see Bardhan 2009, 2010; Chatterjee 2009b; Srinivasan T. N. 2005, 2006 and 2009). The issue, which is perhaps yet to receive a systematic treatment, concerns the scope and nature of the economic transformation and the consequent growth experience. This is particularly true in their relation to early modern growth experiences in Europe, North America, and East Asia.

This chapter employs a supply–demand framework to explain the two countries' economic growth, and then addresses the issue of their long-term prospects. The analysis here is confined only to the "economic" factors that contribute to growth outcomes. Admittedly, there are other factors, such as environmental and institutional factors, that influence a country's growth performance. These, however, are not within the scope of this chapter.

After a brief description of the two growth experiences, the chapter discusses competing models of explaining economic growth, and explains how a supply–demand framework can yield useful information as to how contributing factors relate to the growth outcomes, and how the growth experiences of China and India fit with the conventional growth accounting models.

It then examines the nature and sources of the two economies' observed growth performances to date, and uses the supply–demand framework to analyze the contributions of the input factors. The chapter will then extend the supply–demand analysis to forecast the future growth prospects of the two economies. The supply–demand analysis of the growth outcomes, like the growth analysis of the previous chapter, is an application of the conventional growth accounting mythology and framework, and is thus concerned with direct input factors in growth outcomes, though this chapter employs a broader framework that not only looks at supply-side factors but also demand-side factors. The supply–demand analysis establishes a distinct structure of input factors to growth outcomes and thus helps us to see if a slightly different approach to growth accounting and analysis can lead to more accurate, if not entirely different, descriptions of the growth patterns of the two economies.

1 Competing approaches to economic growth and supply–demand analysis

There have been significant changes to the economies of China and India over the periods of their rapid growth, some as a direct consequence of the growth process itself. China's per capita income is over twice that of India's in price-adjusted, PPP, terms. India's population growth rate is over twice that of China's – a reflection mainly of China's one-child policy. Industry is a significantly bigger contributor to China's GDP than India's, while the service sector contributes more to India's GDP. Income inequality in China is higher than in India, but the ratio of the income share of the top income decile to the bottom is higher in India. India has a much higher proportion of its population in poverty than has China. The proportion of literate persons in the adult population is a lot higher in China. China's economy is much more open than India's, as measured by trade, that is exports plus imports, as a proportion of GDP.

In many respects, the growth patterns of the two economies have not entirely been in keeping with the conventional growth models used by economists to explain observed growth (Basu 2009; Chatterjee 2009b). One of these abnormalities is sectoral sequencing from agriculture to industry, and then services, as anticipated in conventional development economics. A low-income developing country tends to be dominated by agriculture and primary activities; the development process helps enlarge the industrial sector, which attracts both labor and other resources away from agriculture and primary activities. It is only at a much later stage of development that the tertiary sector typically becomes the leading one.

This, indeed, is what one observes, by and large, in the evolution of the Chinese economy. India, however, with a larger agricultural sector than China's, and lower per capita income and adult literacy rate, has a significantly larger service sector share of its GDP. One particular feature of India's growth experience, for example, has been the predominance of its service sector ahead of the more usual industrial sector.

The relevance of this and other similar characteristics generally, and in relation to the two economies, has been addressed in the literature by several commentators (Bhagwati 1984; Bottelier 2007; Chatterjee 2009; Gordon and Gupta 2003, for e.g.). This chapter will examine in general terms these characteristics of the two economies, but in a more contested theoretical framework.

Historically, different economies have, at different times, grown at different rates. What factors and forces cause economies to grow is a question that continues to excite economists and other social scientists. Current literature on economic growth, largely in the field of economics, can be generally viewed according to three groups, each representing a major approach to explaining modern economic growth. The first one is what is often referred to as the post-Keynesian approach, embodied in the works of Roy F. Harrod (1939) and Evsey D. Domar (1946), for example. This group emphasizes the roles of savings and investment. The second approach is the neo-classical models of Robert Solow (1956, 1970) and Trevor Swan (1956), which focus on factor accumulation – particularly the accumulation of physical capital, deriving from investment – as the major determinant of income growth in the short term. This, combined with exogenously given technological progress, influences growth in the longer term. The "endogenous" growth model of the Romer-Lucas genre falls into the third category. Scholars of this tradition treat technical progress as an endogenous (within-economy) process and emphasize knowledge accumulation; that is, the formation of human capital, together with innovation and public infrastructure, as factors promoting growth in the longer term (Barrow 1991; Lucas 1988; Romer 1990).

Following Keynesian macroeconomic analysis (Keynes 1936), growth theorists have long emphasized the close relationship between investment in productive activities and the real income of a country. Since savings act as the source of investment, a rise in the rate of savings can also make the growth rate rise. Savings can be of domestic origin or foreign. For a low-income developing country, domestic savings are usually low. Therefore, access to foreign savings in the form of direct foreign investment is helpful in raising a country's growth rate. The increased international mobility of capital in the post-war period has been a major influence on the observed growth processes of a number of countries – most recently of China and, to a lesser extent, India.

As the transmission channel between savings and income growth is investment, one can discern an induced effect, which flows from increased income to increased investment, via increased savings. While these approaches to explaining growth have a longer history, the more recent advances in the growth-theoretic literature, such as, for example, the endogenous growth theories of Barro, Lucas and Romer alluded to above, re-affirm the crucial role of capital accumulation, via increased investment, in the long-term growth process of an economy.

This chapter follows the above line of inquiry and demonstrates the importance of savings and investment, together with technological improvement, as the crucial contributors to growth. It shows that the interrelationships of these influences on economic growth can be explained further by identifying them as influences from the demand side and the supply side. Both demand- and supply-side factors influence a country's growth performance. The demand factors are domestic consumption and investment spending by the private and the public sectors, while external demand is reflected in the size of the net export earnings; that is, exports less imports. Among the supply-side influences are the availability and the quality of factor inputs such as labor and capital; capital formation; that is, productive investment in physical and human capital, and what is known as total- or multi-factor productivity; that is, enhanced output per unit of a composite of inputs used in the production of goods and services.

2 Demand factors analysis

China's growth has been driven more by investment and net exports than domestic consumption, particularly since the late 1990s. This is in line with the East Asian model economies. China's high savings rate is a topic that has been widely discussed in the literature. Looking closely at this, one finds that the savings rate has gone through three identifiable phases: growing from 30–35 percent of GDP in the early 1980s to 40–5 percent by 1994; falling to around 37 percent by 2000, and then rising again to above 50 percent by 2008. This indicates an annual average growth rate of savings of two percentage points of GDP a year, and a marginal propensity to save of around 60 percent (Ma and Yi 2010).

This, together with large and steady overseas investment flows, saw China's investment rate also rise, from 37 percent of GDP in 1998 to 45 percent by 2008. But since even this high investment rate has still remained lower than China's domestic savings rate, China has had a large and growing current account surplus that has helped to swell its foreign currency reserves from US$403 billion in 2003 to around US $2.27 trillion in September 2009 (Morrison and Labonte 2009: 1).

Much of China's domestic investment has been in infrastructure and industrial development, which, while improving its industrial growth rate and export performance, has kept its levels of consumption and growth rate decidedly modest. The current account surplus and surging reserves have been putting upward pressure on China's currency, the *renminbi* (RMB), or *yuan*.

Since an appreciating *yuan* would dampen its net exports, China has been lending much of its external surplus to deficit countries like the United States by acquiring US dollar assets. While this may have helped the process of China's export-led growth, it is potentially a highly risky strategy too. A decline in the value of a currency such as the US dollar could involve substantial capital loss for China. Likewise, the strategy of export-oriented industrial growth has made about 70 percent of the Chinese economy directly or indirectly dependent on the world economy.

It is worth recalling that, over the initial period of China's economic transition, the US dollar/Chinese *yuan* exchange rate had steadily declined from 1:1.5 in 1980 to 1:8.62 in 1994. This depreciation, combined with its large supply of cheap labor and high rate of capital formation, helped China increase its share of world export trade significantly – from 1.2 percent of GDP in 1983 to 8.9 percent in 2007 – which, in turn, helped its fast economic growth. Its imports also grew from 1.1 percent of GDP to 6.9 percent over the same period, which helped China's major trade partners around the world to achieve higher growth rates via rising exports (to China).

More recently, however, China has faced a unique quandary. While its export-led growth strategy has benefited from a low exchange rate, China's traditionally low and steady domestic inflation has become more volatile, trending upwards in the last few years. This has made currency appreciation a viable policy option to counter the inflationary pressure. Indeed, as inflation reached a peak of 8.7 percent in February

2008, the *yuan*, too, had appreciated by just over 7 percent in the year to January 2008, as part of the 20 percent decline in its nominal rate against the US dollar since the floating of the *yuan* in July 2005. Inflation started to decline steadily from March 2008, however, and remained negative over much of 2009. But it has again been trending upwards to reach 4.9 percent in January 2011. In the year to February 2011, the *yuan*'s nominal rate rose against the US dollar by about 3.8 percent, from 1:6.83 to 1: 6.57 (*The Economist* 2011: February 26th – March 4th: 93). The floating of the *yuan* has thus been helpful in moderating the domestic inflationary pressure in China.

The exchange rate story is more complicated, however, than the nominal rates of the *yuan* might indicate (Morrison and Labonte 2009). Because the US dollar has depreciated against many major currencies in recent periods, and the Chinese *yuan* is still largely tied to the dollar, it too has depreciated against many currencies. The Bank of International Settlements (BIS) reports that China's real trade-weighted exchange rate had appreciated by 18 percent from January 2008 to February 2009, but over the following eight months – to October 2009 – it depreciated by 9.5 percent (Morrison and Labonte 2009: 2). Thus China seems to be hesitant to use the exchange rate as a tool by which to control domestic inflation. It is seemingly trying to protect its net export advantage too, but the increased volatility in its exchange rate is also not a desirable development.

India's GDP growth has been mainly domestic (consumption) demand driven. India's savings and investment rates have been much lower than China's and its share of world exports in 2007, at around 1.8 percent, contrasted sharply with China's 8.9 percent mentioned above. India's imports also grew over the period – from 1.1 percent to 1.8 percent, much less than China's. Strong and sustained growth in private consumption, and the public sector deficits at both central and state government levels, have been the features of India's economic transition over the decade since the mid-1990s. This has started to change in recent years, as we detail below.

The improvement in India's annual GDP growth figures in recent years has prompted the question as to whether it indicates a trend increase in India's GDP growth rate since the middle of 2003.[1] If one breaks down the period 2000–7 into two sub-periods, and examines GDP growth figures in quarterly terms, it emerges that the quarter-on-quarter growth rate crossed the 9 percent mark for the first time in quarter two (Q2) of 2003/04, and had remained above that level in 10 out of the 16 subsequent quarters. In the 13 quarters starting in quarter one (Q1) of 2000/01, GDP growth rate was never above 6.7 percent, and was below

5 percent on five occasions. From the current national income statistics with 1999/2000 as base, it would appear that Indian GDP growth rate had achieved a trend increase from an average of around 4.8 percent to around 8.8 percent between Q2 of 2003/04 and Q2 of 2007/08, an increase of some 80 percent on the quarter-on-quarter growth rate. This is in the 80–90 percent range of China's growth rate.

While this noticeable acceleration in GDP growth may have been reason for optimism among some observers, others felt that the period was too short for firm judgments to be made as to whether this was a cyclical upturn or a genuine structural break which could sustain itself into the future. This skepticism is understandable when it is recalled that something similar in respect of the GDP growth rate was observed over the period 1994/95–1996/97, only to be followed by a prolonged downturn in the growth rate (Jha and Negre 2007: 7). However, the global recession that followed the financial crisis that started in 2007 slowed India's GDP quarter-on-quarter growth down from 9.3 percent in Q3 of 2007/08, to 5.8 percent in Q4 of 2008/09. The growth rate has however registered a sharp increase in recent quarters to reach 8.9 percent in Q3 of 2010, which compares with China's 9.8 percent in the same Q4 of the same year. (*The Economist* 2011: Feb. 26: 93).

Turning now to the observed changes to the way income in India has come to be used up, we note that over the period 2001–07, India's accelerating GDP growth rate was accompanied by a significant increase in gross domestic savings, from around 32 percent in 2000 to over 39 percent in 2007 (World Bank 2011). A less well-known fact about India's generally poor savings performance is that the savings rate of India's household sector, at 30 percent of disposable income in 2005, is even higher than China's 25 percent (Bottelier 2007: 124).

India's much lower national savings rate has historically been due largely to the corporate and public sector's culture of low savings. This started to change, with government deficits falling to a low 2.7 percent in 2007–8, thanks to several reform measures aimed at improving fiscal responsibility adopted by the federal government in 2004, plus the reform of indirect taxation, including the introduction of a value-added tax at the state level. The onset of the global recession, however, has led the fiscal deficit to grow to over 6 percent in 2008/09. The corporate sector had more than doubled its savings rate from under 4 percent of GDP in 2001 to 8.7 percent in 2007–8, but the impact of the global recession has been to slow it down, albeit marginally, to 8.1 percent in 2008/09. The household sector's savings, however, have remained at the same level between 2007/08 and 2008/09.

As already noted, GDP growth declined in both China and India following the onset of the global financial crisis in late 2007, and recession in 2008. The direct impact of the global recession would flow through the channels of trade and of financial transactions. Both countries experienced a decline in their export growth rates – China's real export growth fell from 23.3 percent in 2006 to 8.8 percent in 2008, then rose to 21.8 percent in the first half of 2009. India's high export growth rate of 28.9 percent in 2007/08 fell to 12.8 percent in 2008/09 (World Bank 2009). Thus, while both countries faced declining exports, as the economy with a greater export orientation China's decline was more pronounced. In respect of import growth rate too, both countries have experienced a significant decline. China's imports declined by 11.2 percent in 2009, after having registered positive growth rates of 20.8 percent in 2007 and 18.5 percent in 2008. India's imports, too, which had grown by 35.5 percent in 2007/08 and 20.7 percent in 2008/09, declined to 23.6 percent in 2009/10.

Both countries used monetary and fiscal measures to provide stimulus to their economies in an effort to minimize the impact of the global recession. In the Indian case, because the share of domestic consumption and investment expenditure is high, at more than 80 percent of gross domestic expenditure, the scope for domestic expansion to compensate for falling export growth is somewhat limited. China's domestic demand – being a lot lower, at 68 percent of gross domestic expenditure – has been able to provide stronger demand stimulus. As a proportion of GDP, China's stimulus package has been around 4.4 percent over the period 2008–10, compared to India's much weaker package of around 0.5 percent of its GDP. The measures adopted by China have transformed its fiscal budget from a surplus of 0.6 percent in 2007 to a deficit of 0.4 percent in 2008 and over 4 percent in 2009. In India's case, the central government's fiscal deficit has grown from 2.7 percent in 2007/08 to around 6.8 percent in 2008/09, and higher still if the deficits of the states are included.

3 Supply factors analysis

a Factor-use and factor productivity: China and India compared over 1993–2004

An extensive literature exists on the relative shares and growth patterns of the major sectors, that is agriculture, industry, and services, of China and India (see e.g. Bosworth and Collins 2007; Jha 2007; Srinivasan 2006; Virmani 2004). These findings have been summarized and analyzed in Chatterjee (2009), and we are therefore not going to cover them in detail here. Instead, we explore the influences the supply-side factors have had on the observed growth of the two economies for the period up to 2004 first, and for the more recent years second.

An economy grows by employing factor inputs like capital and labor in larger quantities, and by achieving efficiency gains, captured as total factor productivity. Therefore, by using the information on the growth in labor employment and in output per worker, it is possible to explain the observed growth. One can then go on to compute the relative contributions of the two major ingredients of GDP growth; that is, the use of physical capital per worker and improvement in factor productivity.

Table 3.1 presents the information on these statistics for the total output of the two countries for the period 1993–2004. Although several studies (See Virmani 2004a, b; Srinivasan, T. N. 2005; Jorgenson and Vu 2005, for e.g.) have examined the performance of the two economies over earlier periods, the main reason for choosing this period here is that it was in the 1990s that India launched its major reform program, following the "economic crisis" of 1991, while China continued with its own reforms begun earlier. The impact of these reforms on a major macroeconomic aggregate, that is the GDP of the two economies since the early 1990s, is therefore of particular relevance.

The results, based on the more recent and revised estimates of Bosworth and Collins, cited in Table 3.1, show that labor employment growth contributed more to India's GDP growth than it did to China's, while the opposite was the case with respect to output per worker, China showing a higher contribution from labor productivity. The next logical step of course is to decompose the labor productivity growth by examining how much the physical capital used by labor contributed to the

Table 3.1 Decomposition of observed GDP growth (1993–2004)

	Output	**Employment**	**Output per worker**
China	9.7	1.2	8.5
India	6.5	1.9	4.6
	Sources of output growth per worker 1993–2004		
	Physical capital		**Factor productivity**
China	4.2		4.0
India	1.8		2.3

Unit: Annual percentage change.
Source: Bosworth and Collins 2007.

output growth, and how much an improvement in the overall efficiency of production, that is TFP, did. The results, reported in the bottom part of Table 3.1, clearly show that the contributions of both physical capital and TFP growth are higher for China than they are for India.

India's greater reliance on labor employment relative to China's would appear to be in keeping with the demographic trends of the two countries. India's working age population, at 60 percent of total population in 2005, is projected rise to 61 percent by 2050, and the dependency ratio (ratio of non-working to working populations) to fall from 67 percent to 64 percent (UN 2006). China's working age population, at 67 percent of total population, by contrast, is projected to fall to 53.3 percent by 2050, and the dependency ratio to rise sharply from 57 percent to 88 percent. These trends would suggest that China will need to learn to rely less on increasing labor employment than would India to contribute to its growth process. The evidence cited in Table 3.1, and discussed above, would indicate that this is already happening. We return to this issue later in the chapter.

Going on now to the decomposition of the observed growth of the three broad sectors in agriculture, industry and services, the following observations based on the findings reported in Table 3.2 are pertinent: first, China achieved faster output growth in all three sectors than India; secondly, its growth was sourced more from improved labor productivity, and less from labor employment in both agriculture and industry; and thirdly labor employment in the service sector was higher, and TFP significantly lower than India's. India's performance in agriculture was particularly poor in all respects relative to China's; in respect of labor productivity and TFP, its growth rates were less than one-third of China's. It is only in the service sector that India's performance compares favorably with China's. India achieved high growth in this sector with less additional labor and less capital per worker than did China.

Decomposition of the overall growth figures thus enables identification of the roles of the various factors on the supply side of the growth performance of an economy. The Chinese and the Indian economies have continued to achieve high growth over the period since 2004, as detailed above. However, as yet, no detailed statistical information is available to show the contributions of the supply-side factors to this growth process. So, the question as to whether these economies can sustain their rapid growth is explored in a different manner; that is, by examining the efficiency of their investments overall over the period since 2004. This is very much an aggregate measure, but is meaningful in the context in which it is being employed here.

Table 3.2 Decomposition of growth by major sectors (1993–2004)

	Output	Employment	Output per worker
		Agriculture	
China	3.7	–0.6	4.3
India	2.2	0.7	1.5
		Industry	
China	11.0	1.2	9.8
India	6.7	3.6	3.1
		Services	
China	9.8	4.7	5.1
India	9.1	3.7	5.4
	Sources of output growth per worker 1993–2004*		
	Physical capital		**Factor productivity**
		Agriculture	
China	2.1		1.8
India	0.7		0.5
		Industry	
China	3.2		6.2
India	1.7		1.1
		Services	
China	3.9		0.9
India	1.1		3.9

* Contributions of other factors such as land etc. have been left out.
Unit: Annual percentage change (%).
Source: Bosworth and Collins 2007 and 2008.

A somewhat broad measure of the efficiency of capital use in production processes at the aggregate level is the incremental capital-output ratio (ICOR); that is, the ratio of additional capital investment to the increase in GDP. The lower the ratio, the more efficient is the utilization of capital. Taking the five-year period 2003–8, a period immediately preceding the transmission of the global recession to the two economies, one observes that the Chinese economy grew at an annual average rate of 10.8 percent, and its gross fixed investment was an average of 40.7 percent of GDP. This gives an ICOR of 3.7 percent, which implies that for a 1 percent growth in GDP, 3.7 percent of GDP had been invested. So, with the other growth factors unchanged, if China can either maintain its level of investment at such high levels, or improve its efficiency in the use of capital, that is lower the ICOR, its economy can continue along the recent double-digit annual growth rates.

Turning to the Indian economy over the same period, one observes that the average growth rate of GDP had been 8.5 percent a year, and the share of fixed investment in its GDP was 31 percent, giving an ICOR of 3.7 percent, which is exactly the same as China's. With a rising savings rate, and a modest deficit in the balance of payments, India's capital investment can improve to levels that would see its GDP growth rate potentially also to rise to double-digit levels in the not-too-distant future to match, if not exceed, China's.

The discussion above has laid bare the nature of the economic growth that China and India have experienced in recent decades, and the factors and forces on the demand and the supply side that have influenced that growth. In considering below the long term prospects of the two economies, the possible influences of same factors and forces are examined. A few other potential influences are also brought in briefly as relevant.

4 Forecasting demand and supply as constraints for long-term growth

a Changing demographics and long term growth prospects

The availability and quality of the factor inputs – capital and labor – in particular have a major influence on a country's economic growth, as observed above. Looking at labor first, the continuing reduction in the supply of labor in China has already been commented on. The possibility of "surplus" agricultural labor migrating to the industrial areas to help maintain its competitiveness is more limited in China as the scope for significant further productivity gains in agriculture is unlikely to be large. This shortage will put pressure on the real wage in the industries, and diminish, if not eliminate, China's advantage as a low-wage, labor-surplus economy, specializing in labor-intensive manufactured goods for exporting.

It is industries like this that have attracted the bulk of the expatriate investment in China's Foreign Invested Enterprises (FIEs), which have accounted for over one half of China's exports and imports. Their contribution to China's economic growth had been as high as 40 percent in 2003 and 2004, despite their share in China's GDP being only 20 percent. The possible decline in export growth resulting from the forces alluded to above would tend to reduce the importance of the FIEs and their contribution to the growth process (Whalley and Xian 2006). Any structural shift away from low-skill to higher-skill manufacturing, or to the non-manufacturing, service sector will therefore need to draw more on domestic savings for their required investment. Whether domestic savings can increase further from their already high rates remains to be seen.

The structure of China's population is old, with the population below the age of 15 being around 22 percent, and falling. As its rate of population growth is slow, the population is aging faster. This will further reduce the availability of labor as a "cheap input," as China will graduate from being a classic Arthur Lewis labor-surplus economy (Lewis 1954). On the other hand, China's labor force is generally healthier and more literate than India's, which gives it an advantage that many other developing countries, including India, do not enjoy to the same extent. In the initial phase of China's economic transition, however, the quality of its human capital, as measured by the proportion of the population with a tertiary qualification, was lower, at 1.7 percent, than India's, at 5.3 percent (Li and Zhang 2008). This has changed significantly since the early 1990s as China has surged ahead with its investment in human capital and scientific and technological infrastructure. This has had the effect of transforming China's production structure to more skill-intensive activities.

India, by contrast, has the advantage of having a younger population structure, with 33 percent of the population below the age of 15, and a lower dependency ratio, both at present and into the future, as observed earlier in this chapter. India's rural sector, including agriculture, and other low-productivity activities still employ a large share of its labor force. The ability of the economy to transfer labor to higher-productivity activities is therefore potentially stronger. These advantages, India's so-called demographic dividend (Lee and Mason 2006), can potentially be harnessed by a growing, labor-biased, industrial sector. A major structural shift will however be needed to increase the share of the industrial sectors, especially the manufacturing sector, which alone can possibly absorb the bulk of India's large and growing labor force. This, in turn, will require improved infrastructure, both physical and human, as well as changes to India's labor and bankruptcy laws, which have hindered the transformation of this sector by discouraging fresh investment in it (Srinivasan 2006, 2009).

b Savings, investment and capital formation

China's high savings rate, around 53 percent of its GDP in 2008 (Ma and Wang 2010), has contributed to its high investment rate, as noted earlier in this chapter. Over the period 1998–2008, China's investment as a proportion of GDP increased from 37 percent to 45 percent. Over the same period, India, too, experienced a sharp rise in its investment rate – from 24 percent to 40 percent; its savings rate being around 39 percent (World Bank 2011). A striking difference between the two economies, as alluded to above, is China's large current account surplus, which reflects the excess of its savings over investment. India, on the other hand, has a modest current account deficit. China's international transactions have swung, in a single decade, from a net debtor position of some 10 percent of GDP in 1998 to a net creditor position of 37 percent by 2008, making China a significant capital exporting economy. India is in an unusual position of being also a capital exporter, despite its persistently negative current account balance. Thus, while China lends abroad out of its savings, India does so by borrowing offshore. India also relies more on its domestic savings to finance domestic investment than does China, as pointed out earlier.

This highly investment-intensive domestic demand structure has seen China's private consumption as a share of GDP decline from 47 percent to 36 percent over a decade ending in 2008. India's private consumption share also declined from 64 percent to 55 percent over the same period. However, both economies have been experiencing increased private consumption *growth* in recent years. A rapidly rising GDP makes this possible, despite the declining share of consumption in it. This is likely to continue with rising average levels of affluence, and contribute to the growth process to a greater extent than has been the case so far.

The changing demographic structure of China, with a large section of the population beyond the working age, together with a declining number of potential inheritors within households, is likely to reduce the bequest motive for saving. After an exhaustive survey of the savings behavior of the Chinese economy, Guonan Ma and Yi Wang observe that "China's savings rate is likely to plateau before long and may ease off noticeably from the current 53% or even higher levels over the next 10 years" (Ma and Wang 2010: 24).

India's savings and investment surge, as observed earlier, has occurred much more recently. The increased savings have come from all three major sectors, that is the household, private and the public sectors. Even though the onset of the global recession has had a dampening effect on savings generally, the private sector still had a positive balance of savings over investment in 2008–9 (MOF 2010: 10).

Demographic factors are likely to see India's savings improve as a younger population has a greater savings incentive for both lifecycle and precautionary reasons. Although the inflow of foreign direct investment into India is still decidedly modest in comparison with that of China, the inflow of funds into portfolios and bonds is significantly larger, reflecting perhaps India's more efficient financial system and better organized financial institutions (Huang and Khanna 2003).

Both economies are thus likely to continue experiencing changes to the ways in which they finance their growth as the structure of their economies continues to change, but neither is likely to face severe constraints on the financial front at least.

c GDP growth, inputs, and TFP

The contributions of factor inputs, labor productivity, and total factor productivity to the observed GDP growth of China and India over the period 1993–2004 have been discussed in Section 4 above. Taking a somewhat longer period, for purposes of comparison, Ross (2010) has updated the findings of Jorgenson and Vu (2005) to calculate the changes in the contributions of capital input, labor input, and TFP to the observed growth of China and India. The three periods chosen are 1989–95, 1995–2000 and 2000–5. Let us label the three periods sequentially as period 1 (P1), period 2 (P2), and period 3 (P3).

The gap in India's annual GDP growth, relative to China's, narrowed steadily over the successive periods, from 49 percent in P1 to 68.6 percent in P2 and 75.9 percent in P3. Exploring the factors behind this narrowing, the findings show that India's annual rate of growth of labor input relative to China's had been 141.2 percent, 129 percent, and 158 percent; while its use of capital input relative to China's had been 58.6 percent, 58.2 percent, and 65.1 percent in the three periods respectively. Thus India maintained the stronger labor bias in its production structures; indeed the gap with China in the use of labor had increased by the end of the period. In respect of capital, the gap has narrowed, but only marginally.

It is in respect of TFP growth that the gap has narrowed significantly. India's annual growth of TFP relative to China's having been 23.6 percent, 59.2 percent and 64.1 percent in the three periods. Clearly, the improvement in the growth rate had been very strong from P1 to P2, the improving trend continued, although weakened, over P2 and P3, and so the catching-up process remained on track.

India's progress has been much slower in respect of capital input, again a vital growth ingredient. Combining the annual growth in labor and TFP, Ross (2010) calculates India's growth to have been 45 percent of China's in P1, 78 percent in P2, and 84.6 percent in P3, further confirming the progress India has achieved in the direction of growth-rate convergence with China.

These findings seem to suggest that India lags behind China in respect particularly of its (lower) capital investment as a proportion of income. As observed earlier, India has made significant progress in respect of both its savings and investment performance over the last few years. It would need to continue this trend if the gap in its growth performance is to be narrowed further.

5 Conclusion

This chapter has examined key factor inputs to the growth outcomes and development patterns of the world's two most populous times in recent times, and their future prospects. The findings help explain the factors and forces that have shaped the two countries' economic performance. They also highlight some of the constraints the two giants face as they continue along their growth paths. The two economies, despite their admittedly remarkable achievements in promoting economic growth, have a long way to go to lift their large populations out of the many deprivations they still suffer, as elaborated by Mishra and Ray (2010), for example.

The chapter has attempted to use a supply–demand framework to explain the growth outcomes of China and India. This is helpful to engage a broad range of direct contributing factors for growth accounting and analysis. These factors are framed to allow us better to understand how direct growth contributions are structured. On the demand side, India's GDP has been largely driven by domestic consumption, supported by strong and sustained growth in private consumption and public sector deficits at both central and state government levels, with a recent change to more increasing saving rates and decreased government deficits; while China is experiencing a transition from primarily an export-driven economy to one that is increasingly seeking to expand domestic demand for sustainable growth.

On the supply side, raw employment growth contributed more to India's GDP growth than it did to China's and it was the opposite with output per worker, China showing higher contribution from labor productivity. Overall, the contributions of both physical capital and TFP growth are higher for China than they are for India. Moreover, China achieved faster output growth in all three sectors than did India. China's growth was sourced more from improved labor productivity, less from labor employment in both agriculture and industry but labor employment in the service sector was higher, and TFP was significantly lower than in India. The efficiency of capital use in production process in China is about the same as in India. Finally, while both India and China have continued to achieve high growth, no detailed statistical information is available to show the contributions of the supply-side factors to this growth process.

Clearly, there is a limit to how much the supply–demand model can tell us about the growth experience, particularly what has caused the growth outcomes and what has shaped the growth pattern. This chapter has shown capital investment and savings, labor and employment, and productivity in these two countries and related them to changes in their growth performance and patterns of growth. To provide a more useful insight about these countries' "model," and to determine whether their growth experience constitutes a useful and significant model of modern economic growth that explains what has caused what in growth performance and experience, would require substantive data and evidence beyond the supply–demand model discussed in this chapter, and indeed in most existing growth analysis models or frameworks.

Perhaps, like any working modern capitalist market economy, economic growth and development in China and India are the function of the input of key factors, such as land, capital, labor, and productivity, that have long been recognized as essential contributors to growth outcomes in other modern growth experiences. The configuration and effects of the forces and arrangements enabling or shaping these factors have given the Chinese and Indian growth experiences their own characteristics. This in a way indicates the modern capitalist nature of the emergent Chinese and Indian economies, and there is nothing unique about their growth patterns. Moreover, the supply–demand analysis provides a description of the patterns of factor inputs of the two economies. Other models may look at some other factors and how they relate to the growth outcomes and performance. Beyond these, more profoundly different models would be required to explain the configurations and effects of the forces and arrangements that have enabled and shaped the input of factors to growth.

Note

1. Many of the statistical details used in this subsection are taken from various issues of *The Economic Survey* of the Ministry of Finance, Govt. of India; and *The Handbook of Statistics of the Indian Economy,* published by the Reserve Bank of India.

4

One Economics, Many Recipes: An Institutional Approach to Explaining Economic Growth

Jun Fu

1 China's economic performance in comparative perspective

The Chinese market-oriented reforms and opening up started in 1979. In the past three decades, economic growth in China has been impressive, approaching on average a double-digit growth rate. Put in a historical and comparative perspective, however, the performance is by no means "miraculous." At their respective growth peaks, Japan, South Korea, Singapore, Hong Kong, and Taiwan all achieved similarly high growth rates, averaging at 9.66 for Japan (1951–70); 8.36 for South Korea (1957–76); 9.77 for Singapore (1965–84); 9.03 for Hong Kong (1961–80); and 9.67 for Taiwan (1954–73). The comparable figure was 8.25 for China (1984–2003), and 5.68 for India (1984–2003).[1]

Look at a longer time horizon. According to Angus Madison, about two centuries ago the Chinese population was about one third of the world's total; China was then producing about one third of the world's total GDP. A century later, China's share of the world's GDP declined to about 10 percent, and by the late 1970s, it was further down to less than 5 percent. Today China's population is about one fifth of the world's total; its GDP contribution has gone back to about 10 percent of the world's total. In aggregate amount, China has become the second largest economy in the world. However, its GDP per capita is still below the world average, and stands at the level at which the United States was about a century ago (Fu 2009: 72).

An increase in productivity is, according to Douglas North, the ultimate driving force for economic growth, and a good measure of that is GDP or income on per capita basis (North 2005). Where does China stand by that measure? At present, per capita productivity in China is about 20 percent that of the United States, 25 percent that of Japan, and 30 percent that of South Korea.

What do the above comparative figures tell us? In relative terms China performed much better in history than in modern times (that is, prior to the 1980s). Having achieved very significantly in the past 30 years from an extraordinary low base, China still has great scope for further growth. Indeed, at "normal" performance by China's own historical standard, one fifth of the world's population shall produce one fifth of the world's total GDP.

At the current level of development, however, claims of a "Chinese model" are mostly made *ad hoc*, with little logical consistency, and are therefore theoretically dubious. For theoretical rigor (measured by parsimony, scope, and accuracy), a theoretical model must demonstrate a reasonable level of scope and stability so that it can be replicated across time and space. Thus, instead of "model," I would suggest the term "strategy," embodied in a series of policy choices, to describe the Chinese experience. Indeed, a hallmark of a strategy is flexibility and sensitivity to structural constraints. As Sun Tzu, an ancient Chinese strategist says, a good strategy is like a body of water pushing down a slope, and it turns around the rocks along the way. At a descriptive rather than analytical level, the Chinese experience is rather a story arguably unraveled by "path dependence" (David 2000). It is "crossing the river by groping for stepping stones underneath," so to speak. However, we need theories to explain why the other side of the river is better, or more productive, than this side in terms of relative economic performance.

2 Explaining economic growth – an institutional approach

Why are some countries so rich and others so poor? One way to think about this question is how we spend our time on a daily basis. Without exception, each one of us has only 24 hours a day. We spend each day in three different ways – productive, non-productive, and counter-productive. As humans are social animals, how we spend our time is determined by different institutional settings, consisting of formal rules and informal norms. Economically, a good institution is the one that coordinates our behavior in time-consistent ways[2] that maximize productive hours and minimize non- and counter-productive hours, so that, according to Douglas North, private returns approach social returns.[3] This line of investigation is firmly premised on the micro-foundation; that is, *homo economica*.[4] Indeed, this micro-foundation is a linchpin of theory building in the neo-political economy. It is no surprise that, writing on the Industrial Revolution, T. S. Ashton has argued that the revolution was only incidentally a change in industrial techniques; it was more profoundly a change in industrial organization (Ashton 1955: 105–17),[5] or what in this chapter I call institutional technologies.

3 The MBW model: Market, bureaucracy and wealth

Drawing on the logic of institutional economics, I propose that real economic growth (i.e., the speed of per capita GDP growth is faster than that of population growth) is a function of how sophisticatedly a country develops two sets of institutions – one hierarchical (state) and one horizontal (market). I nickname it the MBW model, where M stands for market; B for bureaucracy (or rather hierarchy); and W for wealth. $W_i = f(B_iM_i)$ in short. For systematic comparisons across countries, with i indicating time in history, W is measured by GDP per capita. What is the appropriate relation between B and M? Logically it echoes the classic question by Ronald Coase; that is, where do we draw the line between the market and the firm? (Coase 1937: 386–405). Theoretically, W would be at its best if management costs in the B dimension equal transaction costs in the M dimension.[6] This institutional logic, I argue, applies not only to China but also to all other countries. India is no exception.

To operationalize our institutional model, in the hierarchical B dimension there are two variables. First, *ceteris paribus*, is whether a country has put in place a sophisticated system of impersonal testing, selection and recruitment of talented people for its hierarchy. Second, since hierarchy begets power and power corrupts, has a country developed a sophisticated web of checks and balances and embedded it in a rule of law system? In the horizontal M dimension, the critical variables are the provisions of personified incentives, property rights protection, and a patent system to encourage innovations, and anti-trust law to keep markets competitive and efficient in allocating resources. If these hierarchical and horizontal building blocks are in place, the model predicts good economic performance.

How well does the model explain China's economic performance? Historically China was the first to develop the *Keju* institution or the civil service examination system. This impersonal testing for the recruitment of officials was initiated in the Sui Dynasty (581–618 AD) and matured in the Song Dynasty (960–1279 AD) (Miyazaki 1976). Little wonder, with all things being equal, that when China systematically had talented people sitting on the hierarchy, for centuries it was ahead of the rest of world in economic performance until well after the Song Dynasty (see Figure 4.1). However, as one can see, China's economic performance stagnated thereafter, if only because there were no more institutional breakthroughs in China subsequent to the Song Dynasty. Why was China subsequently overtaken? By systematic benchmarking, Britain, for instance, learnt from and improved the Chinese civil service

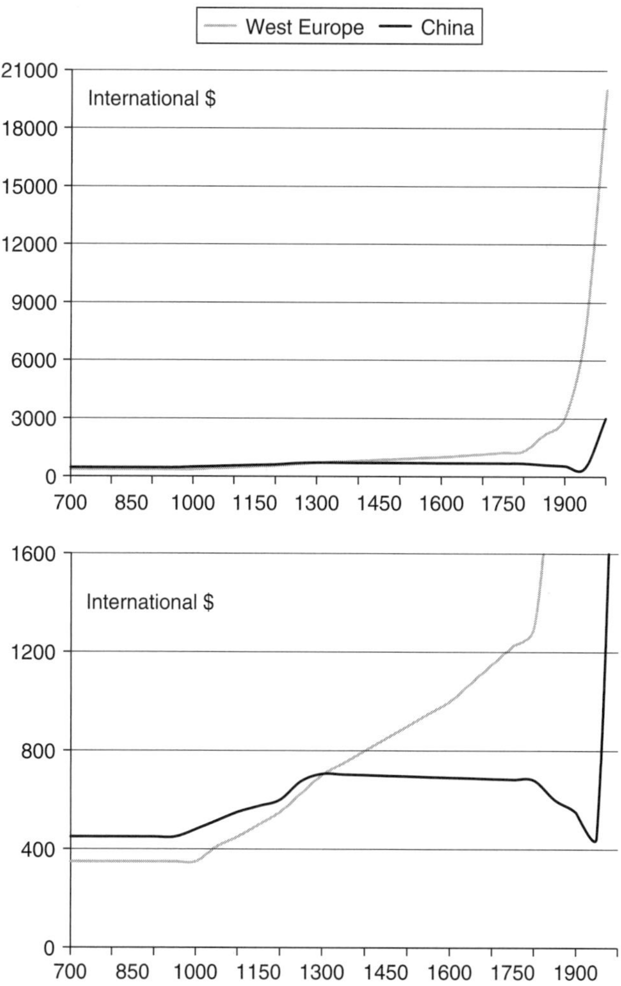

Figure 4.1 GDP per capita comparison, China and West Europe (700–1998)
Source: Maddison 2001.

examination system.[7] More importantly, in line with Lord Acton's warning that absolute power corrupts absolutely, Britain also developed a system of checks and balances based on rule of law starting in the thirteenth century – witness its Magna Carta in 1215. Accordingly, Britain gradually caught up with and subsequently overtook China.

The rest of our story is too long to be elaborated in this short space.[8] Suffice to say that for centuries, the efficacy of horizontal institutional arrangements known as markets was little understood and developed in China. As the Chinese themselves would say, "Everything under heaven belongs to the Emperor." This indicates poor property rights regimes in Chinese imperial times.

In Europe, by contrast, ancient Roman law had a positive effect on property rights protection regimes, and by 1624 Britain had put in place a prototype of the modern patent system, and in 1776 – the same year in which the United States was founded – Adam Smith published *The Wealth of Nations*. This systematically expounded on the efficacy of the market (Smith 1985). In the United States, the anti-trust law known as the *Sherman Act* was enacted in 1888. Within the subsequent two decades, GDP per capita in the United States overtook that of Britain (McCraw 1970: 366). In other words, the US economy took the lead even before World War I – not after World War II, as people would have commonly believed. Why? Because by then the US had assembled all the best institutions that humankind had hitherto invented, including the critical elements of the Chinese civil service examination system, the social contract theory of Jean-Jacques Rousseau, and the separation of powers of John Locke and Montesquieu.

Furthermore, the protection of property rights, including intellectual property rights, was written into the US Constitution. Let us call these sophisticated social arrangements "institutional technologies". What was the economic result of putting together these institutional technologies? According to John Ikenberry, the United States, at its peak in 1948, had about half of the world's total wealth, with a population 6.3 percent of the world's total (Ikenberry 2001).

Indeed, the evidence from history is strong that those countries are most creative and progressive that safeguard the expression of new ideas, and build and adapt institutions based on them. Countries appear to remain vigorous only so long as they are organized to receive and assimilate novel and sometimes unpleasant thoughts.

Viewed in this light, what China has done in the past three decades of market-oriented reforms and opening up is not something unique in human history. Rather, it is a case of GDP per capita convergence with advanced economies (see Figure 4.2) in the industrial era – a process due to and controlled by technological progress[9] and its embodiment in physical capital, as mathematically demonstrated by Hans Danielmeyer (Danielmeyer and Martinetz 2010).[10] In a way, what China has done during the reform years is to make up for its underdevelopment of markets and narrow the technological gap with the advanced economies. Indeed, China's open-door policy puts the country in a better position to duplicate established human knowledge about both hard and soft technologies on a global scale, and entry into the WTO points to the efficacy of market competition on comparative advantages. Such pro-knowledge and pro-competitive institutional re-orientation in line with advanced economies, both hierarchical and horizontal, has been the fundamental driver for China's rapid economic growth in recent decades. And the process of realignment is not finished yet.

Thus, notwithstanding its enormous achievement in the past few decades, China still has a long way to go before joining the wealthy nations, by measurement of GDP per capita.[11] Similarly, market-oriented reforms and integration into the world economy also explains much about India's economic performance. Albeit a decade behind China in initiating reforms, the Indian government has also stepped

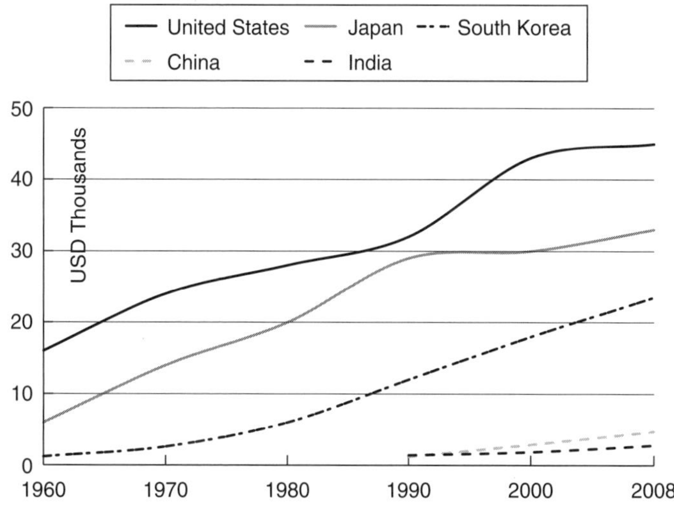

Figure 4.2 GDP per capita convergence with advanced economies
Source: World Bank 2011.

back from micromanaging the economy, letting private enterprise flourish and opening markets to trade and investment. Large numbers of English-speaking workers and familiarity with the West, a legacy of the British rule – was pivotal for the flourishing of India's IT industry. This unique feature by no means vitiates our argument, however. If anything, it only adds to its power, for it shows how a country can

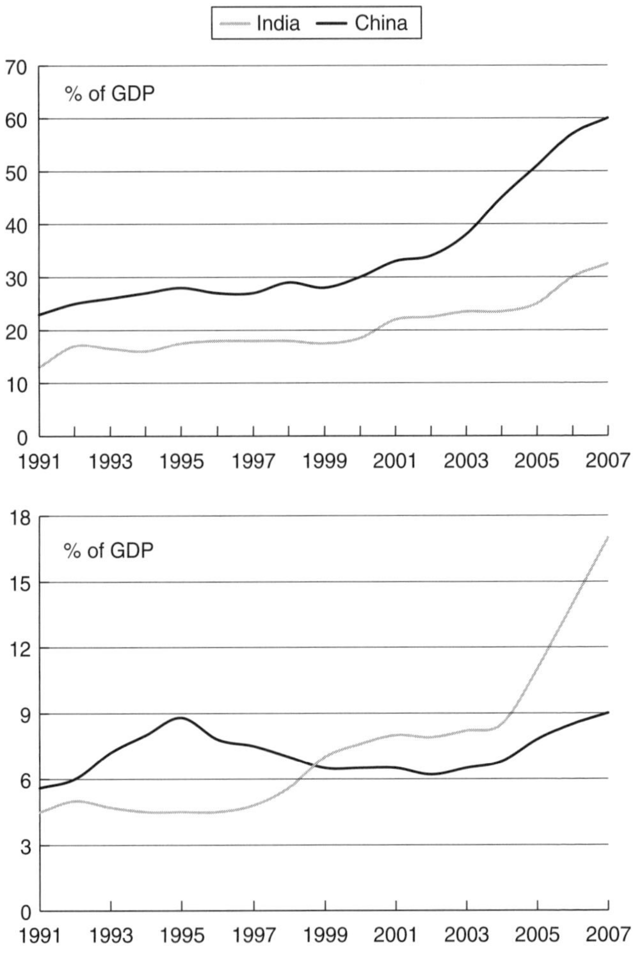

Figure 4.3 Different strategies to the same goal – economic growth. Goods exports (top) and services exports
Source: World Bank 2011.

leverage its human capital in the chains of value of global production. Following the same logic but manifested differently, China becomes the "world factory," focusing more on goods, and India the "world office,"[12] with a greater focus on services (Figure 4.3).[13] Indeed, for markets to create value through trade, geographical distance and associated differences matter.[14]

4 The one economy: Smith, Schumpeter and Lucas

Dani Rodrik has recently published a book entitled *One Economics, Many Recipes: Globalization, Institutions, and Economic Growth* (Rodrik 2007). The title fits our central theme here. China may be unique in many policy choices made in its reform from a planned to a market economy in terms of sequencing and pace. Indeed, its reforms started first in the countryside and then in industrial cities, and experiments were first carried out in the form of special economic zones in coastal areas and then in interior regions. These are features somewhat unique to China, and because they are unique – not generic – they can't be copied automatically elsewhere. Yet behind the broad trajectories of China's reforms and opening up, the logic is consistent with existing economic theories.[15] Let me outline three propositions.

The first proposition draws upon Adam Smith's memorable analogy of the "invisible hand". It speaks about markets being efficient in allocating resources through competition. To mention little else, labor – a critical factor of production – was immobile between urban and rural areas in China prior to the reforms. Removal of that institutional impediment means efficiency gains. Imagine first: prior to the reforms a Chinese peasant worked, say, 3 months a year, for he had little else to do between planting and harvesting. Imagine again: after the reforms, he is now engaged in production 12 months a year. Just by counting the total hours of his work, there is a tremendous increase in productivity. How many Chinese peasants are now mobile (called migrant peasant workers in China)? It is 200–250 millions – a staggering figure, compared to the total labor force of many developed economies.[16]

For individual living standards to improve, per capita growth has to exceed population growth. There, technology makes a difference. Our second proposition thus goes beyond the parameters of neo-classic economic model. By the memorable phrase of "creative destruction," Joseph Schumpeter reminds us of the role of technology in long-term real economic growth (Schumpeter 1942). One is also reminded here that with human cognitive limits, the duplication of established knowledge is easier and faster than pushing forward the technological frontier, because at the frontier there is no superior society from which to copy. What has happened in China on the technological front? By opening up to the rest of the world and sending tens of thousands of students to study overseas, China has been able gradually, or rather rapidly, to narrow the technological gaps in both hardware and software – including those of institutional technologies – with advanced countries, even if China has done very little to push forward the technological frontier. If the Schumpeterian model is correct, the closing of the technological gaps means added sources of productivity gains for China. This indeed is amply reflected in the increasing competitiveness of Chinese products on global markets (Kennedy, Suttmeier, and Su 2008).

Technology is said to come often with tacit, as opposed to explicit, and dispersed knowledge that is not readily transferable to individuals and therefore calls for collective "learning by doing." The implication is that privatization in itself is not a sufficient condition for corporate viabilities. For firms to be viable in competitive markets, effective learning has to take place. What has China done to facilitate learning? Beyond strengthening property rights and corporate governance, the logic of Robert Lucas's endogenous growth model applies here, and it is from this that we derive our third proposition (Robert Lucas 1988). In the Chinese case, to bridge local labor with advanced technology, including international market networks, foreign direct investment (FDI) has played an important role. Indeed, China has been very successful in attracting FDI, and by 2008 the realized amount of FDI reached US$560 billion (Fu 2009). As the world becomes increasingly "flat," to borrow Thomas Friedman's phrase (Friedman 2005), so allowing factors of production to move freely on a global scale, China, with its comparative advantage of low-cost labor, has become a "world factory" (Fallows 2007).

As is obvious, the three propositions outlined above are based on existing theories. Put together, I think they largely cover the ground in explaining the rapid economic growth in China during the past 30 years. In other words, the Chinese experience does not defy the logic of standard economic theories. On the contrary, it only validates them. What are the implications for the future? China must continue to broaden and deepen its access to established human knowledge by keeping the country open. It must further develop pro-market institutions on the basis of the rule of law such that, to use Douglas North's phrase again, private returns approach social returns. Theoretically, barring social, political, and environmental catastrophes, so long as China is still within the phase of industrialization and urbanization, and remains open to the rest of world, the

Table 4.1 Top 10 GDP countries (2010–50)

2050 Rank	Country Name	2010	2020	2030	2040	2050
1	China	2998	7070	14312	26439	44453
2	United States	13271	16415	20833	27229	35165
3	India	929	2104	4935	12367	27803
4	Japan	4601	5221	5810	6039	6673
5	Brazil	668	1333	2189	3740	6074
6	Russia	847	1741	2980	4467	5870
7	United Kingdom	1876	2285	2649	3201	3782
8	Germany	2212	2524	2697	3147	3603
9	France	1622	1930	2267	2668	3148
10	Italy	1337	1553	1671	1788	2061

Unit: USD billions.
Source: Goldman Sachs 2003.

driving force will not diminish until its GDP per capita approaches that of the advanced economies. The same logic applies to India as well.

A glass is both half full and half empty, depending on how you look at it. The fact that GDP per capita for China today is below the world average may sound like bad news; but it also means tremendous scope for further aggregate growth (see Table 4.1), although not of course without challenges.

5 Challenges ahead

Given the current level of integration of the Chinese economy with that of the world, the prospects of the world economy will eventually affect the Chinese, and vice versa. For advanced economies, a key question to ask is: what is the additional source of productivity increase in post-industrial era? Human evolution at the technological frontier[17] – a function of original innovations – is slow by nature. Failure to address this question, I argue, is the foundational reason for the long-term stagnation of the Japanese economy, for its economy, after a rapid phrase of catching up, has been operating at a high equilibrium that approaches, but is not beyond, the human technological frontier. Previously, we were told about the wonders of IT and high value-added services such as investment banking, and accounting and legal services. Now with the burst of the IT bubble and the onset of the world financial crisis, hindsight shows that their efficiency-enhancing effects were apparently exaggerated. In this context, the world economic downturn can be understood as a movement from a high equilibrium prior to the crisis to a low equilibrium that is yet to be ascertained. That said, the point remains that without an additional increase of productivity, the growth trajectories are likely to be a long "L" for advanced economies.[18] What about "reindustrialization" toward a green economy? While this may be a long-term solution, it is no short-term remedy.

What does this mean for the Chinese economy? In the wake of the world financial crisis, while China did not suffer from lack of liquidity it was by no means immune from external demand shocks. Indeed, the very high trade-dependent ratio – reaching 57 percent of GDP in 2008 – has left China very vulnerable to growth slowdowns elsewhere in the world, and particularly in the United States, which accounts for more than 20 percent of China's exports.[19] Even without the world economic downturn, the current growth strategy of the Chinese economy is not sustainable from a long-term perspective. It has depended too much on investments (over 50% of GDP) and exports (net exports over 10% of GDP), but not enough on domestic consumption (below 40% of GDP). Now a severe external demand shock has only exacerbated the unbalanced structure of China's investment-driven and export-led economy. Not surprisingly, of late Chinese Premier Wen Jiabao warned of a Chinese economy that was becoming increasingly "unstable, unbalanced, uncoordinated, and ultimately unsustainable."

A fundamental reason for China's weak domestic consumption and over-reliance on investment and exports is that income growth for domestic labor has not been proportional to the increase in productivity. Labor income as a share of GDP has gone down to about 36.5 percent in 2005 from 56.7 percent in 1983 – a dramatic 20 percent downward slide in 22 years. This misalignment is a reflection of deep institutional flaws, which either weaken or deny labor's ability to articulate and aggregate grievances. Looking down the road, even without considering the environmental impact of China's industrialization and its associated urbanization,[20] the country's current excessive investment-driven and export-led growth strategy is clearly not sustainable.

What is the way out? A critical key lies in boosting domestic consumption, such that supply and demand are reasonably balanced domestically to minimize overcapacity.[21] But that is no easy task. At root, it would call for better representation of different interest groups in the political process of decision-making, and simultaneously involve the learning, designing, and provisioning of better institutional technologies to deal with educational, health, social, and income distribution issues. There, as Yasheng Huang has argued, India, the largest democracy in world, albeit initially slow in coming, may hold better prospects for sustained growth in the long run (Huang and Khanna 2003). China must work very hard at those institutional fronts. Otherwise, the tensions resulting from the widening gap between the rich and the poor[22] will make future development increasingly unsustainable, not only economically, but also socially and politically.[23] Fortunately, China does not always have to reinvent the whole wheel – institutional technologies (software vs. hardware) to ameliorate such tensions are available within the existing frontier of human knowledge. The challenge is to adapt them to the actual conditions of China.

A final cautionary note: currently China has roughly 20 percent of the world's population, uses roughly 30 percent of the world's resources, and produces roughly 10 percent of the world's total GDP. In our formula of $W_i = f(B_i M_i)$, the right-hand side variables can be regarded as a measure of institutional technologies, thus indicating soft-power. With the right-hand side variable (i.e. GDP per capita – an indication of hard power) still below the world's average, at the moment it seems misleading for scholars to talk about a Chinese model and premature for China to project soft power.

Notes

1. Calculated on the basis of the following: OECD, 1995, 2001, 2003.
2. Time consistency means that rules and policies do not depend on the identity of current political officials or dominant political coalitions, but are consistent across generations, thus giving rise to credible commitments that bind political officials to honor property rights. In this context, institutions need to be studied not only statically, but also dynamically – the kind of credible commitments that ensure current institutions survive over time, in spite of individual political leaders. The latter, as a matter of both knowledge and practice, is particularly difficult for developing countries. See Weingast (2010: 28–51).
3. Social returns are defined as private returns plus returns gained by a third party.
4. It assumes that people are self-interested, rational, and utility maximizing.
5. Alien to the Chinese until recently, institutional innovations include giving personhood to non-corporal persons, such as organizations with limited and unlimited liabilities, so that they have legal standing before the law. A legal person is an entity capable of bearing rights and duties. Western law since the Romans has recognized legal persons as combinations of both sets of attributes.
6. This is also implied by Ronald Coase. See Coase (1960: 1–44).
7. Friedrich Hegel, for instance, spoke highly of the Chinese civil service examination, but also pointed out its drawbacks. He said that everyone was equal in the system, but on the other hand they were equally humble before the

emperor. Since only one person's thinking matters over the rest, it was difficult for a society built on that to be continuously dynamic. Accordingly, in learning from the Chinese examination system, civil service systems were made politically neutral in Western countries.

8. For more discussion, see Fu (2009).
9. In our case, this also refers to new institutional arrangements.
10. According to Hans Danielmeyer and Thomas Martinetz, because industrial development is due to and controlled by technical and its embodiment in physical capital, convergence is caused by the inevitable transition from fast duplication of established knowledge to the slow evolution of the industrial culture with education and original innovation.
11. According to a study by Warwick McKibbin, Peter Wilcoxeu and Wing Thye Woo (2008), under "Platinum Age" growth rates, GDP per capita in China could reach that of Western Europe, Japan, and the United States by 2100. But this outcome is not guaranteed, and could be undermined by a fallacy of composition caused by environmental constraints.
12. Referring to out-sourced call centers, data-processing operations and the like (Mattoo, Mishra, and Shingal (2004)).
13. For a good comparison between China and India, see Friedman and Gilley (2005).
14. China probably would not have grown as fast had it tried to make itself a services center. It would have stumbled on language and cultural barriers.
15. In this context, it may be noted that theory building is from specific to generic. In China, it is often the other way around, thus causing much confusion behind the veil of language differences. Many are not aware that a case-specific and *ad hoc* approach defeats the very purpose of theory building.
16. To appreciate how migration restrictions impede productivity in China, see Au and Henderson (2006: 350–88).
17. This would include institutional technologies such as property rights protection, general incorporation laws, corporate governance structures, and independent judicial systems.
18. Indeed, netting out the effects of inflation, global real GDP today is at approximately the level of 2007. Individually, it is at the 2007 level for the United States, 2006 for Europe, and 2004 for Japan. This is also supported by Hans Danielmeyer's empirical finding that, for advanced countries, growth on a longer run has a cycle that starts exponentially, has a long linear part in the middle, and approaches asymptotically a constant final level. Economists are wrong in assuming that growth can go on exponentially and, as a result, the gap between the expectation of exponential returns on investment and the reality of growth from exponential to linear is responsible for all three financial crises of global scale to date.
19. According to a study by Yiping Huang, a 1 percentage-point slow-down in the US economy could lower Asian economic growth by 1.1 percentage points, and Chinese growth by 1.3 percentage points. See Huang (2008).
20. For a good discussion on the environment, also see Day (2005). The urbanization ratio in China is projected to reach 65 percent by 2030. The ratio in 2009 is 46.6 percent in China, lower than that (60%) in Malaysia and the

Philippines, whose average income level is similar to China's. For advanced economies, the average urbanization ratio is over 80 percent.

21. Domestic demand as a share of total demand was 72.8 percent for China in 2008. By comparison, it was 88 percent for India, and 92 percent for the United States.
22. The wealth gap between urban and rural areas in China is 3.33:1; that between coastal and interior parts is 2.2:1. According to the World Bank, the Gini coefficient in China has increased from 0.16 before reforms to 0.47 at present, surpassing the warning line of 0.4. Globally, only 29 countries' Gini coefficients are higher than China's, of which 27 are from Latin America and Africa, and 2 are from Asia (Malaysia and the Philippines). The Gini coefficient in India is 0.36.
23. There are signs that the pressures are mounting. According to a budget report by the Finance Ministry of China submitted to the Chinese National People's Congress in 2010, the budget for "*weiwen*" (maintaining social stability) for 2010 has increased to RBM 514 billion. This is an additional increase of 8.9 percent on top of the 16 percent growth from the year before. By comparison, the Chinese military budget for 2010 is RMB 532 billion.

5
From Dingzhou to Nandigram: Social Conflict, Party Society, and Inter-Governmental Dynamics

Lei Guang

In the hours of dawn on a Saturday morning in June 2005, hundreds of armed men arrived in five buses at a farm field that had long been occupied by local farmers. The farmers had pitched tents and dug trenches on the land for the past 14 months, defying repeated government orders to vacate the land for an industrial project. The municipal government had requisitioned the land in 2001 for a state-of-the-art power plant, but the farmers refused to give it up because of low compensation, alleged corruption, and an uncertain future without land. Prior clashes between the villagers and the power plant contractors had fueled a mutual antagonism. Now, under the cover of dawn, hundreds of unidentified armed men were bused in. They launched a ferocious surprise attack on the rebellious villagers. By the end of the attack, six villagers had died and scores were wounded. Despite the bloodshed, the villagers remained defiant and held on to the disputed land. Fearing escalation, the government responded by sacking the municipal Party Secretary, jailing dozens of perpetrators, and scrapping the land requisition plan (Wang 2005).

On the morning of March 14, 2007, hundreds of police, along with armed men affiliated with the ruling Party, converged on a stretch of rural villages where local farmers had for months blocked roads and built barricades to keep out government officials. The farmers had chased out local officials after a series of fatal clashes with the police in January because they opposed government land acquisition for a chemical hub complex. There had been intermittent violence between local farmers and government workers between January and March. Then, on March 14, hundreds of police and armed militiamen arrived to restore government authority in the region. The confrontation soon turned bloody. "Police fired tear gas and immediately followed with bullets and rubber bullets, chased the people, mostly women and children, hitting out with lathis and iron rods, and firing."[1] By the end of the attack, 14 people had been killed and scores were wounded. The political ripple effects of the violence went far and wide. Prominent politicians condemned the attack. A citizens' tribunal described the episode as a "state-sponsored massacre." Villagers remained defiant while the government was forced to abandon the plan for land acquisition in the area (Kumara 2007; Ramachandran 2007).

These two incidents exhibit remarkable similarity in the nature of the conflict, the escalation of the violence, the governments' handling of land acquisition, and their grudging, partial accommodation in the end to the local farmers' requests. Indeed the nature and dynamics of conflict are so parallel with each other that one might easily place them in nearby localities of the same country and attribute the conflict to the same set of structural conditions. Yet the two incidents took place in apparently different political, economic, and social contexts.

The 2005 incident took place in Shengyou village, part of Dingzhou municipality, Hebei Province, China, about 200 km from the capital Beijing. The whole incident has come to be known as the "Dingzhou Incident" in China's growing list of farmer protests. The more recent violence in 2007 took place in Nandigram, India, a rural area in the East Midnapur district of West Bengal, 150 km from Kolkata. In Shengyou, land was, and still is, collectively owned, and farmers only had cultivation rights under the so-called household responsibility system. For this reason, the state was in a much more powerful position to requisition rural land for industrial use. This was especially so in this case as the land was requisitioned for a state-owned power plant designated as a key infrastructure project.

In Nandigram, successful land reform in West Bengal since the late 1970s had returned land ownership to the farmers. Land became effectively privatized, and varying levels of access are granted to the landowners, sharecroppers, and landless laborers. Politically, life in Shengyou was confined to incipient village-level elections. Shengyou villagers had little, if any, influence over local government officials except through disruptive action or direct appeal to higher authorities. In Nandigram, not only does there exist a tradition of rural self-government through the *panchayat* system, but inter-party competition and electoral politics are an integral part of parliamentary democracy, which affords some protection against predatory government officials.

It is important to point out that Shengyou and Nandigram are not isolated events. Land-based conflicts between villagers and the government have become frequent occurrences in both India and China, as the two countries experience rapid industrial growth, accompanied by cityward migration and urbanization. China's urban development has long been financed by cheap rural migrants and by the seizure of farmland for non-agricultural use. Research commissioned by the Asian Development Bank has indicated that, from 1990 to 2002, over 3.15 million *ha* of farmlands, more than 2 percent of the PRC's total arable landmass, was converted into nonagricultural uses. Over 36 million farmers had lost all or part of their land between 1993 and 2003 (RDI 2007). As a result, land dispute has become one of the most explosive social issues in China during reform.

Basing his evidence from the 1980s and 1990s, Thomas Bernstein cited "taking peasant land" as one of the six major sources of peasant discontent in China as early as in the late 1990s (Bernstein 2000: 96). By the mid-2000s, land-related issues arising from state requisition had become the top cause of rural grievance. Official statistics indicate that there have been 50,000 cases of land disputes in 224 cities between 2003 and March 2008 (Krishnan 2009). According to the Chinese scholar Yu Jianrong, land dispute replaced taxation and fees as the focus of peasant protest after 2002. Indicative of this trend, he reported that 68.7 percent of the phone-in complaints about rural issues at the popular CCTV *Focal Point* program in the first half of 2004 concerned land dispute. A further analysis of petition letters about land dispute reveals that 60 percent of them had to do with government requisition (French 2005; Kahn 2004; Yardley 2004; Yu 2006).

In the case of India, the Nandigram case took place in the wake of several well-publicized violent conflicts between the local governments and farmers on land acquisition. In the middle of 2006, protests broke out in Singur, West Bengal over the state government's attempt to acquire 1000 acres of agricultural land for Tata's Nano car project. Clashes with the police left many villagers injured and as many as 60 villagers arrested in December 2006 (Kumar 2006; *ACHR* 2006). Agitation against Tata Motors continued well beyond the start of its operation in the area (*AWSJ* 2008: 13; *FT* September 14). Earlier in 2006, in the Kalinganagar area of Orissa, 13 villagers were killed by the police while protesting land acquisition by Tata Steel. Shortly after Nandigram, South Korean steel maker POSCO ran into stiff resistance in Orissa, and aggrieved vegetable farmers and vendors in Jharkhand rioted against Reliance Fresh, a major corporate retail store.

Peasant resistance against forced land acquisition had existed in the 1990s, but recent episodes like Singur and Nandigram have spotlighted a deepening crisis in rural India that was brought about by the government's drive for corporate-led industrialization.[2] Central to the government's recent push is the setting up of Special Economic Zones (SEZs), with tax incentives and relaxed labor and environmental regulations in order to attract foreign and domestic enterprises. The Left-Front government in West Bengal has embraced the SEZ strategy with alacrity, and, as it has sometimes found out, with disastrous consequences (*The Economist* 2007: 385: 74).

Though worlds (and years) apart, the Nandigram and Shengyou incidents share some uncanny details about the grievances, the areas of protest, the community, and the process of escalation. The reported complaints by Nandigram and Shengyou farmers were remarkably similar. Farmers from both areas complained about the lack of communication and transparency about the land deals and about local corruption and low compensation for their land. Both Nandigram and Shengyou had been strong regime supporters prior to the land acquisition: Nandigram voters had traditionally voted for the Left-Front government in Bengal; Shengyou village was designated a model "civilized" village by the city government. Both communities were divided, with a minority of Left-Front party activists supporting the government action in India and some pliant villagers from the surrounding areas of Shengyou acceding to surrendering their land.[3] Rumors played a crucial role in galvanizing the villagers in both instances: in Nandigram, a rumor about impending government acquisition sparked the opposition; a rumor about a huge discrepancy between what they were awarded and what they received in compensation motivated the Shengyou villagers to demand a thoroughgoing investigation of the entire land transaction. Finally, before the incidents culminated to the fatal clash in 2007 (in the case of Nandigram) and 2005 (in the case of Shengyou), there had been a prolonged standoff between the government and the villagers. In both cases, smaller-scale violent outbreaks had foreshadowed the final clash.

The question that needs to be asked is why different political, economic, and social conditions in India and China (multi-party parliamentary democracy vs. party-state, private vs. collective ownership of land, differentiated peasantry vs. small peasant holders) should produce similar outcomes in land-related conflict in recent years. By similar outcomes, I refer to the similarity of grievances, the collective and organized form of protest, the violence and its escalation, and the government's apparent post-conflict appeasement of peasants.

In the following, I first identify the different structural conditions in land ownership and regulation that provided the background to the land conflicts in India and China. I then briefly discuss the possibility that a common set of factors at work in both contexts had produced the violence. Not quite satisfied with the common-factors approach, I turn to analyzing the different peasant-state relations in both countries. I argue that while the politicization of India's rural society was largely responsible for the Nandigram-style violence, inter-governmental dynamics were both generative of farmers' protest and, by the same token, responsible for the shape of its final resolution.

1 Land-tenure systems and the conflict over land acquisition in India and China

China has during the reform evolved a hybrid tenure system based on privatized land use, and state and collective ownership. This system has proven to be economically viable, as production of food grain has since increased significantly. Chinese farmers also seem to have embraced the long-term use right under the household responsibility system. The system, however, leaves farmers vulnerable to claims by the state or the collective because they lack formal ownership rights.

There are two principal threats to the farmers' land use right: one comes from periodic adjustment of the household land holdings within the village in response to changes in village population (e.g. deaths, births and marriage) or land addition or loss. Such adjustments tend to be incremental and are generally made on basis of village consensus. A 2005 survey of seventeen provinces showed that a majority of the villages (55%) had conducted two or more re-adjustments since the reform (Zhu, et al. 2006: 775).[4]

The other, more serious, threat comes from government land-takings. The same survey cited above found that incidences of rural land-takings have increased 15 times in ten years before 2005 (Zhu and Prosterman 2007). In a more recent survey in 2008, 29 percent of the farmers report that their villages have experienced at least one land taking by the government, with the highest incidences of land-taking occurring in 2008 (Prosterman et al. 2009). In a majority of such cases, farmers were not consulted about the compensation or even notified about the land requisition in advance. The ambiguity of land tenure system is compounded by the historical legacies of collectivism when local officials freely re-allocated rural land in the commune and by a general lack of rule of law in land administration.

By law, all rural land is owned by the "collective" whose boundary (and hence membership) is sometimes unclear (Cai 2003).[5] Current law also provides that the state may seize collective land for development in the "public interest" as long as reasonable compensation is paid to the farmers.[6] But public interest has been left deliberately vague so that a variety of projects, including commercial enterprises and economic development zones (*kaifaqu*), may pass as public-interest development. One study by the Seattle-based RDI found that, in 2002–3, at least half of the incidents of land-takings were for commercial uses, including real estate projects and industrial facilities.[7] Furthermore, the amount of "reasonable" compensation is decided by administrative fiat, often significantly below the market price. To add to the farmers' sense of injustice, various levels of government and the village collective routinely intercept the land compensation money so that land-losing farmers typically receive only 10–20 percent of the full amount (Zhu and Prosterman 2007).[8]

Throughout China, local governments have taken to land development with zeal and determination during the reform. According to one report, about 4.5 million *mu* of farmland had been converted for non-agricultural uses such as factories, roads, and housing units from 1979 to 2006 (*The Guardian* 2006: May 26). Because of the low valuation of farmland for requisition purpose, the local government stands to gain handsome profit from the transaction and from the tax levied on the factories or real estate development. After the central government reduced peasant tax burdens and abolished agricultural tax in 2006, land development has become the main source of local government revenue. Corruption aside, local authorities have huge institutional incentives to convert farmland into non-agricultural use. Facing protest, they often resort to deceit, coercion, and intimidation in dealing with the ordinary farmers. Insecure land tenure places the farmers in a disadvantaged position to negotiate with the government over large land-taking deals.

In contrast to China, where land disputes may have been caused, or at least aggravated by the lack of clarity over the farmers' land ownership rights, India has had a private land ownership system since independence. In West Bengal, land reform has conferred ownership on millions of sharecroppers, marginal landowners, and agricultural laborers. Yet secure ownership did not turn out to be a bulletproof shield against forced government requisition.

The Indian Constitution allows each state to legislate land acquisition for "public purposes." The legal framework remains the colonial Land Acquisition Act of 1894, with few subsequent amendments. Public purpose usually includes roads, canals, schools, and other infrastructure projects, but its definition has been expanded since 1984 to include the needs of state-owned or controlled corporations, even private projects partially supported by public revenue (Sanyal and Shankar 2009). After the 1990s, "public purpose" was further diluted of its original meaning after the Indian state embraced neo-liberal reform.

More recently, in 2005 India passed the Special Economic Zone Act. Similar to the Chinese practice, the law allows the government to designate entire localities as SEZs and to offer tax, finance, and trade incentives for private investors and industrialists.[9] Unlike their Chinese counterpart, however, the Indian SEZs were established less as an "experiment" in alternative economic systems than as a site of intensified capitalist industrialization, subsidized at the same time by the government (Mitra 2007). Both public and private developers may submit proposals for setting up the SEZs, and the SEZ Act permits the government to exercise the power of eminent domain in order to requisition land on their behalf. As a result, SEZ-related land requisition has displaced an increasing number of rural population in many Indian states since 2005 (Ramakrishnan 2006). Singur and Nandigram were but two prime examples that have gained international notoriety because of the violence involved.

Besides an expanded definition of "public purpose," another contentious issue with land expropriation is who should receive the compensation. A strict legalist approach means that the government would ignore the customary rights of whole classes of non-owners who have a stake in the cultivation of land. They include sharecroppers, laborers, tenants, bargardars (in the case of West Bengal), artisans, and so on. A tendency in the Indian state's land requisition practices has been to emphasize proper remuneration of the legal landowners while neglecting the interests of other stakeholders. This approach has caused deep resentment and resistance among the country's poor, landless, and marginal farmers and tribal communities who stand to lose most in the SEZ-driven land acquisition process. It is somewhat ironic that India seems to have the opposite of China's problem of vague property rights. Adherence to strict legal definitions of land rights is one major cause of agitation among the marginalized social groups against land acquisition.

2 Two common denominator explanations

Given the apparent differences in the land regimes in India and China and the similar increase in land conflicts in both countries, it is tempting to ascribe to a *common* set of explanations about the violent tugs-of-war between the state and peasants in both countries. Chief among them are two explanations: one is political-economic in nature and the other focuses on the political relations between the state and peasants.

The political economy explanation emphasizes the inherent flaws in neo-liberalism and its anti-people nature. This is a point that is emphasized by the traditional Indian left intellectuals who were disillusioned by neo-liberal reform at the central level and specifically by the CPI (M) in West Bengal. They charge that the embracing of neo-liberalism has led to the distortion of "public" interests and made government the handmaiden of capitalist investors. As Prabhat Patnaik puts it, "what we have in India today is not capitalists competing against one another for state government projects, but state governments competing against one another for attracting capitalists." And this gives rise to the scenario where "the only 'industrialization' possible under the neo-liberal policy regime is corporate industrialization; and the type of corporate industrialization that can occur within such a regime is ... necessarily anti-people" (Patnaik 2007). Leftist activists and intellectuals thus call for an alternative industrialization model (based on labor-intensive industries, decentralization, and participation by the poor) as a solution to land conflict in rural areas (Bhaduri 2007).

The other explanation emphasizes the traditional antipathy by the peasants against the state. Peasants are traditionally regarded as a self-sufficient group. They inhabit a bounded cultural community marked by subsistence and moral economy arrangements. They are innately distrustful of outside power, and have staged countless rebellions against external intrusion. On this interpretation, what has transpired in Nandigram and Shengyou may be fitted into the larger historical patterns of peasant resistance to the state: the CPI (M)'s Stalinist legacy in Bengal and local state predation in China.

Empirically, it seems hard to apply both explanations fully to the Chinese case. For one thing, the Chinese farmers have not registered the same degree of dislike of the market reform as the Indians. If given a choice, Chinese farmers would likely press for more secure "private property" rights to the land they own and a market-determined price for it. Chinese intellectuals sympathetic to the plight of peasants insist on privatization of land as the first-line defense against marauding governments.[10] For another, the Chinese farmers' antipathy to the state is perhaps more abundantly clear in their incense at local officials than in their attitude to the central state. Many scholars have noted the bifurcation of Chinese farmers' views of the state. Indeed, as Kevin O'Brien and Lianjiang Li argue, their resistance to the state is predicated on a perceived qualitative difference between the center and the local states (O'Brien and Li 2006; Li 2004).

Analytically, the political economy explanation perhaps has more validity than the timeless state-peasant-conflict model, but both suffer from being too broad to offer any direct purchase on our analytical problem at hand; that is, why the violent resistance in Nandigram and Shengyou took place, and why the state responded the way it did (initial violence followed by partial accommodation). What I offer in the following is a modified state-peasant/society perspective that takes into account the changing nature of the state and the rural societies in China and India today.

3 "Party Society," competitive mobilization and land conflicts in India

In a perceptive article on the changing politics of West Bengal, Partha Chatterjee has pointed out the increasing penetration of political parties in rural West Bengal after successful land reforms and the establishment of new panchayat institutions, unhinged from the traditional caste and land-holding structure. The "party" has become "the elementary institution of rural life in the state ... the institution that mediates every single sphere of social activity, with few exceptions, if any" (Chatterjee 2009). A veritable "party society" has thus arisen in West Bengal where "the party and its local functionaries are the principal arbitrators in all social, family and personal disputes and the principal facilitators when individual villagers need help in matters of health, education, finances, employment or travel" (Chatterjee 2009). Political parties have replaced family, kinship, caste, religion, and even land ownership as the principal institution that binds villagers to the state and local hierarchical power.

The penetration of parties into rural society has fundamentally changed Indian peasantry and its relations to the state. Gone is the traditional bounded subsistence peasant community that is "tied to the land and small-scale agriculture, united by the cultural and moral bonds" standing up to an exploitative state and city-based capital from the outside. The state, as Chatterjee puts it, has "penetrated deep into the interior of everyday peasant life," so much so that the institutions of the state "have become internal aspects of the peasant community" (Chatterjee 2008). Peasants engage the state as an imminent institution, sometimes violently, with the utilitarian logic of seeking appropriate governmental redress to their grievances. Chatterjee calls this the logic of political society (Chatterjee 2004).

Under such circumstances, party leaders derive their authority not so much from their control over economic (e.g. landed property) or cultural power (e.g. caste and religious affiliations) as "from their participation in political movements" orchestrated by the party. India's parliamentary system provides the ideal political platform for this purpose. Thus, party penetration of society has produced a type of politics in West Bengal (and elsewhere in India) that is characterized by intense competition among political parties in rural districts. Ruling political parties engage in clientelist policies to hold their supporters in permanent dependence while opposition parties mobilize the villagers around rural grievances.

I suggest that such "competitive mobilization" is at least partly responsible for the violent outcome in Nandigram: the collective form of farmers' resistance, for the spiral of conflict and violence, and for the CPI (M)'s partial accommodation stance. From news accounts and reports, we learn that Nandigram has had a tradition of militant resistance against outside powers going back to the colonial period, but it has remained a stronghold for the ruling CPI (M) until the 2006 election (Banerjee and Roy 2007). Incipient discontent among Nandigram villagers over land acquisition, however, opened the door for the main opposition party – Trinamool Congress – to coalesce and organize local protest activities.

On January 5, 2007, several opposition groups, chiefly the Trinamool Congress and a local Muslim group Jamait-e-Ulema Hind (JUH), formed the Bhumi Uchched Pratirodh Committee (BUPC, Committee to Prevent Eviction from the Land). The BUPC and Trinamool Congress were instrumental in organizing the farmers' agitation against land acquisition. For two months prior to March 14, 2007, they engaged in a tit-for-tat struggle with local CPI (M) members and supporters, giving rise to a spiral of violence that culminated in the March bloodshed (EPW 2007: 80; Nussbaum 2008). Pro-CPI (M) commentators have disputed the characterization of Nandigram as spontaneous peasant uprising. Instead, they viewed the incident as instigated by BUPC and the opposition parties, and by the class of land agents displaced by government requisition (Bhattacharya 2007; Bose 2007; CPI (M) Elected Representatives 2007). On the opposition side, commentators charged the CPI (M) with orchestrating a "state-sponsored massacre" with the objective of intimidating the villagers who opposed the proposed SEZ (Chaudhuri and Sivaraman 2007).

Faced with fierce resistance from farmers and the likely political fallout of forced acquisition, the CPI (M) adjusted its tactics to include a belated apology by the Chief Minister and to announce openly the abandonment of the SEZ idea in Nandigram. In contrast to the Chinese case, however, the state government did not dismiss any local officials over the incident, nor did it file any charges against the police and other perpetrators of the violence. Instead, it continued to play up the Maoist threats in the region in an effort to legitimize its repressive police action. It engaged in new rounds of recrimination against the opposition parties and leaned on local supporters to counter the efforts of opposition activists, thus perpetuating competitive mobilization at the village level (Chaudhuri and Sivaraman 2007). All this, however, was tempered by the CPI (M)'s realization that the Party had to be attuned to the shifting opinions of the rural electorates.

One might argue that in a parliamentary democracy, elections are one possible auto-mechanism for constraining the perpetual escalation of violence. As early as 2006, when CPI (M) still enjoyed widespread support in Bengal, there were already advance warnings about land acquisition possibly being linked to the loss of elections in some rural districts (EPW 2009: 8). Indeed, as it has turned out, Nandigram and Singur proved to be a turning point in the CPI (M)'s electoral fortune. After 32 years of continuous rule in Bengal, the Left Front coalition suffered major defeats in the 2007 panchayat elections and in the latest 2009 national Lok Sabha election. It seems that the Left Front, at least in the short run, has lost out in its competitive mobilization bid against the Trinamool Congress, the biggest winner to have emerged after Nandigram. Given that the CPI (M) has long been committed to parliamentary electoral democracy, one could make the argument, *prima facie,* that Mr. Bhattacharjee's apology and his decision to call off the SEZ in Nandigram was at least partially motivated by electoral concerns.

To conclude this section, I argue that the violence at Nandigram was produced by a process of competitive mobilization by opposing political parties around a controversial government policy. Competitive mobilization, in turn, was necessitated by changes in state-peasant relations in West Bengal in recent decades. Following successful land reforms, rural Bengal has become a "party society," *à la* Partha Chatterjee, where party agents stake their authority on their ability to mobilize party supporters at the grassroots level and to provide government benefits to them in return. Party cadres unleashed violence to counter the influence of other parties while at the same time trying to contain its spread so as not to let the incident affect the party's electoral fortunes. In this sense, Nandigram-style conflicts are bound to have national repercussions, and local conflicts in India have a way of spilling over to national-level political contests.

4 Inter-governmental dynamic and land conflict in China

In contrast to India, the Chinese countryside in the reform period neither can be called a "party society" in Chatterjee's sense of the word, nor is it characterized by organized partisan mobilization by competing interests. If anything, the Chinese party-state has so thoroughly de-mobilized the countryside it has become a vast administered territory, the mere target of government policies. Important decisions regarding production and welfare are divided between the household and higher-up authorities. Village elections turn on the candidates' technical competence or compliance with authorities, not on their ideological inclination or political visions. Villagers traded in regimented politicized life during the Maoist days for a measure of personal freedom (in work and travel) and for family, religion, consumption, and entrepreneurship.

This is not to say that rural people are content with the administered condition, or that top-down administration has robbed Chinese peasants of their capacity for protest. On the contrary, as our Shengyou case has indicated, the Chinese countryside is simmering with discontent and frustration. Rural grievances, clashes between cadres and farmers, and neighborly or communal disputes are on the rise amid signs of an acute rural governance crisis (O'Brien and Li 2006; Zweig 2003). Still, it is important to remember that these grievances, clashes, and conflicts are not born of an Indian-style politicized rural society, but they coalesce around specific issues (e.g. tax and fees, corruption, land acquisition, etc.) and personalities, and they are mostly confined to the locales of their eruption.

Rural China's governance crisis is partly discernible from the gradual withdrawal of the ruling Communist Party from its traditional rural base. The rural share of party membership has declined steadily since the reform. For example, peasants still made up 46.9 percent of the party rank-and-file in 1979 – already a decline from the historical high of 59.6 percent in 1949 – and they had dropped to 32.5 percent by 2000 (BCRGDXT 2002). Party organizations in the rural areas suffer from chronic recruitment problems and a grave legitimacy crisis. The Chinese press is filled with stories about aging party membership in the rural areas, for example. A report about rural party building from 1994 to 2000 disclosed that almost half (48.8%) of all village party branches were considered weak, backward, paralyzed, or otherwise not functional at one point or another (*Xinhua* 2001: June 14). While omnipresent and omnipotent rural party branches symbolized effective Maoist control over the countryside, as An Chen has observed, "party power is becoming increasingly irrelevant to village governance" during the reform (Chen 2007: 147).

I am not suggesting here, however, that the party has left the farmers alone. Far from it. The party may have ceased to be a *political* machine reaching the bottom of Chinese society, but it has consolidated administrative power, via its cadre appointment system and propaganda control, over various levels of government (from township up) that have in turn ruled the countryside. Equally important, while extricating itself from the rural village the party has not allowed other forms of organization to take its place. Party leaders remain vigilant about new emerging forms of solidarity among the villagers, be they traditional lineage organizations, religious networks, or civic associations. As a result, aggrieved farmers not only lack access to mediating organizations (e.g. associations and interest groups), but they are deprived of organizational resources that they could use to press claims against the local state.

Under such circumstances, ordinary farmers often look *inside* the party-state for allies, sympathizers and other resources, and in doing so they set off an inter-governmental dynamic within the state that responds to or turns against their demand as situations change on the ground. By *inter-governmental dynamic,* I refer both to the horizontal interaction between the same-level governments *and* to the hierarchical relationship between the local government and its supervisory authorities. One could perhaps boil it down to "local state competition" and "central-local relations." For example, local states compete with each other for more investors, bigger projects, and fewer petitioners and "trouble-makers" in China. Dingzhou City, where Shengyou was located, successfully competed for the gigantic power plant in 2001, the state's key project in the Five-year Plan, the No. 1 priority project in the province, the largest investment (9.52 billion *yuan*) in the area since 1949!

Especially pertinent for our analysis here are the central–local relations. I prefer the word "dynamic" to "relations" because the former implies not stasis, but change in response to the pressure emanating from the rural society. China being a unitary political system, the central state has ultimate power to force local governments to comply with the central directives. Yet central and local interests often diverge.

On the issue of land acquisition, the central government is more worried about food grain production, land preservation, and long-term legitimacy in the eyes of villagers, whereas local governments are often interested in pursuing their own institutional interests (e.g. budget) and fast but short-term economic growth. What will set the dynamic in motion are the petitions, protests, and violent confrontations in the society. When the farmers are content and peaceful, the center demands development (and approves the necessary land expropriation) from the local state, and otherwise exercises benign neglect over minor corruption. When the farmers become restive or even violent, the center takes the local state to task for bad governance and for causing instability (*Sinocast* 2004).

The central-local dynamic also reinforces a particular, differentiated view of the Chinese state by the villagers. From the villagers' vantage point, the center often appears as a benevolent and rational power in contrast to the malign and corrupt local other.[11] This view appears justified when one looks at the central government's record and rhetoric in recent years. The center has delivered beneficial policies – from rural education, to the repeal of agricultural tax and experiment with a new rural healthcare system. It has tried to curb local excesses, from corruption to excessive levies to the abuse of power by rural cadres. Most crucially, it continues to broadcast symbols, slogans, and broad statements of socialist values and principles.

All this has instilled in the villagers a deep sense of central benevolence and local injustice. One China expert has noted, a peculiar feature of Chinese political culture is that farmers seek redress at top levels for problems caused by local officials. Citizens use organized protest activities "to circumvent the control of local officials over formal political and legal institutions and prompt the intervention of higher-level officials in resolving citizen grievances" (Minzner 2006). As Xiaolin Guo has nicely put it, "the relationship of the villagers with the central state is political and symbolic, whereas their relationship with the local state is social and economic. The relationship between the central state and the villagers is maintained at a moral level, whereas that between the local state and villagers is more tangible and tied to interests in concrete terms, and the competition for control over economic resources between the two groups forms a major source of social conflicts" (Guo 2001).

To the villagers in Shengyou, unilateral land acquisition by the city government was a policy that went against the central policies designed to protect the farmers' interests. Shengyou villagers were so convinced of their righteousness that the village leaders and party members endorsed and joined the first action to resist government requisition in late 2003 (Wang and Qiao 2005). On the wall of their makeshift memorial hall mourning the dead in the conflict, a giant banner bore the telling sign: "They [the dead villagers] Gave Their Precious Lives In Order To Carry Out the Central Land Policy and Protect Villagers' Interests." Throughout the protest and after, Shengyou villagers repeatedly tried to file petitions in Beijing. Undeterred by jail and local government interception, they kept up hopes of central intervention all the way to the end. One village petitioner is reported to have said after the 2005 violence, "we can only hope the central government will help us to fight for justice as we don't trust local government any more" (Chan 2006).

On the one hand, the bifurcated view of the Chinese state increased the villagers' moral resoluteness in fighting off local corrupt officials. On the other, pressures on the local state to develop the economy and to keep social stability made the local government oscillate between issuing threats and appeasing the protestors. The paramount importance of the largest industrial project in the history of the city must have weighed heavily on the minds of municipal officials as they faced off resistance from the farmers. This must be why the municipal government was shrill in its condemnation of the villagers two months before the fateful clash: "we will strike hard firmly ... on anyone who dare to test the limit of law and are intent on disrupting Dingzhou's environment in favor of development" (Zhang 2005). At the same time, while the municipal government mobilized all local media in support of land requisition, it carefully kept out non-local media organs and kept the lid on a brewing crisis.

A peculiar kind of inter-governmental dynamic was thus set in motion by the protesting villagers. The local government oscillated between appeasement and confrontation with the protesters for a long time while considering possible reactions from the center. When it finally unleashed violence, it did so not directly by deploying its regular police force, but through a business contractor who hired thugs and goons picked up from the city square. Excessive force, and the media exposé, sealed the fate of the local leaders as soon as the Center found out about the savage attacks on innocent villagers. The center intervened and forced the provincial government to cancel the land acquisition in Shengyou, to console the villagers and to charge not only the attackers but also the city's party secretary with crime. Unlike in the Indian case, where future electoral prospects led the CPI (M) to accommodate Nandigram villagers, the appeasement came from the once-obstinate local authorities on the order of the central state.

5 By way of conclusion

What we have here are cases of convergence of local state practices in spite of the fact that they are from very different politico-economic and social contexts. At first sight, it seems that development imperatives trump political distinctions and force the same kind of state behavior toward the citizens. However, I argue that the state-society relations exhibit distinctive differences in India and China. As a consequence, the two localities have arrived at the local land conflicts and at their final resolution via different routes and by distinctively different mechanisms.

In India, increasing politicization has led to what Partha Chatterjee has called a "party society" in West Bengal. Politicians from different parties were locked in incessant struggles whereby social conflict became an extension of electoral politics. Competitive mobilization by different political groups that tap into people's core interests or identities could lead to violent outcomes, as happened in Nandigram and elsewhere. The fact that local politicians would face elections serves as a real constraint on their behavior, but it is often not powerful enough to override their zeal for development, growth, and votes.

In China, unelected local officials are beholden to the central state even though central-local interests often diverge. An inter-governmental dynamic keeps the center above the fray in most social conflicts where local officials bear the brunt of citizen complaints and protest. Deprived of organizational and societal resources, Chinese villagers tend to avoid direct confrontations with the central state but look to explore the fissures and conflicts within the state apparatus – between different levels of government and among different functional units at the same level of government – to create a balance of power that will govern in their favor. All this sets off a situation whereby local conflicts between the state and villagers could get out of hand, especially when the center fails to intervene at opportune moments. To understand the violent outcome and local government action in the tragic Shengyou case, I argue, one needs to pay attention to the inter-governmental dynamic that operates in today's Chinese politics.

Notes

1. *People's Tribunal on Nandigram Report,* available at http://sanhati.com/news/334/
2. For peasant resistance to land acquisition in the early 1990s, see Guha (2007). For more recent cases, see Ramachandran (2007).

3. According to Chinese news reports, Shengyou was the lone holdout village in a group of 12 villages whose land was requisitioned for the power plant project. Reports also indicate that some households, including most definitely the village party secretary, had supported the government requisition.
4. A more recent survey in 2008 found that 34 percent of the villages have carried out re-adjustment of land holdings after 1998, the year when the Land Management Law fixed the farmers' term of lease at thirty years. See Prosterman et al. (2009).
5. As Cai Yongshun has shown, the administrative village, sub-village group, and sometimes even the township, may claim to constitute the "collective" with the right to dispose of collective land in its jurisdiction. In the Shengyou case, the collective in question seems to be the administrative village.
6. The Chinese Constitution grants the state the authority "to expropriate land, in the public interest, for its use." The 1998 Labor Management Law also provides that "[t]he State may, in the public interest, lawfully requisition land owned by collectives." However, the notion of "public interest" is left deliberately vague. Commercial developments are often passed on as public interest projects.
7. RDI Memo on "Land Takings in China: Policy Recommendations," June 5, 2003. However, this assessment is higher than later survey findings that indicate that majority cases of land-takings were for the purpose of road construction (51%) while the building of factories and industrial parks made up about 29 percent. See Zhu et al. (2006: 781).
8. Citing another source, Cai reports that farmer households typically receive only about 10 percent of the total compensation amount, with 25–30 percent going to the village government and 60–70 percent going to higher-level government agencies. See Cai (2003).
9. See http://www.indoresez.nic.in/doc/SEZ. In the case of West Bengal, the Left Front government passed its own SEZ Act even earlier, in 2003. See http://sezindia.nic.in/HTMLS/WBSEZAct.pdf.
10. See interview remarks by Guoying Dang, professor at CASS Institute of Rural Development in *The Guardian* 2006: May 26. Also see Zhang (2008).
11. This view, however, is not confined to the contemporary Chinese villagers. As Eric Hobsbawm and Elizabeth Perry have both noted, modern Europe and imperial China were replete with examples of peasants rebelling against their immediate oppressors while holding the kings and emperors as embodiments of justice. See Hobsbawm (1997); Perry (2008). See also Xiaolin Guo's discussion in Guo (2001).

6

Regime Types, Political Change and Economic Development: The Cases of India and China

Zhiyue Bo

What is the impact of the type of political regime on economic development? Does democracy foster economic growth? Or is an authoritarian regime in a better position to promote material welfare? The conventional wisdom, as detailed by Adam Przeworski et al. (2000), is that the regime type has no impact on economic growth. Democracy neither fosters nor hinders economic development. However, the cases of India and China seem to suggest otherwise. In the past three decades, India – the largest democracy in the world – has sustained a moderate rate of economic growth while China – the largest authoritarian regime – has witnessed an unprecedented period of economic expansion.

Using data on political regimes, political change, and economic growth at the state/provincial level from India and China, this study attempts to understand the impact of political regimes on economic development. This chapter will review the literature on regimes and economic development, highlight the contrast in economic growth between India and China in the past six decades, examine the two countries at the state/provincial level,[1] and explore the impact of local leadership on economic development in a comparative framework.

1 Political regimes and economic development

On the fundamental question of the relationship between political regimes and economic development, we often hear two opposite answers. On the one hand, those who favor growth often caution against democracy because they believe that democratic regimes inhibit growth by diverting resources from investment to consumption (Przeworski et al. 2000: 142–3). On the other hand, those who value efficiency agree that democracies are better for economic growth because of their superior efficiency of resource allocation (Przeworski et al. 2000: 143–4). In recent years, however, a growing literature has subscribed to a third perspective that does not see any differences to prosperity made by different regime types (Przeworski et al. 2000: 145–86).

It is conceivable in a democracy that a political party that is tailored to the interests of the largest number of voters has a better chance to win than its rivals and that a popularly elected party is more likely to adopt a socially popular public policy. "The more democratic a government is," Walter Galenson hypothesized, "the greater the diversion of resources from investment to consumption" (Galenson 1959). Hence the first view that democracy is problematic for economic growth. However, democracy proponents argue that dictatorships are inherently inefficient because they have no incentives to maximize total output and that democracies are more efficient because they protect property rights and thus allow investors to have a long-term perspective (Preworski et al. 2000: 144).

The third perspective that has been articulated is that regime types have nothing to do with economic growth. Democracy neither inhibits nor promotes economic development. This perspective, it should be noted, is nothing new. It was proposed by Samuel Huntington in the 1960s. "The most important political distinction among countries," according to Huntington, "concerns not their form of government but their degree of government" (Huntington 1968: 1). In his judgment, a government is a good government if it can govern. Therefore, there are no fundamental differences between democratic countries such as the United States and Great Britain and authoritarian regimes such as the Soviet Union. "All three countries have strong, adaptable, coherent political institutions: effective bureaucracies, well-organized political parties, a high degree of popular participation in public affairs, working systems of civilian control over the military, extensive procedures for regulating succession and controlling political conflict" (Huntington 1968: 1). In this regard, democracy is not necessarily superior to dictatorship, and vice versa. For Robert J. Barro, regime types do not matter for economic growth because both democratic and non-democratic governments have expanded economic freedoms – in the form of free markets and small governments that focus on the maintenance of property rights – that are conducive to growth (Barro 1996: 1). For James A. Robinson, both regime types are equally likely to suffer stagnation if they adopt bad economic policies (Robinson 1998: 1–46). Based on a dataset of 135 countries over the period of 1950–90, Adam Przeworski, Michael E. Alvarez, Jose Antonio Chelbub, and Fernando Limongi concluded that regimes have effects on neither investment nor the rate of growth of total income (Preworski et al. 2000: 145–58).

2 Political regimes and economic development: India and China

In spite of overwhelming evidence from Przeworski et al., it is important to examine the experiences of India and China in greater detail in terms of regime-growth relationship. First, with a combined population of 2.4 billion, these two countries represent 37 percent of the total world population. The welfare of the people in these two countries is of great importance in itself. Second, India and China are both developing countries. They are still faced with challenges of political, economic, and social development. It will be important to understand whether a particular sequencing might make any difference to the welfare of these and other similarly situated countries in the long run. Finally, the initial conditions of India and China are remarkably comparable except for regime types. Therefore, they constitute almost ideal cases of comparison for studying the effects of regime types on growth.

The two countries had similar conditions. They were both products of World War II. India declared independence in 1947, and the People's Republic of China was founded in 1949. Both had a low level of economic development for a long period since. Real GDP per capita in India in 1952 was US$139, and the similar figure in China was US $59.2 in the same year (Heston, Summers, and Aten 2011). Moreover, both countries adopted the Soviet-type central planning system. India adopted its first five-year plan in 1950, and China's first five-year began in 1953. Both countries experienced economic reforms in recent years. China initiated economic reforms in the late 1970s, and India started reforms in the early 1990s.

Yet the two countries form a clear contrast because of their different political regimes. India is the largest multi-party democracy in the world and China maintains the world's largest Party state. The economic performances of these two countries in the past six decades are clearly in favor of the authoritarian regime instead of the democratic regime. China's annual rate of growth between 1953 and 2009 was 8.1 percent, and India's annual rate of growth during the same period was 4.8 percent (Figure 6.1). In other words, China grew almost 70 percent faster than India did.

One may wonder why China outperformed India in economic growth. Is it because the democratic regime in India diverted too many

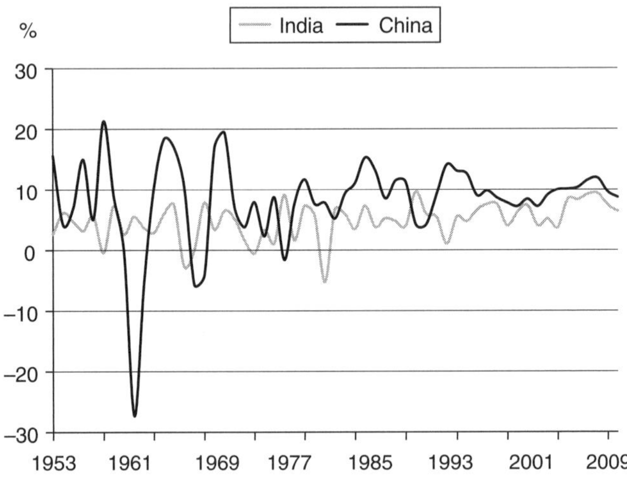

Figure 6.1 Growth rates in India and China (1953–2009)
Source: Author's database.

resources to consumption, thus having the effect of restricting investment? The answer is affirmative. India indeed uses a much larger share of its GDP on consumption than China does. India allocated 86.8 percent of its GDP to consumption on average each year between 1952 and 2004, and China's annual rate of consumption during the same period was only 66.1 percent. In these years, both countries started at high levels and declined in later years; but India maintained much higher levels throughout the period (Figure 6.2).

In the 1950s, India consumed almost 95 percent of its GDP each year on average, with 97.1 percent for 1953. In the meantime, China's annual consumption was only 72 percent of its GDP on average, with the year of 1959 at its lowest level of 56.6 percent. In the 1960s, India lowered its annual consumption to about 91 percent on average while China increased its annual consumption to about 74 percent on average. In the 1970s, India's consumption further declined to 87 percent annually and China's consumption dropped to 65 percent per year. In the 1980s, China maintained its consumption at the 65 percent level while India increased its consumption to 88 percent annually. In the 1990s, India still consumed about 80 percent of its GDP while China's consumption dropped to less than 60 percent of its GDP. In the early years of the twenty-first century, India's consumption was reduced to 75.3 percent of its GDP and China's consumption declined

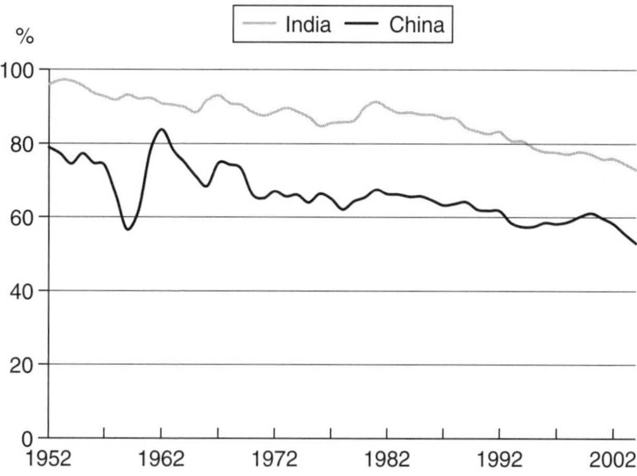

Figure 6.2 Proportion of consumption in GDP: India and China (1952–2004)
Source: Author's database.

to 57.5 percent, with the year of 2004 at 53 percent (the lowest level recorded).

Moreover, consistent with the hypothesis that democratic regimes divert more resources to consumption than authoritarian regimes, India's households take a larger share of the total consumption than do China's households (Figure 6.3).

Between 1952 and 2004, India's household consumption ranged from 83.2 percent to 94.9 percent of the total consumption, with an average of 88.8 percent a year. During the same period, the Chinese households took 80.7 percent of the total consumption on average, with a range from 76.6 percent to 85.1 percent. In other words, the democratic regime in India diverted not only more resources to consumption in general but also more resources to household consumption in particular. In 1953, for instance, India consumed 97 percent of its GDP and China consumed 77 percent of its GDP, representing a different of almost 20 percent. In the same year, India diverted 94.8 percent of the 97 percent of its GDP on households while China used 82.1 percent of the 77 percent of its GDP on households.

Consequently, the Indian government consumes less than the Indian households and the Indian government has fewer resources for itself than its Chinese counterpart. During the period of 1952 to 2004, the Indian government's consumption was 11.2 percent of the total consumption and was only 9.5 percent of its GDP a year on average. In the meantime,

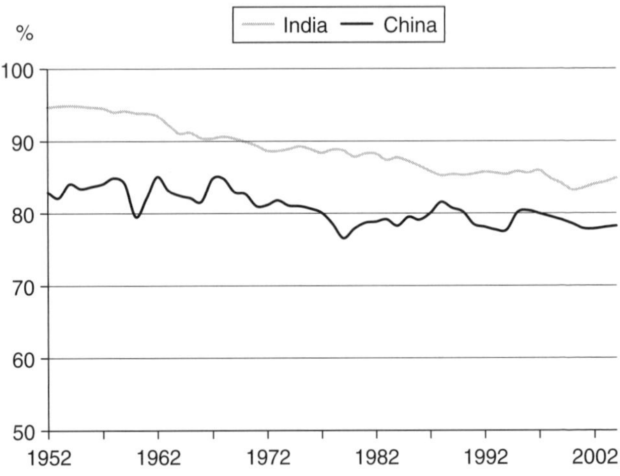

Figure 6.3 Household consumption as a proportion of the total consumption: India and China (1952–2004)
Source: Author's database.

the Chinese government's consumption was 19.3 percent of the total consumption and was 12.6 percent of its GDP on average annually.

As a result of its high consumption India has, understandably, had lower levels of investment. From 1952 to 2004, India's gross fixed capital formation was 17.2 percent of its GDP a year on average. China's rate of gross fixed capital formation during the same period was 27.3 percent, 10 percent higher. In contrast to Figure 6.3, where India maintained higher levels of consumption than China, China's investment was consistently higher than that of India throughout the period (Figure 6.4).

Moreover, although both countries witnessed growth in investment over the years, China's growth was faster than that of India. In 1952, China's fixed capital formation was 11.7 percent of its GDP and India's fixed capital formation was nine percent of its GDP. During the Great Leap Forward, China's fixed capital formation jumped to 25.8 percent, 30 percent, and 31.4 percent of its GDP in 1958, 1959, and 1960, respectively. India's shares in the same years were only 12.7 percent, 11.4 percent, and 11.9 percent, respectively. The gap between China's fixed capital formation and that of India was not significantly narrowed during the years of China's Cultural Revolution (1966–76), and the gap has substantially expanded since 1995. China's fixed capital formation in 2004 was almost 20 percent higher than that of India. China's gross fixed capital formation

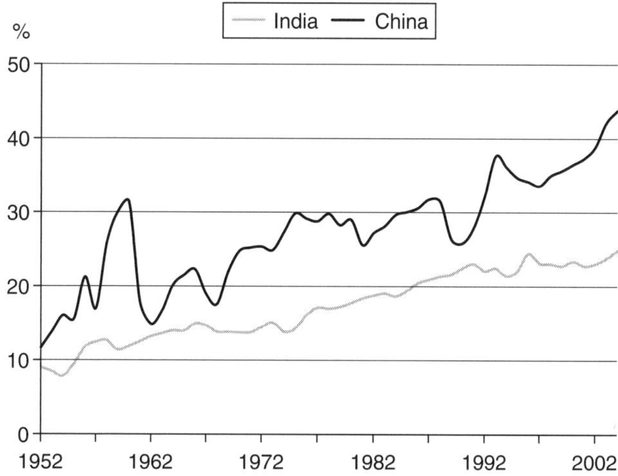

Figure 6.4 Fixed capital formation as a proportion of GDP: India and China (1952–2004)
Source: Author's database.

in that year took 43.8 percent of its GDP, and India's gross fixed capital formation in the same year was only 24.9 percent of its GDP.

A more fundamental reason for India's relatively underperformance is that democratization in an underdeveloped country is the antithesis of modernization. The main social function of democratization in rural areas, as Emilio Willems observed in 1958, is to preserve the existing power structure (Willems 1958: 552). "Electoral competition in postcolonial countries," Samuel Huntington indicated in 1968, "thus seems to direct the attention of political leaders from the urban to the rural voter, to make political appeals and governmental policies less modern and more traditional, to replace highly educated cosmopolitan political leaders with less educated local and provincial leaders, and to enhance the power of local and provincial government at the expense of national government" (Huntington 1968: 445). In contrast, because of its authoritarian nature, the Chinese regime was not subject to the same electoral pressure from peasants. In other words, democratic India is more likely than the authoritarian China to have a rural bias in terms of resource allocations. And this is true especially in the early post-war years of these two countries.

In India, politicians appealed to peasants for votes by making substantial investments in agriculture and rural development. Between

1951 and 2004, India's annual investment in agriculture, that is gross fixed capital formation for agricultural and allied activities, was about 13 percent of the total investment (gross fixed capital formation in India) on average, ranging between 7.7 percent and 23.7 percent.

On the other hand, although the Chinese Communist Party had been propelled to power by peasants' support, Chinese leaders did not have to appeal to peasants by providing similar levels of investment in agriculture. In the period of 1951 to 2004, China's expenditure in agriculture was only 9.8 percent on average, with a range of 3.4 percent to 17.1 percent.

In terms of historical trends in sectoral investment, India and China followed opposite directions initially and then converged in the same direction of decline. India's agricultural investment started at a high point and continuously declined over the years. China's agricultural investment went from a low level to the highest level in the first 14 years and then joined India in the downward trend (Figure 6.5).

Because of its authoritarian nature, China's leadership was able to promote industrialization at the expense of agriculture. As a result, China's secondary sector expanded from 20.9 percent of the total GDP in 1952 to 52.9 percent of the total GDP in 2004, while China's primary sector dropped from 50.5 percent in 1952 to 15.2 percent in 2004. In contrast, India's democratic system hindered its ability to

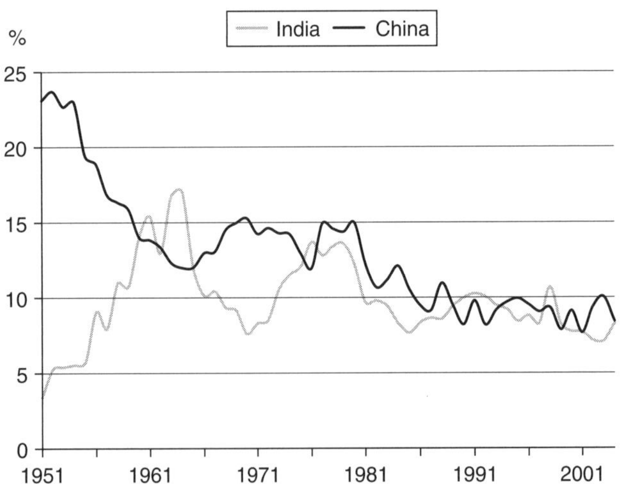

Figure 6.5 Investment in agriculture in India and China (1951–2004)
Source: Author's database.

transfer resources from agriculture to industry. Consequently, India's industrialization progressed at a much slower pace. India's industrial sector in 2007 took only 19.3 percent of its GDP (versus China's 48.1 percent of the same year).

Moreover, China's leadership was able to implement effective family planning policies. China's natural growth rate of population declined from 33.3 per thousand in 1963 to 5.9 per thousand in 2004. In contrast, India's population increased much more rapidly than China's. India's population expanded from 357 million in 1950 to 684 million in 1980 and further to 1130 million in 2007. With an estimated growth rate of 1.4 percent in 2007, India is expected to overtake China as the most populous country in the world by 2030.

Consequently, China's real GDP per capita first caught up with and then substantially surpassed that of India (Figure 6.6). In 1952, China's real GDP per capita was barely 43 percent of India's number. But, 50 years later, China's real GDP per capita was almost two thirds more than that of India. In 2003, China's real GDP per capita reached US$5321 and India's real GDP per capita was only US$3213.

In order to determine precisely how regime types relate economic development, we build a statistical model on the basis of the summary

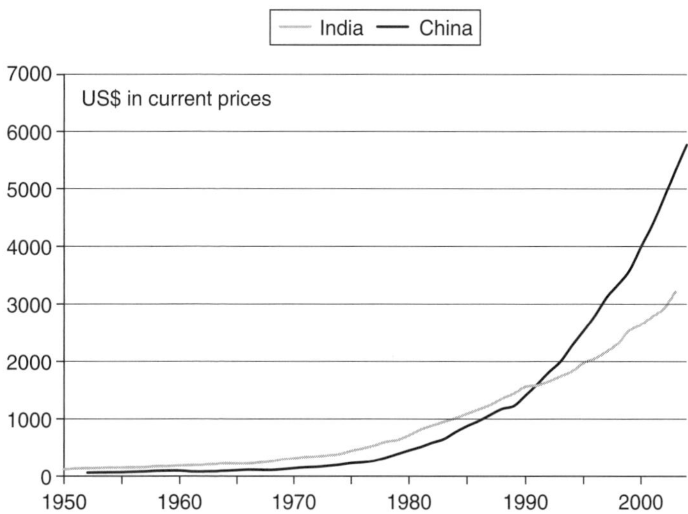

Figure 6.6 Real gross domestic product per capita in India and China (1950–2004)
Source: Author's database.

discussion and data above, with reform as a control variable.[2] The model is

$$Y_{it} = \alpha + \beta_1 (D_{it}) + \beta_2 (R_{it}) + \varepsilon$$

Where
Y_{it} refers to the growth rate of gross domestic product (GDP) of the ith country at t (year),
α refers to the constant,
D refers to regime types (1 being democratic; 0 authoritarian)
R refers to reform policies (1 being years of reform; 0 years of non-reform)
β_1 and β_2 are coefficients of D and R, respectively, and
ε refers to the residual.

Table 6.1 provides results of the regression model. It seems clear from Table 6.1 that both regime types and reform policies make differences in terms of economic growth in China and India. Reform policies were introduced in 1978 in China and in 1991 in India. These two countries grew 2.7 percent faster under reform than previously. India as a democracy grew 2.8 percent slower than China as an authoritarian regime. Both results are statistically significant.

Table 6.1 Regimes and economic growth in India and China

	Model 1	**Model 2**
Democracy	−2.793**	−2.096*
	(1.102)	(1.145)
Reform	2.693**	2.866**
	(1.120)	(1.133)
Investment		0.063
		(0.039)
Constant	6.711***	5.617***
	(0.969)	(1.106)
Adjusted R^2	0.117	0.122
Observations	110	106

Notes:
1. Dependent variable is real GDP annual growth rate.
2. Numbers in parentheses are standard errors.
*p < .10; **p < .05; ***p < .01

Sources:
1. China's data are based on China Statistics Yearbook, various years.
2. India's data are from http://www.indiastat.com/default.aspx.

3 Political variables and economic growth at the local level: India vs. China

How do political variables, including regime types, affect economic development at the state/provincial level in India and China? Do democratic regimes in Indian states have any advantage in terms of economic growth over their authoritarian counterparts in China, or vice versa? Before answering these questions, we need to examine local development in India and China.

a Politics of economic development in Indian states

(1) The evolution of India's state system

India's state system has evolved in the past six decades. During the British colonial period, there were two categories of regions in India. One category is collectively referred to as "British India," regions that were directly administered by the British, and the other is known as "Princely States," or regions that were ruled by Indian rulers. At Independence in 1947, there were 17 provinces under British India and hundreds of Princely States. Upon the Partition of India into the Union of India and Dominion of Pakistan, 12 provinces (Ajmer-Merwara-Kekri, Andaman and Nicobar Islands, Assam, Bihar, Bombay, Central Provinces and Berar, Coorg, Delhi, Madras, Panth-Piploda, Orissa, and the United Provinces) became provinces within India, three (Baluchistan, North-West Frontier, and Sindh) within Pakistan, and two (Bengal and Punjab) were partitioned between India and Pakistan. A further 625 princely states were given a choice of joining either country.

The British Indian province of Bengal was divided into West Bengal (a province of India) and East Bengal (a province of Pakistan), the latter was renamed East Pakistan in 1956 and became the independent nation of Bangladesh in 1971. The British Indian province of Punjab was also divided into West Punjab, later Punjab (Pakistan), and Islamabad Capital Territory; and East Punjab, later Punjab (India), Haryana, and Himachal Pradesh.

India adopted a new constitution on January 26, 1950 and replaced provinces with states and territories. The states would have extensive autonomy and complete democracy in the Union, and the Union territories would be administered by the Government of India. The constitution of 1950 classified 27 states into three types. There were nine Part-A states. They were the former governors' provinces of British India and were ruled by an elected governor and state legislature. There were eight

Part-B states, which were former princely states or groups of Princely States governed by a rajpramukh (who was often a former prince) along with an elected legislature. The rajpramukh was appointed by the President of India. There were 10 Part-C states, which included both the former chief commissioners' provinces and Princely States governed by a chief commissioner (who was appointed by the President of India).

India's state governance went through a fundamental transformation in 1956, providing a foundation for the modern states of India. The States Reorganization Act, which went into effect on November 1, 1956, eliminated the distinction among Part A, B, and C states and reorganized state boundaries along linguistic lines. As a result, India was divided into 21 units, including 14 states and seven union territories. Language played an important role in the restructuring. For instance, the Telugu speaking state of Andhra was renamed Andhra Pradesh and was enlarged by the addition of Telangana, the Telugu speaking region of the Hyderabad State. Consequently, Hyderabad, the former capital of the Hyderabad State, was made the capital of Andhra Pradesh. The states and union territories of India went through a few more changes in the subsequent years.

Currently, India has altogether 35 units, including 28 states and seven union territories. The most populous state is Uttar Pradesh, with a total population of 166.2 million (2001); and the least populous state is Lakshadweep, with a population of only 61,000 (2001). The largest state in territory is Rajasthan (342,000 square kilometers), and the smallest state is again Lakshadweep (30 square kilometers).

(2) Political change in the Indian states

The Constitution of 1950 introduced elections to state governments in India. The first elections were conducted in 1952, with scheduled elections every five years thereafter (Khemani 2004: 125–54). However, a substantial number of state elections occurred in the middle of a five-year term. Out of 107 state elections over the period of 1960–92 in a sample of 14 states, for instance, 36 (34%) occurred in the mid-term (Khemani 2004: 134).

There are three major types of political changes to state leadership. First, there are *ruling party changes* (Figure 6.7). In Indian states, there are multi-party competitive elections. Therefore, it is likely that a ruling party would be replaced by an opposition party in an election. However, ruling party changes in Indian states are rare. Out of 1429 state/years from 1950 to 2009, 228 (16 percent) experienced ruling party changes. However, some years stand out in terms of party changes. In 1967, 10 out of 23 states saw party changes, representing 43.5 percent. In 1977, 15 out of 27 states

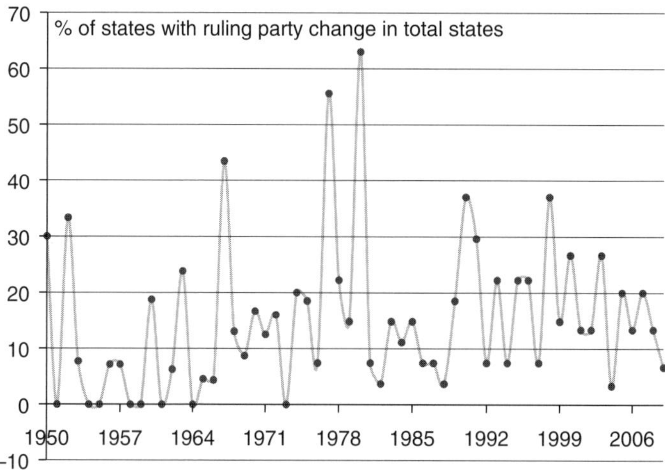

Figure 6.7 Ruling party changes in Indian states (1950–2009)
Source: Author's database.

changed hands from one party to another, representing 55.6 percent. Year 1980 witnessed the peak of party changes, with 17 out of 27 states (63 percent) changing ruling parties. Years 1990 and 1998 are also noteworthy, with 10 out of 27 states (37 percent) changing ruling parties each year.

The second type of political change in Indian states is *party leadership change* – the replacement of an old leader of the same party by a new one (Figure 6.8). This is a bit more frequent than ruling party changes. Out of 1429 state/years, there are 231 changes, representing 16.2 percent. Over the period of 1950 to 2009, there are six peaks of leadership changes. The first peak came in 1952, when a third of leaders were replaced in the elections. Out of 12 states at the time, four had new leaders of the same ruling parties.

The second peak occurred in 1956 when the State Reorganization Act was introduced. Out of 14 states, five (35.7 percent) saw new leaders in that year. Karnataka, for instance, changed two leaders in the year. The third peak took place in the period of 1962–3. About one third (31.3 percent) of 16 states in 1962 replaced leaders of the same party; and more than one third (38.1 percent) of 21 states got new leaders in 1963. Again, Karnataka had frequent changes to the chief minister of the Indian National Congress in 1962. The fourth peak came in 1969 when 10 out of 23 states (43.5 percent) saw new leaders of the same party. The

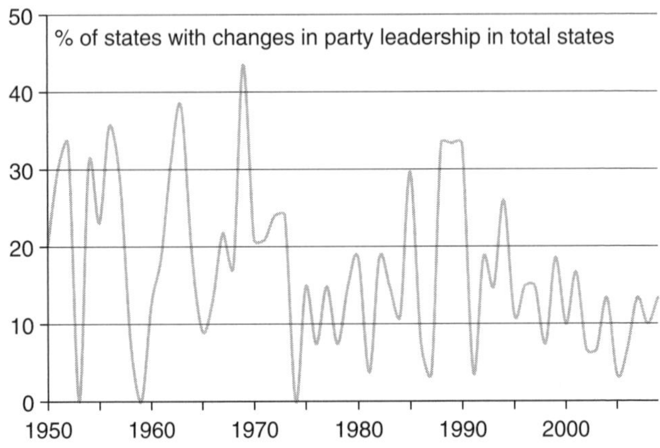

Figure 6.8 Party leadership changes in Indian states (1950–2009)
Source: Author's response.

fifth peak occurred in 1985 when eight out of 27 states (29.6 percent) saw new leaders of the same party. The last peak occurred in the period of 1988 to 1990 when nine out of 27 states (33.3 percent) witnessed new leaders of the same party each year.

The third type of political change in Indian states is the intervention of the central government in local affairs according to the "President's Rule." According to Article 356 of the Constitution of India, the central government has the right to rule in a state when its legislature is dissolved or put in suspended animation. Under the President's Rule, the state governor, who is appointed by the central government, exercises executive authority on behalf of the President of India. It is called the "President's Rule" because it is the President of India who governs the state instead of a Council of Ministers who are answerable to the elected legislature. Since the president has no discretionary powers in India and has to act according to the advice of the Council of Ministers at the center, the administration of the state is practically in the hands of the ruling party at the center. Since 1950, this President's Rule has been used more than 100 times (Figure 6.9).

The President's Rule was used for the first time in 1951 in Punjab of India. Formerly a part of the Punjab region, which also includes the Pakistani province of Punjab and the North-West Frontier Province, the Indian states of Haryana and Himachal Pradesh, parts of Jammu and Kashmir, and the Union Territory of Chandigarh, the Indian state

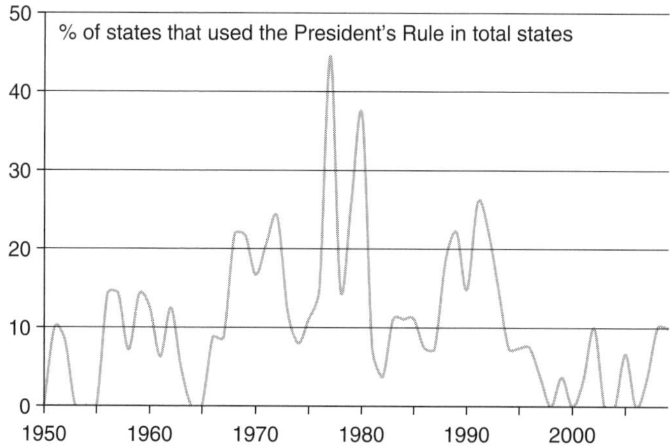

Figure 6.9 Uses of President's rule in Indian states (1950–2009)
Source: Author's database.

of Punjab was under the control of the Indian National Congress. The President's Rule was subsequently imposed in the state of Punjab seven more times, in 1966, 1968–9, 1971–2, 1977, 1980, 1983–5, and 1987–92.

The most well known use (or abuse) of the President's Rule was in the case of Kerala in 1959. After Kerala was inaugurated as a state on November 1, 1956, a new Legislative Assembly election was held in April 1957, producing the world's first democratically elected communist government, headed by E. M. S. Namboodiripad. However, the central government invoked the President's Rule to dismiss the democratically elected, but communist government of Kerala on July 31, 1959, during the "Liberation Struggle" (Vimochana samaram).

In the 1970s and 1980s, the central government used the article to dismiss the state governments under opposition parties under various pretexts. The central government imposed President's Rule in 12 states (44.4 percent) in 1977 and 10 states (37 percent) in 1980. After the landmark case of S. R. Bommai vs. Union of India in 1989, this misuse of Article 356 has become less frequent.

(3) Economic development of the Indian states

Indian states had a remarkable record of economic growth in the period of 1961 to 2005.[3] The average growth rate among 19 states with available information is five percent. The slowest growth rate was –23.4 percent (Goa in 2003), and the fastest growth rate was 41.3 percent (Rajasthan in 1988). Two union territories stand out as the best performers. Puducherry and Delhi had average growth rates of 7.9 percent and 7.3 percent, respectively (Figure 6.10). Three of the largest states, on the other hand, had the slowest growth. Uttar Pradesh, Bihar, and Madhya Pradesh had an average growth of 3.2 percent, 3.3 percent, and 3.3 percent, respectively.

(4) Political changes and economic growth in Indian states

What is the impact of political changes on economic growth in Indian states? The answer is not straightforward (Table 6.2).

First, it seems that the change from one political party to another in a state seems to be a good thing for the local economic growth (Model 1). For each change of the ruling party, there is a corresponding GDP increase of 1.5 percent. This result is statistically significant. Leadership changes and the imposition of the President's Rule seem to slow down local economic growth, but the results are not statistically significant. Moreover, a new variable, "reform," is introduced to the model. This is a dummy variable, with pre-reform years (1961–90) as 0 and reform years (1991–2005) as 1. It seems that "reform" brings about positive changes to the local economy (Model 2). However, when investment was under control, "reform" became liabilities to the local economic growth (Model 3). Finally, it seems both labor and "reform" contribute

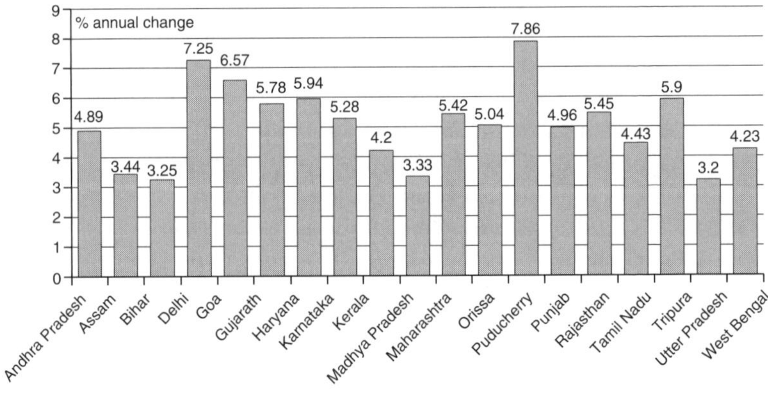

Figure 6.10 GDP growth of Indian states (1961–2005)
Source: Author's database.

Table 6.2 Political changes and economic growth in Indian states

Variables	Model 1	Model 2	Model 3	Model 4
Party Changes	1.426**	1.220*	.930	.969
	(.712)	(.714)	(.868)	(.868)
Leadership Changes	−0.209	−0.123	−0.243	−0.128
	(.586)	(.585)	(.740)	(1.273)
President's Rule	−0.576	−0.266	−0.880	−1.219
	(.905)	(.910)	(1.243)	(1.273)
Reform		1.413**	−1.132	−0.872
		(.551)	(.824)	(.850)
Investment			0.0002***	0.0002***
			(0.0001)	(0.0001)
Labor				−0.303
				(0.247)
Constant	4.898***	4.381***	4.994***	8.965***
	(.310)	(.369)	(.576)	(3.290)
Adjusted R^2	0.002	0.009	0.018	0.019
Observations	805	805	477	477

Notes:
1. Dependent variable is real GDP annual growth rate.
2. Numbers in parentheses are standard errors.
*p < .10; **p < .05; ***p < .01
Source: http://www.indiastat.com/default.aspx accessed on March 30, 2008.

negatively to the economic growth of a locality when they are both under control (Model 4).

b Political leadership and economic growth in Chinese provinces

(1) The evolution of China's provincial system

The system of provinces in China has evolved in the past six decades (Bo 2002: 151–60). First, Taiwan broke away from the rest of China in 1949 when the Nationalists, under the leadership of Chiang Kai-shek, fled to the island province as a result of its military defeat on the mainland. Second, the Central Government of the People's Republic of China merged a number of provinces in the early 1950s and removed regions as a level of government in 1954, reducing the number of provincial units from 51 to 30 (excluding Taiwan).

Third, four categories of provincial units – centrally administered municipalities, autonomous regions, provinces, and special administrative regions – were gradually established and stabilized in later years.

The People's Republic of China initially had 14 centrally administered municipalities. In June 1954, the number of centrally administered cities was reduced to three. Except for Beijing, Tianjin, and Shanghai, all the others were downgraded. Tianjin was also downgraded into a city under Hebei Province in 1958, but its status of a centrally administered city was restored in 1967. Similarly, Chongqing also recovered its "centrally administered city" designation in 1997.

Among the autonomous regions, Inner Mongolia was established the earliest, in 1947. The second autonomous region that came in line was Xinjiang Uyghur Autonomous Region. It was established in 1955. Guangxi Province was made an autonomous region in March 1958, and Ningxia, a part of Gansu Province,[4] was converted to an autonomous region in October 1958. Finally, the Tibetan local government was established in April 1956 and the Tibet Autonomous Region was formally established in September 1965, completing the list of five autonomous regions in China.

With the return of Hong Kong to China, there has emerged a new category of provincial units in China: special administrative regions. Hong Kong was the first special administrative region. It was established in July 1997. Macao became the second special administrative region, in December 1999.

Currently, China has 34 provincial units: 23 provinces (including Taiwan), four centrally administered cities, five autonomous regions, and two special administrative regions. This study is going to focus on 31 of them (Taiwan, Hong Kong SAR, and Macao SAR are not included).

(2) Changes in China's provincial leadership

China's provincial leadership consists of party leaders, government leaders, congressional leaders, and military leaders. For our purposes, we will focus on party and government leaders, in particular provincial party secretaries and governors. I will use the same framework to examine political change as defined in party leadership changes, provincial governorship changes, and how they relate to economic development at provincial levels.

(a) Provincial party leadership. As Figure 6.11 reveals, Chinese provincial party leadership was quite stable over the period of 1949–2004. Out of 1649 unit/years, there were 323 changes, representing 19.6 percent of the total. In the early years of the People's Republic of China, changes occurred when there were major structural transformations. Around the Cultural Revolution, provincial party secretaries were purged for political reasons. Since 1987, provincial party leadership reshuffles have

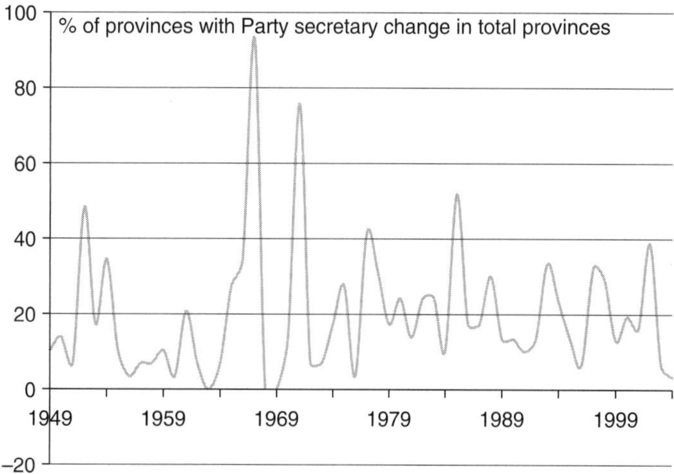

Figure 6.11 Changes in provincial party leadership in China (1949–2004)
Source: Author's database.

become more regularized and have come along with the opening of the National Congress of the Communist Party of China (CPC).

More specifically, there have been several peaks of provincial party leadership changes over the years. The first peak came in 1952, when 14 out of 29 provincial party secretaries were replaced, taking 48.3 percent. Provincial units involved include Shanxi, Tianjin, Jilin, Jiangsu, Zhejiang, Anhui, Jiangxi, Henan, Hunan, Sichuan, Yunnan, Tibet, Shaanxi, and Xinjiang. These provincial units have different stories. Shanxi, Tianjin, Zhejiang, Hunan, Yunnan, and Shaanxi all witnessed frequent changes of their provincial party secretaries in 1952, but their provincial status remained unchanged. Jiangsu, Anhui, Henan, Sichuan, Tibet, and Xinjiang represent a different category. They all went through structural changes in 1952.

The second peak came in 1954 when regional governments were removed as a level of government in China. More than one third of provincial party secretaries were replaced that year. The provinces involved included Liaoning, Shanghai, Jiangsu, Zhejiang, Shandong, Hubei, Guizhou, Shaanxi, Gansu, and Qinghai. The third peak, a relatively small one, came in 1961 when six provincial party secretaries were replaced. The provinces involved were Shandong, Henan, Guangxi, Gansu, Qinghai, and Ningxia. The fourth peak came in

1965 when eight provincial party secretaries were replaced. The provinces involved included Shanxi, Heilongjiang, Shanghai, Guangdong, Sichuan, Guizhou, Tibet, and Shaanxi.

The fourth and fifth peaks came in 1966 and 1967, respectively, when the Cultural Revolution took a toll on China's provincial party leadership as a whole. More than one third of provincial party secretaries were replaced in 1966, and all provincial party secretaries but two were dismissed in 1967. Even in those two provincial units (Inner Mongolia and Tianjin) that seem to have survived the onslaught of the Cultural Revolution in 1967, the provincial party leadership did not escape the fate of their colleagues in other provincial units. The sixth peak came in 1971 when more than 75 percent of provincial party leaders were appointed. This was the year in which most provincial party committees were reestablished.

The seventh peak came in 1975, when Deng Xiaoping was in charge of national affairs in China. Eight provincial party secretaries were replaced that year, representing 27.6 percent of the total. The provinces involved include Shanxi, Liaoning, Anhui, Hubei, Guangdong, Guangxi, Sichuan, and Yunnan. The provincial party reshuffles that occurred in 1977 and 1978 were related to the clean-up of the Gang of Four followers in the provinces. Twelve provincial party secretaries were replaced in 1977, followed by purges of another nine in 1978. The peaks in the early 1980s such as those of 1980, 1982, 1983, and in particular 1985, represent the retirement of veteran leaders at the provincial level. Seven provincial party secretaries were replaced each year in 1980, 1982, and 1983, representing about a quarter of the total provincial party secretaries of the year. In 1985, more than half of the provincial party secretaries were replaced.

Finally, the peaks between 1987 and 2004 seem to have something to do with political cycles around Party congresses. Starting in 1977, the CPC began to hold party congresses on a regular basis. The Eleventh National Congress was held in 1977, followed by the Twelfth National Congress in 1982 and the Thirteenth National Congress in 1987. The Fourteenth through Seventeenth National Congresses were held in 1992, 1997, 2002, and 2007, respectively. The first two peaks came one year after the National Party Congress. Following the Thirteenth Party Congress in 1987, about one third of the provincial party secretaries were replaced in 1988. Similarly, following the Fourteenth Party Congress in 1992, one third of the provincial party secretaries were replaced in 1993. The Fifteenth Party Congress was held in 1997, and provincial party secretaries were replaced in large numbers in both

1997 and 1998. In 1997, 10 provincial party secretaries were replaced, representing about one third of the total. In 1998, nine provincial party secretaries were replaced. In 2002, when the Sixteenth Party Congress was held, 12 provincial party secretaries were also replaced, representing almost 40 percent of the total.

In sum, China's provincial party leadership has been basically very stable over the years, but there have been several peaks of changes in selected years. The changes came about for different reasons. In the 1950s, provincial party secretaries were replaced because of structural transformations; in the 1960s and 1970s, they were mostly purged because of political campaigns; and in the early 1980s, they were retired en masse to make room for younger generations. Since 1987, the changes in provincial party leadership have tended to follow the national Party congress. Provincial party secretaries have been reshuffled as a result of leadership changes at the national level.

(b) Provincial governors. Changes in provincial government leadership in China have largely paralleled those of provincial party leadership (Figure 6.12). Over the period of 55 years, there were 360 changes, representing 22 percent of the total. The first peak came in 1952, the

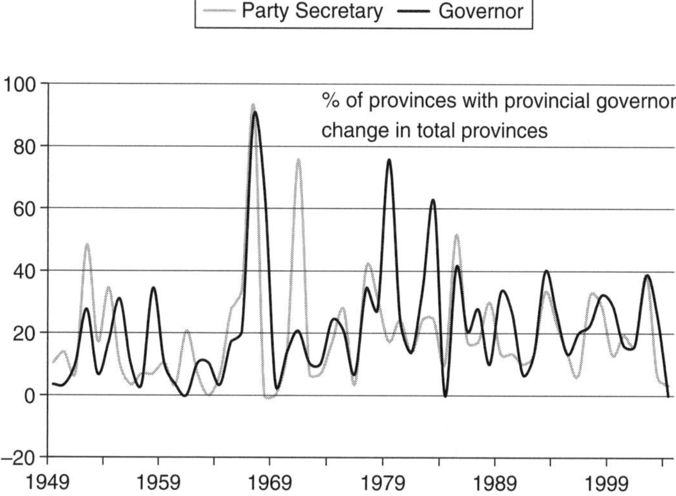

Figure 6.12 Changes in provincial government leadership in China (1949–2004)
Source: Author's database.

same year as the provincial party leadership also went through major changes. Provincial units involved include Tianjin, Hebei, Shanxi, Jilin, Heilongjiang, Hunan, Shaanxi, and Qinghai.

The second peak came in 1955, one year after the second major reshuffle of the provincial party leadership. The third peak came in 1958, the first year of the Great Leap Forward. More than one third of governors were replaced, while very few provincial party secretaries were reshuffled. Governors were mostly purged in the years of 1966 and 1967. Six governors were replaced in 1966, and 26 were purged in 1967.

Provincial revolutionary committees were established in lieu of provincial governments in 1967 and 1968, three or four years ahead of the reestablishment of provincial Party committees. In the aftermath of the "January Revolution" of 1967, in which revolutionary rebels stormed the party and government apparatuses in Shanghai and grabbed power from the power holders, 11 provincial units established provincial revolutionary committees. In 1968, 19 out of 29 provincial units formed provincial revolutionary committees, representing 66 percent of the total. Similar to the provincial party leadership reshuffles in 1977 and 1978, the followers of the Gang of Four were also purged from the provincial government leadership in these years. Ten governors were removed in 1977, and eight were replaced in 1978.

The second largest reshuffles occurred in 1979 when provincial revolutionary committees were abolished and were replaced by provincial governments. In the meantime, governors were no longer concurrent provincial party secretaries. More than two thirds (22) of provincial government leaders were replaced. The only provincial units that experienced no changes include Beijing, Tianjin, Hebei, Inner Mongolia, Liaoning, Jilin, and Hubei.

Similar to the trend in the changes of provincial party leadership, governors who were replaced in the early 1980s were mostly those who had retired. Great numbers retired in 1982–3, two years earlier than the massive retirement of provincial party leaders. In 1983, for instance, 18 governors were replaced, representing 62 percent of the total. In 1985, 12 governors were replaced, representing 41 percent of the total.

The political cycles for provincial government leadership seem to have lagged those of provincial party leadership by one term of five years. Although the pattern of provincial party leadership reshuffles exhibited some tangible patterns of changes from 1987, a similar pattern among provincial governors is not observable until the early 1990s. Since provincial people's congresses are usually held one year after provincial party congresses, the political cycles of provincial government leadership have lagged those of provincial party leadership by one year.

In sum, provincial governors in China have experienced changes for different reasons during different periods. In the 1950s, they were replaced because of structural transformations; in the 1960s and 1970s, they were mostly purged because of political campaigns; and in the 1980s, they were retired to make room for younger generations. Since 1993, the changes in provincial government leadership tend to occur as a result of the elections at provincial People's Congresses. The patterns of political cycles are discernable but not apparent.

(3) Provincial economic development

China's provinces experienced rapid economic growth in the period of 1949–2004 (Table 6.3). The average GDP annual growth rate was 8.9 percent. The slowest growth rate was –57.1 percent (Liaoning in 1961), and the fastest growth rate was 137.3 percent (Beijing in 1953). The frontrunners are Beijing, Shanghai, and Fujian. They all witnessed a double-digit growth in 50-plus years.

Provincial units that had the slowest growth rates include Guizhou, Heilongjiang, Hunan, and Anhui. Their average annual growth rates were all above 7 percent and less than 8 percent. It is remarkable that the slowest growing province in China had an average annual growth rate of more than 7 percent for more than five decades.

Take China's provinces as a group, it is clear that they all performed very well economically. The difference between the fastest growing provincial unit (Beijing) and the slowest growing provincial unit (Anhui) is not huge. It is only 5 percent. The variances among the provincial units are much less than the variances of these provincial units over time.

The history of the People's Republic of China can be roughly divided into two major periods: Mao Zedong's era and Deng Xiaoping's era. Mao's ideology was dominant from 1949 to 1977, and Deng Xiaoping's line has been dominant since late 1978. The economic performance of China's provinces in both periods is impressive. During the Maoist era of 1949–78, China's provinces had an annual growth rate of 7.5 percent, with significant volatility (Figure 6.13). Their best record was 137.3 percent, and their worst record was –57.1 percent. Beijing, Shanghai, and Ningxia were the best performers during this period. The worst performers during this period were Anhui, Henan, Jiangsu, and Guangdong. Their annual growth rates during this period were 3.8 percent, 5.3 percent, 5.5 percent, and 5.9 percent, respectively.

Table 6.3 Economic growth of China's provinces (1949–2004)

Province[a]	Observations	Average Annual Growth Rate (%)	Worst Growth Rate (%)	Best Growth Rate (%)
Beijing	53	12.15	–40.6	137.3
Tianjin	53	9.33	–35.9	33.4
Hebei	55	9.18	–37.0	26.2
Shanxi	52	8.24	–34.6	37.4
Inner Mongolia	52	8.82	–34.7	38.7
Liaoning	52	9.39	–57.1	43.7
Jilin	52	8.13	–31.2	28.3
Heilongjiang	52	7.63	–41.7	40.5
Shanghai	55	10.64	–36.9	38.5
Jiangsu	52	9.00	–10.8	25.6
Zhejiang	52	9.67	–21.9	22.0
Anhui	52	7.20	–28.6	27.4
Fujian	53	10.02	–28.3	24.8
Jiangxi	55	8.33	–12.7	53.8
Shandong	52	9.33	–21.9	29.2
Henan	53	8.01	–40.6	32.9
Hubei	52	8.44	–30.0	29.8
Hunan	52	7.53	–35.5	19.8
Guangdong	53	9.65	–22.0	22.3
Guangxi	52	8.15	–14.3	26.6
Hainan	17	11.48	4.3	40.2
Chongqing	8	9.81	7.6	12.2
Sichuan	26	9.44	2.6	13.0
Guizhou	55	7.81	–37.4	35.3
Yunnan	55	8.18	–24.0	32.2
Tibet	53	7.99	–9.2	45.8
Shaanxi	53	8.90	–33.4	45.2
Gansu	52	8.14	–37.4	27.3
Qinghai	55	8.87	–36.4	42.3
Ningxia	53	9.84	–26.6	40.9
Xinjiang	52	8.48	–22.0	30.0
National	**1533**	**8.87**	**–57.1**	**137.3**

Note:
[a] This refers to provinces, centrally administered cities, and autonomous regions. Hong Kong, Macao, and Taiwan are not included.
Source: NBSC 2005.

China's provincial units did much better in the era of Deng than in the era of Mao. The average annual growth rate for all provincial units is 10.2 percent, with a range from –9.2 percent to 40.2 percent. The volatility is much smaller. The standard deviation is only 4.6, less

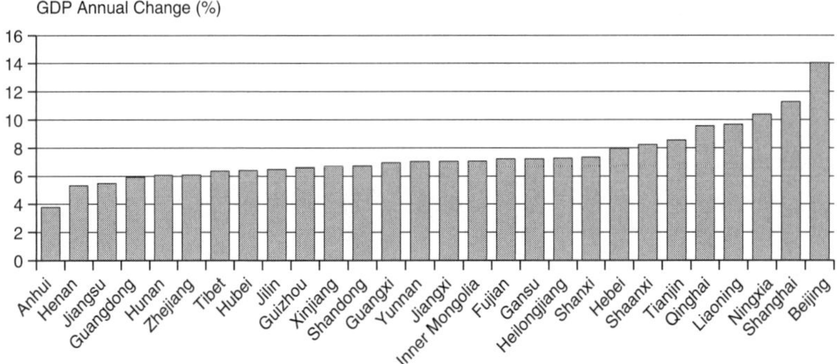

Figure 6.13 Economic growth of China's provinces (1949–1978)
Source: Author's database.

than half of the average growth rate. During this period, coastal provinces such as Guangdong, Zhejiang, Fujian, Jiangsu, and Shandong took the lead (Figure 6.13). On the other hand, only three provinces had a growth rate slower than 9 percent a year for the period of 1979 to 2004: Hunan, Qinghai, and Heilongjiang.

(4) Leadership changes and economic growth in China's provinces

What is the impact of political variables such as leadership changes on economic growth in China's provinces? From Model 1 in Table 6.4, it is clear that the impact of leadership changes on economic growth varies depending on the type of political leaders. Changes of governors seem to bring about positive changes in economic growth, while changes in party leadership may have negative consequences for economic growth. More specifically, when governors are replaced, there is a corresponding 0.8 percent increase in the GDP of the region; when provincial party secretaries are replaced, there is a corresponding 1.7 percent decrease in the GDP of the region. However, the former result is not statistically significant while the latter is statistically significant at the level of $p = 0.05$.

These results are robust when other variables are included. In Model 2, a new variable, "reform," is included. This is a dummy variable, with pre-reform years (1949–78) as 0 and reform years (1979–2004) as 1. Economic reforms did make differences to China's provinces. Their economic performances during the reform era are 2.7 percent better than those of the previous years. To a large extent, the economic growth of China's provinces was driven by investment (Model 3). For each additional percentage point of GDP in investment, there is a corresponding

Table 6.4 Leadership changes and economic growth in China's provinces

Variables	Model 1	Model 2	Model 3	Model 4
Party Secretaries	−1.67**	−1.66**	−1.71***	−1.12*
	(0.705)	(0.699)	(0.660)	(0.577)
Governors	0.79	0.52	0.70	0.64
	(0.668)	(0.664)	(0.625)	(0.548)
Reform		2.72***	2.31***	2.44***
		(0.530)	(0.504)	(0.453)
Investment			0.52***	0.59***
			(0.038)	(0.038)
Labor				0.77***
				(0.070)
Constant	9.03***	7.70***	2.50***	−0.21
	(0.317)	(0.407)	(0.534)	(0.536)
Adjusted R^2	0.004	0.021	0.131	0.243
Observations	1532	1532	1507	1351
X^2	5.79	32.28	225.33	432.72

Notes:
1. Dependent variable is GDP growth in real terms.
2. Numbers in parentheses are standard errors.
*p < 0.10; **p < 0.05; ***p < 0.01.
Sources: NBSC 2005; ZGZZ 2000.

12.3 percent higher growth. To some extent, increase in labor force is also important (Model 4). For each additional percentage point of labor force, there is a corresponding 0.9 percent in GDP growth.

c Comparing India and China at the local level

In order to compare India and China at the state/provincial level, we have pooled our data on two countries and conducted regression analyses.

According to Model 1 in Table 6.5, India, under its multi-party democracy, has been less well performed than China under its single party state in delivering economic performance. Economies under the authoritarian rule grow almost five percent faster than those under the democratic rule. This result is statistically very significant. Reforms seem to be a good thing under either type of regime (Model 2). After adopting reform measures, an economy could grow more than 3 percent faster than previously. In other words, the multi-party pluralist regime in India is less positively related to economic growth but reforms help, while the Party-state non-pluralist regime in China is more positively related to economic growth and reforms can make things much better.

Table 6.5 Regime types and economic growth: China versus India

Variables	**Model 1**	**Model 2**
Democracy	−4.66***	−4.05***
	(.476)	(.479)
Reform		3.25***
		(0.450)
Constant	9.67***	7.91***
	(.273)	(.364)
Adjusted R^2	0.037	0.058
Observations	2456	2456
F	95.80	74.89

Notes:
1. Dependent variable is GDP growth in real terms.
2. Numbers in parentheses are standard errors.

*p < 0.10; **p < 0.05; ***p < 0.01

Source: Author's database.

4 Conclusion

Contrary to the conventional wisdom in the literature, this study has found that regime types matter for economic growth: authoritarian regimes have better records of economic growth than democracies do. For a period of more than half a century, China (an authoritarian regime) outperformed India (a democracy) by a large margin. China's average GDP growth between 1953 and 2009 was 8.1 percent, while India's record for the same period was only 4.8 percent.

India's less impressive performance is largely due to its regime type. Because of democratic pressure for consumption, India diverted much more resources to consumption than did China during the same period. Between 1952 and 2004, India's annual consumption constituted 86.8 percent of its GDP on average and China consumed only 66.1 percent of its GDP annually. Consequently, India's investment level is much lower than that of China. India's annual rate of fixed capital was 17.2 percent of its GDP between 1952 and 2004, and China's rate was 27.3 percent of its GDP in the same period. Moreover, because of electoral pressure, Indian politicians appealed to peasants for votes by making substantial investment in agriculture while Chinese leaders can afford to be single-minded about industrialization without concern for the political consequences.

Furthermore, China, as an authoritarian regime, can have a more effective family planning program and thus has performed even better than India on a per-capita basis. In 1952, China's real GDP per capita was only 43 percent of India's number. But 50 years later, China's GDP per capita was two thirds more than that of India.

Finally, China adopted reform policies much earlier than India, though the difference is not strictly due to different regime types. China officially adopted reform policies in late 1978, and India did not start reform until 1991.

The fact that democracies perform less well than authoritarian regimes holds true at the local levels in India and China. The two local systems were formed around the same time. India began its states system in 1950 when it adopted its constitution and reorganized its states and union territories in 1956. The People's Republic of China consolidated a number of provinces under Communist control in the early 1950s and established the baseline of the current provincial system in 1954. Currently, the two countries have a similar number of local units. India has 35 states and union territories, and China has 34 provincial units, including provinces, centrally administered cities, autonomous regions, and special administrative regions.

In terms of political changes to local leadership, there were different types of change and different patterns of change between India and China. There were three major types of change to the local leadership in India. First, because of multi-party competitive elections, Indian states witnessed regime changes from one political party to another. Over the period of 1950 to 2009, there were 228 party changes in Indian states, representing 16 percent of the total. Second, old leaders of the same ruling are replaced by new ones. In the same period in India, 231 state leaders were replaced this way. Third, the central government of India could also invoke the article on "President's Rule" to intervene in local affairs. The President's Rule has been used more than 100 times in the period from 1950 to 2009. In the early years, this article was abused in favor of the central ruling party. The central government used various pretexts to dismiss local governments controlled by other political parties.

In China, there are no regime changes but only leadership changes of two types of provincial leaders. Provincial party secretaries, the most powerful leaders in China's localities, were replaced quite frequently. Out of 1649 unit/years over the period of 1949–2004, 323 provincial party secretaries were replaced, representing 19.6 percent. In the Mao era, provincial party secretaries were replaced mostly because of political reasons. In the beginning of the Cultural Revolution, in particular, more than 90 percent of provincial party secretaries were purged. In the 1980s, the reshuffles of the provincial party leaders were related to the institutionalization of the political leadership. In 1985, for instance, more than half of the provincial party secretaries were replaced due to the retirement of elderly leaders. From 1987 to 2004, however, changes to the provincial party leadership occurred mostly around national party congresses. Provincial governors, the chief administrators under provincial party secretaries, had similar experiences over the years.

When we look at the impact of political changes on economic performance in India and China separately, we find different patterns. In Indian states, party changes seem to be conducive to economic growth while leadership changes and the President's Rule are not particularly good for economic growth. In China, the replacement of provincial party secretaries is not good for local economic development, while the replacement of provincial governors is not bad for local economic growth. In both countries, however, reform is a good thing because it promotes economic growth.

When we pool the data from Indian states and Chinese provincial units, we have two major findings. One: the political institutions and politics practiced in India are less effective for economic growth than those in China. Two: reform is conducive to economic growth. Since lower economic growth rates are not really intended in the setup of democratic institutions, the negative effect of democracies on economic growth can be regarded as "democratic externalities." It seems that reform policies can offset these externalities to a large extent.

Acknowledgement

The author would like to acknowledge Dr Maathai K. Mathiyazhagan for his initial contributions to the paper on Indian states and to thank Ms. Weng Cuifen for her assistance in compiling a table of Indian states (populations and territories).

Notes

1. Because of the fundamental differences between the two countries, the impact of both regime types and political changes is examined at the local level in this chapter.
2. Since we do not have good data on investment and labor, we have decided to drop these variables.

3. State-wise data are three series of different constant prices. One series of 1960 to 1979 is probably based on the 1960–1 constant price, another series of 1980 to 1992 is based on the 1980–81 constant price, and a third series of 1993–2005 is based on the 1993–4 constant price. Since I do not have access to the deflator from the 1960–61 to the 1980–81 constant prices, I have decided to delete growth rate data for 1980.
4. Ningxia was merged into Gansu at least twice, in 1914 and in 1954.

7 China and India: Education in Paths to Prosperity

Krishna B. Kumar and Ying Liu

The unfolding stories of rapid economic development in China and India have drawn wide scholarly interest in comparison of the strategies each has pursued on the path toward development. In many respects, China and India are similar: both are large and populous, with a significant share of the labor force in agriculture, and reforms instituted to modernize their economies. China started its economic reforms in the early 1970s and India in the early 1990s. GDP per capita has more than doubled in India and increased seven-fold in China.

However, many details of their respective experiences in economic growth are in fact quite different. China stands out for the explosive growth in its manufacturing sector. In contrast, India's growth has been fueled primarily by the rapid expansion of the service-producing industries, challenging the conventional wisdom that the move to services happens only after an economy experiences a phase of manufacturing-led growth.

Among a large number of China-India comparative studies, few have systematically examined the educational development in each country and its contribution to economic growth. This is a critical gap in research given the importance of education in economic and social development. Building upon the authors' previous work in comparing the national education systems of the two countries, this chapter investigates the linkage between educational strategies and economic development patterns in China and India. By highlighting the relative strengths and weaknesses of the education systems of both countries and by broadly comparing their impact on economic growth, we hope to shed light on the effectiveness of the different education strategies on economic development.

Indeed, China and India offer two interesting cases in understanding the complex relationship between education and economic growth. In the late 1940s, both countries embarked on building national education systems under comparable conditions. However, differing historical circumstances and socio-economic policies have led them to different paths, with corresponding strengths and drawbacks. China is often characterized as having a "wide" or "mass" education model. By contrast, India is said to have pursued a "deep" or "elitist" education approach (Baumol, Litan, and Schramm 2007). China largely focused on basic education for the masses while India prioritized for the most part higher education for a few. Both approaches appear to have been successful in their own ways in stimulating aggregate economic growth. Meanwhile, the differing education models are seemingly reflected in the way each country participates in the world economy.

As these two economies have recently evolved in different ways, policymakers in each country have reconsidered their respective national education policies. As a result, we have witnessed a convergence of the strategies pursued by these two countries, with India placing an increasing emphasis on basic education (which had been China's focus) and China on higher education (with an emphasis on English and information technology, which were India's advantage).

How has the education policy changed over time in India and China? How has the education-economy link evolved in each country? We pursue these questions in this chapter. Specifically, Section 1 briefly summarizes the historical path that each country has taken; Section 2 elaborates the "wide" versus "deep" education development patterns; Section 3 links the educational model to economic growth pattern in each country; Section 4 describes the recent convergence of education trends in both countries and its implications on future economic growth; Section 5 discusses broad implications of the experiences of China and India for modern economic growth and development; Section 6 concludes.

1 Historical paths of educational development

Both China and India embarked on building their national education systems around the late 1940s when India gained Independence from the United Kingdom and the Chinese revolution led to the founding of the People's Republic of China (PRC). Despite a fundamental difference in political regime – the PRC was established as a communist country while the Republic of India was founded on the basis of multi-party democracy – both countries shared two important developmental goals: rapid industrialization and the alleviation of social inequality. The then-popular Soviet model convinced national leaders in both countries that a heavy-industry-focused and centrally planned economy was the key to fast track industrialization (Krueger 2002; Yang 2004). Meanwhile, eliminating mass illiteracy was considered key to eliminating poverty and addressing social inequality (Pepper 2000).

Education policy, which was perceived as integral to these developmental goals, shared much in common in China and India during the 1950s and early 1960s. First and foremost, building a large pool of college-educated labor specializing in science and technology became a dominant objective of national education planning in both countries. In India, Prime Minister Jawaharlal Nehru declared the need to renovate the education system to meet the country's scientific, technical, and other manpower needs for a centrally planned economy (Ghosh 2000).

Starting from the Second Five Year Plan (1956–61), India directed much of its education resources to higher education and technical education, particularly to building a large number of engineering institutions (Asuyama 2009). High-quality institutions such as the Indian Institutes of Technology (IITs) and Indian Institutes of Management (IIMs) were set up. In China, nationwide higher education reform began in 1951. Under the advisory of a large number of Soviet experts, universities and colleges were reconstructed to emphasize technical education. During the First Five-Year Plan period (1953–7), the annual growth rate of student admission to institutions of higher education reached 18.2 percent. The number of higher education institutions more than tripled from 1954 to 1960 (Yang, 2004).

Both national governments also envisioned the rapid expansion of primary and secondary education as a way to promote social equality, yet with different successes in implementation. In China, a large number of part-time adult schools were established in both urban and rural areas to teach workers and peasants basic literacy. The majority of these schools were financed by the production brigades of the People's Commune (Asuyama 2009). Mao Zedong, the then paramount leader of China, encouraged "part-time work, part-time study" (*ban gong ban du*) as a virtue. Despite suffering multiple interruptions, work-study schools proved to be an effective way to expand basic education. By 1964, China's literacy rate had already reportedly increased to 66 percent (Asuyama 2009). In India, Mohandas Gandhi envisioned free compulsory education and the teaching of handicrafts to lift the poor out of poverty (Asuyama 2009). The 1950 Indian Constitution included an article on free and compulsory education for all children until age 14 (Ghosh 2000). Nevertheless, this lofty goal did not translate into implementable policy as it was non-binding and no accompanying budget was set aside. The problem of mass illiteracy continued.

The educational paths of the two countries started to diverge in the late 1960s when China began its Cultural Revolution. The political upheaval, initiated by Mao Zedong to revive the revolutionary spirit, halted economic activity nationwide and resulted in years of stagnation and recession. Education turned out to be one of the worst affected areas. The extreme anti-elitist frenzy of the Cultural Revolution brought a virtual halt to higher education. The few colleges and universities that admitted new students selected them based substantially on political virtues rather than on academic performance.

The ten-year Cultural Revolution destroyed much of the Chinese higher education infrastructure. Ironically, there was a gain: the egalitarian forces of the revolution, and Mao's campaign to send millions of urban youth to rural areas to serve as teachers, farmers, and workers, may unintentionally have helped to improve the quality of rural primary education. The number of primary and lower secondary schools continued to increase (Hannum 1999). Overall, the effect was a decided shift in emphasis from higher education to primary education. This trend persisted until China embarked on market-oriented economic reform and restored higher education in the early 1980s.

There was no such tumultuous change in India, where the Nehruvian style of central planning for economic development proceeded for three more decades. India underwent an extended period of steady, yet slow growth – on average less than 3 percent per year, which came to be dubbed the "Hindu rate of economic growth" (Krueger 2002). Also continued was the focus on higher education as suggested by the Soviet model. The proportion of educational expenditure allocated to higher and technical education remained well above one third of the total (Tilak 2005), despite the disproportionately large differential in the number of students enrolled in higher education compared to primary and secondary education.

There has been a sixteen-fold increase in the number of universities, and a twenty-fold increase in the number of colleges, since India's independence in 1947 (UNESCO 2004). Mass illiteracy and universal primary education continued to be neglected, even though the first National Education Policy approved in 1968 re-iterated the goal of free and compulsory education for all children up to the age of 14. In the

1980s, the World Bank took India to task for giving greater priority to higher education over primary and secondary education (UNESCO 2004). Not until 1986, in its New National Policy on Education, did India realize the need for expanding access to primary and secondary education.

2 "Wide" versus "Deep": Education attainment patterns in China and India

Differing historical educational strategies followed by China and India resulted in different patterns of the population's education attainment by the time each country started their respective economic reforms. Overall, China appears to have a "wide" or "mass" educational model. By contrast, India is said to have a "deep" or "elitist" approach.

China

As Figure 7.1 captures, China's educational attainment "pyramid" has a broad base but a narrow pinnacle. The wide base represents China's achievement in extending basic education to its general population: the majority of Chinese people is literate, and has achieved at least primary education; the small bar at the top reflects the very few Chinese students who have had the opportunity to attend post-secondary education. While such a shape is not unique to China, the relative proportion

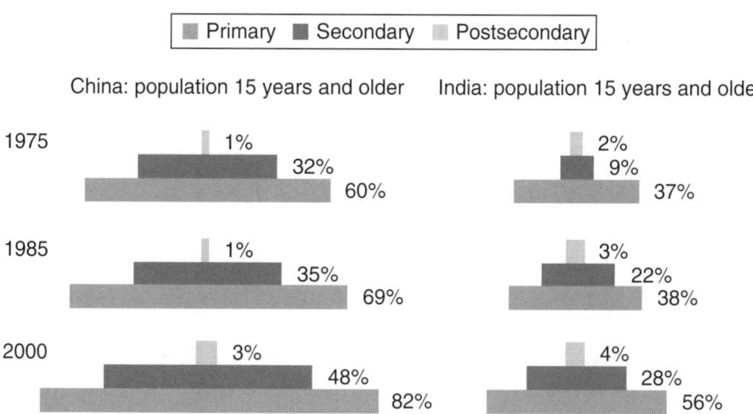

Figure 7.1 "Wide" versus "Deep" education attainment in China and India
Source: Barro and Lee 2001.

of the bottom and the top is quite remarkable when compared to other East Asian countries and India.

China has made great strides in educating its masses since the end of the Chinese Civil War in 1949. The literacy rate, the most basic indicator of a country's education attainment, more than quadrupled in China from the late 1940s to the early 2000s. The literacy rate of adults (ages 15 or older) increased from about 20 percent in the late 1940s to about 91 percent in 2000 (Asuyama 2009; World Bank 2011). The youth literacy rate (ages 15–24), a better indicator of educational opportunities for the current generation of school-age youth, reached 99 percent in 2002 (World Bank 2009). China's remarkable achievement in eliminating illiteracy was praised by a 1982 UNESCO report as "the greatest experiment in mass education in the history of the world. A nation of some 970 million in some 30 odd years had become a nearly literate society" (Bhola 1982).

In addition to a strong commitment to the elimination of illiteracy through mass adult education programs, China has also made great progress in expanding formal schooling among its population. From 1975 to 2000, the average years of schooling increased from 4.4 years to 6.4 years. During the same period, the percentage of the adult population with no schooling decreased from 40.2 percent to less than 18.0 percent; the percentage that attended at least primary education increased from 59.8 percent to 79.9 percent; and the percentage that attended at least secondary education increased from 32.3 percent to 48.1 percent (Barro and Lee 2001). Given the size of the Chinese population (roughly one fifth of the world's total), these numbers represent an extraordinary achievement in increasing the education levels of more than one billion people. In 2007, the UNESCO recognized China's achievement in universal primary education by naming China as a "high" Education-for-All (EFA) country with an overall ranking of 43 out of the 125 countries (UNESCO 2007).

China's education pyramid includes another dimension of width; that is, its strength in mass education lies not only in raising the aggregate educational level of the population, but also in reducing the achievement gaps between the female and male population. As Table 7.1 shows, the gender gap as reflected in the adult literacy rate decreased from 28.1 percent to 8.1 percent between 1982 and 2000. Likewise the gender gap in the youth literacy rate decreased from 13.1 percent in 1982 to 0.7 percent in 2000. From 1975 to 2000, the percentage of adult females who attended at least primary school increased 22.3 percentage points from 47.2 percent to 69.5 percent, which is slightly higher than

Table 7.1 Gender gaps in literacy in China and India

		China		India	
		1982	2000	1981	2001
Adult literacy rate (%)	Male	79	95	55	73
	Female	51	87	26	48
GPI for adult literacy rate*		0.65	0.91	0.47	0.65
Youth literacy rate (%)	Male	95	99	66	84
	Female	82	99	40	68
GPI for youth literacy rate*		0.86	0.99	0.61	0.80

* GPI (gender parity index) = female literacy rate/male literacy rate.
Source: UNESCO 2008.

the change in the percentage for adult males (from 71.7% to 93.9%) (Barro and Lee 2001).

China's most notable weakness has been the low percentage of its students progressing to post-secondary education. The percentage of the Chinese population that attended post-secondary education remained virtually flat at 1.0 percent from 1950 through the mid-1980s. Even as recently as 2000, the percentage of college educated Chinese was still less than 3 percent. China lags not only significantly behind other more developed East Asian regions, including South Korea (26.3%), Taiwan (19.6%), Hong Kong (13.3%), and Singapore (10.0%) on this key indicator, but also other developing countries in the region, such as the Philippines (23.2%), Thailand (10.9%), Malaysia (5.2%), and Indonesia (4.5%). In addition, this number is also lower than that of India's (4.1%) (Barro and Lee 2001). In 2000, less than 10 percent of high school graduates progressed to college. The progression rate for female students was even lower, at about 4.4 percent (UNESCO 2008).

China's unusually low historic rate of college attendance is a result of both intended and unintended state policies that have jointly limited the supply of higher education. First and foremost, the ten-year interruption of higher education during the Cultural Revolution (1966–76) caused tremendous damage to China's higher education and left an entire generation without access to college education.

Even after the Cultural Revolution had ended, state-controlled college admission quotas were set at very low levels throughout 1980s and 1990s, preventing public universities and colleges from expanding their student populations. Private higher education institutions, considered inconsistent with the socialist society, were de facto banned since 1952. It was not until 1997, when the State Council issued its *Regulations of Education Run by Social Forces*, that private institutions of higher education were officially re-legitimized (Yang 2004).

b India

Compared to China's "wide" educational attainment model, the Indian education pyramid has a "deep" shape, in the sense that relatively few Indian youths have had access to basic education, while those who did have access appear to have had a better chance of attending post-secondary education as well. Inadequate access to and attainment of basic education is a well-documented problem in India, which has about one fifth of the world's population but nearly half of the world's illiterate population, despite significant progress made in the past five decades (Kingdon 2007). While the base of India's education pyramid may be small, it has emerged as an important player in the worldwide information technology revolution based on a substantial number of well educated computing and other engineers. This polarized education attainment model is quite unusual and clearly sets India apart from China and its other neighbors in the region.

India has actually made significant progress in expanding education opportunities since achieving independence from the British Empire in 1947. However, its achievement has not been as impressive as China's and those of many other developing countries. In the early 1950s, only about 20 percent of the Indian adult population was literate, a proportion that was comparable to China's level at the time (Asuyama 2009; Rao, Cheng, and Narain 2003). Fifty years later, in 2004, India's adult literacy had tripled to 61.0 percent, and the youth literacy rate had increased even more to 76.1 percent. However, the respective figures for China in 2004 were 91 percent and 99 percent, and the developing country averages were 76.8 percent and 84.8 percent, respectively. Indeed, India's rates of literacy and youth literacy are more on par with Sub-Saharan Africa (61.2% and 72.9% respectively. Kingdon 2007; UNESCO 2008).

The problem of illiteracy in India is a reflection not only of the lack of mass adult education programs aimed at older generations, but also of more limited progress in expanding basic education, particularly at the primary level. From 1975 to 2000, the percentage of the Indian adult population with no schooling decreased by 18.7 percentage points from 62.6 percent to 43.9 percent, nearly four percentage points short of the decrease in China; the percentage that attended at least primary education increased by 18.7 percentage points from 37.4 percent to 56.1 percent, falling just short of half the comparable change in China.

However, the percentage of population with at least a secondary education increased by 19.0 percentage points from 8.9 percent to 27.9 percent, which is about three points higher than the comparable change in China (Barro and Lee 2001). Given this performance, the World Bank's the Education for All Development Index (EDI) project classified India as a "low" EDI country, with an overall ranking of 99 out of 125 countries examined (UNESCO 2007).

The narrowness of India's basic education is also reflected in wide gender inequalities. India's female adult literacy rate of 47.8 percent in 2001 is nearly 26 percent lower than the male adult literacy rate. This represents a gender gap that is more than three times as large as that of China. Similarly, India's female-male youth literacy rate gap, while substantially narrower than that of adults, remained as high as 16 percent as recently as 2000. By contrast, China is very close to eliminating the gender literacy gap among its youth. In addition to gaps in the literacy rate, gender inequality also persists in schooling outcomes in India. Less than 45 percent of India's female population aged 15 and over have ever attended primary school, which is more than 22 percentage points lower than for India's male population of the same age.

The gender inequality further expands at the secondary level, with 19.7 percent of the female population having never attended secondary school compared to 35.6 percent for Indian males (Barro and Lee 2001). Studies have suggested that the female literacy rate has a wide-ranging impact on the economy and society of a given country. Increased female literacy has been linked to decreases in fertility (Drèze and Murthi 2001) and infant mortality (Sufian 1989), and to increases in children's education and economic growth (Behrman et al. 1999). Given these results, steps in India to improve access to education among girls and to provide adult education and literacy training for women in their reproductive years would seem to be highly desirable.

In contrast to its weak performance in literacy and basic education, India has historically enjoyed a competitive advantage over China in post-secondary education. For many decades, India devoted a large proportion of its education resources to higher education, particularly in Science and Technology (S&T). As a result, the percentage of the college-educated population increased faster in India than in China. Between 1960 and 2000, the percentage of the adult population that had attended postsecondary education grew by 3.8 percent in India, but by only 1.9 percent in China. In 2000, 4.1 percent of the Indian population had attended post-secondary education, compared to 2.8 percent in China (Barro and Lee 2001).

This is a significant difference – equivalent to roughly 13 million more college-educated people. In addition to having a larger number of college graduates, India also appears to be ahead of China in establishing flagship higher education institutes that are highly ranked, not only domestically, but also by international peers. Institutes such as the IITs and the IIMs, often called the cradle of the contemporary IT miracle, have benefited from long time collaboration with foreign schools like the Sloan School of Management (MIT) and the Harvard Business School, and are themselves widely considered world-class institutes as of the end of the twentieth century (Agarwal 2007; Singh 2005).

3 Education attainment and patterns of economic growth

Education influences and is influenced by economic growth. While education itself is not sufficient for economic transformation, it is one of the necessary ingredients. The importance of accumulation of human capital – as measured by the educational attainment of the population – to economic development is among the most robust findings of the development economics literature (Barro 2001; Levine and Renelt 1992). Research has shown that human capital acquired through education influences economic growth both directly and indirectly. At the most basic level, education augments cognitive and other skills, which in turn increase the productivity of the labor force (Hanushek and Woessmann 2010).

Education increases adoption of new technologies by supplying people with high skills to conduct research and those with more basic skills to put the results into practice (Barro 2001). Education also provides young people from rural areas with the ability to read, write, and to travel the distance – literally and figuratively – to the urban areas where the jobs are located. In this way, it facilitates the movement of underutilized labor from low agricultural industries into higher productivity manufacturing and services (Birdsall et al. 1995). This helps to broaden the base of industrialization and widen the percentage of the population receiving earnings and participating in the growth process.

Different levels of education appear to contribute to economic growth through different channels. Cross-country empirical studies suggest that secondary and post-secondary education play a more important role for technology transfer (Barro 2001). Once transferred, a large workforce with secondary education is needed for the translation of the technology into wider use. Universal primary education and high coverage of secondary education are generally considered critical contributing factors to a country's manufacturing competitiveness. This is especially true for labor-intensive, low value added manufacturing for which technological imitation – often in the form of reverse engineering – is more important than innovation.

The East Asian "miracle" of low cost manufacturing-led growth that preceded the more recent takeoff by China and India was built on solid achievement in universal primary and secondary educational (Birdsall et al. 1995; Stiglitz 1996). Higher education, on the other hand, plays a bigger role in the model service industries, especially in the areas of banking, insurance, and information and communication technology (ICT) services.

The impact of education on economic development also varies by gender (Barro 2001). Male schooling at the primary level is found to be insignificantly related to growth. However, this level of education is a prerequisite for secondary and higher education, which are significantly related to growth. Female schooling at the primary level does have a significant, albeit indirect impact on economic growth. It stimulates per capita growth by increasing labor market participation among women and inducing a lower fertility rate and better health of children. Slower population growth, in turn, will have positive effects on per capita economic growth rates, both in the short run (fewer children) and by aiding capital deepening and hence productivity growth in the long run.

Different education models in China and India have led to corresponding strengths and weaknesses in the availability of human capital. China's achievements in basic education have left it with a larger labor pool of men and women with primary and secondary education. India's decades of heavy investment in higher education has produced a large number of college-educated, technically savvy, and English-speaking labor. India, however, lags significantly behind China in the coverage of primary and secondary education, particularly among its female population. The differing educational attainment patterns seem to have influenced the patterns of economic development in the two countries in at least three broad areas: sectoral composition, export composition, and employment structure.

Sectoral composition

The overall patterns of sectoral composition in China and India appear closely to mirror their respective comparative advantages in education.

Table 7.2 China and India: Value added by sector

Sector	Country	1985	1995	2005
Agriculture	China	33	19	12
	India	34	27	19
Industry**	China	33	44	48
	India	25	27	27
Manufacturing	China	25	31	33
	India	15	17	15
Services	China	34	37	40
	India	41	46	54

Unit: % of value added (constant 2000 US$) in total GDP.
** Including manufacturing.
Source: World Bank 2011.

As shown in Table 7.2, the share of the agricultural sector, which requires the least schooling of the labor force, has fallen rapidly in both countries, albeit at a faster pace in China. The share of the industrial sector, composed of manufacturing, construction, and utilities, grew tremendously in China and accounted for nearly half of China's GDP by 2005. In India, it increased by a mere two percentage points during the period of 1985–2005. When manufacturing is considered alone, China experienced an eight percentage-point expansion.

By contrast, the share of the manufacturing sector remained virtually unchanged in India. India's most significant growth occurred in the service sector, which increased by 13 percentage points from 41 percent in 1985 to 54 percent in 2005 and accounted for more than half of India's economy by 2005. On the other hand, the service sector in China still accounted for less than one third of economic output as of 2005, despite steady growth in the past three decades. The relative sectoral composition – a larger industry sector in China and a larger service sector in India – is consistent with China's substantial strength is primary and secondary education.

Employment Structure

The impact of differing education attainment models on growth pattern is also reflected in the structure of employment. Overall, the labor-force participation rate is considerably higher in China than in India (Table 7.3). This is hardly surprising since the literacy rate and average years of schooling, two important indicators of a population's basic skill level, are significantly higher in China than in India. Given India's

Table 7.3 China and India: Employment patterns

	Country	1985	1995	2005
Labor participation rate (%)	China	79	79	75
	India	60	60	58
Labor participation rate, male (%)	China	86	84	79
	India	86	84	82
Labor participation rate, female (%)	China	72	72	69
	India	33	35	32
Women employment in the nonagricultural sector as a percent of total women employment (%)	China		39	
	India		14	

Source: World Bank.

particularly low performance in female literacy and school-going outcomes, one would also expect a wider gender difference in employment outcomes. This is indeed the case. India's male labor participation rate is generally on par with that of China. However, India's female labor participation rate has been about 40 percentage points lower than China's. When Indian women do work, they are much more likely to find themselves working in agriculture than their Chinese counterparts.

Due to differences in the definition of employment and in survey sampling frame, estimations of employment by sector – such as those compiled by the International Labor Organization (ILO) – are not immediately comparable between China and India (Bosworth and Collins 2008; ILO 2010; Kumar and Gupta 2008).[1] Nevertheless, several consistent trends have emerged across various estimates. First, a similar percentage of the population was employed in the agricultural sector in both countries throughout 1980s and 1990s.

Starting from mid-1990s, the share of people employed in the agricultural sector has declined in China while it has continued to grow in India. The agricultural sector currently accounts for less than half of the total employment in China. In India, it continued to absorb more than 60 percent of the total labor force even in 1999–2000 (Joshi 2004). Secondly, employment in the industrial sector has been consistently higher in China than in India. In fact, the share of employment in the industrial sector changed very little in India from the late 1970s to the mid 2000s. Thirdly, in China employment in the service sector did not surpass that in the industry sector until sometime well into the first ten years of the twenty-first century. In India, the service sector has employed more people than the industrial sector since as early as the 1990s.

Table 7.4 China and India: Trade composition

Export	Country	1985	1995	2005
Total Exort (% of GDP)	China	24	44	69
	India	13	23	43
Goods in Total Export (%)	China	89	87	91
	India	74	82	65
Services in Total Export (%)	China	11	13	9
	India	26	18	35
Computer and information services (2003 data in millions of US $)	China	1,102		
	India	11,366		

Source: UNCTAD 2009; World Bank 2011.

Trade composition

Increased openness was a key factor in the recent economic takeoff of both China and India. The two countries' comparative advantages in education are perhaps best illustrated by the ways in which each country participates in the global economy. As a share of total GDP, trade more than doubled in China and more than tripled in India, albeit starting from a lower level (Table 7.4). The vast majority of China's exports is composed of goods, reflecting China's strength in large-scale, labor-intensive manufacturing. Indeed, China has firmly established itself as the "world's factory."

India's export encompasses a significantly larger share of services. India's competitive edge in service export is particularly salient in the computer and information services (databases, data processing, software design and development, maintenance and repair, and news agency services), for which India's large stock of English-speaking, college-educated technical labor force is a key strength. In 2003, exports of these services were ten times larger in India than in China. Including export in communication services (telecommunications, business network services, teleconferencing, support services, and postal services), India leads all other developing economies in the export of ICT services as a share of total service exports – 42 percent in 2006 (World Bank 2009).

4 Recent convergence of educational paths and its implications on growth

Interestingly, China and India have been moving towards each other in their educational strategies in recent years. In China, higher education has regained importance and expanded over time. In India, more resources have been invested in improving access to primary education.

The ending of the Cultural Revolution in 1976 marked a new era of Chinese history. Deng Xiaoping, the new national leader and architect of the market-oriented reform, re-appraised the importance of science and technology in economic modernization. The ten-year cessation of higher education during the Cultural Revolution left a mass skill shortage. Throughout the 1980s, the Chinese focused on restoring and promoting higher and vocational education. By 1995, the gross enrollment ratio for higher education had increased from about 2 percent in 1985 to slightly more than 5 percent (UNESCO 2008). The number of students enrolled in higher education per ten thousand people grew from 328 to 461 (TFHES 2000).

In the 1990s, private demand for college education grew exponentially due to the improvement in household income over the previous decade. The government responded by expanding the entrance quota for public universities. Between 1999 and 2006, the number of Chinese students enrolled in higher education increased fivefold (Yang 2004). At the primary and secondary levels, enrollment first declined in the early 1980s, partly due to agricultural de-collectivization. Families found it economically advantageous to have children work at the farm or at home rather than send them to school. The declining trend, however, was stopped after the Communist Party issued a decision to promulgate nine-year compulsory education in China (Yang 2004).

In India, a critical policy change occurred when the government announced a new National Policy on Education (NPE) in 1986 (DHE 1986). The NPE identified basic education – including primary and secondary education – as an area of policy priority and called for increased financial and organizational support. The NPE represents a fundamental shift in India's national education strategy. Since then, the share of public educational expenditure allocated to primary education has increased significantly while that allocated to higher education has decreased proportionately (Figure 7.2).

Under the close scrutiny of the United Nations EFA program, the Indian government introduced several national initiatives to expand children's access to primary education and improve its quality, particularly in rural areas and among traditionally disadvantaged subpopulations (UNESCO 2004). Prominent examples include Operation Blackboard (1986), the Total Literacy Campaign (1988), Minimum Levels of Learning (1989), and the District Primary Education Program (1994) (Kingdon 2007). Perhaps as a side effect of the shift of focus to

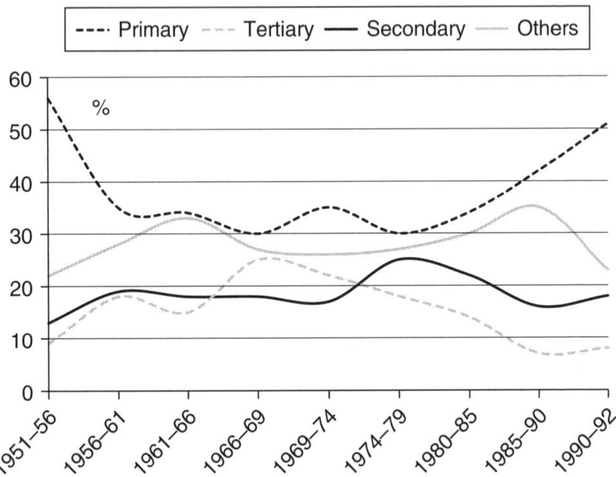

Figure 7.2 Public education expenditure by level of education, India
* The "Others" category includes adult education and technical education.
Source: Tilak 2005.

basic education, the percentage of public funding invested in higher education has decreased significantly in recent years.

To compensate for the shortfall in higher education funding, the Indian government has since allowed public universities and colleges to start charging tuition for self-financing courses and distance education programs. It also opened doors to private participation. As a result, private institutions have proliferated in recent years. These institutions are particularly active in the areas of great market demand, such as engineering, medicine, computer science, and business. Foreign participation is another new trend in India's higher education landscape. Foreign institutions usually offer joint programs with Indian institutions and have remained moderate in size (Agarwal 2007).

While it might take another decade or so to observe the impact of recent policy changes on population education attainment, China and India have started to converge in enrollment trends. As shown in Figure 7.3, India is very close to catching up with China in terms of gross enrollment ratio at the primary level, which has historically been China's strength. China, on the other hand, surpassed India for the first time around the year 2000 in the gross enrollment ratio for tertiary (higher) education.

Shifted educational priorities have presented different sets of opportunities and challenges for China and India as each country has strived to take its economy to the next level. China's success in manufacture initially benefited from an abundance of cheap and basically educated labor. As China moves up the manufacturing value chain, demand for low-skill labor is gradually replaced by demand for high-skill labor (*Forbes* 2010: Mar. 15). On the supply side, more and more younger Chinese are no longer willing to work for low-paying and physically-demanding jobs after a three-decade increase in their real income (*WSJ* 2010: Feb. 22: *China Real Time Report*).

This combination has led to higher costs of low-skill labor and pushed some labor-intensive manufacturing industries to look for alternative

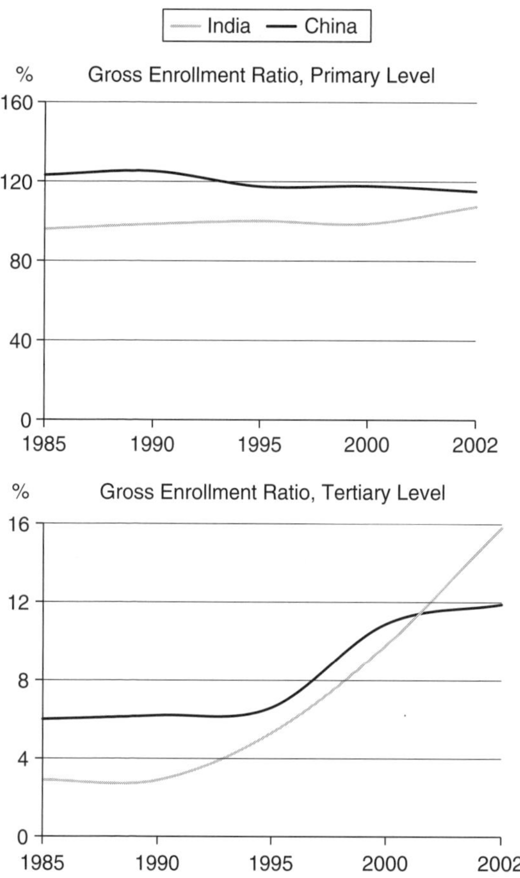

Figure 7.3 Converging trends in education in China and India
Source: UNESCO 2005.

production bases such as Vietnam, Bangladesh, and India. Ongoing economic structural adjustment also further increases the private demand for higher education since future job vacancies are more likely to exist in sophisticated manufacturing industries that require higher levels of skill. As the numbers of college graduates and English-speakers continue to rise, China might have the potential to compete with India in areas that have traditionally been India's advantages.

With improved outcomes in primary and secondary education, India has the potential to better position itself in the labor-intensive manufacturing sector. Compared to aging China, India also enjoys the so-called demographic dividend of a younger population (Bloom et al. 2002). To realize such potential, however, India will have to continue committing itself to removing obstacles – such as rigid labor laws, backward infrastructures, and lack of access to finance – that are widely considered to be responsible for India's low performance in manufacturing (Kumar and Gupta 2008). Another challenge India faces is a shortage of skilled labor in its fastest growing global outsourcing industries, including software and the service industry.

While India's leadership in global outsourcing had originally benefited from a large highly trained and English-speaking labor pool, the demand for such skilled workers has greatly outstripped the supply in recent years (*NYT* 2006: February 16). The problem is further acerbated by the falling share of public funding in higher education due to the government's shifted priority to primary education. A common complaint among business leaders is that good public universities generate too few graduates, and new private colleges are producing graduates of uneven quality (*AP* 2005: June 8). Some companies have resorted to in-house training as a temporary solution while others have started to consider alternative outsourcing destinations (*NYT* 2006: February 16).

5 Broad implications

China and India have shown that both the "wide" and "deep" models of education can set a country on the path toward development. However, it might be too early to tell which model will eventually outperform the other. As seen above, there are signs of convergence in educational strategies and it may be difficult to apportion credit to either model. Neither China nor India may be an ideal model for other countries. As we have shown, both countries' growth experiences have been highly contextual and the result of unique historical circumstances, political design, and good luck.

Nevertheless, economic scarcity has dictated that policies designed to promote higher education compete directly for resources with policies designed to expand basic education. While a literate workforce is necessary for sustained levels of economic growth, the effect of secondary and higher levels of education on economic growth has a much shorter time lag than primary education. It is useful to ask what lessons the rest of the developing world, especially countries in Africa and the rest of Asia, can draw from the contrasting experiences of China and India.

A few factors bear consideration. First, Baumol, Litan, and Schramm (2007) note that the two models are likely to produce very different distributional outcomes. Widespread basic education enables a large share of the population to participate in and benefit from a modern economy. This in turn contributes to the growth of a middle class, reducing the polarization in the income distribution that is characteristic of the poorest of the developing countries (Psacharopoulos 1985).

By contrast, countries with concentrated educational attainment often face the challenge of how to spread the economic fruit to the general population and therefore are more likely to see higher income disparity. Japan and the East Asian "Tigers" are good demonstrations of the former, while Latin America is often cited as an example of the latter. China has so far done a good job in integrating the millions of its rural population with basic literacy in economic modernization with its manufacturing-led growth model. India's service-led model, on the other hand, has had limited impact on employment expansion and has raised concerns about the prospect of a "jobless growth" (Joshi 2004).

Studies comparing the relative distribution outcomes of recent economic growth in China and India, however, have produced at best mixed results. Various estimates of the Gini index,[2] though differing among themselves, largely show that China had more equitable income distribution throughout the 1980s but the situation was reversed sometime in the mid- to late-1990s (Deininger and Squire 1996; Gajwani et al. 2006; IMF 2007). Statistics from the International Monetary Fund (IMF) that examine the per capita income growth by income quintile reveal some additional details of each country's inequality pattern.

In China, the per capita income has grown steadily, yet by an accelerated rate when one moves from the lowest quintile to the highest quintile. By contrast, the per capita income in India grows significantly faster for the top quintile than for any other quintile. In fact, the remaining four quintiles do not appear to differ in income growth rate (IMF 2007). Such evidence appears to be consistent with the popular perception that the elite, who have best access to higher education, have benefited most from India's recent economic development.

Not only is inequality an undesirable development outcome, it is often argued that persistent inequality might derail economic reforms by removing the political support for them (Birdsall et al. 1995). Some economists have suggested that high inequality is often associated with real barriers to upward mobility for those at the bottom. Limited access to good schooling and credit, and the racial and ethnic discrimination that are sometimes correlated with low income, are examples of an unlevel playing field that can discourage effort. A low level of income inequality, on the other hand, stimulates economic growth by inducing large increases in savings and investment by the poor, and by increasing market demand for domestic producers (Birdsall et al. 1995).

Last but not least, while the takeoff of India's information industry was built upon a large number of technically educated workers both at home and abroad, these individuals account for only a very small percentage of the Indian population. Yet the sheer size of India's population has ensured that even this small percentage amounts to a critical mass. India's success in attracting global services outsourcing has also benefited from a broad base of English-speaking workers. Other developing countries might not have the luxury of a large enough population – let alone an English-speaking one – to pursue a similar approach. These observations lead us to believe that the Indian experience is the more unusual of the two and the conventional strategy of broad and universal education that China has followed might be a safer option for others to emulate.

6 Concluding remarks

Rapid growth in China and India is transforming the global economy. This experience poses new challenges for understanding the process of transition and growth. While there is ample evidence that the potential for rapid change and catch up is enormous, there is no single model of how that potential can be unleashed: the ways in which it has happened vary from country to country. The comparison between China and India suggests there are different patterns of growth and development as well as differences in the role education plays in this process. There is a huge opportunity for comparative analysis aimed at understanding which policies work and which do not – a task that will continue as more economies start growing at the pace of China and India's.

Notes

1. For example, the Chinese data in the ILO excluded armed forces and reemployed retired persons. The Indian data in the ILO database included only employment in the public sector and establishments of non-agricultural private sector with 10 or more persons employed. Bosworth and Collins (2008) used the national household survey data in India to project annual employment in India. For China, they used a variety of sources and noticed inconsistency among different sources.
2. The Gini index is a measure of inequality with a value of 0 expressing total equality and a value of 1 maximal inequality.

8

Labor Movement and Economic Growth: Shaping and Managing the Lewis Transition in China and India

Jason Young

The economic rise of China and India provides a unique opportunity to compare the role of internal labor flows in the development of two nations with agricultural populations of unprecedented scale. This chapter puts forward a comparison of the formal institutional arrangements of China's *hukou* institution and the predominantly informal arrangements that shape labor migration and segmentation in India and questions the assumption that development entails free rural to urban migration in the classic Lewisian sense. It finds that contrary to arguments in favor of a coherent development model, significant differences in development trajectories are apparent. In China, formal institutional arrangements continue to shape the development process and act as intervening variables distorting the push-pull and transition forces anticipated in economic models of migration such as the Lewis transition, while in India, this process remains predominantly informal. The chapter argues that both formal and informal institutional arrangements can shape labor migration and constitute an important and oft-neglected feature of development. Significant differences between China and India's management of labor transfer provide a partial explanation for their divergent economic trajectories and suggest that the development experience is too complex to be captured by one model alone.

China's GDP based on purchasing power parity (PPP) valuation as a percentage of US GDP has risen from 9 percent in 1980 to 69 percent in 2010. India's GDP (PPP) has risen from 10 percent in 1980 to 28 percent in 2010 (IMF 2011).[1] Both countries are also somewhat anomalous in the nation-state system with each country having populations over a billion, together representing over a third of humanity. As developing countries with large rural populations, both China and India face similar economic challenges moving away from agrarian-based economic systems through the creation of employment in emerging secondary and tertiary sectors. This transition is ongoing and is a core feature of their development. While the economic re-emergence of China and India is reshaping the global economic system, domestically both are still struggling with the transition from agricultural-based economies to economies based on urban manufacturing and service industries.

This chapter examines whether the role of formal and informal institutions in this transition constitutes a coherent development model in the cases of China and India. The first section discusses development literature before introducing the Lewis transition in the second. The third section presents data comparing key indicators of the Lewis transition in China and India: urbanization and internal migration; employment in agricultural, secondary, and tertiary industries; productivity of secondary and tertiary labor. The fourth and fifth sections compare the role of formal and informal institutions managing the Lewis transition in China and India. The final section returns to the question of how institutions shape the Lewis transition and asks if this constitutes a development model for countries with large agrarian populations.

1 The emergence of development models

Before the emergence of European economies, China and India made up the bulk of global economic power (Frank 1998; Maddison 1998 and 2001, and earlier chapters in this volume). But in the nineteenth and early-twentieth centuries, both civilizations experienced humiliation and dependency at the hands of European powers as their economies dramatically stagnated in comparison to the growing might of the Western economies. After a long struggle for political and economic sovereignty, the two powers emerged in the post-war period as independent nation-states but were hampered by prolonged and chronic underdevelopment, with large and growing populations and a high reliance on the subsistence economy of the agricultural sector. China's communist revolution isolated its economy from the rest of the world and introduced the socialist planned economy. Falling out with the Soviet Union further forced its leaders to follow a policy of economic autarchy. While India maintained relations and trade with other countries, it too leaned heavily towards the Soviet model and, under the leadership of Nehru, the economy was also structured along the socialist model.

In more recent decades, leaders in both countries have promoted a more pragmatic approach to development, integrating their economies into the world economy and utilizing the existing pools of capital, technology, and know-how with ever-increasing returns. China has come to be known as the manufacturing center of the world and India as a global service center. India and China have drastically increased their GDP, developed their education and health services, and improved their infrastructure and productive output. Goldman and Sachs predict China's GDP (USD) will overtake US GDP in the late 2020s and India will be the third largest economy by the early 2030s (Wilson and Stupnytska 2007). Clearly, both India and China are in the midst of a remarkable period of growth and development. This provides a unique opportunity to compare growth strategies in the world's most highly populated nations to ascertain whether a coherent development model can be observed.

Early in the post-war period, development studies were dominated by what came to be known as modernization theory. The dominant strand of this theory postulated "a uniform evolutionary vision of social, political, and economic development" and had deep roots in classical theory (Chirot and Hall 1982). Stages of economic growth were prescribed universal properties over varying periods of history. W. W. Rostow, perhaps the most well-known advocate, argued that it is "possible to identify all societies, in their economic dimensions, as lying within one of five categories: the traditional society, the preconditions for take-off, the take-off, the drive to maturity, and the age of high mass-consumption" (Rostow 1960: 4). A less than complimentary strand of modernization theory also explained development in the West through a social-psychological model. It argued that Westerners "were possessed by a high need for achievement and rationality" and that this explained how the West became more developed than other parts of the world (Chirot and Hall 1982: 82).

These theories gave way to sustained criticism from many scholars. Samuel Huntington, in his "Political Development and Political Decay" essay, provided a compelling critique of the body of work and re-conceptualized political development as institutionalization (Huntington 1965). The critique from world systems theory looked to deep structural factors as an explanation for the problem of economic development in non-western countries, rejecting both the argument of European exceptionalism and the idea that non-Western countries had "traditional" economies (Chirot and Hall 1982). The Wallerstein-Frank school of economic development proposed autarkic closure to break the dependency on the developed world, something reminiscent of Lenin's theory of imperialism.

Both China and India show this influence, as both experienced a period of development during which the state moved to forms of self-reliance and broke away from the established international economic system. Then, beginning in the late 1970s in China and the late 1980s in India, a return to development models based on integrating into the world economic system saw both countries' governments turn full circle in their efforts to promote economic development. This time, however, the experience of Japan and the East Asian Dragons and Tigers was touted as a new development model to follow (Cohen 2000).

The East Asian "miracle" is a term popularized by a World Bank report on eight high performing Asian economies over the period 1965 to 1990 (World Bank 1993). These East Asian economies each experienced three decades of rapid economic growth at breakneck speeds (Huang 2005). This success caught the eye of development theorists, who argued it characterized a particular model of development in which the government, motivated by a desire for rapid economic growth and development, intervenes in industrial affairs (see Johnson 1982; Woo-Cummings 1999). Various scholars have also focused on factors such as land reform, improved investment, the release of human resources (labor), investment in education (particularly vocational), some effort to control fertility, trade liberalization, business networks and growth alliances, corporate governance, foreign direct investment, industrial policy, and export-led growth (Fatemi 2002).

When China's economy also "took-off," government strategies were compared to the model of development established by the East Asian Dragons and Tigers (Baek 2005). Studies have highlighted a similar emphasis on export-led growth, the importance of foreign direct investment, and the significance of planning boards and a government with the unity and strength to put in place economic policy with short-term upheaval but long-term growth outcomes. The emergence of Indian growth raises similar questions. A significant difference is, however, apparent when comparing the economic conditions of China and India and the East Asian economies. Clearly, the size of the population in China or India is far higher than even Japan. Development in China and India must therefore differ significantly to other East Asian countries due to the massive challenges population flows of such proportions present.

2 Labor transfer and the Lewis transition

While the majority of political economic studies concerned with migration have focused on the estimated 200 million migrants that cross international borders, the number of migrants estimated to live within their home country but outside their region of birth is an astounding

740 million. This mobility is integral to the process of development (UNDP 2009), but a detailed explanation of what role it plays has yet to be fully incorporated into development studies (Skeldon 2010). Any role for the state is downplayed or outright rejected.

Ronald Skeldon argues "it seems unlikely that [migration] can be easily manipulated, increased, decreased or changed in a direction to suit certain desired policy objectives" (2010: 335). In general, there remains a dearth of research on the strategies governments employ to manage population and labor movements. As such, economic models that largely ignore the role of the state still form the basis of our understanding of the role that internal migration and urbanization play in the development process. The early work of Arthur W. Lewis is used here to outline the importance of population, urbanization, and labor transfer to the development process in countries with large agrarian populations.

The "Lewis transition" or "Lewis model" focuses on the transfer of agricultural sector "surplus labor" through internal migration and urbanization in developing countries with large populations and was made known in his article "Economic Development with Unlimited Supplies of Labor" (Lewis 1954). It was "the received 'general' theory of the development process in 'labor surplus' Third World nations during most of the late 1950s and 1960s" (Todaro 1976: 21). The model dichotomizes the economy of developing countries into two sectors: a traditional rural subsistence sector (low productivity; "surplus labor"), and a high productivity modern urban industrial and service sector. Development entails transfer of "surplus labor" from the low productivity subsistence sector to the high productivity urban sector through growth of employment in the urban sector.

Moreover "modern sector growth and employment expansion is assumed to continue until all 'surplus' rural labor is absorbed in the urban industrial sector. Thereafter the labor supply curve becomes positively sloped and both urban wages and employment will continue to grow. The structural transformation of the economy will have taken place with the balance of economic activity shifting from rural agriculture to urban industry" (Todaro 1976: 23). The Lewisian turning point comes when the supply of rural labor from the countryside begins to taper off. At this point non-agricultural wages begin to rise. This signifies a significant turning point in a country's development.

Lewis identified the problem of "underemployment" in countries with large populations where a high percentage of the population is involved in agriculture. "In the over-populated countries the farmers, the petty traders, the domestic servants, and many classes of casual labor are not fully occupied. As economic development occurs there is a shift to the new types of employment which open up, and the reduction of 'disguised unemployment' shows itself in a relative contraction of the trades which have been carrying the surplus" (Lewis 1955: 333).

From these observations, Lewis concludes one of the best measures of economic growth in a developing country is the measure of the proportion of the labor force involved in agriculture. Lewis argues that the move from pre-modern conditions to modern conditions requires productivity gains in the agricultural sector that release the "underemployed" to move to urban areas to labor in the secondary and tertiary sectors. If the industrial and services sectors are not developed to the extent that they can absorb this labor, then the majority of these laborers will remain "underemployed" in the agricultural sector. This makes the proportion of the labor force involved in agriculture a good measure of economic development.

The Lewis transition requires urbanization and changing spatial distribution of the population. Lewis points out that the speed of urbanization can be problematic in countries where economic growth is just beginning. As the population is still growing rapidly and potential laborers are drawn to the high growth in urban areas, overpopulation of these areas can become a problem. This issue is especially problematic in China and India where the size of the rural "underemployed" agricultural population remains incredibly large.

Lewis was also acutely aware of the importance of population growth for economic development and warned "the individual country which goes through a phase of high birth and low death rates has to pay a substantial economic price for doing so" (Lewis 1955: 310). As the rural populations of both India and China have historically been very high, it is expected that both Chinese and Indian governments are aware that over-population of urban areas could cause swamping of the developing urban industries. It is also expected that the Lewisian turning point is still some time away and continues to present major challenges for policymakers. Demographics suggest China is far closer than India to this turning point, also suggesting that China's economic development, as measured by the Lewis transition, is further ahead than India's.

3 The Lewis transition in China and India

The following figures (Figures 8.1–8.4) show the size of the rural and urban populations in China and India over the period 1981 to 2007.

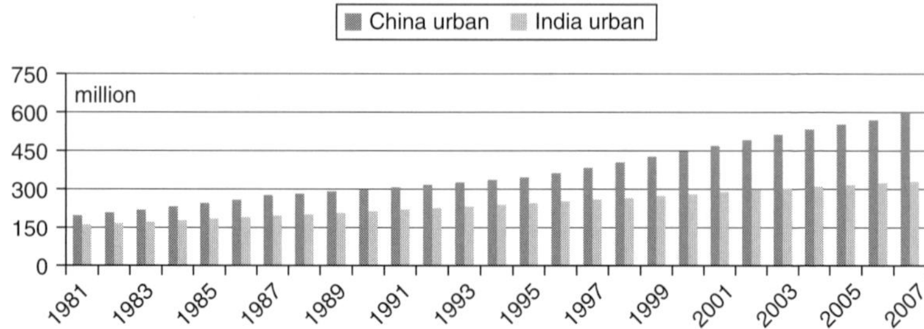

Figure 8.1 Urban populations in China and India (1981–2007)
Source: UNSD 2010.

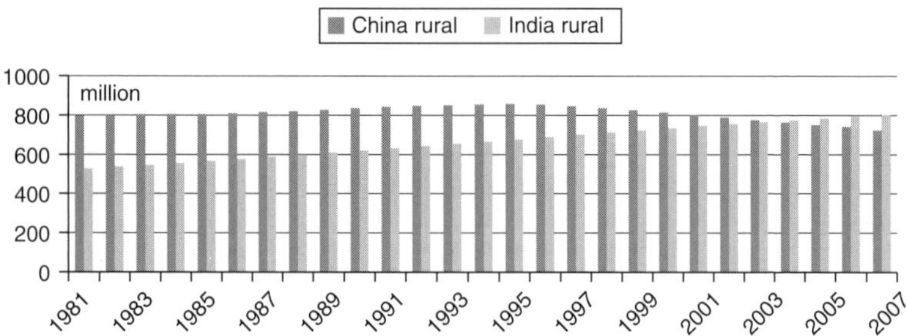

Figure 8.2 Rural populations in China and India (1981–2007)
Source: UNSD 2010.

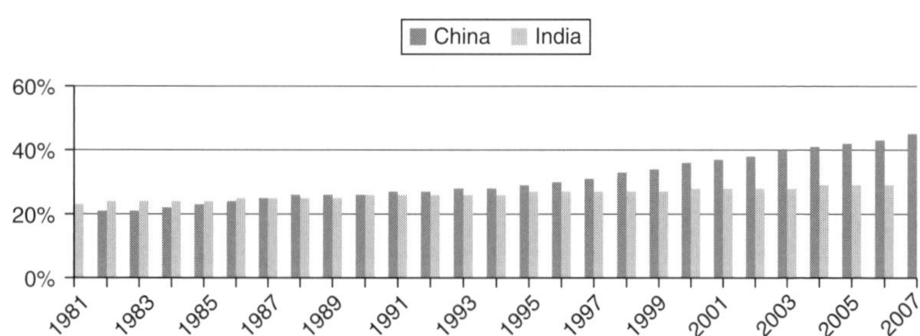

Figure 8.3 Level of urbanization in China and India (1981–2007)
Source: UNSD 2010.

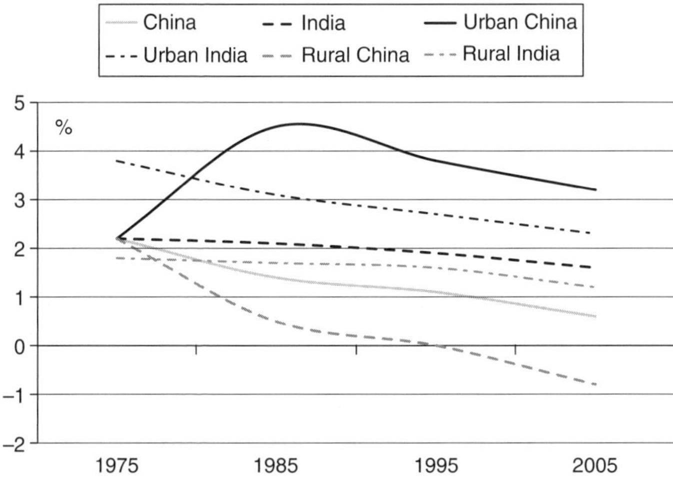

Figure 8.4 Annual rate of population growth in rural and urban areas in China and India (1975–2005)
Source: UNSD 2010.

China's urban population has outstripped the growth of the Indian urban population (Figure 8.1) while India's rural population overtook the Chinese rural population in 2004 (Figure 8.2). Urbanization in China overtook India in 1988. From the mid-1990s, the Chinese rate of urbanization began to outpace urbanization in India (Figure 8.3). While India's urban population continued to grow, doubling between 1981 and 2007, China's tripled.

Moreover, as seen in Figure 8.4, China's rural population first stagnated and then decreased, while India's rural population continued to grow. Growth rates for the total Chinese population have dropped from over 2 percent annually to close to zero. Growth rates in urban areas jumped from 2 percent annually to over 4 percent and remain above 3 percent, while annual growth in the rural population has stagnated and is now negative. India by comparison started out with the same overall annual growth rate but the decrease over the period has been far less significant, dropping only to 1.6 percent annually, a full 1 percentage point higher than China. The urban population growth rate has gone from being higher than China's in 1975 to lower than China's by an almost consistent 1 percentage point from 1985 to 2005. Perhaps the starkest difference is evidenced in the continual growth of the rural population in India, which in China has moved to negative growth.

Internal migration is also lower in India than in China. Bell and Muhidin's comprehensive *Cross-National Comparisons of Internal Migration* (2009) presents data that shows that while internal migration in Asia in general is lower than developed areas such as Europe and Australasia, it is significantly higher in China than in India. The 2000 census recorded 73 million interprovincial lifetime migrants in China, while in India the 2001 census recorded only 42 million interstate lifetime migrants. China's level of internal migration intensity was 6.193 percent compared to India's 4.141 percent (Bell and Muhidin 2009). Evidence of both population mobility and urbanization are on these scales higher in China than in India. These demographics therefore suggest the Lewis transition is more advanced in China than in India.

Lewis (1954) argued an important part of the Lewis transition was not only urbanization but the transfer of labor from the agricultural sector to industrial and services sectors and the increasing contribution of these industries to economic growth. Again, the evidence suggests that China has gone further along this process than India. The following figures (Figure 8.5, Figure 8.6, and Figure 8.7) show the value added of agriculture as a percentage of GDP from 1981 to 2007 and the level of growth and employment in the agricultural, industrial, and services sectors of the Chinese and Indian economies. Significantly, the contribution of agriculture to GDP has dropped faster in China than India and the industrial and service sectors are more productive, employ more people, and earn more revenue for China than India. The transition away from an economy primarily based on agriculture to one with

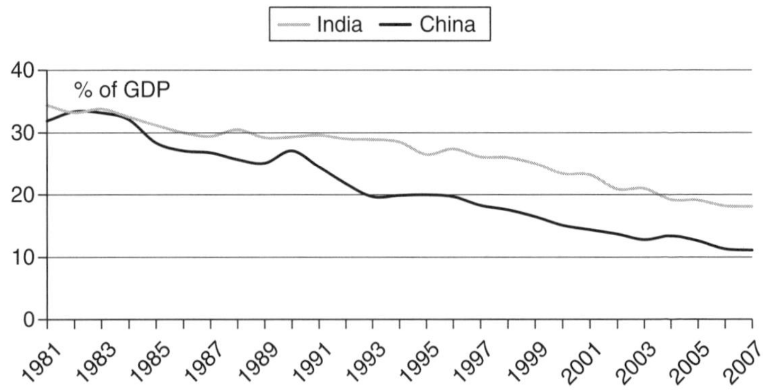

Figure 8.5 Contribution of agriculture in China and India to GDP (1981–2007)
Source: UNSD 2010.

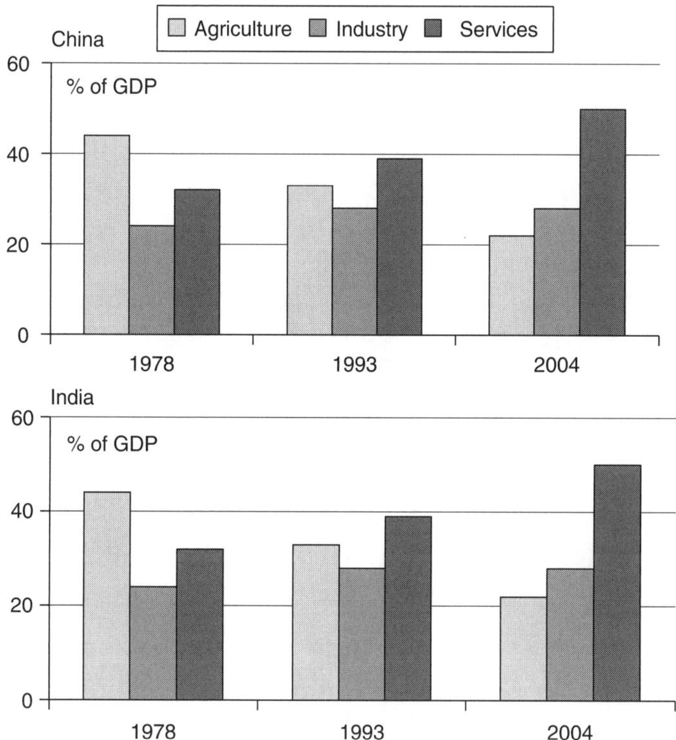

Figure 8.6 Value added by sector in China and India
Source: Bosworth and Collins 2008: 57.

highly productive secondary and tertiary industries has occurred faster in China than in India.

The growth of the manufacturing sector in China is particularly striking compared to the growth in India. Moreover, growth in the service industry shows that Chinese services are not only more productive but they also employ more people than in India. This evidence should also, according to Lewis (1955), be a good measure of the level of economic development. As the Lewis transition proceeds and more rural labor moves into the economically productive tertiary and secondary sectors, Lewis argues, capital should accumulate and trade and industry flourish. The following data (Figure 8.8 and Figure 8.9) supports this assertion as they show China's growth outstripping India's as expected by China's more rapid transition through the Lewis model. China has

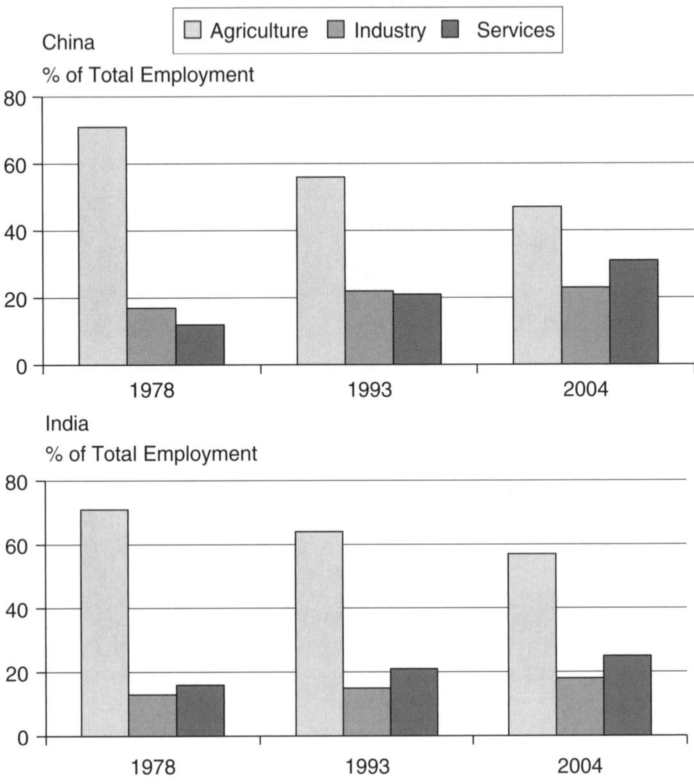

Figure 8.7 Employment by sector in China and India
Source: Bosworth and Collins 2008: 57.

both a higher gross domestic product than India and a higher GDP per capita. India's GDP per capita was higher than China's until 1991, about the same time that China's population growth dropped in rural areas but increased in urban areas and overall GDP expanded considerably.

These results suggest population growth and spatial distribution are an essential aspect of the development process. India's economic development, compared to China's, is hampered by continual growth in rural areas and limited urbanization. As growth in rural areas continues, the mass transfer of labor from rural to urban employment becomes increasingly difficult. China by comparison has been able to transfer rural labor to the productive urban industries and this is a large part of the success of its emergent secondary and tertiary industries.

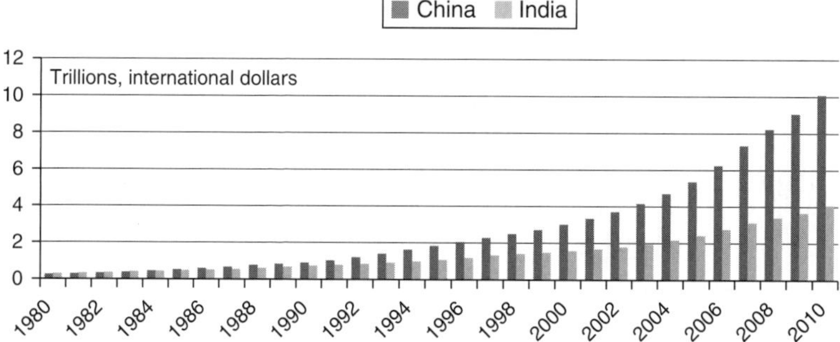

Figure 8.8 India and China GDP (1978–2010)
Source: IMF 2011.

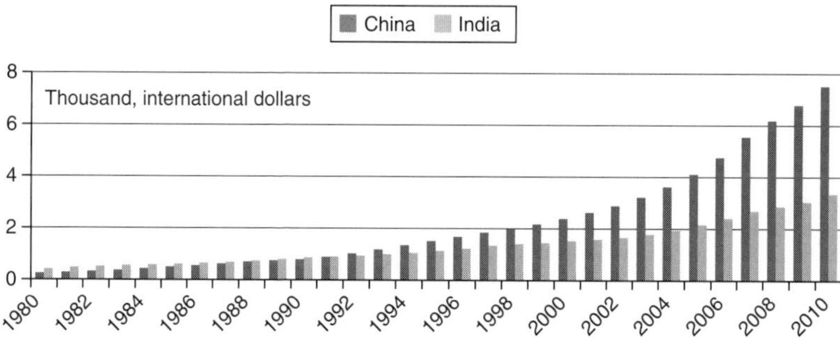

Figure 8.9 India and China GDP per capita (1975–2010)
Source: IMF 2011.

China's urbanization is more advanced than India's not only because of a higher rate of transfer from rural to urban, both through migration and expansion of urban areas, but also through the slowing birth rate. As China's birth rate has slowed this creates opportunities in urban areas and urbanization drains the population from rural areas to meet these opportunities. China's economy has developed faster than India's, and this is reflected in the proportion of people involved in agricultural and non-agricultural employment as well as the proportion of people living in urban areas.

Governments in both countries recognize the importance of managing the Lewis transition, as evidenced by data in the *2005 World Population Policies*' synopsis of government views and policies relating to population growth, spatial distribution, and urbanization (United Nations 2008). While in 1976, 1986, 1996, and 2005, Indian officials considered the population "too high" and had policies to lower growth, Chinese officials moved from considering the population "too high" to "satisfactory" in 1996.

Moreover, by 2005, Chinese officials had reportedly adjusted the policy of lowering the size of the population to one of maintaining it. In terms of spatial distribution, Indian officials have consistently desired major change and have sought to lower rural to urban migration, especially migration to urban agglomerations. Chinese officials reportedly only desire minor change and in 2005 declared a policy to raise rural to urban migration, including to urban agglomerations. In summary, both demographic and economic statistics as well as United Nations' reports on government policy suggest the Lewis transition is much more of a concern for Indian officials than Chinese, who seem to have been able to manage the transition and be well on the way to reaching the Lewisian turning point. The following sections compare efforts to shape and manage this transition in each country.

4 Managing the Lewis transition in India

The previous section showed demographic and economic evidence of the Lewis transition in India and China and found that urbanization, internal migration, and economic growth through non-agricultural industries is significantly lower in India. India's lack of population mobility, in particular urbanization, is particularly striking when compared to similar developing countries with large populations. Rates of urbanization in India remain low compared to rates in other developing economies (Figure 8.10). India's urban population accounted for 28.4 percent of the total population in 2000, roughly 15 percent lower than urban population rates in countries with similar levels of GDP per capita (Deshingkar and Anderson 2004). This is true even though incomes in urban areas have been rising faster than incomes in rural areas, accentuating the classical push and pull of economic rationales to urbanize.

This raises the important question of why this is so. Three possibilities are explored. The first is that the Indian government has formal institutions to restrict internal mobility and urbanization and this has prevented urbanization. The second explores the importance of informal institutions, culture, and society and asks if there is something unique about Indian society that has led to comparatively lower levels of urbanization. The final possibility explored is that India's level of

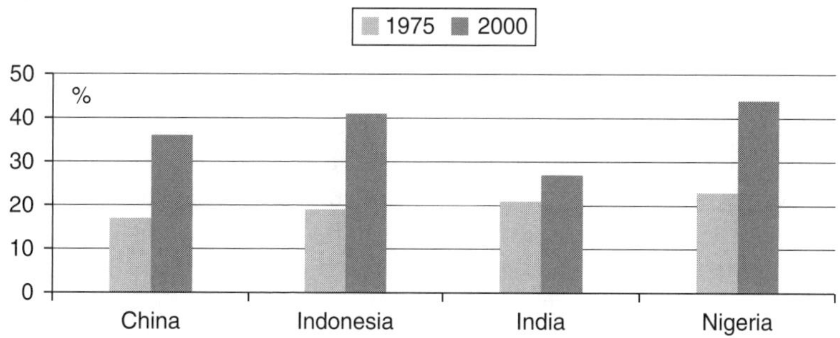

Figure 8.10 Urbanization in China, Indonesia, India, and Nigeria
Source: Adapted from Munshi and Rosenzweig 2009:41.

economic development, and, more importantly, its form of economic development, has not provided urban employment and this has discouraged would-be migrants from leaving their rural homes. The first two explanations suggest that there are intervening forces shaping the Lewis transition in India. The final explanation suggests that the lack of labor mobility is more a symptom of India's slow uptake to modern economic arrangements.

The first trend that becomes clear in the literature on India's labor regulations is the strong historical approach to protecting the rights of Indian workers from exploitation and poor working conditions. Labor advocacy and autonomous unions have a history of effecting change in labor relations between employer and employee, and while the power of unions has been rolled back to some extent in recent decades, employees in India clearly have a better record providing good working conditions for their employees. Some scholars studying India's economic development over the last few decades have argued that these "pro-worker" labor regulations are in fact a hindrance to economic development and labor mobility.

Besley and Burgess (2004) conducted a study of state amendments to the Industrial Disputes Act (1947) from 1958 to 1992. Their comparison of "pro-worker" or "pro-employer" amendments with the growth of manufacturing led them to conclude "that pro-worker amendments to the Industrial disputes Act are associated with lowered investment, employment, productivity and output in registered manufacturing. Regulating in a pro-worker direction is also associated with increases in urban poverty" (Besley and Burgess 2004). This shows that there is some evidence that India's economic development, as compared to the development of China, is slower due to labor regulations that protect the rights of workers and uphold labor standards. If labor standards lower economic growth, they also reduce the opportunity for labor mobility and can therefore be seen as an intervening variable in the form of government regulation of the Lewis transition.

Another important feature of the government's role in managing the Lewis transition is the absence of a regulatory mechanism for slowing, managing, directing, or controlling movement and residency within the Indian state. This is particularly surprising considering the low rate of migration and urbanization in India. Some studies have shown that residency in China has a large impact on the rate of internal migration and urbanization, particularly permanent migration (see next section), but a review of Indian residency laws suggest that a system similar to China's *hukou* system is not in place. Formal laws and regulations in fact act in the opposite direction.

The Indian Constitution (amended in 2007) states that all citizens have the right to equality, including the right not to be discriminated against on grounds of place of birth. Titles and "untouchability" have been constitutionally abolished. Article 19 of Part III of the constitution, the *Right to Freedom*, clearly states that all citizens have the right to move freely throughout the territory of India, to reside and settle in any part of the territory of India, and to practice any profession, or to carry on any occupation, trade, or business (Government of India 2007). Formally, the Government of India does not impede labor and population mobility; in fact these freedoms are clearly protected in the constitution. Qualifying for a change of residency in India is also far simpler than in China. The right to vote is constitutionally protected and each citizen over the age of 18 has the right to vote in the area in which they "ordinarily reside." If a migrant moves to a new area they fill in a form notifying the electoral office of their change of residency and they have the same rights as local citizens do to vote (Election Commission of India 2010). Therefore, the formal institutions of government are not structured to inhibit migration by reducing the rights of migrating citizens.

The next consideration is the importance of informal institutional practices. While the actual regulations and laws of the state do not act as an impediment or as an intervening variable in the movement of Indian citizens, various informal characteristics of the bureaucracy are problematic. The most serious issue concerns corruption and the misuse of constitutional and legal mechanisms. Corruption in India is considered to be institutionalized, accompanied by a general belief that the status quo cannot be changed.

Moreover, the constitution and legal rulings originally intended to protect India's civil service from arbitrary dismissal has led to long protracted legal rulings that act to guard the civil service from allegations of corruption and misuse of power (Dwivedi and Jain 1988). Recent news reports concerning the state of corruption and bureaucratic governance suggest this issue is still very much of central concern for India's economic and political development (*NYT* 2010: March 22).

This will have a detrimental effect on population mobility and urbanization because migration involves a change of residence, a change of electoral entitlements and, in many cases, the re-issuing or confirmation of ration cards and important documents such as marriage certificates. A dysfunctional and corrupt bureaucracy will significantly increase the costs of migration through the addition of bribes and the problem of time wasting. Furthermore, the 2009 *Human Development Report* argues that seasonal workers are excluded from voting in elections when they fall during peak movements, and migrants living outside their registered district do not get subsidized food or health care and cannot vote (UNDP 2009: 17, 1) due to issues in changing residency. These informal practices likely reduce mobility.

A further consideration for the lack of population mobility in India is the role Indian cultural values and norms play, especially in rural areas. Some studies suggest that these practices are not conducive to migration and urbanization for a large section of the Indian populace. The caste system has been singled out in this regard. One study suggests that the persistence of low spatial mobility in rural India is due to the existence of sub-caste networks that provide mutual insurance to their members (Munshi and Rosenzweig 2009). Rural workers in India are less likely to out-migrate because the act of migration separates them from these informal networks, which provide much of their social and economic security as well as their cultural, ethnic, and religious identity.

The final observation rests on the nature of the relationship between economic development and population mobility as theorized by the Lewis transition. If population mobility is a prerequisite for economic development in the form of rural labor moving into the more productive secondary and tertiary sectors in urban areas, economic development is also a prerequisite for migration. Labor transfer cannot occur without the creation of urban jobs through economic development and economic development requires the movement of the rural labor force. The two factors are concomitant and it is hard to tease out the causal relationship between the two.

The Lewis transition is a predominantly economic theory that states that an important part of the economic development of a national economy is the move from economic arrangements characterized by a high proportion of the labor force being employed in the agricultural sector to economic arrangements where the majority of employees are involved in highly productive work in secondary and tertiary sectors in urban areas. In India, we have seen that the economy has developed rapidly over the period of study. However, we have also noted that the population has continued to grow at a rapid rate. If the population continues to grow, it is expected that economic growth can occur *without* a major transfer of labor from rural areas.

Rather, the natural growth in urban areas will continue to supply developing industries, and the growth in rural populations will remain underemployed in the agricultural sector and only very little will be transferred to urban employment. Here, the argument is not that India's economy has failed to grow but rather that the growth in the Indian economy has not been sufficient (as measured by the growth in rural population) to allow for a mass transfer of labor from rural areas. In this case, the Lewis transition is obscured and limited by continual growth in the rural population. Moreover, the form of growth is also significant. The lack of manufacturing employment in India severely decreases the available employment opportunities for potential migrants. China's comparative advantage lies in labor-intensive manufacturing while India's lies in the export of skilled services, making unskilled or semi-skilled work secondary to development (Deshingkar and Anderson 2004: 4).

Finally, when utilizing the population and urbanization data presented by the Indian Government, it is important to consider if the entire population residing in India, especially in urban areas, is accounted for. The issue of homelessness questions the ability of the state to competently measure the true number of the urban population as "homelessness is also associated with the lack of a ... ration card, and reflects disconnection from society and the loss of citizenship ... street homeless people do not have ration cards making them entitled to important nutritional supplements, the right to vote and access a range of services" (Speak and Tipple 2006: 10). Local area studies also suggest that, as in China, urbanization and migration is increasing rapidly: "a number of recent village studies from different parts of India show a sharp increase in population mobility, including long term and temporary migration as well as commuting" (Deshingkar and Anderson 2004: 2). The advent of slums in places such as New Delhi also attests to the increasing prevalence of rural to urban migration on an increasingly permanent basis.

In summary, this case suggests population mobility and urbanization in India is low compared not only to China but also to other countries of similar development levels. Leaving the debate over the influence of pro-worker regulations to one side, formal institutions of governance are not designed to impede or slow urbanization directly or manage the Lewis transition. Informal practices of government and various cultural and social norms do however play a role. The government has not directly tried to manage the Lewis transition but this is still occurring through informal institutional and cultural practices.

Moreover, India's form of economic development has not created the necessary urban employment, especially considering the continual growth of the rural population. Questions also remain concerning the true number of urban migrants in India's urban centers. The next section presents the case study of China and seeks to ascertain what role the government has had in managing the Lewis transition there. As will become clear, the response of Chinese officials to the massive task of developing the economy and shifting the rural labor force into more productive urban labor has been astoundingly different to that of Indian officials.

5 Managing the Lewis transition in China

Turning to China a very different story emerges. Perhaps one of the most significant findings for China is the growth of urban areas. Not only has China's urban population increased dramatically over the period of study, but so too has the actual size of urban areas (Deng et al. 2010). Urbanization in this case is not only attributable to rural to urban migration but also to the expansion of urban areas into rural areas. While this expansion does not necessarily mean rural citizens are accorded "urban residency," it does mean they undertake non-agricultural employment and live urban lives, the fundamental requirement of the Lewis transition.

The following figures (Figure 8.11 and Figure 8.12) outline the level of employment in agriculture, industry and services over the period 1978 to 2007. Agriculture has dropped from accounting for 70 percent of all employment to 40 percent in 2007. The number of people working in industrial and services sectors has accounted for the drop in agricultural employment as a proportion of the whole. Employment in urban areas, as shown in Figure 8.13, has grown from 20 percent to 40 percent of all employment.

As the population has moved from rural employment in agriculture to urban employment in industry and the services sector, China's

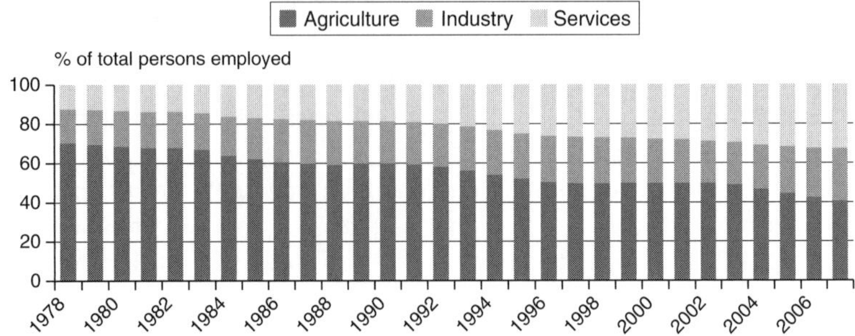

Figure 8.11 Percentages of employed persons in China by sector (1978–2007)
Source: NBSC 2008:18.

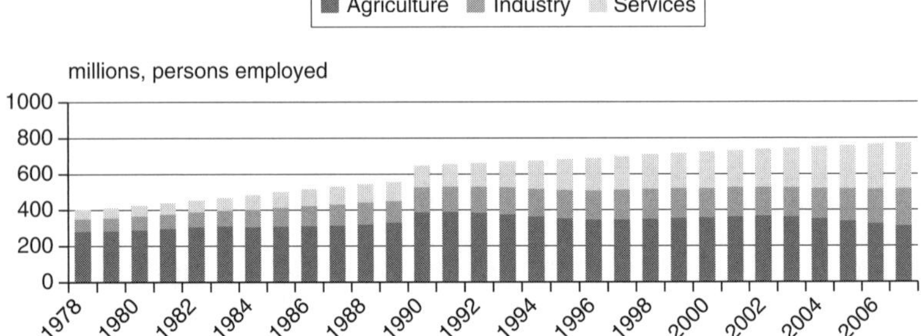

Figure 8.12 Numbers of employed persons in China by sector (1978–2007)
Source: NBSC 2008:18.

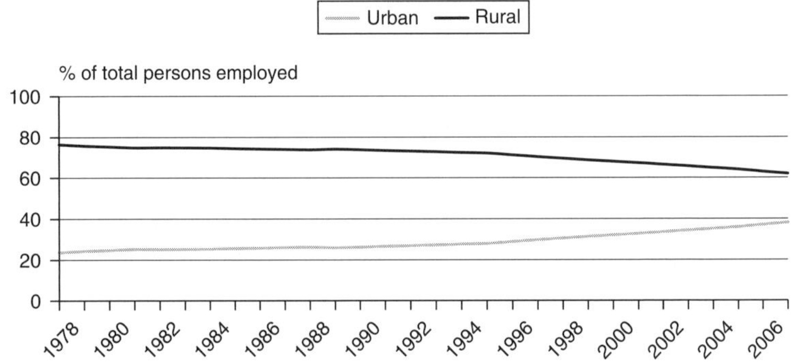

Figure 8.13 Employed persons in rural and urban areas (1978–2007)
Source: NBSC 2008:17.

economy has grown rapidly. Figure 8.14 and Table 8.1 show the drop in the contribution of agriculture as a percentage of GDP and the outstanding growth of industrial and services sectors.

From this we can see that compared to India, China is urbanizing at a far quicker pace. It is also clear that China's economy has higher GDP and a higher GDP/capita rate. More people work in non-agricultural employment, and these industries create greater wealth for the overall economy through higher rates of productivity. This all suggests that the Chinese economy is progressing rapidly through the Lewis transition and approaching the Lewisian turning point. The timing of this turning point is a highly debated field of research in China (see Cai 2008). The question of utmost interest to this study however is what role the Chinese state has played in this transition. Turning to an analysis of state policy over the reform era it becomes clear the state has been an active participant in the development process through the maintenance and adaptation of the *hukou, huji,* or household registration system.

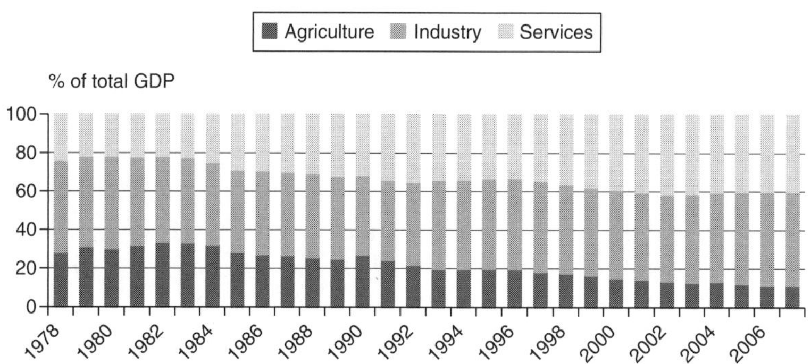

Figure 8.14 GDP by sector (1978–2007)
Source: NBSC 2008: 33.

Table 8.1 Growth in three sectors

	1978	**2007**	**Growth factor**
Agriculture	102.8 billion	2.8 trillion	27 times
Industry	174.5 billion	12 trillion	70 times
Services	87.3 billion	10 trillion	115 times
Total	364.5 billion	25 trillion	68 times

Unit: Yuan, 2008 prices.
Source: NBSC 2008: 33.

The *hukou* system is a formal institution of nationwide residency permits that guide migration and residency in China. The critical feature of these permits is the entitlements they provide their holders. *Hukou* is "China's first credential" (Tian 2003) and entitlements to *hukou* are decided by local government officials. Permanent *hukou* residency is strictly controlled by officials wary of overpopulation in desirable urban areas and mounting service delivery costs. Because of the tight control over *hukou* transfer (transferring one's residency to a new area) hundreds of millions of Chinese migrants fail to obtain a change of residency at their destination. The majority of these migrants are rural laborers with agricultural *hukou* status.

The *hukou* system remains poorly understood even after recent attempts by a group of editors in China to highlight the significance of it to the Chinese governing system made international headlines (Branigan 2010). This group of editors put out a joint call for an end to *hukou* dualism and the discrimination of migrants. They highlighted migrant's inability to change their residency from "agricultural" or "non-local" when migrating into urban areas to take work in the developing secondary and tertiary sectors. The joint editorial was issued at the time of the annual National People's Congress sitting and called on representatives to reform the system to conform to the constitution (*Daily Editors* 2010: March 1). Regrettably, this joint appeal has not significantly changed state policy to date.

Hukou has a long history in China and its importance to dynastic ruling systems should not be understated (see Lu 2003; Wang 2005). However, it was not until the late 1950s that the current regulation dividing urban and rural populations was implemented. The *People's Republic of China Hukou Registration Regulation* was adopted by the Standing Committee of the National People's Congress on January 9, 1958. Article 1 clearly sets out the rationale behind the measures, stating, "This regulation is formulated in order to maintain social order, protect the rights and interests of citizens, and to be of service to the establishment of socialism."[2] Lu Yilong (2002) argues that the regulation was designed primarily to establish social order and stability and to decrease migration pressures on the cities struggling with unemployment after decades of upheaval as well as to allow the government to establish "work order" through the socialist planned economy.

Both outward and inward migration, temporary and permanent, are managed by the Public Security Bureau. Migration, most importantly permanent migration, from rural areas to urban areas was strictly controlled by a process of applying to leave, to migrate, and to enter a new area. Without the required residency permits access to state services were withheld. The *hukou* institution acted as a fundamental feature of the command economy as "work units" and cooperatives became responsible for *hukou* administration and applications, giving central planners extensive powers of management and social control.

The *hukou* system has two fundamental forms of dualism, agricultural/non-agricultural and local/temporary. The first division has traditional antecedents that go back as far as the very beginnings of political life in China (Wang 2005). In the late 1950s, the division of agricultural and non-agricultural *hukou*[3] institutionalized the traditional division of rural and urban areas. Non-agricultural *hukou* holders were allocated employment in China's urban command economy while agricultural *hukou* holders were organized into rural collectives that passed on set state quotas of grain and other agricultural products to supply the industrial development in urban areas. The "breakdown" of this division is one of the fundamental features of the reform era in China.

The second dualism in the *hukou* system is the division of local and non-local status. Prior to the reform era the division was simple. All citizens in China were allocated their *hukou* status in a set *hukou* zone based on the location of their mother's *hukou* status. Local status provided the bearer with local provision of employment, state services, healthcare, and education (varying widely over rural/urban and differing areas of development). Movement "outside the plan" was essentially shut down because without changing one's *hukou* status a citizen did not have access to what Dorothy Solinger describes as the "urban rationing regime" (Solinger 1999). However, since the early 1980s an increasing number of migrants have moved outside their *hukou* zone, predominantly from rural areas to engage in non-agricultural employment in the rapidly growing secondary and tertiary industries. This has created another class of migrant who have been institutionalized by government regulations introducing "temporary permits" for what are known in China as non-*hukou* or non-*huji* residents. This has created the following hukou categories in China's urban areas (Table 8.2).

Non-local *hukou* status has significant disadvantages for migrants. Firstly, they are not entitled to a range of local government entitlements and services such as education and healthcare subsidies. Secondly, they bear the brunt of employment discrimination. Thirdly, they are considered temporary, making integration into the established socio-economic environment in urban areas extremely difficult. While some cities are slowly abolishing the agricultural/non-agricultural division

Table 8.2 Categories of urban workers by Hukou status in China

	Agricultural	Non-agricultural
Local	Local *nongmin* (agricultural *hukou* holders) swept up in the "urban sprawl"	The permanent urban *hukou* population
Non-local	Temporary workers from rural areas with temporary residency	Temporary workers from other urban areas with temporary residency
	Temporary workers from rural areas without temporary residency	Temporary workers from other urban areas without temporary residency

(Chan and Buckingham 2008) and many cities are experimenting with greater levels of *hukou* transfer (Wang and Liu 2006) these divisions remain significant to emerging migration and urbanization patterns because agricultural *hukou* holders who migrate to urban areas in search of employment and livelihood opportunities are relegated to a second-tier institutional status. They fail to obtain non-agricultural local *hukou* status but lose the benefits of their local rural *hukou*.[4] They become *nongmingong* or what is known as the "floating population," non-agricultural, non-local temporary *hukou* holders who nonetheless live urban lives and contribute to the non-agricultural urban economy (Figure 8.15).

Local *hukou* holders with agricultural *hukou* also exist as urban workers and are also relegated to a second-tier institutional status. As such, the number of people counted as urban remains far higher than the number of people with non-agricultural *hukou* status. The statistics presented earlier in this section showed that China is far ahead of India in terms of urbanization. However, even though China's urban population reached around 600 million in 2007, the number of non-agricultural *hukou* holders was a mere 431 million.[5] *Hukou* acts to slow population mobility, especially permanent or long-term migration to urban centers, by decreasing the desirability of rural to urban migration by withholding urban residential rights. The level of urbanization on average sits 10 percent higher than the level of non-agricultural *hukou* status. *Hukou* rates, temporary permits, and strict *hukou* transfer policies constitute a development strategy providing tools for the state not only to slow the rate of urbanization but also to shape the direction and flows of people to areas of China deemed in the interests of local and central

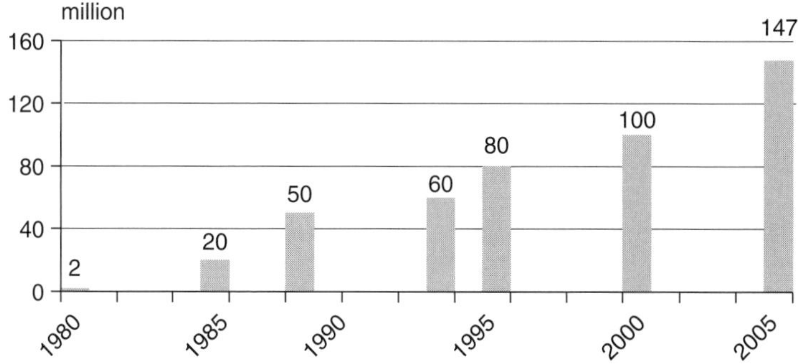

Figure 8.15 National floating population (1980–2005)
Source: NBSC 2006:114.

Table 8.3 Urbanization and Ministry of Public Security Hukou type in 2007

	Total population	**Urban**	**Proportion**	**Rural**	**Proportion**
Level of urbanization	1321	594	45%	727	55%
	Total population	Non-agricultural	Proportion	Agricultural	Proportion
MPS *Hukou* type	1309	431	33%	878	67%

Source: NBSC 2008: 5,293.

planners. This questions Lewis's and other development models, which assume rural to urban labor transfer is a function of the development of the labor market, as they fail to consider government policy as an intervening variable in this process.

"Urbanization from below" is a term denoting official efforts to urbanize less densely populated areas of China as part of the Chinese developmental process (Fan 1994). The state uses *hukou* status as a means to influence the direction of migration. This is done by maintaining strict criteria, as seen in Table 8.3, on both the distribution of temporary permits and especially on the allocation of *hukou* transfer in areas that are already heavily urbanized and over-populated.

Areas to which the state wishes to promote rural to urban migration can then lower the entry criteria for permanent *hukou* transfer and thus encourage migrants to settle there. *Hukou* status is a significant determinant of life opportunity in the city as non-*hukou* migrants with agricultural *hukou* status are generally relegated to the lower end of the economic employment spectrum. Migrants who obtain *hukou* transfer are significantly advantaged as they have the same political and economic rights as the local population. Therefore, the state has a powerful instrument by which to shape urbanization and population mobility processes. The following table sets out a selection of regulations that have been used by the state to provide incentives for potential migrants to settle in areas assigned by the state.

A series of regulations (Table 8.4) have also been designed to encourage migration of people with particular characteristics into highly sought after urban areas through *hukou* transfer. This began with the localization of *hukou* management in the late 1980s and early 1990s through the increasing advent of illegal *hukou* sales by local government and a series of Green/Blue Chop *Hukou*. Blue Chop *Hukou* were intermediary *hukou* close to permanent local *hukou* status and far above the temporary status most rural migrants are relegated to. Obtaining this type of *hukou* required significant investment in the urban area or employment skills deemed relevant to local development.

This was followed by a series of local moves to set out *hukou* transfer policies that encouraged the inward migration of not only party cadres, military personnel, and relatives of locals, as historically had been the case, but also the inward migration of talented employees, highly educated graduates, business entrepreneurs, and property owners. These competitive *hukou* transfer procedures act as an important development tool at the local government level and further show not only that the market shapes the migration and urbanization process in China but also

Table 8.4 Regulations encouraging urbanization from below

Year	Regulation
1984	State Council Notification Regarding the Problem of Nongmin Settling in Market Towns, *Guowuyuan guanyu nongmin jinru jizhen luohu wenti de tongzhi*
1997	Blueprint for Experiments in Small City and Town Huji Management Reform, *Xiaochengzhen huji guanli zhidu gaige shidian fangan*
2001	Recommendations Regarding Accelerating Reform of the Small City and Town Huji Management System, *Guanyu tuijin xiaochengzhen huji guanli zhidu gaige yijian de tongzhi*

that the state has the regulatory means to manage the Lewis transition through the *hukou* system.

In summary, the role of the *hukou* system in China is significant. Development specialists and economists need to pay more attention to the way it shapes urbanization and population mobility. The state has made significant efforts to manage the Lewis transition through the *hukou* system, in particular to stimulate economic growth through the creation of temporary permits and the targeted migration of citizens, to maintain stability through the surveillance and security of the population, to manage and direct the flow of urbanization through the creation of differing residency schemes for potential migrants, and to encourage migrants with particular skills or capital to transfer into local areas. The comparison with India, where the state does not directly manage the Lewis transition, and China, where the state is very effective at managing it, raises a series of questions relevant to development models for the early process of economic development in states with large rural populations.

6 The end of development models?

Finally, we return to the original question of development models in developing countries. The debates that pervaded the second half of last century focused on the role of government in economic development and led to a selection of development models being ascribed to the process of development, particularly in East Asia. This chapter has gone some way to showing that government regulation of urbanization and migration is also a means to influence economic development through the management of the Lewis transition.

In countries with large rural populations it is perhaps unsurprising to find a role for government in this transition. In China, the role has been lessening as the transition reaches the critical Lewisian turning point, though past results may make it hard for local government in particular to relinquish control over residency. In India, the role of government in the transition, while formally absent, informally remains important, and socio-cultural attitudes and norms act powerfully to shape the movement and residency of Indian citizens within the bounds of the nation-state. Overall, China is both more advanced as measured by the Lewis transition and the government more formally in control of the process.

The evidence collected here suggests a well-planned development strategy in China for managing the Lewis transition, while in India it is a more informal process. For India, the Lewis transition is controlled more through informal institutions and a strong cultural tendency hindering a large section of the poor in society from being able to urbanize and be socially mobile. In both cases evidence of the Lewis transition was found but China was found to be far closer to the Lewisian turning point than India. China has controlled population growth, targeted the transfer of labor from agricultural to non-agricultural employment, developed the secondary and tertiary sectors while maintaining strict residency criteria, and introducing a new sub-residency institutional tier. This suggests three things. First, the Lewis transition can be managed to some degree by government regulations and enforcement. Second, management of the Lewis transition favors prolonged and controlled economic growth in the early stages of development. Third, management of labor transfer in China and India does not represent a coherent model of development.

In countries with large rural populations, managing the early stages of the Lewis transition as the Chinese state has done with the *hukou* institution can be beneficial to macro-economic growth. By controlling population growth in particular, Chinese officials have shaped conditions more conducive to the mass movement of people from rural to urban areas. This movement has been guided and managed, reducing some of the more negative issues associated with rapid uncontrolled urbanization. However, this has not been without a cost. The creation of a new intermediary institutional status of "temporary residents" suggests the Lewis transition has been retarded, with present and future economic and political ramifications.

As the economy develops, such restrictive and blunt instruments create a danger of either dampening the political and economic vibrancy and dynamism so necessary for a developed economy or creating ideal conditions for social instability and regime change. In this sense, the *hukou* system should be seen as a temporary feature of development and plans should already have been made to liberalize the system to avoid firstly, political instability in the form of *nongmin* protests and civic disobedience, or secondly, in the form of a distorted and malfunctioning domestic market economy. Future economic development and political stability is premised on the ability of the state to liberalize mobility *and* residency in urban areas and to put in place policy that can help improve conditions in rural areas to reduce rural-urban disparity.

The opposite is true for India. Here informal practices manage migration and urbanization patterns. A corrupt bureaucracy increases the costs of movement and dissuades potential migrants from stimulating the urban economy. Social and cultural practices, especially in rural areas, still intervene in the Lewis transition by dissuading people from migrating outside of their kin networks or relegating migrants to employment based on these networks. The Indian government would do well to set up programs to encourage and guide rural to urban migration in order slowly to break down these informal practices.

Furthermore, as India is very much in the early stages of the Lewis transition, policy needs to address the continuing growth of the population. Uncontrolled population growth threatens the potential for future economic growth to transfer the majority of the rural underemployed into productive urban employment. Clearly India is developing and urban areas are growing, but at the same time India's rural areas continue to grow and population mobility is comparatively low. This is preventing India from making a speedier transition to modern economic arrangements. Efforts need to be made by government to, firstly, lower the birth rate in both rural and urban areas; secondly, to improve the health and education standards of the rural population; thirdly, to improve basic infrastructure, roads, railways, and communications to facilitate mobility; fourthly, to encourage rural to urban migration and population movement from one area to another; and finally, to direct this mobility to ensure rural workers can be productively integrated into the urban economy. These policy recommendations can be achieved without severely encroaching upon the fundamental rights of the Indian population.

These issues are important for debates on the process of development in India and China. At the heart of this debate is the larger question of what the relationship between development and governance is. Seemingly, there are no simple answers. What is clear is that authoritarianism is neither necessary nor sufficient for development (Bardhan 2009), thus rejecting the overall governance model of China. At the same time the argument that democracy is a prerequisite for development is also found to be untrue in this case. Further complicating the debate is the claim that while authoritarian countries can develop under un-democratic conditions, these states post-development will be faced with the choice to move towards democracy or face economic and political stagnation or chaos. The challenge of negotiating the Lewis transition can be met by both democratic and authoritarian governments so long as they effectively addresses the key challenges of reducing population growth, creating secondary and tertiary employment, and guiding the movement of underemployed rural laborers into urban secondary and tertiary industries, after which time the question of the form of government becomes more significant.

7 Conclusion

The Lewis transition remains an important challenge for developing economies with large "underemployment" in agriculture. There is a role for government in managing this transition, and in China this role has been performed through the *hukou* institution; in India, however, there is a marked absence of formal governance in this area. Instead, population mobility and urbanization are managed by informal institutional practices and cultural and social norms. In the early stages of economic development in countries with large rural populations, it is advantageous for the state to play a developmental role by managing population growth and mobility. China has both a far more restrictive model of population growth and mobility and a higher degree of economic development and rate of urbanization. India has a good level of economic development and a steady growth of urban areas, but is not transitioning as rapidly due to continued growth in rural areas and a general lack of population mobility. It is suggested that China's current management of labor transfer is, however, only applicable temporarily, for as the Lewisian turning point is reached and wages start to rise, such a restrictive approach to the management of labor flows can become an impediment to further economic development through distortions in the market or political instability as citizens struggle for equality of civic rights. For India, increased government intervention in population growth and mobility is required.

The cases of India and China show that states can approach the challenges of negotiating the Lewis Transition in a variety of ways and that these methods can also change considerably over time. Such divergent strategies reflect the complex array of economic, political, and cultural conditions of each country at any given time. As both India and China are experiencing rapid economic growth and development, it would be overly constricting to try to contain the complexity of developmental experience to a single development model alone. Instead, it is more productive to analyze what strategies work well for which countries under what conditions through a comparative developmental approach.

Notes

1. US GDP (PPP) in 1980 (2.788) and 2010 (14.658); China GDP (PPP) in 1980 (0.248) and 2010 (10.086); India GDP (PPP) in 1980 (0.288) and 2010 (3.645) – trillions.

2. People's Republic of China Hukou Registration Regulations, *Zhonghua renmin gonghe guo hukou dengji tiaoli* (1958).
3. *nongye hukou* and *fei nongye hukou.*
4. The major benefit being farming the plot of land allocated by the state.
5. This is still 100 million higher than India's urban population. Note: some non-agricultural *hukou* holders live in rural areas, such as village cadres or as schoolteachers.

9

China's Economic Growth Engine: The Likely Types of Hardware Failure, Software Failure, and Power Supply Failure

Wing Thye Woo

1 The bust in doom-and-gloom talk (so far)

Predictions of doom and gloom for China have a long tradition among China economists. For example, in the mid-1990s, Nicholas Lardy of the Peterson Institute for International Economics started highlighting the de facto insolvency of the Chinese banking system with the implication that a bank run leading to financial sector collapse, which would then be likely to send the economy into a tailspin, was a strong possibility in the medium term.[1] The twenty-first century began with the claim by Gordon Chang (2001) that China's imminent accession to the World Trade Organization (WTO) would cause such widespread unemployment within China's already alienated population that China's economic and political systems would collapse.

These two dire predictions have turned out to be wrong. China, in fact, accelerated its annual GDP growth to double-digit rates after 2001. Nicholas Lardy was wrong because while the banks were indeed bankrupt, the Chinese government, which owned them, was not bankrupt and could hence afford to bail out the banks when necessary. The fiscal strength of the government made it irrational for depositors to contemplate a bank run. Gordon Chang was wrong because the WTO membership quickened the pace of job creation in China by greatly increasing the volume of FDI inflow. The WTO membership made China more attractive to FDI because it guaranteed the access of Chinese goods to the US market by eliminating the need for China to get the most-favored-nation (MFN) status annually from the US Congress (McKibbin and Woo 2003).

The most recent literature on China's future growth has once again become pessimistic. One of the most astute of China analysts, Minxin

Pei (2006a), has argued that China is now in a *trapped transition* that is described as "a transformative phase in which half-finished reforms have transferred power to new, affluent elites" (Pei 2006b) who are using crony capitalism to generate high economic growth that is not sustainable. Pei felt that meaningful reform to ensure continued high growth was improbable.[2]

Pei's pessimism about the inevitable exhaustion of China's growth momentum is shared by another leading China scholar, Yasheng Huang (2008). In Huang's contrarian assessment, China in 1999 was actually less capitalistic than China in 1989. He asserted that the administration of Jiang Zemin and Zhu Rongji, which ended in March 2003, had reversed the march toward capitalism by systematically promoting the growth of large state-owned firms in the urban areas and suppressing the activities of the privately owned small and medium firms in the countryside. Huang has attributed the deterioration in income distribution across classes and across regions to this re-occupation of the commanding heights of the economy by state-controlled companies, often in cahoots with foreign private companies, and the intensification of discrimination against the domestic private firms. Huang believes that the state-controlled firms are intrinsically less innovative than the domestic private firms, and he therefore concludes that China is unlikely to be able to move on to the next stage of economic development in the near future, at least not before India does so.[3]

2 The road to prosperity might not be a smooth one

This long tradition of forecasting doom and gloom about China is really quite surprising because China's economy has been like a speeding car for almost 30 years. Hence, not surprisingly, it is becoming more common to hear glowingly optimistic assessments of China's future than dismissively pessimistic ones. For example, Jim O'Neill, Dominic Wilson, Roopa Purushothaman and Anna Stupnytska (2005) of Goldman Sachs have predicted that, even should China's GDP growth rate slow down steadily from its average annual of 10 percent in the 1979–2005 period to 3.8 percent in the 2030–40 period China's GDP would surpass that of the United States in 2040.[4]

I think that a good guide to how one should regard the new optimism and the traditional pessimism is found in the discussions of the sixth Plenum of the 16th Central Committee of the Communist Party of China (CPC), which concluded on October 11, 2006. The sixth Plenum passed a resolution to commit the CPC to establishing a harmonious society by 2020. The obvious implication from this commitment is that the present major social, economic, and political trends within China might not lead to a harmonious society or, at least, not lead to a harmonious society fast enough.

Among the disharmonious features mentioned in the fifth paragraph of the "resolutions of the CPC Central Committee on Major Issues Regarding the Building of a Harmonious Socialist Society" were a serious imbalance in the social and economic development across, and within each of, China's provinces; worsening population and environmental problems; grossly inadequate social safety nets, and medical care system; and serious corruption. The harmonious socialist society proposed by the sixth Plenum would encompass a democratic society under the rule of law; a society based on equality and justice; an honest and caring society; a stable, vigorous, and orderly society; and a society in which humans live in harmony with nature.

What is the origin of the CPC's decision to change its primary focus from "economic construction" to "social harmony"? And why include a target date of 2020? I believe that this switch in emphasis from "economic construction" to "social harmony" occurs because the Hu–Wen leadership is well aware that the political legitimacy of CPC rule rests largely on maintaining, first, an economic growth rate that is high enough to keep unemployment low; and, second, a growth pattern that diffuses the additional income widely enough. Specifically, the Hu–Wen leadership recognizes that without accelerated institutional reforms and new major policy initiatives on a broad front, the 1978–2005 policy framework, which had produced an average annual GDP growth rate of almost 10 percent, is at odds with environmental sustainability and with international concerns about China's persistent trade imbalances. More importantly, unless their new policies could produce significant improvements in social harmony by 2020, social instability would reduce China's economic growth, hence making the leadership of CPC in Chinese politics unsustainable.

To return to the analogy of China's economy being like a speeding car, the Hu–Wen leadership saw that that car could crash in the near future because there were several high-probability failures that might occur and cause an economic collapse. To be specific, there are three classes of failures that could occur: hardware failure, software failure, and power supply failure.

A hardware failure refers to the breakdown of an *economic mechanism*, a development that is analogous to the collapse of the chassis of the car. Probable hardware failures include a banking crisis that causes a credit crunch that, in turn, dislocates production economy-wide, and a budget crisis that necessitates reductions in important infrastructure and social expenditure, and possibly generates high inflation, and balance of payments difficulties as well.

A *software failure* refers to a flaw in *governance* that creates frequent widespread social disorders that disrupt production economy-wide and discourage private investment. This situation is similar to a car crash that resulted from a fight among the people inside the speeding car. Software failures could come from the present high-growth strategy creating sufficient inequality and corruption to, in turn, generate severe social unrest, which dislocates economic activities; and the state not being responsive enough to rising social expectations, hence causing social disorder.

A *power supply failure* refers to the economy being unable to move forward because it hits either *a natural limit or an externally-imposed limit,* a situation that is akin, respectively, to the car running out of gas or to the car smashing into a barrier erected by an outsider. Examples of power supply failures are an environmental collapse, for example climate change, and a collapse in China's exports because of a trade war. In a sense, the repair of a power supply failure is more difficult than either the repair of a hardware failure or the repair of a software failure because a large part of the repair has to be undertaken in collaboration with other countries. For example, the lowering of trade barriers requires China to negotiate with other countries; and the reversal of environmental damage could require an advance in scientific understanding, an outcome that is more likely to occur when the entire scientific talent in China and the rest of the world is focused on the task.

The discussion of the many events that could make China's high growth unsustainable is beyond the scope of this chapter. I will limit my discussion to one or two of the most likely precipitating events in each class of failures. Section 3 identifies the weakening of China's fiscal position by nonperforming loans in the state banks as the likely type of hardware failure that would occur. Section 4 discusses the outbreak of social disorder as the likely type of software failure. For power supply failures, I think that the two most likely ones are (a) the erection of trade barriers against China's exports, to be discussed in Sections 5; and (b) an environmental collapse, especially a shortage of water, to be discussed in Section 6.

3 Fiscal stress from the state-owned banks could cause hardware failure

Among doomsayers, one favorite mechanism for the forthcoming collapse of an economy is the inevitable fiscal crisis of the state. What is noteworthy is that this fiscal mechanism is used by doomsayers of all stripes. James O'Connor (1973), a Marxist economist, predicted that the dynamics of capitalist America would precipitate a fiscal crisis that would destabilize the economy completely. In turn, Gordon Chang (2001), a capitalist lawyer, predicted that a fiscal crisis could be the triggering event in the unavoidable disintegration of socialist China.

This fixation of the doomsayers upon a large negative fiscal shock as a totally destructive systemic shock is understandable because fiscal imbalance is the proximate cause in most crises. The reason is that the state budget is often faced with the task of defusing the cumulative tensions unleashed by deeper, more fundamental social processes. To a first approximation, fiscal capacity is a fundamental determinant of system stability because economic sustainability depends on the ability to cover production costs, and political viability depends on the ability to reward one's supporters and to pay off one's enemies.

The reality in many cases is that fiscal sustainability is the prerequisite for both economic sustainability and political viability, and that economic sustainability and political viability are intricately linked and mutually reinforcing. To see the mutual interdependence of the two, one has only to recall the many times that near-bankrupt governments have been driven out of power after raising the prices of a subsidized item like food, petrol, or foreign exchange.[5] One could indeed go so far as to say that the degree of economic and political resilience of a state can be measured by the state's ability to cover an unexpected, prolonged increase in expenditure or an unanticipated, protracted shortfall in revenue.

An OECD (2006) report has raised grave concerns about China's fiscal management. Specifically:

> China's officially reported spending figures reflect only about three-quarters of total government spending. Extra-budgetary spending, social security outlays and central government bond financing of local projects are not part of the official budget. Notwithstanding recent reforms, the government remains overly exposed to extra-budget and off-budget activities, which make public expenditures difficult to plan and control and which impair their accountability

> and transparency. Contingent liabilities have been a major source of unplanned spending and pose perhaps the greatest risk to the controllability of future expenditure.
>
> (OECD 2006: 10)

The fact that fiscal sustainability is central to economic management can be seen in the two fiscal targets that the original Growth and Stability Pact of the countries in the Euro-Zone specified for its members to meet: that the consolidated government budget deficit should not exceed 3 percent of GDP except in case of unusually severe downturn; and that the debt-GDP ratio should be brought down to 60 percent or lower.

Table 9.1 gives an international perspective on the fiscal situation in China by comparing it with those in the OECD countries. I chose the year 2001 for China because I want to postpone until later the discussion on the fiscal consequences of the ongoing recapitalization of the state-owned banks (SOBs). I use the year 2003 for OECD because the cross-country data were conveniently available for this year.[6] Table 9.1 reports that China's official debt-GDP ratio was 16.4 percent, which compared very favorably with the OECD average of 75.3 percent. If the tiny state of Luxembourg is treated as an exception and excluded from the comparison, then the lower half of the OECD distribution of debt-GDP ratios ranges from 18.6 percent (South Korea) to 55.5 percent (Denmark); and the upper half of the distribution ranges from 58.1 percent (Hungary) to 154 percent (Japan).

As China's debt-GDP ratio of 16.4 percent is below the 18.6 percent of South Korea, and China's annual budget deficit has almost always been below three percent of GDP, it would seem that China has a sounder fiscal situation than all the OECD countries. Such an impression needs to be qualified, however. Many analysts have noted that China's official debt-GDP ratio understates the extent of China's fiscal burden because it does not include the nonperforming loans in the SOBs that the state would have to take over during recapitalization, and it does not include many contingent liabilities, for example pension schemes of state enterprises that the state would have to assume responsibility for in order to preserve economic and social stability. Citigroup (2002), for example, has estimated that the cost for SOB recapitalization was 46.9 percent of GDP, social security obligations was 26.1 percent, and external debts were 15.6 percent.

Part II of Table 9.1 uses estimates from Citigroup (2002) and Fan (2003) to revise China's official debt-GDP ratio. The outcomes are

Table 9.1 Comparative perspective on the size of China's national debt as % of GDP

	General government gross financial liabilities		**Total tax revenue**	
	1995	**2003**	**1995**	**2003**
(I) OECD's Fiscal Situation				
Luxembourg	6.7	6.7	42.3	41.3
Korea	5.5	18.6	19.4	25.3
Australia	43.4	18.9	29.8	31.6
Ireland	81.2	31.1	32.8	29.7
New Zealand	51.7	32.0	36.9	34.9
Iceland	59.4	41.4	32.1	39.8
United Kingdom	52.7	41.9	35.1	35.6
Czech Republic	19.3	46.8	37.5	37.7
Slovak Republic	n.a.	49.7	n.a.	31.1
Norway	40.5	50.4	41.1	43.4
Finland	65.1	52.0	46.0	44.8
Poland	n.a.	52.1	37.0	34.2
Spain	68.8	54.8	31.8	34.9
Denmark	77.6	55.5	49.5	48.3
Hungary	n.a	58.1	42.4	38.5
Sweden	82.2	59.8	48.5	50.6
Netherlands	87.0	61.9	41.9	38.8
United States	74.2	63.4	27.9	25.6
Germany	55.8	64.6	37.2	35.5
Portugal	69.9	66.6	33.6	37.1
Austria	69.6	69.4	41.1	43.1
France	62.6	71.7	42.9	43.4
Canada	100.8	75.7	35.6	33.8
Belgium	135.2	103.2	44.8	45.4
Greece	108.7	108.8	32.4	35.7
Italy	125.5	121.4	41.2	43.1
Japan	87.0	154.0	26.7	25.3
OECD total	72.8	75.3	35.7	36.3

(II) China's Fiscal Situation

	Debt-GDP (%)	**Revenue-GDP (%)**		
	2001	**1995**	**2001**	**2008**
Official data	16.4	10.7	16.8	20.5

	Revised debt-GDP ratio in 2001 after taking into account:	
	(a) 2nd recapitalisation costs	**(b) all contingent liabilities**
Citigroup (2002)	65.9	114.9
Fan (2003)	57.4	74.7

OECD data from: http://stats.oecd.org/wbos/viewhtml.aspx?QueryName=2&QueryType=View&Lang=en.

China revenue data for 1995 and 2001 are from China Statisctical Yearbook 2005, and revenue estimate for 2007 is from Deutsche Bank (2009).

that China's debt-GDP ratio is 57.4 to 65.9 percent when only SOB recapitalization is undertaken; and 74.7 to 114.9 percent when all contingent liabilities are recognized. This change in China's debt-GDP ratio moves China from the bottom of the OECD distribution to the top half of the distribution; and, in the worst case scenario, puts China in the group of the five OECD countries with the highest ratios; 74.7 to 114.9 percent for China vs. 75.7 percent for Canada, 103.2 percent for Belgium, 108.8 percent for Greece, 121.4 percent for Italy, and 154 percent for Japan.

Should the much higher revised debt-GDP ratio raise concern about China's fiscal sustainability? Our cautious reading of the evidence is that a fiscal crisis is not imminent in China. China's ratio not only falls within the OECD experience, its worst-case ratio of 114.9 percent is still lower than Italy. Most importantly, China's ratio is still substantially lower than the highest OECD ratio of 154 percent, Japan.

While I believe China's fiscal regime to be sustainable, there are two fiscal features that have rendered the fiscal system vulnerable to a crisis. The first fiscal feature is that China has a lower capacity to service its public debt than all the OECD countries. While China's revenue-GDP ratio has increased rapidly from 10.7 percent in 1995 to 16.8 percent in 2001 and to an expected 20.5 percent in 2008, the 2008 level is still too low by OECD standards. The average revenue-GDP ratio in the OECD in 2003 was 36.3 percent, with the three lowest ratios (25.3% for Japan and South Korea, and 25.6% for the United States) higher than China's. While China's best-case debt-GDP ratio of 57.4 to 65.9 percent puts it in the same group as Denmark (55.5%), Hungary (58.1%), Sweden (59.8%), and the Netherlands (61.9%), China's revenue-GDP ratio is only 20.5 percent compared with Denmark's 48.3 percent, Hungary's 38.5 percent, Sweden's 50.6 percent, and the Netherlands' 38.8 percent. For the OECD countries with debt-GDP ratios that are similar to China's worst-case debt-GDP ratio of 74.7 to 114.9 percent, all of them also have higher revenue-GDP ratios: 20.5 percent for China vs. 33.8 percent for Canada, 45.4 percent for Belgium, 35.7 percent for Greece, and 43.1 percent for Italy.

The important point about this first fiscal feature is that, as China's public debt rises from 16.4 percent of GDP to 74.7 percent with the incremental assumption of the contingent liabilities, the state will have to reduce expenditure steadily to accommodate the additional debt service unless there is an increase in state revenue.

The second fiscal feature that renders China vulnerable to a fiscal crisis is the constant need to recapitalize the SOBs. In 1998–9, the government injected new capital into China's banks and transferred a large proportion of the NPLs to the state-owned asset management corporations (AMCs), in order to raise the capital adequacy ratio (CAR) of the four largest state-owned banks, commonly referred to as the Big Four,[7] from 4.4 percent at the end of 1996 to over 8 percent at the end of 1998. However, the rapid appearance of new NPLs after 1998 has lowered the average CAR of the Big Four to 5 percent by the beginning of 2002.

The outcome was that China undertook a second round of recapitalization of the SOBs in 2003. Some unorthodox methods were used. For example, in late 2003, Bank of China and China Construction Bank received a capital injection US$22.5 billion each from the foreign reserves of the People's Bank of China.[8] The results of this second recapitalization, and the rapid expansion of loans in the last two years, is that the NPL ratio has improved, and the CAR of the Big Four was about 8 percent respectively at the end of 2004.

The important question is how many more rounds of bank recapitalization can China afford without generating a fiscal crisis? The simple fact is that fiscal sustainability lies at the heart of whether a banking crisis would actually occur. As long as the state is perceived to be able and willing to bail out the SOBs, depositors would retain their confidence in the SOBs regardless of the actual state of their balance sheets. Since the stock of publicly acknowledged government debt in 2004 is only about 33 percent of GDP, it is usual to hear official assurances that the current fiscal deficits of less than 2 percent of GDP do not pose a problem for debt servicing by the state.[9] However, the current value of the debt-GDP ratio is not a good indicator of the sustainability of the existing fiscal policy regime; a better indicator would involve working out the evolution of the debt-GDP ratio over time.

To put the issue formally, the evolution of the debt-GDP ratio is given by:

$$d\,(\ln[Debt/GDP]) \,/\, d\,t = r + [GDP/Debt]\cdot[f + b] - y$$

where

r = *real interest rate on government debt*

f = *primary fiscal deficit rate*

= *[state expenditure excluding debt service – state revenue] / GDP*

b = *NPL creation rate*

= *[change in NPL in SOBs] / GDP*

y = *trend growth rate of real GDP*

As long as $y > r$, then the debt-GDP ratio will have a steady-state value that is nonzero when sum of $(f + b) > 0$. Specifically,

$$(Debt/GDP)_{steady\text{-}state} = (f + b) \;/\; (y - r) \text{ when } y > r$$

China appears to belong to this case because its post-1978 annual growth rate has averaged 9.4 percent; its growth rate in the next ten years is likely to be above 8 percent; and the real interest rate has been about 4 percent. For the generation of likely future scenarios, I will make the conservative assumptions that y is 8 percent, f is 1 percent, and r is 6 percent.[10] It is difficult to predict b, the rate that banks would generate NPLs, because it depends on the type of banking reform undertaken. If no meaningful reforms are undertaken, then b is likely to remain at the historic value of 6 percent.

So conditional on the effectiveness of reforming the SOBs, the steady-state ratio is:

$$(Debt/GDP)_{steady\text{-}state} = 350 \textit{ percent when } b = 6 \textit{ percent}$$
$$(Debt/GDP)_{steady\text{-}state} = 200 \textit{ percent when } b = 3 \textit{ percent}$$
$$(Debt/GDP)_{steady\text{-}state} = 100 \textit{ percent when } b = 1 \textit{ percent}$$

The noteworthy finding from the above scenarios is that China will produce a level of $(Debt/GDP)_{steady\text{-}state}$ that is high by international experience despite the optimistic assumptions that long-run growth rate is 8 percent, that b will be lowered from 6 percent of GDP to 1 percent. The most optimistic outcome is still two thirds larger than what the European Union has set to be the "safe" debt-GDP target (60%) for its members. The banking system has made China vulnerable to a fiscal crisis, even though there is a theoretical steady-state level for the debt-GDP ratio. Of course, the creation of NPLs cannot be attributed entirely to the SOBs. Their chief customers, the embezzlement-ridden and inefficiency-ridden SOEs,[11] deserve an equal share of the blame.

The important point from this second fiscal feature is that the present ongoing recapitalization of the SOBs is the last time that the government can afford to recapitalize the SOBs, and possibly the last time that the government can do so without upsetting confidence in the financial markets about the soundness of China's fiscal regime.

Now, how difficult is it to stop losses in the SOBs in order to ensure fiscal sustainability? The solution lies in imposing a hard budget constraint on the SOBs. SOB managers have to be convinced that the present recapitalization is indeed the last free supper, which the 1998 recapitalization was announced to be, and that their compensation and promotion will depend only on the profitability of the SOBs relative to the profitability of private banks.

At the same time, the prudential supervision and monitoring of bank operations will have to be strengthened to prevent asset stripping and discourage reckless investments fostered by the asymmetrical reward system under the soft budget constraint.[12] The operations of SOBs could be further improved by bringing in foreign strategic investors who would be part of the management team, and by removing the influence of the local governments on bank operations.

One additional way to harden the budget constraint faced by the SOBs is to privatize some of their branches, and use the performance of the new private banks to gauge the performance of the remaining SOBs. The privatization of some branches will also help convince the SOB managers that the government is indeed serious about the present SOB recapitalization indeed being the last free supper.

The NPL ratio has stayed low since the second round of recapitalization in 2003. It is, hence, more frequent now to hear claims that the SOBs have improved their internal incentives and risk assessment ability so much that large NPL ratios are a thing of the past. I think, however, that it is premature to pronounce victory on SOB reform because the 2003–8 period has been one of high growth.

The very aggressive fiscal-monetary policy mix undertaken by the government to combat the Global Finance Crisis that hit China at the end of the third quarter of 2008 may yet create a large amount of bad bank loans. The sharp export decline brought GDP growth in 2008:4Q down to 1.5 percent from the double-digit growth rates in the first three quarters. The resulting drop in demand for production financing caused bank loans to fall by 9.8 percent in November 2008.

The Chinese government responded with a fiscal stimulus of 4 trillion RMB that was undertaken in 2009–10, an annual stimulus of about 7 percent of GDP. Monetary easing has been even more dramatic. The annualized growth rate of bank loans in the November 2006 to December 2008 period was in the range of –9.8 percent of 43.6 percent, with an average growth rate of 16.2 percent. Since December 2008, the credit quotas have been relaxed and bank managers have been encouraged to lend generously. The result has been a quantum leap in bank lending in 2009. Bank loans increased 89 percent in January 2009, 48 percent in February 2009, and 94 percent in March 2009. It might be too naive believe that this recent rapid increase in bank lending in such a short period would not lead to the emergence of a large amount of NPLs in the future.[13]

4 Flaws in governance could cause software failure

The satisfactory functioning of a market economy requires a wide array of regulatory institutions that range from straightforward law-and-order administration to complicated legal adjudication that would, for example, have the prerequisite scientific understanding to determine whether a patent case involves real technological innovation or not. China's strategy of incremental reform combined with the fact that institution building is a time-consuming process meant that many of its regulatory institutions are either absent or ineffective. The results have been governance failures on many fronts, of which the most well-known recent examples are the violations against the welfare of consumers and workers.

There have been significant regulatory failures in keeping China's food supply and pharmaceutical products safe. The misuse of chemicals to lower production costs has resulted in the addition of poisonous substitutes into toothpaste (*NYT* 2007: May 22, July 1), cough medicine (*NYT* 2007: May 6), and animal feed (*NYT* 2007: April 20, May 9); the application of lead paint to children toys (*NYT* 2007: June 19; FT 2007: August 2);[14] and the over-employment of antifungals and antibacterials in fish farming (*NYT* 2007: June 29, July 3). Most of these above abuses received enormous attention because these items were exported to other countries and their harmful effects were reported widely in the international press.[15] Clearly, Chinese consumers have been suffering much more from such types of malfeasance, the scope of which has not been realized because of the considerable press censorship in China (*NYT* 2007: June 5).

Dereliction in duty by government officials is the fundamental reason for such governance failures. The most well known recent case was the conviction of Zheng Xiaoyu, the former director of China's Food and Drug Safety Agency, for accepting bribes to approve production licenses for pharmaceutical companies and food companies. Such dereliction in official oversight has resulted in

> [t]ens of thousands of people ...[being] sickened or killed every year as a result of rampant counterfeiting of drugs, and tainted and substandard food and drugs. For instance, last year 11 people died in China with an injection tainted by a poisonous chemical. Six people died and 80 others fell ill after taking an antibiotic that had been produced ... with a substandard disinfectant. Small drug makers in China have long been accused of manufacturing phony or

> substandard drugs and marketing them to the nation's hospitals and pharmaceutical companies. And mass poisonings involved tainted food products are common.
>
> (*NYT* 2007: May 30, July 13)

There have also been significant regulatory failures in the treatment of labor, especially in the areas of occupational safety and wage payments. One of the most recent horrifying accounts involved forced labor of kidnapped children in the brick kilns of Shanxi and Henan provinces (*China Daily* 2007: June 16).[16] The official *China Daily* reported, "as many as 1000 children may have been sold into slave labor in central China" (*China Daily* 2007: June 15). This deplorable affair was exposed partly "because of an open letter posted online by a group of 400 fathers appealing for help in tracking missing sons they believed were sold to kiln boss" (*NYT* 2007: June 18). A parent visiting the brick kilns in her quest to find her son found that the local police were not only unwilling to help but also demanded bribes instead (*NYT* 2007: June 16). In one case, the brick kiln was owned by the son of the village Party secretary (*NYT* 2007: June 18).

Perhaps the two most dismaying revelations from the news reports on the brick kiln slavery are that this sad state of affairs had been going on for a decade;[17] and the "forced labor and sexual exploitation have increased as the trend in human trafficking in China has taken a turn for the worst" (*China Daily* 2007: July 27). Yin Jianzhong, the senior official at the Ministry of Public Security who identified the worsening trend in human trafficking in China, recognized a reason for the negative development to be "the loopholes in the legal and labor systems ... [Specifically,] the Criminal Law on human trafficking protects women and children only and leaves out grown-up and teen males. It doesn't have provisions for punishing those trafficking people for forced labor or prostitution" (*China Daily* 2007: July 27). The fact that such legal loopholes exist supports our contention that the main cause behind the administrative failures in China is the "dereliction of duty by government officials."[18]

Inadequate institutions of governance are not the only cause of social tensions in China, however. The present economic development strategy, despite its ability to generate high growth, also generates high social tensions because, in the last ten years, it has had great difficulties in reducing extreme poverty further and in improving significantly the rural-urban income distribution and the regional income distribution; see Woo, Li, Yue, Wu, and Xu (2004), and Démurger, Sachs, Woo, Bao,

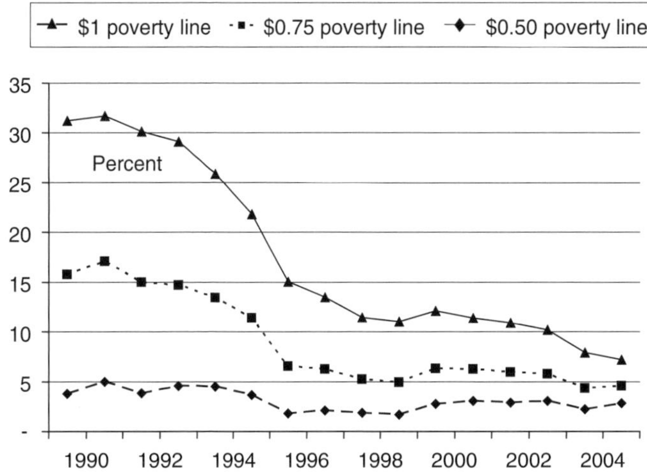

Figure 9.1 Proportion of rural population below poverty rate line

Chang, and Mellinger (2002). As seen in Figure 10.2,[19] in the first half of the 1990s, the \$1 poverty rate[20] dropped rapidly from 31.3 percent in 1990 to 15.0 percent in 1996. But in the following six years, the decline was only 5 percentage points. The \$1 poverty rate stayed in the 10–12 percent rate in the 1998–2003 period even though the GDP growth rate averaged 8.5 percent annually. It was only after the sustained large-scale effort to develop western China began in 2001 and the post-2002 rise in the GDP growth rate to 10 percent or higher that the \$1 poverty rate dropped to 7.9 percent in 2004 and then to 7.2 percent in 2005.

However, the progress in poverty alleviation in the last decade is considerably much less impressive when the poverty line is lowered. The \$0.75 poverty rate stayed unchanged from 1998 (4.6%) to 2005 (4.2%); and the \$0.50 poverty rate actually increased from 1.9 percent in 1998 to 2.8 percent in 2005. In short, the higher growth rate in the 2003–5 period did not cause income to trickle down to the poorest 5 percent of the rural population, and hence caused income inequality to worsen.

In the 1985–7 period, China's Gini coefficient was below 0.3.[21] According to a report in the official *China Daily* in June 2005:

> China's income gap widened in the first quarter of the year [2005], with 10 percent of the nation's richest people enjoying 45 percent of the country's wealth ... China's poorest 10 percent had only 1.4 percent of the nation's wealth ... No precise Gini coefficient was

> provided [by the state statistical agency], but state press reports in recent weeks said the value was more than 0.48 and approaching 0.5 ... Most developed European nations tend to have coefficients of between 0.24 and 0.36, while the United States has been above 0.4 for several decades.
>
> (*China Daily* 2006: June 19)

The Asian Development Bank (2007) recently conducted a study of income inequality in 22 Asian countries over the 1992–2004 period. For 2004, only Nepal had a Gini coefficient (47.30%) that was higher than China's (47.25). However, in 2004, China's income ratio of the richest 20 percent to the poorest 20 percent (11.37) was the highest in Asia; significantly higher than the next highest income ratio (9.47 for Nepal). China is probably the most unequal country in Asia today.

Table 9.2 presents the income inequality in China within the international context. China's income inequality today is generally lower than that in Latin America but generally higher than that in Africa. The steady increase in China's income inequality since 1985 raises the possibility that China is heading toward the Latin American degree of income inequality.

Table 9.2 China's income inequality across time and space

		Gini Coefficients		**Income Ratio of Top 20%/Bottom 20%**	
	Period	**Initial Year**	**Final Year**	**Initial Year**	**Final Year**
Nepal	1995–2003	37.65	47.30	6.19	9.47
China	1993–2004	40.74	47.25	7.57	11.37
India	1993–2004	32.89	36.22	4.85	5.52
Indonesia	1993–2002	34.37	34.30	5.20	5.13
Taipei,China	1993–2003	31.32	33.85	5.41	6.05
South Korea	1993–2004	28.68	31.55	4.38	5.47
Japan	1993	24.90		3.37	
Colombia	2003		58.60		25.30
Brazil	2004		56.99		23.00
Cote d'Ivoire	2002		44.60		9.70
Nigeria	2003		43.60		9.80
United States	2000		39.42		8.45
United Kingdom	2002		34.37		5.59

Sources: Asian Development Bank (2007) and UNDP (2006).

Doing more of the same economic policies in today's China will not produce the same salubrious results of quick reduction in poverty and slow increase in inequality as in the early phases of economic reform. The reason is that the development problems have changed. In the first phase of economic development, the provision of more jobs, through economic deregulation, was enough to lower poverty significantly. At the present, many of the people who are still poor require more than just job opportunities, they need an infusion of assistance, for example empowering them with human capital through education and health interventions, first in order to be able to take up these job opportunities. Effective governance for equitable growth has now become even more challenging, and so the probability of improving social harmony has been diminished.

Furthermore, the present mode of economic development also generates immense opportunities for the embezzlement of state assets, seizure of farmlands for industrial development, and corruption because of the absence of effective mechanisms to supervise government employees (see Woo 2001). These features certainly make social harmony hard to sustain.

The data on social unrest are consistent with the hypothesis of rising social disharmony. First, the incidence of public disorder, labeled "social incidents," has risen steadily from 8700 in 1993 to 32,500 in 1999 and then to 74,000 in 2004. Second, the average number of persons in a mass incident has also risen greatly, from eight in 1993 to 50 in 2004.[22] It should be noted, however, that these numbers might not portray accurately the degree to which social unrest has increased because the data include disco brawls and gambling den raids as well as social protests.

Clearly, the number of mass incidents would have been lower if China had better governance. There would have been more pre-emptive efforts at conflict mediation by the government and less abuse of power by government officials if the government's actions had been monitored closely by an independent mechanism and the government had also been held more accountable for its performance.

One main source of recent social unrest in rural China has been the conversion of farm land to industrial parks without adequate compensation to the farmers. It is interesting therefore that the No. 1 Document issued jointly in January 2006 by the CPC Central Committee and the State Council pledged not only to "stabilize and regulate the transfer of land-use rights and accelerate land acquisition reforms," but also to "expand channels to express public opinions in the countryside and improve the mechanism to resolve social conflicts" (*SCMP* 2007: January 30).[23]

The desire by the Hu–Wen leadership to improve the institutions of governance is also borne out by the following report from the *South China Morning Post* about what Premier Wen said when he met a group of Chinese citizens in Japan in April 2007 (*SCMP* April 16, 2007):

> During 30 minutes of impromptu remarks, he said the key to pursuing social justice, the mainland's most important task, was to "let people be masters of their houses and make every cadre understand that power is invested in them by the people."
>
> Although he did not deviate from the official line and spoke informally on both occasions, Mr. Wen is known for being careful about what he says, whether in prepared remarks or speaking off the cuff. The fact that he highlighted, in the presence of Hong Kong and overseas journalists, the need for political reform is uncharacteristic and interesting; particularly in the context of the leadership reshuffle looming at the Communist Party's 17th congress later this year.
>
> There have been signs that the leadership under President Hu Jintao is under increasing pressure to undertake drastic political reforms to consolidate the party's grip on power and stamp out widespread corruption.

While there are reasonable grounds for an analyst to doubt either the sincerity of Premier Wen's words or his ability to act on them, the analyst cannot doubt that Premier Wen is at least aware that democracy is one way to solve many of China's problems of governance. The embrace of the Harmonious Society program by the Hu–Wen leadership reveals CPC's acknowledgement that democracy, rule of law, and a stable income distribution comprise an indivisible combination that is necessary to ensure the social stability that will keep the economy on the high growth path to catch up with the United States, a vision that acts as the bedrock of CPC's legitimacy to rule.

5 The first likely type of power supply failure is trade protectionism

China's emergence as a major trading nation has been accompanied by increasing conflicts with the European Union and the United States about China's trading practices and its exchange rate policy. The dissatisfaction over trade with China is evident from the following two press reports:

> Peter Mandelson, the EU trade commissioner ... called various aspects of China's trade policy "illogical", "indefensible" and "unacceptable" and accused [China] of doing nothing to rein in rampant counterfeiting ... Mr. Mandelson also refused to grant China market economy status ... [because it has] fulfilled [only] one of five criteria.
>
> (*FT* 2007: June 13)

> After years of inconclusive skirmishing, trade tensions between the United States and China are about to intensify ... "We are competing not only with a country with low wages but with very high and heavy subsidies and a rigging of their currency ..." says Rep. Sander Levin, D-Mich, chairman of the House Trade Subcommittee ..." I hate the term trade war because it is always used when you try to get a fair break ...," he says: "Sometimes pressure works."
>
> (*US Today* 2007: June 13)

While the trade deficit is many times identified as the cause of the trade tension, the true cause is the ongoing large shift in the international division of labor that has been set in motion by the post-1990 acceleration of globalization and by the continued fast pace of technological innovations. The next two sections will set out the case that the trade tensions reflect, one, the pains of structural adjustment in the United States because of its very inadequate social safety nets (Section 5a); and, two, the dysfunctional nature of China's financial system (Section 5b).

a Trade protectionism against China created by defects in the US economy

It is not uncommon to encounter allegations that the bilateral US–China trade deficit represented the export of unemployment from China to the United States, and that it lowered the wage for labor. These allegations are not supported by the facts, however. Table 10.3 shows that the steady rise in the trade deficit from 1.2 percent of GDP in 1996 to 5.9 percent in 2006 was accompanied by a fall in the civilian unemployment rate from 5.4 percent in 1996 to 4.6 percent in 2006, and by a rise in the total compensation, measured in 2005 prices, received by a full-time worker from $48,175 in 1996 to $55,703 in 2005.[24]

What is fueling the resentment toward imports from China when the median US worker is experiencing neither more unemployment nor lower compensation? The explanation is that the US worker is feeling more insecure in the 2000s than in the 1980s because of the faster turnover in employment. Globalization and technological innovations have required the worker to change jobs more often and he finds that there are considerable costs associated with the job change because of the inadequacies of the US social safety nets.

The more frequent change in jobs is documented in Table 9.3 by the declining trend in the length of the median job tenure for older male workers. The median job tenure for males in the:

> *33 to 44 age group*, decreased from 7.0 years in 1987 to 5.1 years in 2006;
>
> *45 to 54 age group*, decreased from 11.8 years in 1987 to 8.1 years in 2006; and
>
> *55 to 64 age group*, decreased from 14.5 years in 1987 to 9.5 years in 2006.

Table 9.3 Trace balance, unemployment rate, total compensation for labor, and job tenure in selected year in the United States

	1987	1996	2000	2006
Trade Deficit as percent of GDP (%)	3.1	1.2	3.9	5.9
Unemployment Rate (in percent)	6.2	5.4	4.0	4.6
Total compensation for a full-time equivalent employee (at 2005 prices)	$46,041	$48,175	$52,728	$55,703
Median tenure at job for male workers by age group (in years)				
33 to 44	7.0	6.1	5.3	5.1
45 to 54	11.8	10.1	9.5	8.1
55 to 64	14.5	10.5	10.2	9.5

Trade deficit and unemployment data are from U.S. President (2007).
Data on compensation in real terms are from Gary Burtless (2007).
Compensation under column 2006 is actually for year 2005.
Data on average job tenure in 1996–2006 are from the Bureau of Labor Statistic website: http://www.bls.gov/news.release/tenure.t01.htm
1987 data are from Burtless (2005).

Table 9.4 Distribution of the global labor force (Unit: million USD; SIC countries: former Soviet bloc, India and China)

		The non-SIC countries			The SIC countries			
	Global Total	Non-SIC Total	Developed Economies	Developing Economies	SIC Total	China	India	Soviet bloc
1990	2,315	1,083	*403*	*680*	1,232	*687*	*332*	*213*
2000	2,672	1,289	*438*	*851*	1,383	*764*	*405*	*214*

Source: Freeman (2004). Our figure for "total" in 2000 is different from that in Freeman.

In terms of social safety nets, Gary Burtless (2005) reports that within the G-7 in 2004, only the United Kingdom has a less generous unemployment benefits scheme than the United States. An unemployed person in the US received initial unemployment benefits that equaled 53 percent of previous income compared to 78 percent in Germany, 76 percent in Canada and France, 61 percent in Japan, 60 percent in Italy, and 46 percent in UK. The duration of unemployment benefits was six months in the US compared to 12 months in Germany, nine months in Canada, 30 months in France, ten months in Japan, and six months in Italy and the UK.

There are two major factors behind the more frequent changes in jobs. The first factor is globalization, especially the post-1990 integration of the labor force in the former Soviet Union, India, and China (SIC) into the international division of labor. Table 9.4 shows that the number of workers already engaged in the international division of labor in 1990 was 1083 million and the combined labor force of the SIC was 1232 million. The international division of labor in 1990 was certainly an unnatural one because half of the world's workforce had been kept out of it by the SIC's autarkic policies.

The economic isolation of the Soviet bloc started crumbling when the new non-communist Solidarity government of Poland began the marketization and internationalization of the Polish economy on January 1, 1990.[25] For the Chinese elite, the end of the Soviet Union in August 1991 confirmed that there was no third way in the capitalism-versus-socialism debate. In early 1992, Deng Xiaoping entrenched China firmly on the path of convergence to a private market economy.[26] In 1991, India faced a balance of payments crisis, and it responded by going well beyond the administration of the standard corrective macroeconomic medicine of fiscal-monetary tightening and exchange rate devaluation into comprehensive adjustments of microeconomic incentives.

A decade after the start of the deep integration of the SIC economies into the world economic system, the number of workers involved in the international economic system in 2000 had increased to 2672 million, with 1363 million workers from SIC (see Table 10.4). The Heckscher-Ohlin model would predict that this doubling of the world labor force, achieved by bringing in cheaper labor from SIC, would lower the relative price of the labor intensive good and hence reduce the real wage in the industrialized country.[27] Furthermore, the fact that US capital could now move abroad to set up production facilities in the SIC economies to service the US market as well as third markets also gave globalization another channel to lower the US wage.

However, the US real wage has not fallen (Table 10.3). The reason is that the remarkably high growth in US productivity since the late 1980s, perhaps enabled in large part by the information and communications technology revolution, prevented the real wage from declining. Furthermore, as the import competition is focused on the good that uses low-skilled labor intensively, the wage gap between low-skilled labor and high-skilled labor in the US has widened. In short, the economic impact of globalization in the US is therefore manifested in, one, a diminished labor share of GDP rather than in a lower real wage; and, two, an increased dispersion in US wages.

While the Heckscher-Ohlin model does provide a coherent mechanism for globalization to have the above two wage outcomes, the inconvenient truth is that China might not be the most influential factor in these developments, even though it accounted for 764 million of the combined SIC labor force of 1383 million in 2000. China is unlikely to be the most important culprit because there have been three other independent developments that also had important consequences for US wages.

First, there have been many technological innovations that have substituted capital for labor; for example, fewer secretaries are now needed because today's answering machines can convert messages into voice files and email them to traveling professionals. Technological innovations have also transformed many of what have been traditionally non-tradable services into tradable services, allowing jobs to be outsourced to foreign service providers. For example, the ICT revolution has allowed offshore call centers to handle questions from US customers, offshore accountants to process US-based transactions, and offshore medical technicians to read the X-rays of US patients. The empirical literature suggests that technological innovations are likely to have had a bigger influence on US wages than import competition from China.[28]

Second, there have been institutional changes that attenuated labor's share of income. Union membership has declined, reducing the bargaining power of labor. There has also been an upward shift in the compensation norms for high-level executives. Third, there has been increased immigration into the United States – before 2001, especially, a disproportionate inward immigration of low-skilled labor.[29]

In short, much of the popular outcry in the United States and EU against China's trade surpluses is misplaced. A widening of the US trade deficit creates additional stress on US labor because US imports are more labor-intensive than its exports. However, even if China's trade balance was zero, the pains of structural adjustment and income redistribution caused by technological innovations, institutional changes, globalization, and immigration would still be there; and the amount of worker anxiety they generated collectively would be much larger than the additional worker anxiety generated by the widening trade deficit.

The reduction of trade tensions between the United States and China would be helped if the United States now strengthened its social safety nets to lower the cost of changing jobs. Specifically, the US Congress should quicken the reduction in fiscal imbalance, and expand trade adjustment programs, especially those that upgrade the skill of younger workers. The Trade Adjustment Assistance (TAA) program still functions inadequately after its overhaul in 2002. Lael Brainard (2007) reported that:

> Participation has remained surprisingly low, thanks in part to confusing Department of Labor interpretations and practices that ultimately deny benefits to roughly three-quarters of workers who are certified as eligible for them. TAA has helped fewer than 75,000 new workers per year, while denying more than 40 percent of all employers' petitions. And remarkably, the Department of Labor has interpreted the TAA statute as excluding the growing number of services workers displaced by trade … Between 2001 and 2004, an average of only 64 percent of participants found jobs while they participated in TAA. And earnings on the new job were more than 20 percent below those prior to displacement.

The TAA program is in clear need of further improvement. Brainard's (2007) proposal for the establishment of wage insurance is an excellent way to bring the US social safety net more in line with the type structural adjustments driven by globalization and technological changes.

b Trade protectionism against China created by defects in the Chinese economy

China's chronic and growing overall trade surplus reveals a serious deep-seated problem in China's economy, its dysfunctional financial system. This problem is revealed by the aggregate-level accounting practice that the overall current account balance[30] is determined by the fiscal position of the government, and the savings-investment decisions of the state-controlled enterprises (SCEs) sector and the private sector, which together make up the non-government sector.[31] Specifically:

$$CA = (T - G) + (S_{SCE} - I_{SCE}) + (S_{private} - I_{private})$$

where CA = current account in the balance of payments

$CA = (X - M) + R$

X = *export of goods and non-factor services*

M = *import of goods and non-factor services*

R = *net factor earnings from abroad (i.e. export of factor services)*

T = *state revenue*

G = *state expenditure (including state investment)*

S_{SCE} = *saving of the SCEs*

I_{SCE} = *investment of the SCEs*

$S_{private}$ = *saving of the private sector*

$I_{private}$ = *investment of the private sector*

The Chinese fiscal position ($T - G$) has for the last decade been a small deficit, and so it is not the cause of the swelling current account surpluses in the 2000s. The current account surplus exists because the sum of savings by SCEs and the private sector exceeds the sum of their investment expenditures.

Why has China's financial system failed to translate the savings into investments? Such an outcome was not always the case. Before 1994, the voracious absorption of bank loans by SCEs to invest recklessly kept the current account usually negative and the creation of nonperforming loans (NPLs) high. When the government implemented stricter controls on the state-owned banks (SOBs) from 1994 onward, for example removing top bank officials whenever their bank lent more than its credit quota or allowed the NPL ratio to increase too rapidly, the SOBs slowed down the growth of loans to SCEs. This cutback created an excess of savings because the SOB-dominated financial sector did not then re-channel the released savings, which were also increasing, to finance the investment of the private sector. This failure in financial intermediation by the SOBs is quite understandable. Firstly, the legal status of private enterprises was, until recently, lower than that of the state enterprises; and, secondly, there was no reliable way to assess the balance sheets of the private enterprises, which were naturally eager to escape taxation. The upshot was that the residual excess savings leaked abroad in the form of the current account surplus. Inadequate financial intermediation has made developing China a capital exporting country!

This perverse current account outcome is not new. Taiwan had exactly this problem up to the mid-1980s when all Taiwanese banks were state-owned and were operated according to the civil service regulation that the loan officer had to repay any bad loan that he had approved. The result was a massive failure in financial intermediation that caused Taiwan's current account surplus to be 21 percent of GDP in 1986. The reason why China has not been producing the gargantuan current account surpluses seen in Taiwan in the mid-1980s is because of the large amount of SCE investments.

Why is the savings rate of the non-government sector rising? The combined savings of the SOE and non-SOE sector rose from 20 percent in 1978 to 30 percent in 1987, and then went above 45 since 2004. In discussions on the rise of the savings rate, a common view is that the rise reflects the uncertainty about the future that many SOE workers feel in the face of widespread privatization of loss-making SOEs. We find this explanation incomplete because it seems that there also been a rise in the rural saving rate, even though rural residents have little to fear about the loss of jobs in the state-enterprise sector because none of them is employed there.[32]

We see two general changes that have caused both urban and rural saving rates to rise significantly. The first is "increased worries about the future." The steady decline in state subsidies to medical care, housing, loss-making enterprises, and education, and mismanagement of pension funds by the state have led people to save more to insure against future bad luck, for example sickness, job loss, to buy their own lodging, to build up nest eggs for retirement, and invest in their children.

The second change is the secular improvement in the official Chinese attitude toward market capitalism. Given the high rate of return to capital, this increasingly business-friendly attitude of the Communist Party of China has encouraged both rural and urban residents to save for investment, that is greater optimism about the future has spawned investment-motivated saving.[33]

In our explanations for the existence of the current account surpluses and the growth of the surplus, there is a common element in both: China's financial system. The fact is that savings behavior is not independent of the sophistication of the financial system. An advanced financial system will have a variety of financial institutions that would enable pooling of risks by providing medical insurance, pension insurance, and unemployment insurance; and transform savings into education loans, housing loans, and other types of investment loans to the private sector. *Ceteris paribus*, the more sophisticated a financial system, the lower the savings rate. China generates the current account surplus shown in Table 9.2 because of inadequate financial intermediation, and the surplus grows over time because the dysfunctional financial system fails to pool risks to reduce uncertainty-induced savings and fails to provide loans to reduce investment-motivated saving.

What is to be done in China? The obvious short-run policy package has three components. First, the steady process of *yuan* appreciation begun in July 2005 should be quickened, and be used more aggressively as an anti-inflation instrument. Second, import liberalization should be accelerated, for example implementing seriously the commitments made in negotiations for WTO membership like IPR protection, and expanded beyond WTO specifications.

The third component of the short-run policy package is to have an expansionary fiscal policy, for example rural infrastructure investments, to soak up the excess savings, with an emphasis on import-intensive investments (e.g. buying airplanes and sending students abroad). It is important that time limits be put on the expanded public works and SCE investments because, in the long-run, the increased public investments could follow an increasingly rent-seeking path that is wasteful, for example building a second big bridge to a lowly-populated island to benefit a politically-connected construction company as in Japan, and the increased SCE investments could convert themselves into nonperforming loans at the SOBs.

Clearly, the optimum solution to the problem of excess saving is not for the government to absorb it by increasing its budget deficit but to establish an improved mechanism for coordinating private savings and private investments. The establishment of a modern financial system will not only achieve the objective of intermediating all of domestic saving into domestic investment, it will also enhance welfare and lower the savings rate by pooling risks through vehicles like medical insurance and pension insurance. In a nutshell, China's main challenge today is to develop smoothly-functioning financial, planning, and regulatory systems that can employ the remaining rural surplus labor (as indicated by an average wage of about $120 per month for 480 million rural and migrant workers) and surplus capital, which shows up now as China's sustained current account surplus and rising foreign exchange reserves.

The important conclusion from this section is that US–China trade tension would be lowered much more if both countries were to undertake corrective policies rather than if China acted alone, and that a wider range of policy instruments should be employed, for example wage insurance program in the United States and financial market development in China, rather than relying just on exchange rate adjustment alone.

6 The second likely type of power supply failure is environmental collapse in China

The present mode of economic development has given China the dirtiest air in the world, is polluting more and more of the water resources, and is, possibly, changing the climate pattern within China. The reality is that the CPC's new objective of living in harmony with nature is not a choice, because the Maoist adage of "man conquering nature" is just as unrealistic as creating prosperity through central planning. China's fast growth in the last two decades has done substantial damage to the environment. Elizabeth Economy (2004: 18–19) summarized the economic toll as follows:

> China has become home to six of the ten most polluted cities in the world (Economy 2004: 18–19). Acid rain now affects about one-third of China's territory, including approximately one-third of its farmland. More than 75 percent of the water in rivers flowing through China's urban areas is [unsuitable for human contact (Economy 2004: 69)] ... deforestation and grassland degradation continue largely unabated (Economy 2004: 65)[34] ... The [annual] economic cost of environmental degradation and pollution ... are the equivalent of 8–12 percent of China's annual gross domestic product.

Water shortage appears to pose the most immediate environmental threat to China's continued high growth.[35] Presently, China uses 67 to 75 percent of the 800 to 900 billion cubic meters of water available annually, and present trends in water consumption would project the usage rate in 2030 to be 78 to 100 percent (*SCMP* 2004: January 3). The present water situation is actually already fairly critical because of the uneven distribution of water and the lower than normal rainfall in the past fifteen years. Right now, "[about] 400 of China's 660 cities face water shortages, with 110 of them severely short (*Straits Times* 2004: January 3)."[36]

The extended period of semi-drought in northern China combined with the economic and population growth have caused more and more water to be pumped from the aquifers, leading the water table to drop three to six meters a year (*SCMP* 2001: August 11). And a study using measurements from satellites (the Global Positioning System) has established that the part of China north of the 36th parallel latitude has been "sinking at the rate of 2 mm a year" (*Straits Times* 2004: January 3). Specifically, "Shanghai, Tianjin, and Taiyuan are the worst hit in China, with each sinking more than two meters (6.6 feet) since the early 1990s" (*Agence France-Presse* 2004: July 23).

The overall water situation in northern China is reflected in the fate of the Yellow River,

> which started drying up every few years from 1972, did so for increasing periods of time over longer distances in the 1990s until 1997, when it dried up for almost the entire year over a stretch of several hundred kilometers.
>
> (*Straits Times* 2007: January 3)

The utilization rate of Yellow River's water is 60 percent, far exceeding the internationally recommended utilization limit of 40 percent. All the mentioned factors have contributed to lowering the "amount of Yellow River water feeding into the Bohai Sea" from an annual 49.6 billion cubic meters in the 1960s to 14.2 billion cubic meters in the 1990s to the present 4.65 billion cubic meters (*SCMP* 2006: November 7).

Water shortage and the increasing pollution of what water there is[37] are not the only serious environmental threats to the economy of northern China. The desert is expanding at a possibly accelerating pace, and man appears to be the chief culprit. The State Forestry Administration reported that 28 percent of the country's land mass was affected by desertification in 1999, and 37 percent was affected by soil erosion. The report identified about 65 percent of the desert as having been created by "over-cultivation, overgrazing, deforestation and poor irrigation practices" (*SCMP* 2002: January 30). The rate of desertification is 3900 square miles a year,[38] an annual loss of a land area twice the size of Delaware. One direct upshot is a great increase in the frequency of major sandstorms[39] that play "havoc with aviation in northern China for weeks, cripples high-tech manufacturing and worsens respiratory problems as far downstream as Japan, the Korean peninsula and even the western United States (*NYT* 2004: April 11). In the assessment of Chen Lai, Vice-Minister of water resources: "It will take nearly half a century for China to control the eroded land and rehabilitate their damaged ecosystems in accordance with China's present erosion-control capabilities" (*SCMP* 2002: January 30).

While northern China has been getting drier and experiencing desertification, nature as if in compensation, or in mockery, has been blasting southern China with heavier rains, causing heavy floods, which have brought considerable deaths and property damage almost every summer since 1998.[40] The sad possibility is that the northern droughts and southern floods may not be independent events but a combination caused by pollution that originates in China. I will have more to say about this possibility later.

Clearly, without water growth cannot endure. And in response, the government began implementation in 2002 of Mao Zedong's 1952 proposal that three canals be built to bring water from the south to the north: an eastern coastal canal from Jiangsu to Shandong and Tianjin, a central canal from Hubei to Beijing and Tianjin, and a western route from Tibet to the northwestern provinces. Each canal will be over a thousand miles long (*SCMP* 2002: November 27). Construction of the eastern canal (which would be built upon a part of the existing Grand Canal) started in 2002, and of the central canal in 2003.

The scale of this water transfer project is simply unprecedented anywhere:

> Together, the three channels would pump about 48 billion liters of water a year – enough to fill New York's taps for a quarter century. Only a tenth as much water flows through the next-largest water diversion project, in California.
>
> (*SCMP* 2002: November 26)

This massive construction project will not only be technically challenging but also extremely sensitive politically and fraught with environmental risks. The central canal will have to tunnel through the foot of the huge dyke that contains the elevated Yellow River, and the western canal will have to transport water through regions susceptible to freezing. The number of people displaced by the Three Gorges Dam was 1.1 million, and this water transfer scheme is a bigger project. The enlargement of the Danjiangkou Dam (in Hubei) alone to enable it to be the source of the central canal will already displace 330,000 people (*FT* 2002: August 27; 2004: July 26). Moving people involuntarily is certainly potentially explosive politically. The project could also be politically explosive on the international front as well. One plan for the western canal calls for "damming the Brahmaputra river and diverting 200 billion cubic meters of water annually to feed the ageing Yellow river," a scenario that is reportedly "giving sleepless nights to the Indian government ... [which is concerned that this 'Great Western Water Diversion Project' could have immense impact on lower riparian states like India and Bangladesh" (*Times of India* 2006: October 23).

The environmental damages caused by this project are the most serious for the central and western canals. In the case of the central canal,

> environmental experts [in Wuhan where the Hanjiang River flows into the Yangtze] are worried about ... [whether the annual extraction of eight billion cubic meters of water could affect] the river's ability to flush out the massive pollution flows released by the thousands of factories and industries along the tributaries ... The reduced flows could increase the frequency of toxic red algae blooms on the Yangtze near the confluence with the Hanjiang River. There have already been three blooms ... [by May of that year, 2003].

The western canal has generated a lively controversy. Some scientists are contending that it "would cause more ecological damage than good" (*WSJ* 2006: October 23), because it "could cause dramatic climate changes ... [and] the changed flow and water temperature would lead to a rapid decline in fish and other aquatic species" (*American-Statesman* 2006: September 10).

Many opponents of the water transfer project have argued that water conservation could go a long way toward addressing this problem because currently a tremendous amount of the water is just wasted, for example only 50 percent of China's industrial water is recycled compared to 80 percent in the industrialized countries (*Strait Times* January 2004), and China consumes 3860 cubic meters of water to produce US$10,000 of GDP compared to the world average of 965 cubic meters Strait Times June 10 (*Straits Times*: 2006: March 8). The most important reason for this inefficient use of water lies in the fact that "China's farmers, factories and householders enjoy some of the cheapest water in the world" (SCMP March 8, 2006), even though China's per capita endowment of water is a quarter of the world average (*Straits Times* 2004: June 10).

There is, however, the unhappy possibility that neither the price mechanism nor the three canals can solve China's water problem and make its growth sustainable unless the present mode of economic development is drastically amended. There is now persuasive evidence that China's voluminous emission of black carbon (particles of incompletely combusted carbon) has contributed significantly to the shift to a climate pattern that produces northern droughts and southern floods of increasing intensity (Menon, Hansen, Nazarenko, and Luo 2002; Streets 2006). The biggest source of what has been called the "Asian brown cloud" in the popular media is burning of coal and bio-fuels in China. If the pollution-induced climate change analysis is valid, it means that China's massive reforestation program will not succeed in reducing sandstorms in the north because trees cannot survive if the amount of rainfall is declining over time; and the number of south-north canals will have to be increased over time in order to meet the demand for water in northern China; until China reduces its emission of black carbon significantly (presuming no new large emissions from neighboring countries like India).

The general point is that effective policy-making on the environmental front is a very difficult task because much of the science about the problem is not known. For example, China must no longer select its water strategy and its energy strategy separately. A systems approach in policymaking is necessary because the interaction among the outcomes from the different sectoral policies can generate serious unintended environmental damage. If part of the shift in China's climate is integral to global climate change, then a sustainable development policy would require a complete rethinking of the location of population centers, and types of enhanced international cooperation on global environmental management.

The uncomfortable reality for China is that unless ecological balance is restored within the medium-term, environmental limits could choke off further economic growth. And the uncomfortable reality for the rest of the world is that the negative consequences of large-scale environmental damage within a geographically large country are seldom confined within that country's borders. The continued march of China's desertification first brought more frequent sand storms to Beijing and then, beginning in April 2001, sent yellow dust clouds not only across the sea to Japan and Korea but also across the ocean to the United States. China's environmental management is a concern not only for China's welfare but for global welfare as well.

In discussing the environmental aspects of the water transfer plan, it is important to note that there is now an open controversy in

China involving a key government infrastructure project, and that this controversy is not limited to members of the technocracy. The very public nature of the controversy and the involvement in it of more than just scientists, engineers, and economists reveal how very far social attitudes have progressed. The important point is that this change in social expectations will require any government in China to live in harmony with nature. However, any government will have great difficulties in doing so even if it wants to because a green growth policy involves a systems approach, and scientific understanding of many ecological sub-systems and the nature of their interactions is still rather incomplete.

Proper management of the environment has now become critical for China if it is to continue its industrialization process. The unexpurgated version of a 2007 World Bank reported that "about 750,000 people die prematurely in China each year, mainly from air pollution in large cities" (*FT* 2007: July 2);[41] and a 2007 OECD study has estimated that "China's air pollution will cause 20 million people a year to fall ill with respiratory diseases" (*FT* 2007: July 17). Pan Yue, the deputy head of the State Environmental Protection Agency, summed up the present situation in China very well when he said:

> If we continue on this path of traditional industrial civilization, there is no chance that we will have sustainable development. China's population, resources, environment have already reached the limits of their capacity to cope. Sustainable development and new sources of energy are the only road that we can take.
>
> (*FT* 2004: July 26)

The bad news is that there is no sign of significant progress in China's efforts to reduce pollution. China failed to meet its 2006 target for modest improved energy efficiency (*FT* 2007: January 11); and the Netherlands Environmental Assessment Agency has claimed that China became "the world's top producer of carbon dioxide" in 2006 (*SCMP* 2007: June 21). The worrying sign is that there might not be significant progress in the near future because of the concern that environmental protection might slow growth down too much. This concern might be the reason for the recent suspension of the release of green GDP estimates (WSJ 2007: July 17: SCMP 2007: July 24), and for the planning agency's objection to the proposed new auto emissions standards (*FT* 2007: June 19).

7 Conclusion

In appraising whether the attainment of the October 2006 vision of a Harmonious Society would be sufficient to sustain high economic growth in China, the greatest inadequacy I see is the absence of an objective to build a harmonious world. A harmonious society cannot endure in China unless there is also a harmonious world, and vice-versa. China's pursuit of a harmonious society requires it actively to help provide the global public goods that make a harmonious world possible; and the two global public goods that come readily to mind are the strengthening of the multilateral free trade system, and the protection of the global environmental commons.

China has benefited immensely from the GATT-WTO free-trade regime, and yet it has, up to this point, played a very passive role in pushing the Doha Round negotiations forward to completion. By default, Brazil and India have assumed the leadership of the developing economies camp in the trade negotiations. According to Susan Schwab, the US Trade Representative, at the G4 (US, EU, Brazil and India) meeting in Potsdam in June 2007, Brazil and India retreated from their earlier offers to reduce their manufacturing tariffs in return for cuts in agricultural subsidies by the developed economies because of "their fear of growing Chinese imports" (*FT* 2007: June 22). The Brazilian-Indian action caused the Potsdam talks to fail and hurt the many developing economies that were agricultural exporters.

China should now seek a leadership role in the Doha Round negotiations that is commensurate with its participation in international trade. Failure of the Doha Round could set in motion the unraveling of multilateral free trade because the present international atmosphere is right for protectionism. The US, which has traditionally been at the forefront for expanding the multilateral free trade system, is now beset by self-doubt for three major reasons.

First, the US was willing to put up with the pains of structural adjustments in the 1960–90 period to accommodate the growing imports from Japan, South Korea, Taiwan, and ASEAN because they were front-line allies in the Cold War. With the end of the Cold War, it is natural for the US to re-consider the economic cost of structural adjustment because the security and ideological benefits from it have gone down.

Second, the amount of required structural adjustment in the US to accommodate the rise of the SIC bloc is far greater than the earlier adjustment to the rise of its Cold War allies. As noted, the entry of the former Soviet, Indian, and Chinese economies has doubled the labor force participating in the international division of labor.

Third, the strongest lobby for free trade in the US has been the economics profession, and the free trade doctrine has come under strong internal criticism in the last few years. Paul Samuelson has made many fundamental contributions to the development of the standard trade models that convinced mainstream economists that free trade is the best policy, and it was therefore an intellectual earthquake when he argued in 2004 that under free trade, where outsourcing accelerates the transfer of knowledge to the developing country, there could be a decline in the welfare of the developed country (Samuelson 2004). Intellectual apostasy is spreading; for example, as in 2005, Alan Blinder joined Paul Samuelson in criticizing free trade fundamentalism.

While it is not yet clear about the veracity of the Samuelson hypothesis, it is clear, however, that the hypothesis reflects the widespread pains of structural adjustment that they witness around them – a phenomenon captured by the decreasing length of median job tenure. In April 2007, the US bypassed multilateralism in free trade by agreeing to form a Free Trade Area (FTA) with South Korea. With the US weakening in its resolve to protect the multilateral free trade system, China should now become more active in the Doha Round negotiations to deregulate world trade further. Such a role will be very much in China's interest because Brazil is now bypassing multilateral trade liberalization by entering into FTA negotiations with the European Union. The fact is that a growing number of nations like Brazil "are increasingly wary of a multilateral deal because it would mandate tariff cuts, exposing them more deeply to low-cost competition from China. Instead, they are seeking bilateral deals with rich countries that are tailored to the two parties' needs" (*WSJ* 2007: July 5). It is time for China to show that it is a responsible stakeholder by joining in the stewardship of the multilateral free trade system.

The global environment is the second area where China can help to build a harmonious world system. Specifically, China should be mobilizing international consensus to form an international research consortium to develop ways to burn coal cleanly because China is now building a power station a week and is hence able to facilitate extensive experimentation on prototype plants to burn coal cleanly. If successful, this global cooperation on clean energy research will unleash sustainable development in China as well as in the rest of the world.

We realize of course that while the need to maintain high growth could motivate China to become more active in supplying global public goods, it might not be allowed to do so however because of the usual reluctance of the existing dominant powers to share the commanding heights of world political leadership. The sad experience of Japan being denied permanent membership in the Security Council of the United Nations is a case in point. Harmonious international relations are the omitted item in China's perception of a Harmonious Society in 2006, and it could turn out to be a very soft spot in the Chinese growth engine. Besides, the competent management of economic issues is also fundamental to maintaining China's high growth path. The most important realization on this front is that in today's China doing more of the same economic policies will not produce the same salubrious results on every front because the development problems have changed.

On the fiscal management front, my analysis suggests two main policy suggestions to reduce the vulnerability of China to possible future fiscal difficulties. First, the extractive capacity of the state should be enhanced so that the revenue–GDP ratio would increase to 25 percent in the medium term. This extra revenue will be the fiscal cushion that allows the state to accommodate unexpected expenditure demands or revenue shortfalls. As noted earlier, the collection of revenue might probably first require overcoming the challenge of forging the political consensus for a tax increase. Second, the management of state assets and the regulation of the financial sector should be reformed to eliminate the phenomenon of repeated recapitalization of the SOBs. The privatization of some units of the SOBs, and the emergence of large domestic private banks will help in strengthening the budget constraints perceived by the managers of SOBs.

The fact is, however, that the probability of a software failure and the probability of a power supply failure are both higher than the probability of a hardware failure. This means that development policy-making in China has become more challenging. There must now not only be more adroit, but also fuller accommodation, of domestic social demands in order to keep China's growth rate high. The reality is that popular satisfaction with the status quo depends inversely on the level of expectations, and the expectations of the Chinese people towards their government have risen dramatically along with income, and, more importantly, risen along with their growing knowledge of the outside world. A Chinese government that consistently fails to produce results in line with the rise in social expectations runs the increasing risk of being challenged by another faction within the CPC, culminating into an open split with each side seeking the support of non-party groups.

To complicate matters there have been not only rising expectations but also diversification of expectations. In this new situation, the greater use of democratic procedures, the establishment of an independent judiciary, and the restoration of a free press might be inevitable if CPC is successfully to accommodate the rising social expectations and mediate the emerging differences in social expectations. What will happen will depend on whether the CPC is sufficiently confident that it will be politically skillful enough to lead the democratic transition and emerge afterward as the most important political force. History tells us that the French monarchy and the British monarchy reacted very differently to the popular requests for reform, and the outcomes were very different in each case.

Notes

I am deeply grateful to Xiaoming Huang, Iikka Korhonen and Aaron Mehrotra for incisive comments that improved this chapter tremendously. I am also deeply grateful for the guidance on my analysis that I received from the participants in the conferences where this work has been presented.

1. Lardy wrote, "China's major banks are even weaker than most official data suggest. On a realistic accounting, these banks' capital adequacy is negative, and they are insolvent (1998: 95) ... The failure of China's largest financial institutions would disrupt the flow of credit and disrupt the payments system, leading to a collapse of economic activity. The failure of major banks also could have long-term implications for the household savings rate. A lower savings rate would mean a lower rate of investment and slower growth, in turn depressing the rate of new job creation, leading to sustained higher levels of unemployment" (143–4).
2. According to Minxin Pei (2006b): "In a 'trapped transition,' the ruling elites have little interest in real reforms. They may pledge reforms, but most such pledges are lip service or tactical adjustments aimed at maintaining the status quo."
3. Huang (2006) sees that India does not discriminate against its indigenous capitalists in favor of foreign capitalists, and predicts that unless "China embarks on bold institutional reforms, India may very well outperform it in the next 20 years."
4. For a review of the debate on how to interpret China's high growth in the 1978–2000 and why China, unlike the economies of the former Soviet bloc, did not experience a recession when it made the switch from a centrally-planned economy to a market economy, see Sachs and Woo (2000), and Woo (2001).
5. For example, President Soeharto of Indonesia was pushed out of office in May 1998, one month after raising fuel prices.
6. http://stats.oecd.org/wbos/viewhtml.aspx?QueryName=2&QueryType=View&Lang=en
7. The Big Four are Agricultural Bank of China, Bank of China, China Construction Bank, and Industrial and Commercial Bank of China.

8. The People's Bank of China established an investment company (Central Huijin Company) under the State Administration of Foreign Exchange to undertake this injection of capital. This gave Huijin 85 percent of the ownership of China Construction Bank, and 100 percent of Bank of China.
9. One should really use the consolidated debt of the state sector because it includes at least some part of the contingent liabilities (e.g., foreign debts of SOEs and SOBs, and unfunded pension schemes in the SOE sector) that the state might have to assume responsibility for when the state-owned units default on their financial obligations.
10. f has been above 1.5 percent for the past seven years. r was 4 percent in the past only because the interest rate was regulated. I think that the implementation of financial deregulation that is necessary for normal healthy development of the financial sector will render r to be at least 6 percent because, one, according to Solow (1991), the stylized fact for the real interest rate in the United States is that it is 5 to 6 percent; and, two, both the marginal rate of return to capital and the black market loan rate have been more than 20 percent.
11. See Woo, Hai, Jin, and Fan (1994), and Woo (2001).
12. The asymmetry is from the absence of financial punishment when a loss occurs.
13. See Woo and Zhang (2010) for a detailed discussion of the Chinese macroeconomic policy response to the Global Financial Crisis.
14. The first article also reported the recall of a ghoulish fake eyeball that was filled with kerosene, and of an infant wrist rattle that was a choking hazard.
15. For example, radial tires were manufactured without the gum strips that prevented the tires from separating; see *NYT* 2007: June 26.
16. *The New York Times* reported that: "The workers endured prison-like confinement with fierce dogs and beatings ... Released workers were shown on television with festering wounds and emaciated bodies" (2007: June 18).
17. This point was made by the popular tabloid *Southern Metropolis Daily*, see *NYT* 2007: June 18.
18. This point was made by the Shanxi governor, Yu Youjun, who said: "For a long time, relevant government departments did little to regulate rural workshops, small coal mines and small factories, and they are basically out of control and are not being supervised ... The dereliction of duty by civil servants and the corruption of individuals have made it possible for illegal labor to exist, particularly the abductions of migrant workers, and forced labor of children and mentally disabled people" – see *SCMP* 2007: June 23.
19. The 1990–7 figures are from World Bank (2001) Annex 1, Table 3, and the post-1997 figures are computed by Ximing Yue (private communication).
20. The proportion of rural population receiving a daily income of $1 or less.
21. The Gini coefficient has a value between 0 and 1, and the higher the value, the greater the degree of income inequality.
22. The 1993 number is from Keidel (2006: 1), and the 2004 number is from Pei (2005) who wrote that, in 2004, there were 74,000 "mass incidents" involving 3.7 million people compared to 10,000 such incidents involving 730,000 people in 1994. Possibly, because of the widespread attention in the Western media on the marked rise in mass incidents, the post-2004 definition of

mass incidents appeared to have been changed, making post-2004 data not comparable with the 1994–2004 data.

23. No. 1 Document designation is designed to show that this is the most important task in the New Year.
24. This positive wage trend for the average worker is also seen in that for the average blue-collar worker; see Woo (2008).
25. The economic transition and political disintegration of the Soviet bloc became irreversible when Yeltsin replaced Gorbachev as the unambiguous leader of Russia in August 1991 and implemented market-oriented reforms in January 1992.
26. Today, under the heading of a socialist market economic with Chinese characteristics, the Chinese constitution gives private property the same legal status as public property, and the Chinese Communist Party accepts capitalists as members.
27. More accurately, the wage of the formerly isolated SIC worker would rise while the wage for the worker in the industrialized country would fall.
28. There is a large empirical literature on relative impact of technological changes and globalization on the US wage rate, e.g. Sachs and Shatz (1994), and Feenstra and Hanson (1996).
29. Ottaviano and Peri (2005) are good discussions of this topic.
30. Of which, in China, the overall trade account is the biggest part.
31. The SCE category covers companies that are classified as SOBs (state-owned companies); and joint-ventures and joint-stock companies that are controlled by third parties, for example legal persons, who are answerable to the state.
32. Economist Intelligence Unit (2004: 23) reported that "farmers' propensity to save seems to have increased."
33. Liu and Woo (1994) and Woo and Liu (1995) contain formal modeling and econometric support for the investment-motivated saving hypothesis.
34. "degradation has reduced China's grassland by 30–50 percent since 1950; of the 400 million or so hectares of grassland remaining, more than 90 percent are degraded and more than 50 percent suffer moderate to severe degradation" (Economy 2004: 65)
35. Air pollution is a serious problem. Of the twenty cities in the world identified by the World Bank as having the dirtiest air, sixteen of them are located in China. It is shocking that lead and mercury poisoning are more common than expected, see *FT* (December 18, 2004); and *WSJ* (September 30, 2006).
36. The shortage is reported to be most acute in Taiyuan in Shanxi and Tianjin (Becker (2003)).
37. Examples of serious water pollution are recorded in *SCMP* 2003: June 6; *Straits Times* 2003: September 18; *NYT* 2004: September 12; *SCMP* 2006: May 8; and *NYT* 2006: September 4.
38. This is average of the 3800 square miles reported in *NYT* 2004: April 1, and the 4014 square miles reported in *SCMP* 2002.
39. The number of major sandstorms in China was five in the 1950–59 period, eight in 1960–69, 13 in 1970–79, 14 in 1980–89, 23 in 1990–99, 14 in 2000, 26 in 2001, 16 in 2002, and 11 in 2003 according Yin (2005).
40. NDRC (2007) reported: "The regional distribution of precipitation shows that the decrease in annual precipitation was significant in most of northern

China, eastern part of the northwest, and northeastern China, averaging 20–40 mm/10a, with decrease in northern China being most severe; while precipitation significantly increased in southern China and southwestern China, averaging 20–60 mm/10a ... The frequency and intensity of extreme climate/weather events throughout China have experienced obvious changes during the last 50 years. Drought in northern and northeastern China, and flood in the middle and lower reaches of the Yangtze River and southeastern China have become more severe."

41. 350,000 to 400,000 died prematurely from air pollution in Chinese cities, 300,000 from poor air indoors, and 60,000 (mostly in countryside) from poor-quality water.

10
Comparing National Sustainability in China and India

Bruce Gilley

China and India have experienced several decades of rapid economic growth. Much social science theory predicts that rapid growth will bring a host of destabilizing factors: rising income inequalities – the "Kuznets curve" hypothesis (Kuznets 1955); insatiable demands for political participation – the "Kings dilemma" of Huntington (Huntington 1968: 177); weakening social solidarity – the "Durkheim nightmare" (Durkheim 1893); and a population explosion – the so-called demographic transition (Thompson 1930). Recently, the problems of environmental degradation have been added to the list, in particular rising air and water pollution, increased deforestation, rapid biodiversity loss, and soaring greenhouse gas emissions – the "environmental Kuznets curve" (Panayotou 1997).

In all cases, the models have assumed that the threats *increase* during the period of rapid growth and then *decrease* during the period of growth deceleration as a result of both structural and policy responses – the familiar "inverted-U" trajectory. Income inequalities are resolved by redistribution, social anomies by a new form of organic solidarity, population explosion by declining fertility, and political participation demands by institutional inclusion. In the case of the environment, the threats can be brought under control by a transition away from industry, increased resources available for environmental protection, and rising social demands for effective regulation.

There is no promise however that the threats will decline or that existing institutions will not collapse in the face of them. Navigating across the upper portion of the inverted-U, or avoiding it altogether by "tunneling" to the other side, is the central issue for the social theory of developing nations and one of the most pressing contemporary challenges for both China and India.

Various versions of the inverted-U models – economic, political, social, and environmental – have been tested on cross-national data and the results are usually mixed. Yet models are useful not just as descriptive predictors but as heuristic devices for the interrogation of particular country experiences. Thinking about the China and India experiences using the expectations of inverted-U models and through an explicitly comparative framework helps us to better understand the precise challenges faced by both countries. For policy-makers engaged in long-term planning, these models remain indispensable even if their fit with the empirical reality of these countries (and others) is imperfect.

In this chapter, I will first reconceptualize the inverted-U challenges in terms of sustainability and then proceed to examine contemporary evidence from both China and India. This is followed by a discussion of the future pathways both countries will follow and a concluding section evaluating their comparative performance. I find that both countries require immediate adjustments in their growth models in order to protect their sustainability systems. The required adjustments differ, however, and the potential options also vary. China and India have outgrown development models, but the period in which they must consider sustainability models is just beginning.

1 A sustainability approach

Since the challenges of the inverted-U models are diverse, there is a need for a higher-order concept that brings together the various questions related to the core issues of human survival and well-being: health, material resources, freedoms and opportunities, security, social resources, and so on. The concept of "sustainability" – literally the ability to endure – is apt for this purpose. Early writers on human sustainability (Brown 1954; Kohr 1957) considered it essential for all nations to consider their long-term durability rather than only their immediate economic development. The question of sustainability began with a specific focus on the well-being of the natural environment. In recent years, it has crossed over into a more humanistic, or anthropocentric, focus on the well-being of human societies. In this context, it refers to the ability of human societies to endure at or above their current levels of well-being. Sustainability is seen as the logical successor to gross domestic product or the Human Development Index (HDI) as the best measure of human well-being because it recognizes the multidimensional sources of human well-being and because it explicitly takes into account future generations (Parris and Kates 2003).

The greater the number of future generations taken into account and the more broadly we conceptualize human well-being, the more aggressively a human society must confront sustainability challenges today. Richard Posner (Posner 2004: 150–55) suggests in light of uncertainty and technological progress that a reasonable view is a "grandchildren rule" that applies a zero discount rate to only two generations beyond the current one or about 100 years. This translates into an implied discount rate for infinite future generations of about one percent per year. Sustainability must therefore focus on whether systems are being maintained today to protect human well-being at or above current levels for the next 100 years, or at only one percent per year below those levels forever.

As to the breadth of the concept of "well-being," Julian Marshall and Michael Toffel (Marshall and Toffel 2005) warn against including every desirable attribute of human society. We must allow that a sustainable human society can be far from just, pleasant, or progressive. Instead, human well-being must be defined in terms of those attributes necessary to live minimally productive and healthy lives. Both China and India are today societies that deliver human well-being to most members despite being unjust and brutish in many respects.

Thus, to restate the inverted-U challenges in terms of sustainability, we are concerned with the implications of rapid growth in China and India for the systems that support human well-being in the two countries for the next 100 years. This concept might be called "national sustainability,"[1] since we are concerned not with political systems, economic growth, or the environment per se but only with these things as they relate to the well-being of the human communities found in each state, the "nations." Since these two countries account for 37 percent of the world's population, this covers a large part of the sustainability picture for humanity as a whole.

Simon Bell and Stephen Morse have defined sustainability in terms of the underlying sub-systems that allow human societies to endure at their current levels of well-being. They together constitute "the sustainability system." Thus, sustainability is "a situation where [the system] quality remains the same or increases" (Bell and Morse 2008: 12). The relevant sub-systems certainly include the natural environment and, for the moment, the threats to the natural environment appear to be the biggest challenge to human sustainability. However, other parts of the overall system – political, economic, and social – also need to be studied because of their contributions to human well-being and because of their impacts on the environmental sub-system itself.

At present, an agreed framework for measuring national sustainability is only in its infancy (WGSSD 2008). Different approaches stress sub-system inputs, often termed the "capital" approach; sub-system policies, often termed the "policy" approach; and sub-system outputs and outcomes – direct measures of human well-being. In the following sections, I will make use of widely available indicators of inputs, policy, and outputs/outcomes to assess the quality of sustainability sub-systems in China and India: economic, environmental, social, and political (Table 10.1). In each case, I use the maximum and minimum values of each data set to construct simple quintile categories, with each representing one fifth of the total range. The two countries can then be rated in terms of their quintile ranking, from 1 (best) to 5 (worst).

Table 10.1 National sustainability: China and India

Indicator	**Quintile (1-Best to 5-Worst)**	
	China	**India**
ECONOMIC		
Economic Risk Indicator (Euromoney 2010)	1	2
Sovereign Risk (Standard & Poor's 2010)	2	2
ENVIRONMENTAL		
Environmental Performance Index (YCWLP 2010)	3	4
Global Climate Risk Index (German Watch 2010)	5	5
Proportional Environmental Impact (Bradshaw, Giam, and Sodhi 2005)	5	4
SOCIAL		
Multidimensional Poverty Index (UNDP, 2010)	1	3
Gender Inequality Index (UNDP 2008)	2	5
Life Satisfaction (NEP 2005)	2	3
Social Trust (WVS 2006)	2	4
POLITICAL		
Political Stability (Kaufmann et al. 2010)	3	3
Government Effectiveness (Kaufmann et al. 2010)	3	3
State Fragility (SFT 2008)	2	3
Political Weakness (Rice and Patrick 2008)	4	2
Security Weakness (Rice and Patrick 2008)	2	3
Average* Quintile (1-Best to 5-Worst)	**2.6**	**3.2**

* Average of means of each of the four sub-systems.

I then consider the dynamics of overall system quality, asking how and whether China and India can respond to the challenges of the inverted-U for national sustainability.

2 Current assessments

Rapid economic growth in China and India is nothing new. China's human development index rose by 50 percent between 1950 and 1973, compared to a gain of 32 percent in India, while life expectancy rose from around 40 in both countries to 66 in China and 56 in India. Life expectancy in China is now 74 compared to 64 in India. India's HDI rose at the same pace as China's from 1980 to 2010 – leaving a roughly 20 percent gap between the two in terms of their material development. China and India are both growth success stories. And that growth shows no signs of slowing.

The rapid growth of the economic system is the source of many of the challenges to human sustainability represented by the inverted-U. However, as a positive source of human sustainability it must also be protected against collapse. While "catch-up" models assume that rapid growth (in the 8–10% range) will continue in both China and India at least until 2020 (Li and Zhang 2008; Rawski and Dwight 2008), and more likely until 2030, the economic sub-systems in both countries face unique threats. National sustainability requires not only that the threats caused *by* economic sub-systems be met, but also that the threats *to* them be met.

The composite economic risk index compiled by *Euromoney* combines credit, finance, debt, structural variables relating to labor and investment/savings, and growth. From this perspective, both countries have economic systems that are highly stable, consistent with the premise here that they are rapidly growing economies far from the frontier and are likely to continue growing. Indeed, the economic sub-systems are the only ones that are very "healthy" in international comparison, perhaps too "healthy" for the good of other sub-systems. As developing countries, China and India have also both been remarkably successful in establishing the trust in their sovereign debt,[2] as shown by the Standard & Poor's sovereign risk ratings.

Most comparative analysis suggests that China leads India with respect to its economic system, although both are success stories (Prime 2009). China's economic sustainability has been proven through three distinct crises: the domestic banking crisis of the 1990s, the Asian Financial Crisis of 1997–8, and finally the global economic crisis of 2008–9. India, meanwhile, has sustained rapid growth since the initiation of market reforms in 1991, although it has embarked on a much less sustainable fiscal trajectory than China.

It is also important to note the different ways that the two countries have arrived at similar levels of economic sub-system quality. China has led India in terms of transportation and telecommunications infrastructure, but India has led China in terms of skilled labor for information technology and complex manufacturing-based operations (Prater, Swafford, and Yellepeddi 2009). China has made itself a base for flow-through export demand, while India has concentrated more on domestic demand. As a result, the main threats to economic sub-system quality in China are the transition to value-added manufacturing and services including the financial sector, while India's challenges revolve around infrastructure constraints and the related low level of savings.

The quality of the environmental sub-system that supports human sustainability includes a wide range of factors. These include access to basic environmental needs like water, air, and land, as well as protections against natural disasters. Every national society also depends on a broader regional and global environmental system for its sustainability. Management of the environment has to be consistent with human survival for many generations, taking into account uncertainty about the ecological needs of humans that may not be well understood at present.

Existing comprehensive measures of environmental systems for India and China generally put the two countries as roughly similar, as both having seriously degraded environments. Both the Environmental Performance Index (EPI), which looks primarily at the management of domestic environmental systems, and the Global Climate Risk Index (GCRI), which is based on retrospective economic and human losses from extreme weather, put the countries in the fourth and fifth quintiles respectively. In the latter case, both China and India are among the 20 nations most vulnerable to climate change because of their huge populations, widespread poverty, and environmental degradation caused by rapid growth. Only the Proportional Environmental Impact (PEI; Bradshaw, Giam, and Sodhi 2010) indicator, which considers environmental quality and vulnerability as well as the quality of policies and regulations in place, rates India as better than China.

Consistent with so-called environmental modernization theory – a linear or logarithmic function – and the second half of the (quadratic) inverted-U model, countries that are wealthier tend to have better records of environmental management. This fact can be seen visually if we compare the EPI ratings to income per capita (Figure 10.1). What this chart shows is that China, given its income, is a large *underperformer* whereas India is a less severe underperformer. India's environmental system is in relatively better health than China's given that it is poorer.

Studies of within-country variation confirm environmental modernization theory. In their 44-indicator measure of social, economic, and environmental sustainability in 2339 county-level units in China in 2005, Liying Sun and colleagues (Sun, Ni, and Borthwick 2010) find that the most sustainable areas are overwhelmingly rich coastal cities while the least sustainable are poor inland rural areas. Despite lower population densities and more abundant natural resources, the poorer parts of China in the west are unable to generate social and economic resources, and that in turn degrades environments.

Jared M. Diamond refers to China as a "lurching giant" because rapid economic development both degrades the environmental system through direct impacts and enhances it through technological and policy solutions. Diamond is impressed with China's "unique form of government, top-down decision-making" that makes environmental improvements possible. However, Indian castes, he notes, have long provided an equally effective bottom-up mechanism of sustainability by limiting different groups to the exploitation of just one natural resource such as a stream, certain farming, certain lands, and so on that they pass on to their

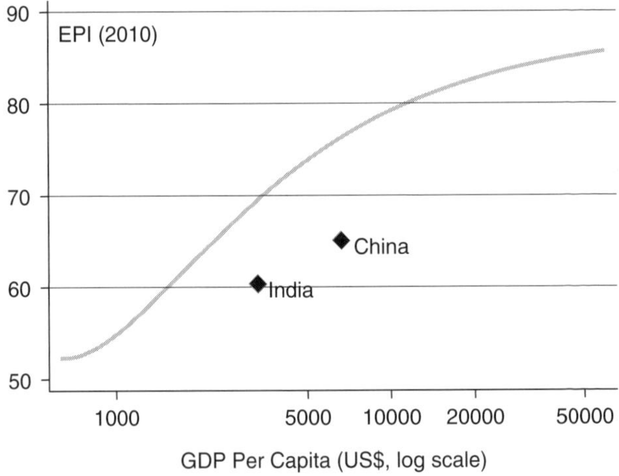

Figure 10.1 Income and environmental system quality (n = 149 countries)
Sources: World Bank 2011; YCELP 2010.

children (Diamond 2005: 377). Modernization poses a threat to both mechanisms, however – one reason that their environments may have declined so precipitously.

Stephen Morse (2008: 80) warns that the assumption that increased wealth will improve the environment is comforting "especially to those countries undergoing rapid economic development such as China." Yet as he notes, the purely environmental quality components of the EPI without the socio-economic impact and policy response components more closely approximate the (quadratic) inverted-U environmental Kuznets curve, consistent with the PEI. In other words, the greater sustainability of coastal areas in China may reflect the more extensive policy response and resources for managing impacts. Stripped of these GDP-driven factors, the environmental degradation of those regions would stand out as worse than that of the poor but undeveloped inland, as others have argued (De Groot, Withagen, and Zhou 2004).

In other words, in comparative terms, China is already underperforming its income-level peers in environmental protection and, stripped of income-related components, its environmental record may be worse still. China therefore has likely accumulated severe quality problems in its environmental sub-system when compared to the more typical India. China's environmental sub-system may have reached a point of near-collapse, whereas India's still has the chance of avoiding the worst parts of the inverted-U. As Thomas Homer-Dixon puts it: "By degrading its environment, drawing down its energy resources, and creating appalling disparities between its rich and poor, China is stretching the limits of its elasticity, perhaps close to the breaking point" (Homer-Dixon 2006: 276).

The social system that underpins human sustainability refers to the norms and structures that facilitate social cooperation. From the standpoint of objective structural challenges to social cooperation such as poverty and gender inequality, as well as subjective experiences of life satisfaction, China's social system is in better shape than India's. However, all of these measures except perhaps social trust have a positive linear, rather than inverted-U, relationship to development levels. Growth has made both countries more sustainable in terms of their social systems.

The more pressing aspect of social systems is social trust and conflict, which is usually hypothesized to follow the inverted-U pathway as rapid growth loosens traditional social bonds before new structures and resources can be brought to bear on creating a new social stability. For instance, ethnic alienation and conflict has been escalating in both countries as they have grown rapidly, in Tibet and Xinjiang for China, and Kashmir and the Northeast states for India. Rapid growth has stimulated sub-national identities and perceptions of deprivation. The social trust indicator thus shows China as having unusually strong social fabric (consistent with a culturalist theory of Chinese exceptionalism that has underpinned its social and political stability despite rapid growth) while India looks more typical of a rapidly growing country caught at the top of the inverted-U.

Finally, political system quality refers to the ability of institutions to deliver valued public goods such as security, stability, conflict resolution, and welfare. Both countries have often been seen as teetering on the brink of political collapse (Akbar 1985; Chang 2001). That neither country has collapsed tells us nothing about the value of these predictions – they might be good ones that simply did not come to pass. Several multi-country research projects seek to theorize the causes of political collapse and then rate countries accordingly. In most cases, China comes out ahead of India. The reason is that threats to the state's coercive monopoly seem less severe in China than in India, while the effectiveness of state institutions in formulating and implementing policies seems greater in China than in India. In effect, state dominance is used as the metric for most political system quality measures.

This essentially Weberian notion of political sustainability is much like the "political order" theories of Huntington. He admired North Korea with its "well-organized, broadly-based, complex" political system and called China "one of the most outstanding political achievements of the mid-twentieth century." However, it is often forgotten that Huntington also believed that India had achieved significant political order as a result of the highly institutionalized Congress Party and Indian Civil Service (Huntington 1968: 84, 342, 343). More to the point, political system quality may depend more on the ability of a political system to manage social conflicts and maintain legitimacy than simply to dominate society. Pranab Bardhan argues that because of its relatively greater social heterogeneity, India is better at managing conflicts even if China is better at solving collective action problems. Yet over time, he argues, it is countries that manage conflicts that are more likely to endure – especially as they ride over the hump of the inverted-U. "Indian heterogeneity and pluralism have ... provided the basis for a better ability to politically manage conflicts, which I am not sure China's overarching homogenizing bureaucratic state has so far acquired, even though this ability is likely to be sorely needed in the future years of increasing conflicts inevitable in a fast-growing internationally-integrated economy with mounting disparities and tensions" (Bardhan 2003: 17).

The Economist Intelligence Unit (EIU) states: "India's democratic institutions are firmly entrenched and resilient, with orderly and generally accepted transfers of power. The risk of political collapse is therefore much lower than in most other developing countries in Asia" (EIU 2010: 5). By contrast, its assessment of China notes that "corruption, and a growing gulf between the political leadership and the mass of the public whom they are meant to represent, are the most obvious consequences of the failure to introduce political checks and balances" (EIU 2009: 9).

One political stability rating system, by the Brookings Institution, finds that India is on a more sustainable political trajectory than China because of its democratic system – which accounts for 40 percent of its overall political strength rating. Brookings also includes gross human rights abuses as an indicator in a lack of security for citizens vis-à-vis the state. This factor, coupled with more accurate measures of civil unrest in China's far western Xinjiang and Tibet regions, leads to a closer measure of security in the two states as well. As Brookings notes: "Contrary to some conventional usage, we do not equate 'strong' states with authoritarian or semi authoritarian regimes that impose their will within or beyond their borders, a criterion that would make North Korea, for example, a strong state (rather than a weak one, as we regard it). Instead, a state's strength or weakness is a function of its effectiveness, responsiveness, and legitimacy across a range of government activities" (Rice and Patrick 2008: 3).

Perhaps this explains why, as Guang shows in this volume, local officials in China are increasingly responding to land disputes in an "Indian manner," although they would be loathe to admit as much. As Edward Friedman relates: from "Gandhi's supposed romanticism to various environmental movements, India is experienced by the politically conscious in China as weakened by a lack of a Nietzschean-like will to power and domination. India's surrendering power and political will to societal forces in a liberal democracy, is, from the perspective of CPC nationalism, imagined in Beijing as diffusing effort, capacity and possibility away from a strong central state which would supposedly have the will and wherewithal to struggle in the anarchic and amoral international world so that the nation could win" (Friedman 2009: 85).

To the extent that democratic mechanisms support this political resilience, India is clearly ahead of modernization expectations, whereas China is increasingly behind. The basic problem is a tendency to conflate bureaucratic authoritarian rule with political system quality and to view politics as a threat to states rather than as a process of state-building (Hameiri 2007). If political sustainability depends upon the creation of institutions that both deliver public goods and manage political conflicts, then again we are left with a mixed comparison between China and India.

In sum, the systems underlying national sustainability in both China and India have come under significant stress as a result of rapid growth. Both face severe environmental stresses, while India confronts social stresses and China political stresses.

Integrated comparative assessments remain very tentative (Gilley 2011), however. Because of this, we need higher-level theories that explain national "collapse" in terms of a hierarchy of sub-systems. There is at present no such hierarchy that can predict social collapse. Diamond (Diamond 2005) has argued for the centrality of environmental sub-system and the contributing role of political and social sub-systems, while Tainter's earlier theory and its successors (Caldararo 2004; Railey and Reycraft 2008; Tainter 1988) centered on the degradation of political and economic sub-systems as a result of excessive complexity. Most, like Homer-Dixon (2000; 2006), admit the interrelatedness of the sub-systems, and the inherent unpredictability of their effects.

China, by virtue of being richer, has the resources to be a more sustainable society than India under ecological or political modernization theories. However, in practice, it is "straying from the path" of becoming more environmentally and politically sustainable as development proceeds. As development has progressed, it has accumulated rising environmental and political sustainability deficits without enjoying the concomitant windfalls that might allow it to swing back into equilibrium. As a result, it requires ever-faster economic growth to prevent rising dissatisfaction. In short, China is caught in a razor's edge sustainability race.

India, by contrast, has all the problems associated with a lower level of development. But it is along, or, in the case of political sustainability, ahead of the modernization trajectory, meaning that it is more sustainable than would be expected given its income level. As development has progressed, India has accumulated rising environmental and political sustainability surpluses, such that the strains and stresses of modernization are accommodated. Perhaps as a result, India is less driven to deliver high growth.

The dilemma of growth models – that they create problems even as they create resources for solving them – only raises the key question: can political leaders in China and India leverage new resources to make the necessary changes?

3 The Dynamics of Sustainability

While sustainability challenges are only now becoming acute, political leaders in both China and India have thought about the issue for several decades. In China, beginning in the 1980s, growing worries among intellectuals about the need to assure national sustainability began to affect policy. By far the most prominent voice in this debate has been government researcher Hu Angang, who has analyzed in turn the challenges to the nation of population pressures (Hu 1989), fiscal incapacity (Hu and Wang 1993), regional inequalities (Hu, Wang, and Kang 1995), environmental decay (Hu 1997), political corruption (Hu 2001), and global integration (Hu 2002). The collapse of communism in the Soviet Union in particular prompted this sort of wide-ranging analysis of the environmental, social, political, and economic problems that had accumulated within China's development model. Creating sustainable institutions and practices was tied to the responsibility to protect the Chinese nation and the CPC.

As part of the Five-Year Plan beginning in 1995, the Party adopted a new maxim of "sustained, fast, and healthy growth." A *People's Daily* commentary of 1995 said: "The rapidity we need is a sustained rapidity rather than a rapidity over one or two years. Therefore, when setting a speed, we must leave some margin, and the current speed must aim at creating favorable conditions, rather than placing obstacles, for future speed ... If we fail to attend to these problems at an early date, a sustained economic development will be unlikely and we will become powerless before environmental and social problems" (*People's Daily* 1995: October 17: 1). Thus for China, sustainability has been embedded in a grand strategy of survival for nation and regime. As Lo notes of China: while "the CPC is solidly entrenched, it remains nervous about the sustainability of economic growth, tightening resource constraints and ethnic tensions. It worries about its continuing capacity to deliver good governance and maintain regime legitimacy" (Lo 2010: 2).

In India, by contrast, the idea of sustainability was more integrated into the founding myths and ideology of the regime. Gandhi's many sustainability-linked concepts included holism, localism, participation, naturalism, ecological stewardship, and limits to consumption (Cox 2004; Gruzalski 2002; Khoshoo and John 2009; Lal 2000). Whereas activists like Hu Angang in China have struggled to connect sustainability concerns to their country's political and cultural heritage, those in India have had the opposite problem of being trapped within the overpowering influence of Gandhi.

Gandhi's ideas were of course honored more in the breach than the observance by socialist planners under Nehru. But India was always open to the idea of sustainability because of Gandhi's influence, whereas the idea of limits to growth were tantamount to political treason under Mao. India presented one of the key papers to the Earth Summit in Brazil in 1992 (while China did not participate). The idea of sustainability was incorporated into India's Ninth Five Year Plan in 1997. While both countries aim at national survival, India's goals have not been couched in the language of regime or government survival. Moreover, India's strategy explicitly integrates social, economic, political, and environmental sustainability (consistent with the Gandhian heritage) whereas for China, political sustainability is treated as a separate project.

Political leaders in both countries have strengths that could help them to manage sustainability stresses better than in other countries in Asia (compared, say, to Thailand, the Philippines, or Burma) and their economic growth trajectories will provide new resources for change. Both can draw upon significant civilizational resources. Indeed, that is why they are both ancient civilizations. A tentative conclusion is that both countries fit the "lurching giant" description of Diamond – meaning they are subject to "changes for the better and changes for the worse, often in rapid alternation" (Diamond 2005: 374). This may be precisely because they are getting closer to the top of the inverted-U where one would expect to see a simultaneous existence of extreme challenges with the sudden influx of structural and policy solutions to them. The dynamics of lurching in China and India raise a number of issues, in particular how far can they lurch without collapsing, or putting themselves on a trajectory of collapse that is virtually impossible to reverse? Many have argued that India's social fabric is torn beyond repair or that China's political system is likewise irreparable.

It may be that there is a sort of "double movement" in sustainability paths that parallels the nineteenth-century "double movement" of market expansion and market protection paths by Polanyi (Polanyi 1944). China may be more prone to sudden lurches historically than India because of its particular civilizational features, such as centralization vs. decentralization, homogenization vs. pluralism, and so on.

Threats to the sustainability system resulting from rapid growth *can* be ameliorated through structural and policy responses. However, for countries like China and India, this transition will be dramatic and risky. It is *dramatic* in the Myrdalian sense of an intense, immense story that speeds towards a climax with an uncertain ending. The ending will be written by choices made by civil society and elites in the societies who can choose to undertake the difficult tasks of embracing reforms to ensure sustainability. "The action in this drama is speeding toward a climax. Tension is mounting: economically, socially, and politically" (Myrdal 1968: v. 1, 34).

The transition is *risky* in the sense that by definition, inverted-U transitions are most unstable just as they reach that climax, the peak of unsustainability. "The only way onward is to keep wringing new loans from nature and humanity" (Wright 2004: 84), which unfortunately have both been pushed to their limits. The choice then is to make radical changes to restore the underlying sustainability sub-systems. But the political will to change course may be too little, or it could simply be too late. Policy-makers might believe that they can tunnel under the inverted-U somehow, averting the worst phase of unsustainability. But it may be too late. The Asian Drama of today is the drama of sustainability choices in China and India (Lam and Lim 2009).

Optimistic assessments of the potential of these Asian giants to lurch their ways back to sustainability are common. Gary Jefferson and colleagues believe that China's institutions will respond effectively to the social challenge on inequality, if for no other reason than China's leaders have a vested interest in the reform process (Jefferson, Hu, and Su 2006: 45). Frauke Urban (2009) argues that both China and India have an opportunity to make a transition to low-carbon energy through the use of domestic natural resources and the choice of technology. He stresses the importance of not assuming past models apply because, for instance, countries like China and India can achieve technological leapfrogging, going straight to best-practice low carbon energy, and because they often have options such as local bio-fuels and nuclear fast reactors that provide immediate Pareto (win-win) gains, a point made by others (Raj and Rajan 2007).

The Chinese and Indian growth "miracles" have been useful illustrations of catch-up-based growth. However, the early development models were deficient in not paying attention to the question of sustainability. The transition to lower growth at the technological frontier requires structural, sectoral, institutional, and strategic adjustments. There is certainly no singular sustainability model and yet both countries could learn from one another in many respects. India could feasibly borrow from Chinese experiences in economic system quality by paying more attention to fiscal probity and in social system quality by paying more attention to its spatially dispersed urbanization-driven poverty alleviation strategies. China could feasibly borrow from Indian experiences in environmental system quality by more carefully managing industrialization and in political system quality by allowing for more participation and voice in decision-making. Both countries should learn from each other to understand the complex dynamics of human sustainability systems.

Doing so requires political leadership and social support. There is no saying which country will do better in this "second transition" following the "first transition" to rapid growth. The contingent and interactive nature of development decisions in any large developing country like China or India means that the world can only watch and wait.

Notes

1. *minzu kechixuxing* in Mandarin Chinese, *jatiya nirantaratā* in Hindi.
2. A good measure of external views of their economic stability.

11
The "Living Wisdom" of China's Development Experience

Zhenglai Deng

1 Development experience and knowledge

In recent years, particularly since the outbreak of the global financial crisis in 2008, there has been flooding of declarations and claims, among the academics and public commentators in China, of "the end of the West," "China is saving capitalism," "China rules the world," or "the Chinese model." Regardless of how we see these declarations and claims, one thing has become clear: that changes in China and the world in these years have raised significant new challenges and opportunities for China studies. Much in my view reflects the poverty of the intellectual tools we employ to understand growth and development experience of China for the past 30 years or even beyond.

I argue in this chapter that existing models for explaining China's development experience are insufficient, as most of them are empirically incapable of reflecting the full range of endogenous forces and dynamics that have shaped the experience to become what it is, and epistemologically inflexible to allow valid descriptions and inferences of historically and civilizationally different growth experiences. Understanding China's development experience requires greater intellectual space for analytical frameworks appropriate for China's development experience, ones that allow exposure and analysis of forces and dynamics in China's development experience that are untreatable in existing social sciences models and theories. These analytical frameworks, one of which is proposed in this chapter, amount to a "knowledge transition" in our thinking, conceptualizing and framing in the social sciences and in China studies in particular. It requires a rediscovery of China, a reframing of China's development experience, and a reorientation of China studies to flourish on broader intellectual and epistemological foundations.

"To *re*discover China," of course, is not to throw away all existing theories and frameworks on China's development experience, but rather to suggest that we should be conscious of the contemporary conditions for China's development experience, the evolving nature of the problem of development, broader cultural and intellectual resources available in China and yet untapped in popular studies of China's development experience, and appropriate research methods and analytical frameworks that a full understanding of the conditions and problems would require. To re*discover* China, moreover, is not to intend to find a universal theory and method for such an exercise, but rather, to suggest that we take a more critical approach toward existing theories, concepts and frameworks, so as to develop a "paradigm" that can effectively explain the way of existence and development of the Chinese civilization. Finally, to rediscover *China* is not to presuppose a definitive and essentialist China, but rather to understand and describe a civilization on a solid ethic foundation. It is not to focus exclusively on an economic China with an outstanding performance in economic development, but rather, a historical China with a deeply rooted tradition, but also as part of the contemporary world structure.

The analytical framework I propose here therefore concerns four mutually related dimensions: (1) a theoretical explanation of the link between China's development experience and the Chinese traditional culture; (2) a theoretical construct of the discourse on globalization and China; (3) a description of resources in Chinese culture and philosophy that are universally applicable and compatible with modern conditions; and (4) a theoretical explanation of the Chinese "living wisdom."

This chapter will examine the fourth issue and bring the whole discussion to bear on the first issue. I shall develop my discussion around the concept of living wisdom and demonstrate the relationship between China's living wisdom and its development experience, which in my view form the core of a development model of living wisdom. Given the critical importance of the concept to the whole thesis here, and perhaps its significant deviation from mainstream theories and concepts in explaining China and its development, I will not start with a normative judgment of the "development model of living wisdom," but rather focus this chapter on how the concept and the model built around it analyzes and explains.

I shall proceed with the task in three sections in this chapter. In the first section, I will discuss living wisdom as a general theoretical concept. This is necessary and critical for my overall thesis here. It involves a theoretical concern that scholarly attempts to explain China's development experience shall be sensitive to the real issues in China's development practice rather than be informed simply by theoretically constructed problems on the basis of institutional indicators that are easy to generate scholarly communication in popular discourses, but have little to do with the practices and real life in China.

This implies an interest in exploring a possible philosophical spirit that underlies the link between China's development and uniquely Chinese cultural tradition. The value of such a philosophical spirit as an analytical tool is important for the following reasons. If one believes there is no social science research that is absolutely value neutral, then any social science research would be informed by some form of philosophical and ideological commitment. An absolutely value-neutral social scientific theory is non-existent. Social science research, as long as it aspires to be thoughtful, will have to resort to certain philosophical promises. Immanuel Wallerstein suggested that scientists are deeply embedded in their natural and living environment. This is the material basis for the link between one's intellectual activities and philosophical and ideological bias (Wallerstein 1996: 100).

In the second section, I shall critically examine key theories of the Chinese model of economic development, particularly those popular among Chinese academics. I will demonstrate that these popular theories are largely "knowledge oriented" and "institution oriented," and are inappropriate for an effective understanding of China's development experience. The last section will outline a theoretical framework on a model of China's development centered on the concept of living wisdom.

2 A general concept of living wisdom

The concept of living wisdom in China's development experience can be summarized in the following seven propositions.

Proposition 1 Theories and discourses of the Chinese model of economic development mostly are not wisdom oriented, but knowledge oriented. Research and studies of this kind presuppose that human society and human nature are accessible to human knowledge, and therefore that they are explainable and understandable through knowledge. This presupposition overlooks or disregards, however, the intuitive nature of human activities and relations, and consequently the shaping power and generating capacity of living wisdom in human society.

My distinction between knowledge and wisdom is inspired by the notion of two different categories of knowledge as developed in the works of Michael Polanyi, Friedrich Hayek, and Michael Oakeshott.

In their view, human knowledge can be divided into two types: technical knowledge – explicit knowledge or theoretical knowledge, and practical knowledge – or tacit knowledge. For the former, "its chief characteristic is that it is susceptible of precise formulation, although special skill and insight may be required to give it that formulation." As for the latter, "the method by which it may be shared and becomes common knowledge is not the method of formulated doctrine ... Its normal expression is in a customary or traditional way of doing things, or simply, in practice" (Oakeshott 1991: 12, 15).

Oakeshott further points out, "The heart of the matter is the preoccupation of the Rationalist with certainty. Technique and certainty are, for him, inseparably joined because certain knowledge is, for him, knowledge which does not require to look beyond itself for its certainty; knowledge, that is, which not only ends with certainty but begins with certainty and is certain throughout" (Oakeshott 1991: 16). On this, however, Hayek argues that mentality is rather a social and cultural construct, where there is a close connection between the order to be sensed by everyone, that is Hayek's "sensory order," and the inexplicable knowledge, that is "tacit knowledge." In other words, tacit knowledge is superior to other kinds of knowledge. Tacit knowledge enables organic beings to "exist continuously," born out of and closely related to human senses of responding to events that will influence the way of being (Hayek 1952: 82).

This "tacit knowledge" is what I call "tacit wisdom." Living wisdom is therefore a different kind of knowledge, acquired and accumulated through every day life and practice in responding to different kinds of challenges in the real world of life. It is about what is true or right and what the best to act in response is. In this chapter, knowledge, as in knowledge-oriented studies, refers specially to technical knowledge while wisdom, as in wisdom-oriented studies, refers to living wisdom as defined here.

Proposition 2 By definition, all knowledge-oriented studies have a presupposed value judgment or an ideological commitment, whether they are claimed to be "normative" or "scientific." Consequently, they are unable to concern, let along carefully examine, the living wisdom that shapes human activities, relations, and society, and the living philosophy that provides foundational support for such living wisdom. The purpose of living wisdom is to survive and develop, and therefore it is fundamentally not free of value or ideological judgment.

Logos is a core concept in philosophy and even in the wider science and social sciences in the West. From there modern rhetoric, logics, science, and rationalism have developed. The meaning of *Logos* in Heraclites' original sense has undergone significant change along with the development of philosophy, particularly since the Enlightenment, following the rise of natural science ever since Galileo. Most notable is the transformation of philosophy from being spirit based to being mathematics-based, and science-dominated (Zhang 2004). As a consequence, scientism, rationalism, and "logos-centrism" have become core values and principles of the modern social sciences.

Value judgment and ideological commitment in logos-centrism led to the tradition of binary opposition in Western metaphysical tradition – soul vs. body, nature vs. culture, man vs. woman, and truth vs. falsehood, one often negating the other. Not only does logos-centrism tend to be ideologically presupposed or biased, it is unable to concern the living wisdom, particularly the Dao-based core philosophy of Chinese culture. In contrast, living wisdom is non-value presupposed, non-ideological. It is a living centered, non-logos philosophy, free of values and ideologies.

Proposition 3 Knowledge-oriented studies are inherently about seeking knowledge accumulation. Hence, these studies are inevitably conceptual or logical exercises within the established framework of knowledge. They become meaningless when they are outside the framework. Consequently, there is no study so far investigating the significance of knowledge increment studies and their relations with knowledge frameworks.

Knowledge-oriented studies follow what I call "the Iron Law of Knowledge" (*zhishi tielü*), a rule that governs knowledge traditions and accumulation. All our knowledge has developed within our intellectual traditions and trajectories. Without these traditions and trajectories, there would be no knowledge accumulation. Scholarly traditions and trajectories are therefore the only benchmark by which we can assess whether a particular research is creative or not. Without intellectual traditions and trajectories built up through generations of scholars and intellectuals, we are unable to see whether research is accumulation. The notion of living wisdom challenges this iron law of knowledge, and fundamentally reflects upon knowledge, the logics of knowledge production, and the basic assumptions of scientism in knowledge-oriented researches.

Proposition 4 Knowledge-oriented studies, by definition, are constructivist, logic based, definitive, generalized, and even ideological. They are inherently committed to generalization. Living wisdom, in contrast, is historical, contemporary, and even futurist. It is in the spirit of the people. There is always "tacit knowledge," in the sense Hayek uses the term, in Chinese culture – a hybrid of traditional, present, and future wisdom.

Living wisdom is a tacit knowledge – *tacit* in the sense that it is implied. It emphasizes the way we know something (know how) rather than our ability to describe what we know (know that). As Hayek has pointed out, *know-how* is embedded in the mode of rule-based behavior. We may be able to discover these rules, but we do not have to describe these rules in order to follow them. Among other things, tacit knowledge has two important qualities. First, tacit knowledge is closely related to cultural traditions and this relationship is achieved through reproduction among individuals and groups. Tacit knowledge provides consistent guidance for people to act in various circumstances. It is independent of rationality and gained though learned and explained experiences, and through cultural traditions inherited through things such as those for Chinese family education. In other words, this know-how tacit knowledge is not preserved and spread through formal institutions, but embedded in the informal social institutions and networks. At the centre of this are the norms for daily social activities.

Second, tacit knowledge is highly individualized knowledge. While this tacit knowledge embedded in cultural traditions and informal social institutions and networks, the content of tacit knowledge of an individual is not determined by cultural traditions or informal social institutions and networks. It is dependent upon the individual or the knower. This tacit knowledge reflects the environment and conditions the knower finds for himself in his learnt wisdom through informal family education, communication, and social experience. The reflection is no doubt very specific for the individual and thus it has very limited possibilities to be communicated or reproduced. The knowledge living wisdom explores therefore is not technical knowledge emphasized in conventional knowledge-oriented studies that seeks certainty and universality, but rather tacit or practical knowledge that is uncertain and particular.

Proposition 5 Living wisdom is wisdom outside knowledge frameworks that are closely intertwined and interacts with knowledge and valid ideologies. Living wisdom does not subscribe to principles, but it has its own principles – living principles. It does not subscribe to universal values or morals, but follows particular values or morals. It is value free or ideology free. However, at the same time, it disguises itself in knowledge and valid ideologies.

The ethical or moral principles in living wisdom are what Max Weber calls "responsibility ethics." Weber separates an ethic of responsibility from an ethic of ultimate ends based on the value of an action and its foreseeable consequences. Unlike an ethic of ultimate ends, which appeals to universal ethic principles, an ethic of responsibility follows specific ethical rules guided by the foreseeable consequences of an action. As he argued, "there is a profound opposition between acting by the maxim of the ethic of conviction (putting it in religion terms: 'The Christian does what is right and places the outcome in God's hands'), and acting by the maxim of the ethic of responsibility, which means that one must answer for the (foreseeable) consequences of one's actions" (Weber 1994: 359–60). Also, "The person who subscribes to the ethic of conviction feels 'responsible' only for ensuring that the flame of pure conviction (for example, the flame of protest against the injustice of the social order) is never extinguished" (Weber 1994: 360). Therefore, the ethic of conviction follows universal moral principles while ethic of responsibility emphasizes consequence-led particular moral principles.

This point is particularly relevant to the dual structure of ideology in China.[1] Living wisdom in China is often disguised in naturally valid official ideology. Here, different kinds of knowledge, including technical knowledge, are valid under the official ideology and form interactive relations with living wisdom or incorporating into its own, insofar as they satisfy the principles of the ethic of responsibility, that is, living principles.

As we can see, living wisdom suggests an interactive structure among the production and reproduction of wisdom and knowledge, the Weberian ethic of responsibility and ethic of ultimate ends, as well as dualism in ideological structure. It highlights and explains the complex interactions in the real world with the principle of living as the highest principle.

Proposition 6 Living wisdom is therefore local, though it differs from what is in Geertz's "local knowledge" (Geertz 1983). It is living, valid, flexible, and to some extent, imitable and communicable. It comes largely from family education and socialization, rather than from knowledge, disciplines, and scientific paradigms in formal school education. It differs over time, across places, according to one's social position, and even because of different personal character. Its quality and validity are therefore particular, contextual, and temporal. It does not recognize any ideological commitment to any individual, but only functions within its own boundary of validity. This fundamentally means that living wisdom is a highly individualized local knowledge in its mode of existence, spreading, production, and reproduction.

Proposition 7 It is worth emphasizing that knowledge of social sciences is by definition people-centered, and informed by the imperatives of modern order in state, social, and international systems. It essentially excludes nature, treating it as an object. Even when it does concern nature, it treats nature as external. Living wisdom, however, is ecological, and concerns humans and nature as an integral one. It is not informed by the imperatives of modern order in state, social, and international systems. This fundamentally means that living wisdom is congruent with the *Nomos* of ethnic groups or communities, and is in harmony with "external" nature and internal "nature."

3 The China model and its theories

The concept of living wisdom is intended to bring our attention to the need for greater intellectual space for knowledge and knowledge acquisition, and particularly to the value of wisdom-oriented knowledge. This is critically important for our efforts to understand one of the great human achievements in recent human history, the development experience of China. Since Joshua Cooper Ramo, a senior consultant at Goldman Sachs and a senior editor at the *Time* Magazine, coined the concept of "Beijing Consensus," China's development experiences have been grouped under the topic of the Chinese model and have gained tremendous popularity in the Chinese and international scholarly communities. To explain China's development experiences we will need, therefore, first of all to examine the whole debate concerning the Chinese model.

The Chinese model debate has been dominated by two different groups of contending arguments. One group, led by Qin Hui, Deng Xiaomang, and János Kornai, is very critical of the notion of the Chinese model. Members of this group either offer very critical interpretations of the Chinese model, or singly refuse to accept that such a model of economic development exists. For Qin, the Chinese model symbolizes the comparative "advantage of low human rights" endowment in the globalizing world, suggesting that China has not integrated into world civilization (Qin 2010). Deng, commenting on the recent case of the waves of Foxconn employee suicides, argues that it is wrong to suggest that China has invented a development "model." The so-called Chinese model is largely the Western model of the nineteenth century, perhaps with some "Chinese characteristics." The fact that we have this very old model in today's China has something to do with the weakness of solidarity of the working class in China (Deng 2010: 92–3). During a recent interview by a Chinese newspaper, Kornai argued that "model" as a concept refers to a true process made up of a series of historical events. China is the most populous country in the world, with distinct cultural traditions. This makes its development experience hard to copy, and it therefore makes little sense to speak of a "Chinese Model" (Kornai 2010).

The other group, including leading scholars such as Pan Wei and Yao Yang, endorses the concept of the Chinese model. These scholars provide preliminary explanations of the Chinese model, naturally framed in the institutionalist paradigm. Pan, for example, argues that the Chinese model is a unique and excellent form of interest equilibrium. Its success challenges the dichotomy of plan vs. market in economics; democracy vs. authoritarianism in political science; and state vs. society in sociology. Pan sees the Chinese model as consisting of three dimensions: a societal model of *sheji* (state-embedded) with the integrated whole of the state and its members; a political model of *minben* (people-centered) with the single Party representing the people to govern; and an economic model of *guomin* (national) with the dominance of the SOEs (Pan 2009: 3–85).

While the two groups appear to oppose each other in their arguments, these arguments are very much framed in the same way, sharing similar paradigmatic assumptions. The Chinese model, both for those who support it and those who oppose it, is of a series of distinct institutional factors, such as national development strategy, institutional arrangements, and decision-making that differ from other models, especially the Soviet or Western models. The debate about the Chinese model between these two groups centers on the following issue areas: on politics, either defending the unified Party leadership or appealing to democratic transition; on the economy, either supporting a state-led market economy or arguing for further market liberalization; on society, either advocating a harmonious society for stability or emphasizing full protection of human rights and liberty; and on external relations, either insisting on an independent, autonomous, and peaceful foreign policy, or opposing money diplomacy, taking more responsibilities as a major power, and protecting the environment and human rights (Lin and Yao 2006; Zheng 2010).

These theories and arguments about the Chinese model are knowledge oriented and they all share several additional problems. Firstly, they all focus on institutional factors and assume consistency, harmonization, and complementarity of these factors in a top-to-bottom deployment model. However, research has shown that in China's development experience such consistency, harmonization, and complementarity is not possible in practice. They are largely imagined. Post-war political theory, particularly public policy theory, has recognized the importance of policy implementation in public policy process. In these studies, problems in policy implementation arise because of the following reasons. First, there are various technical difficulties in policy implementation, some of which are difficult to overcome as they are complex, unique, and interdependent, and implementation often concerns a series of policies rather than a single policy. The diversity of the problems a particularly policy responds to also makes implementation difficult. The larger, and more diverse the target groups of a policy, the more difficult it is to use preset instruments to influence the target groups. Moreover, the extent of change a policy expects from target groups largely determines the level of difficulty. Those policies concerning change in cultural tradition – to eliminate ethnic discrimination, for example – are hard to implement within a short span of time (Howlett and Ramesh 1995: 234–40). The theory that public policies can be consistent and free of distortions in their top-to-bottom implementation has little empirical evidence to support it.

The reform and social transition in China that underlie its development experience have two outstanding features. One is the insufficiency of involved institutions and the historical circumstances for that. The other is that the reform is a historical process of interest differentiation and realignment. China's reform, particularly since the 1990s, took place with a strong disillusion over the Soviet planning model and Western mainstream development models. It took shape with no preset target model or a design for a development strategy. Those institutional factors identified in our scholarly discussions and analyses formed in this historical process, which is a process of "crossing the river by groping for stepping stones underneath" (*mozhe shitou guohe*).

Moreover, social resources that used to be under the state's direct control started to be distributed and transferred (*fangquan rangli*) during the reform. This has led to significant change in social groups and structure.[2] It has also brought change in the relations between central and local government. In particular, the reform of the taxation system in 1994 (*fenshuizhi gaige*) to separate central and local taxes has transformed local governments into legitimate units of self-interest.[3] While the Central Government represents broad national interests, ministries of the Central Government and governments at provincial, municipal, county, and township levels all started to have their special interests, and, driven by these interests, to take what Jürgen Habermas would call strategic actions.[4] The Chinese saying, that government above has a policy, but people in the real world have a strategy (*shang you zhengce, xia you duice*), echoes exactly this point. Without understanding this, it would be hard to understand why there are various models – Sunan, Wenzhou, Shandong, and so on – in China's development experience. How is it possible that we can have all these apparently different, or even antithetical, local or regional models under one singular Chinese model? The Chinese model is therefore not a single formula. If we only see it as a grand macro strategy, policy, and directive at the national level, we will not be able to explain how units of different interests interpret, frame, or even distort those institutional factors from their own interests and local circumstances.

Second, whether they endorse or reject the Chinese model, those in the debate all focus on aspects of the institutional factors that are different from the West. The institutional factors in Western experiences are the primary points of reference. The only difference between these two groups of opposite views is that those who support the Chinese model look for factors in it that are not found in Western experiences: one-Party government, state embeddedness, and so on; and those who reject the Chinese model direct their attention to the factors that are not found in Chinese institutions: democracy, human rights and liberty, labor organizations, and so on.

The problem appears to be that China's development experience, whether matters at the state or grassroots levels, has little to do with what was instrumental in the Western experiences. On the contrary, China's development practice, particularly since the early 1990s, has amounted to a "farewell" to the West, advancing Chinese reform and transition according to China's own unique socio-historical conditions.[5] Clearly, with a Chinese model framed in the Western experiences, we would be blind to endogenous practices at the state and civil levels, and their overall complexity.

Third, whether supporting or opposing the Chinese model, those in the debate are inevitably inclined to frame their claims in a rationalist framework, as if the Chinese model is an unfolding of a preset rational design. This seems to neglect the fact that the process of China's development has been a body of unintended outcomes or a process of unintended expansion. I conducted some research on the three privately owned bookstores in Beijing, Wansheng Bookstore, Fengrusong Bookstore, and Guolinfeng Bookstore, as a case study to explain the process of the unintended expansion of China's privately-owned bookstores. My research indicates that as part of the development of self-employed business (*getihu*) and privately owned enterprises, the development of privately owned book stalls and bookstores has been constrained within the large environment of reform. In their natural growth itself, though, the reform of economic institutions aimed at fostering market forces and arrangements has provided conditions for the development of the private business sector, thus generating necessary conditions for the emergence of civil society organizations.

This makes privately owned bookstalls and bookstores part of civil society, acquiring special "value addition" and being able to reflect the complex interaction between state and civil society organizations in knowledge production and dissemination. This interaction has furthermore resulted in an unintended expansion, allowing the state and other governing organizations progressively rather than revolutionarily to respond to new issues and challenges arising from this development process, adjusting themselves and law and policy, and directing economic interests to bear unintentionally on political outcomes, eventually leading to profound change in governing institutions and techniques in areas for which no reform was initially designated. This bookstore story symbolizes the same process on a much larger scale – the formation of social order. In the spirit of Carl Menger and Friedrich Hayek, the position of each factor in a social order is not a result of the concerted arranging function of an external or internal force. Rather, it is the result of the action of each factor.[6]

Fourth, these theories also overlook the influence of China's ideology and culture, as well as their interaction in the process of China's reform. They overlook the role of Chinese living wisdom in China's development. A key special feature of China's reform is its pragmatism. There are no preset ideal prospects or core values to serve as a basis for social mobilization and solidarity, which in a way makes the mainstream ideology rather open and tolerating. This opening and tolerance has been crucial in China's development experience and is, in my view, one of the great achievements in contemporary Chinese political practice. This of course is an unintended consequence. Contemporary Chinese ideology nicely mixes Marxism, which proposes a full scale assault on the political economy of capitalism; Maoism, which advocates "popular democracy"; and the thought of Deng Xiaoping, which holds that "development is of overriding importance," as well as "*minben* politics" (people-centered politics), the "rule of the virtuous" (*yide zhiguo*), and the "harmonious society" (*hexie shehui*) in Chinese cultural tradition.

This mixture has preserved the broad thinking space in the "ideal prospect" for China, but also provided multiple moral justifications for China's reform and development. It further provides broad space for practice and development of the Chinese living wisdom under the large context of dualism in form and substance in Chinese traditional culture.

A case in point. Chen Dingmo, former party secretary of Longgang Town, Wenzhou, Zhejiang, is a key figure in the development of this small town in the 1980s to become the "Number One Rural City in China," with a GDP 10 Billion *RMB* (US$1.5 billion) and a population of 300,000. Chen is someone who has a deep understanding of the Chinese living wisdom, reflected in his ability and skill in utilizing ideological openness and tolerance to guide local economic development. As early as the mid-1980s, prior to the official recognition of the right of land use in the 1988 amendments to the Constitution, Chen turned to the Marxian theory of "differential land rent," and began to charge fees for land use as fees for "public infrastructure." This solved the problem of capital shortage for the development of public infrastructure, but also stood up against ideologically motivated challenges from both government and the public about the legitimacy of charging fees for public properties. He also used lines from Marx, Mao, and Deng to provide ideological support for various new measures, devices and arrangements such as "gratis fund pooling" (*wuchang jizhi*), "compensated fund fooling," and "public and private pool capital" to fund schools, environment projects, and public services. There is no question that the openness and tolerance of China's official ideologies have enabled Chen to use his living wisdom creatively in charting the successful development of Longgang Town.

In sum, a practice-oriented explanation of the Chinese model centered on the notion of living wisdom and unintended results can be a relatively effective approach to understanding China's development experience. Living wisdom is in and of itself a practical wisdom and a main force shaping and conditioning unintended consequences. It allows us to grasp the essence of the Chinese model in the real, concrete, and substantive practice, and to construct future prospects as unintended consequences of China's development.

4 The development model of living wisdom as an ideal type

How does all of the above help us to develop an understanding of China's development experience? In this section, I will attempt to explain the development model of living wisdom, taking the ideal type[7] approach of Max Weber.

The contributions of living wisdom to China's development can be easily observed and described. For economic development, this is demonstrated primarily in what I call the *Able Person phenomenon* or Able Person model that emerges in the development of social units such as economically more advanced regions, enterprises, and even universities or social groups. As has been observed elsewhere, a key feature of China's economic development is that those economically more developed regions or enterprises have long been shaped by such able persons. We have Wu Renbao for Huaxi Village, Wang Hongbin for Nanjie Village, Zhang Ruimin for Hai'er, Liu Chuanzhi for Lenovo, Chen Dingmo for Longgang Town, and so on.

Theoretically, this Able Person phenomenon is the embodiment of authoritarian rule at the grassroots level. It is an instance of the functional logic of Weber's charismatic rule. To be sure, an authoritarian regime provides a broad institutional background for Able Person governance at grassroots levels. It also serves as an environment for the charismatic leaders to exercise their living wisdom. Charismatic leaders at the grassroots in China not only need passion, responsibility, and judgment, as Weber argues (Weber 1994), but also living wisdom. Within the boundaries of the nation-state, grassroots units face not only competition from other units at the same level for survival and living, but also the challenge of bargaining with governments at the upper levels. During the initial period of reform and opening up, there was a very strong opposition from the extreme leftists (*jizuo*). Grassroots leaders had to face very complex, fierce political pressures to do things right. They not only needed political leadership, but, more importantly, a high level of living wisdom, particularly political wisdom.

One excellent example of these grassroots charismatic leaders is Wu Renbao, someone behind the miraculous development of Huaxi Village. Wu enjoyed absolute authority in Huaxi Village, derived from his personal soft power; that is, the personal influence sourced largely in his moral character, and from the effective political capacity that originated from his living wisdom. The combination of these allowed the miracle of Huaxi Village and the miracle of Wu himself (Zhang 2003). Living wisdom shaped the Able Person model as exemplified in Wu's Huaxi Village case in the following ways. It enabled the bypassing of ideological restraints with a careful selection of ideological arguments to legitimize local economic development or to allow ideologically based arguments of opposing views to neutralize themselves; and resortde to local resources, cultural and material, and packaged new measures and arrangements in official political language.

To extend the case above to a broad framework for explaining China's development experience, the following are key elements of an ideal type of China's development model of living wisdom.

First of all, as far as it relates to economic development, living wisdom has two interconnected aspects: a self-centered community of relations with networks of family-based relations, place-based relations, business-based relations, and a Chinese diaspora network, aimed at the ethic of responsibility for local economic development (Hu 2005: 7–8); and a unit-centered community of political and economic interests that carries out strategic actions and transactions through acquaintances,[8] seeks reliable political patronage through political exchange, and secures ideological support through utilizing the performance assessment system of developmentalism.

Different from the individual-centered society in the West, China is a group-centered society, derived from family-centered society. Key to a group-centered society is the paramount importance of relations (Fei 1998: 24–30; Liang 1990: 93). On the basis of a decade-long empirical study on Chinese villages, Hu Biliang and others found that relations are a set of special rules that play a significant role in peoples' daily lives. They also contribute in a significant way to local economic development at regional levels and advance the process of regional modernization (Hu 2005: 3). The community of relations has a great impact on economic exchange: relations-based rules serve as an alternative mechanism to the "market" in a market economy in allocating resources in such economic activities as attracting Foreign Direct Investment and facilitating trade. While market rules have gradually made their way into China since reform and opening-up, and the government's administrative adjustment and control have also played an increasing important role, relations-based rules have continued to play an important alternative role in resource allocation. This is because the level of development of the market in China is still not high. Market rules have not yet fully developed. The cost of using these rules or approaching these rules is high (Chen and Hu 1996: 123–6).

The effects of the community of relations are found not only on economic exchange, but also on political exchange. The market economy in China is still state-led. There are therefore no pure economic activities, but rather economic exchanges that are affected by politics, closely related to politics, and protected through politics. Economic logic is therefore intertwined with political logic. This is true for private entrepreneurs as well as grassroots leaders. Therefore, principal players in economic activity, particularly grassroots leaders, understand the rules of the market economy, and exercise living wisdom with regard to politics. A person of living wisdom is an entrepreneur who has a good sense of market rules, and a politician who has the ability to use administrative rules and relations-based rules. In political exchange, this living wisdom reflects in one's ability to expand his community of relations inside the political system, to develop trust and patronage, and to make best use of the openness and tolerance of the official ideology to provide political support for the economic growth of one's unit.

Second, living wisdom, seen in the perspective of ethics, provides the common interest or common good of a particular living community – family, work unit, region or nation, and so on – over the broad interests of a larger community. Since early modern times, there has been a constant debate in ethics over right and good, and their relationship. This debate started in Hegel's criticism of Kant's moral universalism. More recently, the tension between liberalism and communitarianism took this debate to a higher level. The question of whether "right" or "good" has primacy over the other concerns not only our moral philosophical position, but also the complex conditions that modern society faces.

According to Habermas, accompanying value pluralism in post-conventional society is a divorce of social expectations from the cultural mode of self-determination and self-realization, that is to say, a separation of moral judgment and ethical recognition. "'Turning away from rigid conventions,' which are socially enforced, burdens the individual, on the one hand, with moral decisions of his own and, on the other hand, with an individual life project arising from the process of ethical self-understanding" (Habermas 1993a: 183). What set of values a community adopts reflects its collective identity. This collective identity further concerns the community's understanding of what are legitimate norms; that is, in the sense of Kant's universal moral for mankind. It also concerns an imagination of lifestyle by members of the community; that is, in the sense of Hegel's notion of a particular ethical identification with a lifestyle on the basis of individual peculiarity, which is not exchangeable with others.

At the individual levels, according to Habermas, this reflects the different requirements of the moral and the ethical on the individual. The former concerns interpersonal relations and symbolizes the socialized individual's interest in normality in interpersonal exchange and self-determination. The latter is about the relationship between the individual and self, and symbolizes the pursuit of non-exchangeability and self-realization by the individualized self (Habermas 1993: 1–17, 1998: 25–6, 55). It is worth noting, given the fierce competition for survival and development in modern society, that how an individual chooses values and a lifestyle is what self-realization is all about, and is what is implied in the whole idea of individual liberty.

This is also true for a living community with collective interests or common good. As long as the external environment for living is not of great harmony, it would be some form of legitimacy in a living community to allow its collective interests or common good to surpass the general interests of the parent community. From the perspective of moral philosophy, therefore, Deng Xiaoping's proposition to "let some people and some regions to get rich first, so as to bring the whole population to common prosperity" means that it might be morally right to let the collective interests of some groups – to get rich first – surpass the greater good of the whole population.

Separating right from good and the notion of the common good of community also finds a good foundation in economic theory. The Smithian problem in Joseph Schumpeter's theory, for example, arises from Smith's assumptions in *The Wealth of Nations* and *A Moral Sentiment* of human relations driven by different aspects of human nature. It is thus a problem of coordinating these two different aspects of human nature: *ego* and *sympathy*. While the Smithian problem is often interpreted as a logical contradiction in his theory, this represents multiple-dimensions of human nature and the complexity of forming a good social order. The overall teaching of Smith's theory is that the market as an invisible hand is an effective mechanism that coordinates public and private interests. It can advance public interests as an unintended consequence of self-interest activities (Jiang et al. 1997: 18–19).

In terms of economic development and living wisdom in China, we can argue that the living wisdom of differential love centered on the economic interests of the unit can also advance public welfare – such as overall national economic development – as an unintended consequence. Moreover, in Chinese reform practice, under the general ideology of common prosperity various living communities reach a level of economic development, and then expand the community as part of efforts to practice general morals on a larger scale. The case of Huaxi Village is a case in point. More recently, Huaxi Village has made notable efforts to extend the village boundaries.[9]

In the political theory of ethics, Weber's ethic of responsibility, as discussed earlier, provides theoretical support to grassroots leaders for "whole-hearted dedication to development" (*yixin yiyi mou fazhan*). All politics for each economic unit are framed in the language of the ethic of responsibility to promote economic development. The justification for this ethic of responsibility is the new ideological principle that "development is the iron principle" (*fazhan jiu shi ying daoli*). Any measures, programs, and arrangements that benefit the economic development of the unit would be supported. Under such an "ideology," '"economic development as defined by development, productive power and competitiveness becomes the primary aims of the state." Without promising equality or social welfare in development, the state "avoids tensions in its aims." In the meantime, the government does not passively support the invisible hand of market, but rather actively guides economic development, especially through top-down rational planning and special industrial policies (Yu 2008).

Moreover, the political legitimacy of this ethic of responsibility is the ideal of "for the people" (*minxiang*) compatible with the Chinese cultural tradition, rather than that of "by the people" (*minzhi*). Whether in the "Three Favorables" (*sange youliyu*) of Deng Xiaoping, the "Three Represents" (*sange daibiao*) of Jiang Zemin, or the "Three For the People" (*sange weimin*) of Hu Jintao, the core idea is *minxiang*, encouraging Communist cadres truthfully to represent "the fundamental interests of the overwhelming majority of the people," or "advance welfare for the people" (*weimin mouli*) (Zhu 2009: 624–5).

Third, living wisdom is ideologically attached to a legitimate and effective ideological discourse framework such as economic development, common prosperity, and so on. Consequently, the dual structure of the ideology that results from utilizing projections from such an ideological framework is a natural feature of living wisdom.

Ideologies in China exist in various different forms, including both officially sanctioned mainstream ideology and civic ideologies that are normatively and practically effective. The official ideology itself, as we have demonstrated earlier, has a great deal of openness and tolerance. The actual substance of the ideological discourse is more interesting. The reform and opening-up in China has followed the following path. From the time when he proposed "Adhere to the Four Cardinal Principles" (*jianchi sixiang jiben yuanze*) in the 1980s, Deng Xiaoping effectively removed the substance of socialism and Marxism from the practice of China's reform, and legitimized Chinese politics on the regime's continuation of the symbols of socialism, and Marxist-Leninist-Maoist thought. In Jiang Zemin's times, Jiang took a more forward-looking approach and attempted to use the "Three Represents" to fill the vacuum in this symbolic framework. This of course led to embarrassment and anxiety resulting from its inability to reconcile contradictory elements in the ideological frameworks of discourse.

It is in Jiang's period that China has developed mechanisms to experiment and test ideology, in order to seek the best combination of discourse frameworks to fit the political order in China, rather than continuing to reconcile internal tensions in the existing ideology (Wang 2010: 216–17). The development of these mechanisms is an exemplary illustration of how the ruling Party uses living wisdom – political wisdom – to lead to a dynamic interaction among competing discourse frameworks, and the emergence of the dual structure in China's mainstream ideology, which legitimizes the structural model of the function of living wisdom at grassroots level. Under this overall ideological environment, key propositions such as "development is the hard truth" (*fazhan shi yind daoli*), "scientific development" (*kexue fazhan*), "harmonious society" (*hexie shehui*), "rise of powers" (*daguo jueqi*), "national renaissance" (*minzhu fuxin*), people-centered (*yi ren wei ben*), "eight honors and eight disgraces" (*barong bachi*), and even the "tribute system" (*chaogong tixi*) all have the function of ideological discourse (Wang 2010: 217–22).

In this ideological context, it becomes an important part of the living wisdom (political wisdom) of grassroots leaders to use some effective ideological discourse framework(s) to justify policy, methods, and arrangements in economic development (i.e. political correctness). It is apparent that the consequent separation of form and substance in such ideological discourse, especially by those leaders doing the left but saying the right, or doing without saying, reflects their living wisdom and responses to policy and institutions.

In summary, all of these are critically important for China's economic development. Living wisdom as a model of development consists of some key elements, such as to seek ideological validation and legitimation, to pursue common interest or common good for a given community, and to resort to traditional resources of *guanxi* and shared ethics. Using living wisdom as an analytical framework to understand China's development experience allows us to see China's economic development in the past 30 years as a historical process of unintended expansion shaped through living wisdom under the protection of the dual structure of ideology, in the mode of transactions through acquaintances in economic exchange and strategic actions in political exchange, justified in the shared interests or common good of living communities at different levels, and with the aim of economic development as the highest ethic of responsibility. This is an untended outcome because it is not the result of a rational design. Rather it is an outcome of the function of non-logical living wisdom of people at various levels of society, particularly those at grass roots levels.

In Lieu of a conclusion

In lieu of a summary discussion of living wisdom and the development model of living wisdom, I wish to respond to two potential challenges. First of all, we shall not shy away from the universal significance of the development model of living wisdom, but rather analyze and understand its universal significance. As I have demonstrated above, the development model of living wisdom has its universal significance. Seeing it as a universal model places a greater demand on individual capabilities and personal qualities. Individuals under such a model would have acquired some form of living wisdom, in addition to support and assistance from the environment around, as well as positive interaction between themselves and their environment. The model of living wisdom would be broadly applicable under these conditions. Without these conditions, however, the successful story of development would be hard to replicate.

Second, there is the problem of transaction costs. On the surface, development facilitated through living wisdom might have much higher transaction costs, particularly the costs of socialization. In terms of the overall benefits of transactions, however, whether such a model incurs high transaction costs is questionable. The development experience in China shows that transaction costs, particularly the costs of socialization, are real for enterprises in China because of the insufficient support of the institutional environment. For many Chinese enterprises, transaction costs can be as high as 50 percent of their annual revenue (Liu 2008). The question here is why are businesses willing to accept such high transaction costs. And with such high costs of socialization placed on Chinese enterprises, how does China still have such an impressive performance in economic growth and development? These are difficult questions. Answers to them would require a Chinese version of the *Wealth of Nations*.

Notes

1. The concept of dual structured ideology reflects the complexity of ideology in China. In my view, there are two sets of ideologies in today's China. On the one hand, there is the official ideology used in formal documents and communications and are still very much framed in the classical works of Marx and Lenin and official guidelines of political discourses. One the other hand, there is a dominant ideology in practice that reflects much of the real world or what is actually guiding the real world. These two sets of ideologies maintain close interaction and nevertheless fulfill very different functions in Chinese society today.

2. There are two aspects to change in social structure. First, new social classes emerged outside the formal system, including the self-employed, freelancers, owners of private entrepreneurs, and senior employees of joint, foreign-owned, or private enterprises. They hold an increasing amount of social resources. Second, there are changes in social classes within the formal system, where there was an internal social stratification within the old classes of peasants, workers, and cadres. See Zhang (2000).
3. While there are different views on the 1994 taxation reform and the purpose of the reform was to increase the capacity of the central government for macro control and management, the reform in fact for the first time has established the financial autonomy of the local government in formal institutional arrangements. Through the reform, taxes are divided between central and local governments according their categories; a new transfer payment system and its working principles have been established, and there are separate taxation jurisdictions and authorities for central and local governments. For more detailed discussion on the taxation reform and its consequences; See Chen (2010); Huang and Zheng (1997); Wang (1997); Xiong (2005).
4. For Habermas, a success-oriented *strategic action* is opposite to an understanding-oriented *communicative action*. On the basis of the notions of *normatively regulated action* and *dramaturgical action*, especially *teleological (strategic) action*, Habermas proposes the concept of "communicative action." In his view, "The teleological model of action is expanded to a strategic model when there can enter into the agent's calculation of success the anticipation of decisions on the part of at least one additional goal-directed actor" (Habermas 1984: 85).
5. As part of the official ideology, this farewell to the West was disguised under the name of "socialist market economy." Cui Zhiyuan was among the first scholars to take note of this. In an article in 1994, he summarized this farewell as the second movement of ideological liberalization (*dierci sixiang jiefang*). The first, according to him, was the ideological liberalization movement starting in the late 1970s, aimed at Mao's socialist ideas and institutions. In this second movement of ideal liberalization at a new critical point of history in reform and transition, the overall purpose is not entirely clear. In this historical conjuncture of confusion, dynamism, and intricacy, the conventional dichotomous frameworks, such as private vs. state-owned, market vs. plan, China vs. West, liberal vs. conservative, and so on, are no longer sufficient, or effective, for capturing the reality and forecasting what will come next. A second ideological liberalization was therefore needed, to expand the thinking space for institutional innovation, rather than simply to overcome conservative resistance; to explore opportunities for institutional innovation, rather than dwelling on either or no dichotomies (Cui (1994)). Fourteen years later, facing the breakout of a global financial crisis, another scholar, Gan Yang, revisited the concept of a second ideological liberalization, arguing that this movement will break us from the past obsession with the American model (Gan (2008)).
6. What is noticeable is that in the history of political thought, this thesis of "unintended result" was not exclusively suggested by the Menger–Hayek School. There have been different propositions on how international social actions can result in unintended results in the formation of human social order, including Émile Durkheim's "causal analysis" and "functional

analysis"; Sigmund Freud's emphasis on sub-consciousness; and Robert Merton's "actors intending and knowing certain consequence that is helpful to systematic adaptation or adjustment" and "objective consequence neither intended by nor known to actors."

7. Ideal type is a central concept in Weber's methodology. First, it is value concerned with separating itself from logical positivism. Second, the purpose of ideal type as a methodology is not to demonstrate categorical similarities among different cultural phenomena, but rather to show their differences. Weber's ideal type is employed to show the differences among different cultures from the information provided in different ideal types while ensuring that these differences are significant on the same analytical logic; and to keep some distance from the empirical facts, to help the researcher grasp empirical objects relevant to the research interests. See Zheng (2006: 59, 63).
8. It should be pointed out that "acquaintance transaction" (*shuren jiaoyi*) excludes economic corruption through low price and insiders' deals. Instead, this concept refers to various kinds of strategic actions adopted by leaders of economic units to construct a unit-centered "*guanxi* community" (economic interest community), as well as to use this community for economic exchange and the promotion of economic development.
9. For a long time, Huaxi Village had adopted the institution of "one separation, five unifications" as initiated by Wu Renbao, namely the separation of village and enterprise, unified management of economy, unified deployment of cadres, unified arrangement of labor force under equal conditions, unified distribution of welfare, and unified planning of village infrastructure. Since 2002, Huaxi Village, via "one unification, five separations," merged with the neighboring 16 villages into a Greater Huaxi Village, with its area expanding from 0.96 to 30 square kilometers and its population from 2000 to over 30,000. See Liu (2010).

12
Conclusion: The End of Development Models?

Xiaoming Huang

The contributors in this volume were asked three sets of broad questions to help us understand the nature of rapid economic growth and development in China and India, and how they relate to the broad world experiences of modern economic development: Is there a shared pattern of economic growth and development between China and India? Does that shared pattern constitute a unique model of modern economic growth and development? How do the growth experiences of China and India fit with other experiences of modern economic growth and development?

1 Findings

The chapters in this volume have either demonstrated or made their case on the premise that there is a shared pattern in rapid and prolonged economic growth and development in China and India in the past 30 years. They both had the experience of a failed "socialist" economy and long-lost opportunities to take off in the first decades after World War II. The economic crisis and social turmoil associated with the failure led to economic reform with liberal, market institutions and processes. Since economic reform, opening, and liberalization, both countries have seen a substantial period of high-speed economic growth, social development, and national transformation.

The authors have used different frameworks and focused on different indicators in comparing the two countries' growth performance and development achievements. While a similar pattern of rapid and prolonged economic growth and social change on such a large scale under a similar set of historical conditions is clearly seen in both China and India, there is a broad consensus among the contributors that China seems to have performed better than India; and that China and India have developed different sets of unique features in their growth input structures and growth enabling systems. Moreover, views vary as to what we should make of their growth and development experiences. Das and Chatterjee in their conventional growth accounts have established the historical pattern of growth and development in the two countries, and, along with other contributors, have found that China's growth performance is much better than India on key indicators. Beyond these assessments, Woo raised concerns over whether the 1978–2005 policy framework, so successful in the past, can continue to produce the same level of growth performance; while Gilley believes that in the long term the slower and less dramatic growth record of India is perhaps an indicator of a more sustainable growth model.

Beyond the historical pattern of rapid economic growth and social development, findings on a model of economic growth between the two depart sharply. Given that the two countries differ on almost every indicator of significance for modern economic growth – except sharing the similar set of historical conditions, and the same experiences of economic reform and liberalization – one would naturally suspect that liberal reform, market institutions, and the private sector are perhaps the driving force for their rapid economic growth. Evidence from the initial description of the growth patterns in the introduction gives us no confidence in affirming this. Not only do India and China differ significantly on many of the indicators of levels of economic liberalization and marketization, their levels in international comparison are in the medium, if not lower range, of the world.

If a shared pattern is primarily of growth performance and historical path, rather than of causal relationship, would China and India each present a contrasting pattern in their growth enabling factors and forces? Many popular studies have precisely this in mind when comparing China and India. Contributors in this volume have taken case studies on some of the possible categories of theorizing about the causing factors. Through conventional growth accounting and analysis that looks at the contributions of land, capital, labor, and total factor productivity to growth outcomes, Das and Chatterjee found no clear pattern from the growth experiences of China and India to suggest that either one has been driven by a causally significant structure of inputs factors for their growth. India had lower rates of saving than China but has been quietly moving up. This is also true of government debts. India had much high government debts than China and the situation has significantly improved over the years. China had its growth financed through oversea Chinese investment, export earnings, and FDI. Sectoral contributions have come mainly from the service sector for India, and from manufacturing for China. The agricultural sector has contributed to growth in India while a significant part of growth activities has shifted to the industrial sector for China. While demand for growth in China has come significantly from export earnings, India's growth demand has been driven largely by domestic consumption.

Reconstructions of the structure of input factors have suggested that there is a unique pattern of factor contributions to growth outcomes in each of the countries, and the two do not match in their patterns. More importantly, the structures of factor inputs to growth outcomes in these two cases have raised many serious questions to the established models of modern economic growth and development. For example, standard development economies would expect that the service sector would develop when growth in industrial sector has accumulated enough skilled labor and capital, which is expected to occur at the late stage of economic development. India's growth experience displays the opposite. Its "catch up" growth has been led by the flourishing of the service sector while the agricultural sector still dominates. For another example, established development economics would expect extra labor from the agricultural sector to move to the industrial sector, thus pushing urbanization as part of the rebalancing of the labor structure when the agricultural and industrial sectors. This occurred in China in a constrained fashion, as Jason Young's chapter here has demonstrated. In India, on the other hand, such movement has not been significant.

Research and analyses using mainstream growth accounting models, frameworks or methods, as seen in Chapters 2 and 3 in this volume, suggested that like any other capitalist market economies, the Chinese and Indian economies and their historical growth experiences can be analyzed and explained using standard factors-of-production analysis. After all, the two economies are no different from the US or Japanese economies – they are all constituted by and therefore accountable to the same key contributing factors. Fu in his chapter takes his broad universalistic perspective of modern capitalist economy to a more profound level. In his institutional approach, Fu spelt out his MBW model where M is for market, B is bureaucracy and W for wealth. The B hierarchical dimension entails a sophisticated system of impersonal testing, selection, and recruitment of talented people, and a sophisticated web of checks and balances and embedded it in a rule of law system. The horizontal M dimension involves provisions of personified incentives, property rights protection, and a patent system to encourage innovations and anti-trust law to keep market competitiveness and efficient in allocating resources. If these hierarchal and horizontal building blocks are place, the model predicts good economic performance.

The China story, in Fu's view, is not something unique in human history, and the notion of the Chinese model is simply misleading. The past 30 years have been for China to make up for the underdevelopment of its markets and narrow the technological gap with the advanced economies. Behind the broad trajectories of China's reform and opening-up, the logic is consistent with existing economic theories and with the basic institutional logic that has driven modern economic growth in Europe, North America, and East Asia, and now China and India. Indeed, what is called "the Chinese model" is largely a strategy to catch up and institutionally realign in response to one's structural conditions.

We have seen in the first part of this volume that growth models can refer to patterns of growth, structures of input factors, and distinct features of growth activities, and that all these models are different manifestations of the fundamental logic of a modern capitalist market economy. This can be seen more clearly when we move from growth "accounting" to growth "explanation." Growth explanations look at the large setting beyond the immediate factors of production – forces, structures, and arrangements that enable and shape factor inputs to growth outcomes. East Asian model economies were the latest examples of modern economic growth and development to have generated various theories and hypotheses at this level.

China and India, being the two largest developing countries in Asia, allow an almost automatic reference to the East Asian growth model. China and India differ on almost every indicator of the forces that are seen to have shaped the East Asian model. The chapters here have focused on some key indicators to explore further how these factors relate to their growth and development experiences: the role of the state, political institutions, education, and labor migration. On the role of the state and political institutions, chapters by Guang and Bo have provided more sophisticated explanations as to how regime types and political institutions relate to economic growth and development. There is an established view in the literature on the East Asian economic model that the state in East Asian countries is "developmental." This more assertive, interventionist, corporatist, or even authoritarian "state" played a significant role in the success of the East Asian model economies. Moreover, because of the textbook contrast between China and India in their regime types and political institutions, the debate about regime types and economic development becomes acutely relevant and interesting. Bo's chapter picks up the classical debate between the East Asian model advocates and mainstream institutional theories over regime types and political institutions. Building up regression models between political institutions and political change on the one hand and economic growth on the other hand at both national and local levels, the study has found that regime types do matter, and, in this case, China, as a non-liberal regime with non-pluralist political institutions, has performed better than India.

Guang went beyond the regime type debate, and demonstrated in his case study how political institutions under different regime types actually function. In his investigation of the similar patterns of growth related social conflict, political reaction, and solution, Guang has found that it is the party society in India and inter-government dynamics in China that explain the very similar patterns of conflict and conflict resolution in their modern economic development. In a sense, regime types in abstract ideological terms are not much use in explaining dynamic and sophisticated development behaviors.

The chapters on education and labor migration give further evidence to how the East Asian or other growth and development models become less relevant when we make a controlled comparison between China and India. Kumar and Liu examined the role of education in economic growth and development. They found that there have been different patterns of education policy in China and India, wherein China has a more mass-based education that provided a broad range of basic education and training to a wide range of sectors of society while India has a more elitist approach to education provision. These different patterns of education provision, or education paths, have a clear impact on the growth model where the mass based education provision allowed a supply of workers with the necessary literacy level, skills, and knowledge for manufacturing industries while in India, the elitist provision of education in postgraduate studies and research allowed the booming of the service sector. The authors have further found that there have been clear adjustments in both countries to a more balanced provision of education at both mass and advanced levels. It is evident from this research that the role of education in economic development as a general model of economic growth has little value as each country will take a different path of education provision. It is at this level of education paths that we see how education provision may shape industrial structure of an economy.

Development models as theoretical explanations are built to help us understand growth outcomes that are unable to be accounted for in conventional growth accounting models. Development models offer one single factor or one set of factors, as the cause of growth. The problems are known for such models because of the complexity of the social system in which economic growth takes place, path dependence and contingency of forces shaping economic growth and development, and the empirical difficulties in establishing accurate and realistic descriptions of factors and their relations. The four chapters in the second part of this volume have provided good evidence of the problem of theorizing causes of growth. Guang's chapter has demonstrated how different political institutions and dynamics can lead to similar development behavior, while Bo has turned the whole theory of regime-growth link upside down. The study by Kumar and Liu suggests that single factor generalizations are not of much value unless we have sufficient empirical evidence to exactly what has shaped what. Young has taken the whole developmental state theory to task.

The problem with development models are not confined to growth accounting and explanation. Growth models are also developed as alternatives to modern economic growth and development, and as strategies for transforming to alternative modes of development.

These alternative development models often begin with questions about the premises upon which conventional growth models are conceived. Sustainable vs. catch-up growth, for example, represents one alternative thinking on the parameters of modern economic growth and development. Woo centered his discussion on the sustainability of the current model in China. The Chinese economic growth engine, in his view, consists of three parts: hardware, which involves economic institutions and mechanisms; software, which concerns governance; and power supply – the natural and externally imposed limits on growth. Failure of each part is likely and therefore there is a substantive challenge for sustainable growth and development. For Woo, the 1978–2005 policy framework can no longer continue to produce the same growth performance as it did in the previous 30 years and adjustments are required for sustainable development. Woo lays out a grant strategy or platform for China to deal with these possible failures.

Gilley takes the problem of sustainability to a different level of debate that would require a fundamental paradigm shift in thinking about economic growth and development. Gilley's chapter makes a case that the earlier development models are built upon catch-up-based growth. Such models are premised on the amount and speed of GDP and income increases, and how various factors and institutions facilitate this. These models, in Gilley's view, were "deficient" in not paying attention to the question of sustainability, where the well-being of humans in the long run is the ultimate purpose for economic growth and development. Instead of analyzing, measuring, and assessing how factors and institutions facilitate the growth of GDP, this sustainability approach looks at growth and development as a system, and measures the quality of economic, environmental, social, and political subsystems in support of sustainability. Gilley argues that the sustainability approach is more integrated into the founding myths and ideology of the regime in India, while in China sustainability has been embedded in a grand strategy of survival for nation and regime, reflected particularly in the much-celebrated move in recent years in development strategy towards "scientific development." The second transition to lower growth at the technological frontier requires structural, sectoral, institutional, and strategic adjustments as well as political leadership and social support.

There is a shared view among the contributors that growth and development models are essentially about the strategy to bring required resources and arrangements together for growth and development. Both Woo and Gilley are of the view that a good national strategy is required for the transition of the Chinese economy to sustainable growth and development. Fu also shares the same view on the development model as a strategy. In his view, China's growth experience has been the working of a strategy to shape the institutional environment that allows the logic of modern economic growth to play fully on its own.

The final chapter by Deng brings this prescriptive take of growth and development models much further. The problem with existing development models, in his view, is not so much that they have mistaken the purpose and value of economic growth and development; it is that they are fundamentally unable to capture the dynamic, intuitive, contingent, and strategic nature of growth activities and development experiences. Much of the literature on development models is satisfied with mutual referencing within the paradigm framework and little engaged with real experiences.

The problem is at two levels: at the empirical level, China's development experience is the function of the living wisdom of people in China. Such living wisdom is "tacit knowledge" in the sense used by Polanyi, Hayek, and Oakeshott. Tacit knowledge is something one accumulates through individual and collective experiences in understanding how things work, what matters, and what is the most effective way to get a desired outcome. As a way of practical activity, tacit knowledge is accumulative, not definitive or precise. People exercise their "living wisdom" in growth and development activities. These activities are individualized and purpose oriented, strategically calculated, and setting-specific (content, environment or network of relations). Accumulatively they constitute the large picture of growth and development, and the outcomes of these activities are not always as intended. More importantly, the growth and expansion of these economic activities often defies the paths envisaged in rationally designed models.

At an intellectual level, social sciences pursue "technical knowledge." Such knowledge is required to be precise, definitive, and rational. Based on clearly identified and measurable cause-effect relations, social sciences have not found a way to capture tacit knowledge. Existing development models therefore have significant difficulties in describing and explaining growth and development experiences. The whole China model debate, for example, has spent quite a lot of capital trying to understand why economic growth and development was possible without a clear guiding "model"; how incompatible institutional arrangements can co-exist in the dual track transition; and why do we have problem applying transaction costs and rule of law to China? Why is the "model" of China's reform and transformation an *ex post* coherence and not an *ex ante* grand design? Why is Chinese reform and change piecemeal, gradual, and non-radical? How can property rights be ambiguous and yet help growth activities? Deng suggests that perhaps not only is there a need for a "second transition" in growth and development as suggested by Gilley, but also a need for a transition in knowledge: What do we know and how do we know about growth experiences? What the growth experiences of China and India have forced us to think is not only what they are doing wrong or right in their growth and development but, rather, what we have done in turning these rich experiences into useful knowledge. The various models we have seen have clearly not achieved that.

2 Model as pattern, framework, theories or strategy

The discussion above and the large literature on development models seem to suggest that people may mean different things when they use different models. What is a model of economic development? Economic growth and social development have been major challenges of our times. There are significantly different ways of organizing economy and society; different timings by which the modern economy took shape and the corresponding institutions formed in different societies; different internal and external environments and dynamics that affected the society's ability to respond to modern conditions, and the interplay of forces and interests in such a response; and differences in the consequent growth and development experiences. Consequently, it has become a real enterprise to find appropriate frameworks to reflect accurately individual modern development experiences as a way of explaining why some societies have started earlier in modern development, and done better than others; why many have taken different paths, experiencing hardships, disruptions, delays, failures, or "decay"; and how one can learn from other great achievers.

But the perceived value of development models goes beyond that. As chapters in this volume have demonstrated, there are three different ways of using the term "model" in this field. A model of economic growth and development is first and foremost *descriptive*. Growth analysts and theorists have increasingly realized that modern economic growth, even under the same conditions and the same logic of the capitalist market economy, can take different forms. The literature on comparative capitalism, particularly the substantive work comparing the Anglo-Saxon and Rhine models, is largely intended to demonstrate the distinctive patterns and styles of organizing the capitalist market economy in different Western industrial societies: how they stand on the balance between state and market, between efficiency and welfare, and between competition and corporation. There is no ideological judgment or performance assessment involved in distinguishing these models. The main thrust of the efforts is to justify the differences within the framework of the capitalist market economy.

A model of economic development can also be *explanatory*, linking a particular set of forces, factors, and institutions, and the way they relate to one another, to growth outcomes and development performance. This is a particular feature of works on the East Asian economic model. This model identifies government, export, industrial policy, corporate organization, saving, Confucian values, and so on as key variables that enable prolonged, high-speed economic growth and profound social development. Studies focusing on each of these individual variables further develop frameworks that capture the actual, hopefully causal, relationship between these variables and economic performance: export-led growth (Hong and Krause 1981), the Confucian affectional model (Tai 1989), the *chaebol/kereitsu* model (Hamilton 1991; Kang 1996; Ungson, Steers, and Park 1997), and the developmental state model (Johnson 1982; Wade 1992). While such a link is often proclaimed as causal, what is actually established in the models is often associational.

Finally, a model of economic growth and development can also be *prescriptive*. As Janos Kornei suggests, "model refers to a real process of a series of historical events, and such a process can be an exemplar for other countries to imitate" (Kornai 2010). There is a mixture of the descriptive and prescriptive elements here. The MBW model in Fu's chapter, the model of sustainable development in Woo's three-part engine model in Chapter 9 and Gilley's discussion in Chapter 10, and Deng's living wisdom in Chapter 11 are all prescriptive in nature. A prescriptive model implies a strategy for action, at least, it is often perceived so.

This important tradition of development experiences as a model for others to follow has been carried on from one to the next of each major wave of the successful stories of modern economic takeoff, rapid growth, and significant achievement in the development of a modern economy, society, and state: notable among these experiences are the early "rise of the West" (North and Thompson 1973) and the "East Asian miracle" in more recent times (World Bank 1993). North and Thompson advise us that intellectual property rights arrangements and their associated economic, legal, and political institutions are essential for modern economic growth. The World Bank experts insist that public policy – efficiency and effectiveness – are the key to the miraculous performance of the East Asian model economies. Indeed, almost every version of the East Asian economic model is attached to some form of prescriptive expectation – so much so that, as soon as the Asian economic model is mentioned, one will never fail to hear the next question: can it be copied; that is, can it be transferred to other developing countries? One will inevitably end up with a paradox: either the answer is yes (and then one would have to work hard to demonstrate that the model is one of causal relationship so that it can be empirically reproduced), or one would have to accept that there is no such thing as the Asian economic model or there is no value in searching and proposing one.

3 China, India and development models

Finally, let us return to the original questions we put to our contributors to this volume. It is perhaps safe to say that in the descriptive sense of a development model, there is a shared historical pattern of modern economic growth and development in China and India – socialist economic experiences; lost opportunities for early economic takeoff and industrialization; economic reform, opening and liberalization; and prolonged, high speed economic growth and development. Beyond that, there is no clear theoretically meaningful pattern of factors-of-production contributions to growth outcomes, and growth enabling activities and arrangements. In the various descriptions of their growth experiences, even in paired comparisons, we learned little except what happened, how each indicator measures up, and how the two countries compare on these indicators, and thus what the unique features of their growth experiences are.

Going one step further to see models as analytical or explanatory frameworks and use them to explain why and how, we have four sets of findings. First, the descriptive analyses are usually not sophisticated enough to suggest, let along establish, a causal model and to measure what factors contribute to growth and how much. The original growth accounting was designed for this, but this is rarely the case with developing economies. Much of the fanfare about the growth and development of China and India stops short of that.

Second, in the style of the East Asian growth models, where a single or set of non-economic factors are identified and their perceived causal relationship to growth outcomes demonstrated, we have no single model developed from the growth experiences of China and India. In each case – state-society relations, political regime, education, labor – we have found no consistent evidence in support of or against the established models of rapid economic growth and development, particularly those from the East Asian model debate. In some cases, the evidence is conflicting. In others, enabling factors simply become irrelevant. In most cases, China and India are different on almost every indicator deemed essential for successful economic growth and development by the East Asian model literature. And yet both seem to have achieved impressive economic growth and development.

Third, one thing that requires a controlled comparison between the two for an explanation is the extent of the growth where China is seen to have performed better than India. This can perhaps be explained by the fact that China started reform, opening and liberalization earlier than India. In terms of different stages of catch up growth, China is at a more advanced stage of the growth process and is expected to show better performance on indicators such as the size of the economy, GDP per capita, productivity, and accelerated pace of growth and greater improvement on development indicators.

Finally, models can also be prescriptive and function as a strategic blueprint. This goes in two directions. Scholars who have problems with the notion of model and therefore often refuse to recognize the existence, or possibility of, a model of growth and development are often troubled by the prescriptive intentions of model advocates. Often the line of argument is that countries are different, so it is hard for growth experiences to transfer across national (institutional or cultural) boundaries; therefore, there is no such thing as a Chinese model, or an Indian model. Since our studies here have found no consistent evidence for a model in either the descriptive or analytical sense in Chinese or Indian growth experiences, this is less of a problem for us.

In another direction, however, a model can be prescriptive for the country itself. The sustainability models discussed by Woo and Gilley are good examples. Model in this context is synonymous with strategy. The old, outgrown model of catch up growth is wrong or problematic, and the new model sets the imperatives and direction for action to make it right.

Perhaps in a broader historical and intellectual perspective, the growth experiences of China and India are indeed not so profoundly unique to require a model to capture their form and substance. They are simply the latest instances of the growth and expansion of the modern capitalist economy at the global level. As Fu points out, once the conditions for this are in place, it should not be a surprise to see such "miracles" occur. This happened in Europe in the eighteenth and nineteenth centuries; in continental Europe and East Asia since World War II; and it is happening in China and India.

Or, perhaps, the forms and substance of their economic growth and development are so peculiar – because of culture, local conditions, living wisdom, path dependence, and so on – that any attempt to capture them in the form of a "model" would only do injustice to the growth experiences themselves, and to those who are still trained to believe that we shall be able to learn social experiences from others because this is cost effective, allowing "curve-tunneling" or "leapfrogging" in modern economic growth and social development. If models are of this function, the evidence and arguments presented in this volume suggest that they are largely irrelevant to real growth experiences. China and India have experienced substantial economic growth and social development in spite of the predictions and advice of many development models in the past. It is therefore comforting to see, ironically, that there has been little enthusiasm in looking for new development models in comparing China and India.

Bibliography

ACHR (Asian Center for Human Rights). 2006. "Atrocities at Singur, India: A Matter of Rights of the Dispossessed," *ACHR Weekly Review* (accessed 7 December 2009, from http://www.achrweb.org/Review/2006/144-06.htm).

Agarwal, Pawan, 2007. "Higher Education in India: Growth, Concerns and Change Agenda," *Higher Education Quarterly*, 61 (2): pp. 197–207.

Ahya, Chetan and Andy, Xie, 2004. *India and China: A Special Economic Analysis* (New York: Morgan).

Akbar, M. J., 1985. *India: The Siege Within* (New York: Viking Penguin).

Albert, Michel, 1993. *Capitalism vs. Capitalism: How America's Obsession with Individual Achievement and Short-term Profit Has Led it to the Brink of Collapse* (New York: Four Walls Eight Windows).

AM, 2009. "The State of the CPI (M) in West Bengal," *Economic and Political Weekly* 44 (30): p. 8.

Andreas, Joel, 2008. "Changing Colours in China," *New Left Review*, 54 (Nov/Dec): pp. 123–42.

Ashton, Thomas, S., 1955. *An Economic History of England: The 18th Century* (London: Methuen).

Asian Development Bank, 2007. *Key Indicators: Inequality in Asia*. (Manila: ADB).

Asuyama, Yoko, 2009, "Skill Formation Systems of China and India," in Ohara Moriki, and Koichiro Kimura (eds) *Comparative Study on Industrial Development Process in China and India. Interim Report* (Chiba, Japan: Institute of Developing Economies) pp. 27–75.

Au, Chun-chung and J. Vernon Henderson, 2006. "How Migration Restrictions Limit Agglomeration and Productivity in China," *Journal of Development Economics*, 80 (2): pp. 350–88.

AWSJ Asian Wall Street Journal (http://www.wsj-asia.com).

Aziz, Jahangir, Steven, Vincent Dunaway, Eswar Prasad and International Monetary Fund, 2006. *China and India: Learning from Each Other: Reforms and Policies for Sustained Growth* (Washington, DC: International Monetary Fund).

Baek, Seung-Wook, 2005. "Does China Follow 'The East Asian Development Model'?" *Journal of Contemporary Asia*, 35 (4): pp. 485–98.

Banerjee, Partha and Dayabati Roy, 2007. "Behind the Present Peasant Unrest in West Bengal," *Economic and Political Weekly*, 42 (22): pp. 2048–50.

Bardhan, Pranab, 2003. "Crouching Tiger, Lumbering Elephant: A China–India Comparison," in Kaushik Basu, Pulin Nayak and Ranjan Ray (eds) *Markets and Governments* (New Delhi: Oxford University Press), pp. 60–73.

Bardhan, Pranab, 2006. "Awakening Giants, Feet of Clay: A Comparative Assessment of the Rise of China and India," *Journal of South Asian Development*, 1 (1): pp. 1–17.

Bardhan, Pranab, 2009. "India and China: Governance Issues and Development," *The Journal of Asian Studies*, 68 (2): pp. 347–57.

Bardhan, Pranab, 2010. *Awakening Giants, Feet of Clay: Assessing the Economic Rise of China and India* (Princeton and Oxford: Princeton University Press).

Barro, Robert, J., 1991. "Economic Growth in a Cross Section of Countries," *Quarterly Journal of Economics*, 106 (2): pp. 407–73.

Barro, Robert, J., 1996. "Democracy and Growth," *Journal of Economic Growth* 1 (1): pp. 1–27.

Barro, Robert, J., 2001. "Human Capital and Growth," *The American Economic Review*, 91 (2): pp. 12–17.

Barro, Robert, J. and Jong-Wha Lee, 2001. "International Data on Educational Attainment: Updates and Implications," *Oxford Economic Papers*, 53 (3): pp. 541–63.

Basu, Kaushik, 2009, "China and India: Idiosyncratic Paths to High Growth," *Economic and Political Weekly*, XLIV (38): pp. 43–56.

Baumol, William, J., Robert E. Litan and Carl J. Schramm, 2007. *Good Capitalism, Bad Capitalism, and the Economics of Growth and Prosperity* (New Haven: Yale University Press).

BCRGDXT (Beijing City Research Group on Deng Xiaoping Theory [Beijingshi Deng Xiaoping Lilun Yanjiu Zhongxing Ketizhu]), 2002. "Zhongguo gongchandang dangyuan duiwu shehui chengfen de lishi kaocha (Historical Assessment of the Social Backgrounds of the CCP Members)," *Zhongguo tese shehuizhuyi yanjiu* (Studies of Socialism with Chinese Characteristics) (1): pp. 46–50.

Behrman, Jeremy, Andrew Foster, Mark Rosenzweig and Prem Vashishth, 1999. "Women's Schooling, Home Teaching and Economic Growth," *Journal of Political Economy*, 107 (4): pp. 682–714.

Bell, Martin and Salut Muhidin, 2009. *Cross-National Comparisons of Internal Migration*, Human Development Research Paper, pp. 2009–30 (Geneva: United Nations Development Programme).

Bell, Simon and Stephen Morse, 2008. *Sustainability Indicators: Measuring the Immeasurable?* (London: Sterling; VA: Earthscan).

Bello, Walden and Stephanie Rosenfeld, 1992. *Dragons in Distress: Asia's Miracle Economies in Crisis* (London: Penguin).

Berstein, Thomas, 2000. "Instability in Rural China," in David Shambaugh (ed.) *Is China Unstable* (Armonk: Sharpe), pp. 95–111.

Besley, Timothy and Robin Burgess, 2004. "Can Labor Regulation Hinder Economic Performance? Evidence from India," *Quarterly Journal of Economics*, 119 (1): pp. 91–134.

Bhaduri, Amit, 2007. "Alternatives in Industrialization," *Economic and Political Weekly*, 42 (18): pp. 1597–601.

Bhagwati, Jagdish N., 1984. "Splintering and Disembodiment of Services and Developing Nations," *World Economy*, 7 (2): pp. 133–43.

Bhattacharaya, Swapan, K. and Biswa N. Bhattacharyay, 2007. "Gains and Losses of India–China Cooperation: A Gravity Model Impact Analysis," *CESifo Working Paper Series*, no. 1970, April (Frankfurt, Germany: Munich: CESifo Group).

Bhattacharya, Malini, 2007. "Nandigram and the Question of Development," *Economic and Political Weekly*, 42 (21): pp. 1895–8.

Bhola, Harbans S., 1982. *Campaigning for Literacy* (Paris: UNESCO).

Birdsall, Nancy, David Ross and Richard Sabot, 1995. "Inequality and Growth Reconsidered: Lessons from East Asia," *The World Bank Economic Review*, 9 (3): pp. 477–508.

Bloom, David, E., David Canning and Jaypee Sevilla, 2002. *Demographic Dividend: A New Perspective on the Economic Consequences of Population Change* (Santa Monica: RAND).

Bo, Zhiyue, 2002. *Chinese Provincial Leaders: Economic Performance and Political Mobility* (Armonk: Sharpe).

Boltho, Andrea and Maria Weber, 2009. "Did China Follow the East Asian Development Model?" *European Journal of Comparative Economics*, 6 (2): pp. 267–86.

Bose, Deb Kumar, 2007. "Land Acquisition in West Bengal," *Economic and Political Weekly*, 42 (17): pp. 1574–5.

Bosworth, Barry and Susan M. Collins, 2008. "Accounting for Growth: Comparing China and India," *Journal of Economic Perspective*, 22 (1): pp. 45–66.

Bosworth, Barry and Susan M. Collins, 2007. "Accounting for Growth: Comparing China and India," *National Bureau of Economic Research Working Paper*, no. 12943 (Massachusetts: Cambridge).

Bottelier, Pieter, 2007. "India's Growth from China's Perspective," *Journal of Applied Economic Research*, 1 (1): pp. 119–38.

Bowles, Paul and John Harris, 2010. *Globalization and Labor in China and India: Impacts and Responses* (Basingstoke: Palgrave Macmillan).

Bradshaw, Corey, J. A., Xingli Giam and Navjot S. Sodhi, 2010. "Evaluating the Relative Environmental Impact of Countries," *PLoS ONE* 45 (5): pp. 1–16.

Brainard, Lael, 2007. "Testimony on Meeting the Challenge of Income Instability, Joint Economic Committee Hearing," 28 February 2007, Washington, DC, http://jec.senate.gov/Documents/Hearings/02.28.07%20Income%20Instability/Testimony%20-%20Brainard.pdf.

Branigan, Tania, 2010. "Chinese Newspapers in Joint Call to End Curb on Migrant Workers," *The Guardian*. 1 March, http://www.guardian.co.uk/world/2010/mar/01/chinese-newspapers-migrant-workers-rights.

Brown, Harrison, 1954. *The Challenge of Man's Future* (New York: Viking Press).

Brown, Robert, S. and Alan Gutterman, 1998. *Asian Economic and Legal Development: Uncertainty, Risk, and Legal Efficiency* (Boston: Kluwer Law International).

Burchfield, Shirley, Haiyan Hua, Dyuti Baral and Valeria Rocha, 2002. *A Longitudinal Study of Integrated Literacy and Basic Education Programs on Women's Participation in Social and Economic Development in Nepal*, United States Agency for International Development.

Burtless, Gary, 2005. "Income Supports for Workers and Their Families: Earnings Supplements and Health Insurance," Paper presented at the Workforce Policies for the Next Decade and Beyond conference, 11 November (Washington, DC: Urban Institute).

Burtless, Gary, 2007. "Income Progress across the American Income Distribution, 2000–2005," Testimony for the Committee on Finance, US Senate, 10 May 2007, Washington, DC: Brookings Institution.

Bussiere, Matthieu and Arnaud Mehl, 2008. "China's and India's Role in Global Trade and Finance: Twin Titans for the New Millennium?" *Occassional Paper No. 80* (Frankfurt: European Central Bank).

Cai, Fang, 2008. *Renkou yu Laodong Lupishu* (Green Book of Population and Labor): *Zhongguo Renkou yu Laodong Wenti Baogao No.9*: *Liuyisi zhuanzhedian Ruhe yu Kuzinieci Zhuanzhedian Huihe* (Reports on China's Population and Labor No. 9, Linking up Lewis and Kuznets Turning Points) (Beijing: Shehui kexue chubanshe).

Cai, Yongshun, 2003. "Collective Ownership or Cadres' Ownership? The Non-Agricultural Use of Farmland in China," *The China Quarterly*, 175 (September): pp. 662–80.

Cai, Yongshun, 2008. "Disruptive Collective Action in the Reform Era," in Kevin O'Brien (ed.) *Popular Protest in China*, pp. 163–78 (Cambridge, MA: Harvard University Press).

Caldararo, Niccolo, 2004. *Sustainability, Human Ecology, and the Collapse of Complex Societies: Economic Anthropology and a 21st Century Adaptation*, Mellen Studies in Anthropology (Lewiston: Edwin Mellen Press).

Chai, Joseph, C. H. and Kartik C. Roy, 2006. *Economic Reform in China and India: Development Experience in a Comparative Perspective* (Northampton: Edward Elgar).

Chan, Kam Wing and Will Buckingham, 2008. "Is China Abolishing the Hukou System?" *The China Quarterly*, 195 (September): pp. 582–606.

Chan, M., 2006. "Villagers Keep Up Demands for Justice," *South China Morning Post*. March 28, p. 5. (Hong Kong).

Chang, Gordon, G., 2001. *The Coming Collapse of China* (New York: Random House).

Chatterjee, Partha, 2004. *The Politics of the Governed* (New York: Columbia University Press).

Chatterjee, Partha, 2008. "Peasant Cultures of the Twenty-first Century," *Inter-Asia Cultural Studies* 9 (1): pp. 117–18.

Chatterjee, Partha, 2009a. "The Coming Crisis in West Bengal," *Economic and Political Weekly*, 64 (9): p. 43.

Chatterjee, Srikanta, 2009b. "Anatomy of the Growth and Transformation of the Economies of China and India," in Subrata Ghatak and Paul Levine (eds) *Development Macroeconomics: Essays in Memory of Anita Ghatak*, pp. 26–48 (London: Routledge).

Chaudhuri, D. R. and S. Sivaraman, 2007. "Nandigram: Six Months Later," *Economic and Political Weekly*, 42 (41): pp. 4103–6.

Chaudhuri, S. and M. Ravallion, 2006. "Partially Awakened Giants: Uneven Growth in China and India," *Policy Research Working Paper No. 4069* (Washington, DC: World Bank).

Chen, An, 2007. "The Failure of Organizational Control: Changing Party Power in the Chinese Countryside," *Politics & Society*, 35 (1): pp. 145–79.

Chen, Huasheng, 2010. "*Dalu fenshuizhi gaige dui zhongyang yu difang guanxi ji difang guanxi ji difang caizheng jingji yingxiang zhi fenxi* (An Analysis on the Influence of Separate Taxation Reform on the Central-Local Relations and Local Fiscal Economy in Mainland China)." Accessed, 20 August at http://new.21ccom.net/plus/view.php?aid=2078.

Chen, Jiyuan and Hu, Biliang, 1996. *Dangdai zhongguo de cunzhuang jingji yu cunluo wenhua* (Economy and Culture in Contemporary Rural China) (Taiyuan: Shanxi jingji chubanshe).

Cheru, Fantu and Cyril Obi, 2010. *The Rise of China and India in Africa: Challenges, Opportunities and Critical Interventions* (London: Zed Books).

Chirot, Daniel and Thomas D. Hall, 1982. "World-system Theory," *Annual Review of Sociology*, 8: pp. 81–106.

Citigroup, 2002. *Greater China Insights*, 14 June.

Clifford, Mark, 1994. *Troubled Tiger: Business, Bureaucrats and Generals in South* (New York: Sharpe).

Coase, Ronald, 1960. "The Problem of Social Cost," *Journal of Law and Economics*, 3 (1): pp. 1–44.

Coase, Ronald, 1937. "The Nature of the Firm," *Economica*, 4 (6): pp. 386–405.

Cohen, Warren I., 2000. "The Resurgence of East Asian Economic Power," in Warren I. Cohen (ed.) *East Asia at the Centre: Four Thousand Years of Engagement with the World* (New York: Columbia University Press).

Cooper, Richard, N. 2006. *How Integrated are Chinese and Indian Labor into the World Economy?* WCFIA Working Paper, February. Cambridge: Harvard University.

Cornwall, John, L., 2010. "Economic Growth," in *Encyclopædia Britannica*. Retrieved 16 December 2010, from Encyclopædia Britannica Online: http://www.britannica.com/EBchecked/topic/178400/economic-growth.

Cox, Peter, 2004. "Re-evaluating Gandhi: Swaraj and Swadeshi in 'Environmental' Activism Ecotheology," *Journal of Religion, Nature & the Environment*, 9 (1): pp. 105–23.

CPC (Communist Party of China), 2004. "Resolution on Strengthening the Building of the Party's Governing Capacity," 19 September, Section 1.

CPI(M) Elected Representatives. 2007. "Nandigram Situation: Myths and Reality," *People's Democracy*, Retrieved 7 December 2009, from http://pd.cpim.org/2007/1118/11182007 nandigram%20governor.htm.

Crafts, Nicholas, 1997. "The Human Development Index and Changes in Standards of Living: Some Historical Comparisons," *European Review of Economic History*, 1 (3): pp. 299–322.

Crouch, Colin, Wolfgang Streeck, 1997. *Political Economy of Modern Capitalism: Mapping Convergence and Diversity* (London: Sage).

Cui, Zhiyuan, 1994. "*Zhidu chuangxin yu dierci sixiang jiefang* (Institutional Innovations and the Second Thoughts Liberation), *Ershiyi Shiji* (Twenty-First Century): (8).

Dailami, M. and P. Masson, 2009. "The New Multi-polar International Monetary System," *Policy Research Working Paper No. 5147* (Washington, DC: World Bank).

Danielmeyer, Hans and Thomas Martinetz, 2010. "The Long Term Development of China, India, and the USA," Paper presented at the Wellington Conference on Contemporary China 2010, Wellington, New Zealand.

Das, Dilip, K., 2006a. *China and India: A Tale of Two Economies* (London: Routledge).

Das, Dilip, K., 2006b. "China and India: An Era of Escalating Economic Interaction," *China and World Economy*, 14 (4): pp. 105–19.

Das, Dilip, K. 2008. *The Chinese Economic Renaissance: Apocalypse or Cornucopia* (Houndmills: Palgrave Macmillan).

Das, Dilip, K., 2009a. "Short- and Long-term Prospects of Indian Economic Growth: A Dispassionate Analysis," *International Journal of Trade and Global Markets*, 20 (2): pp. 194–210.

Das, Dilip K. 2009b. "Globalization and an Emerging Global Middle Class," *Economic Affairs*, 29 (3): pp. 89–99.

Das, Dilip K. 2010. "Indian Economy: Recent Growth Performance and the Impact of Global Financial Crisis," *Harvard Asia Pacific Economic Review*, 11 (1): pp. 43–7.

David, Paul, 2000. "Path Dependence, Its Critics and the Quest for 'Historical Economics'," in P. Garrouste and S. Ioannides (eds) *Evolution and Path Dependence in Economic Ideas: Past and Present* (Cheltenham: Edward Elgar).

Day, Kristen, 2005. *China's Environment and the Challenge of Sustainable Development* (Armonk, N.Y.: M. E. Sharpe).

De Groot, H. L. F., C. A. Withagen and M. L. Zhou, 2004. "Dynamics of China's Regional Development and Pollution: An Investigation into the Environmental Kuznets Curve," *Environment and Development Economics*, 9 (4): pp. 507–37.

Deininger, Klaus and Lyn Squire, 1996. "A New Data Set Measuring Income Inequality," *World Bank Economic Review*, 10 (3): pp. 565–91.

Démurger, Sylvie, Jeffrey D. Sachs, Wing Thye Woo, Shuming Bao, Gene Chang and Andrew Mellinger, 2002. "Geography, Economic Policy and Regional Development in China," *Asian Economic Papers*, 1 (1): pp. 146–97.

Deng, Xiangzheng, Jikun Huang, Scott Rozelle and Emi Uchida, 2010. "Economic Growth and the Expansion of Urban Land in China," *Urban Studies*, 47 (4): pp. 813–43.

Deng, Xiaomang, 2010. "Fushikang de '*zhongguo moshi*' (The 'Chinese Model' of Foxconn)," *Nanfeng chuang* (13).

Deng, Zhenglai, 2003a. "*Zhongguo faxue de chongjian, pipan yu jiangou* (The Reconstruction, Critique and Construction of China's Legal Science." *Jinlin daxue shehuikexue xuebao* (*University Journal of Social Sciences*) 5.

Deng, Zhenglai, 2006. *Zhongguo faxue xiang hechu qu* (Chinese Jurisprudence, Where to Go?) (Beijing: Shangwu chubanshe).

Deng, Zhenglai, 2009a. *Shui zhi quanqiuhua? he zhong fazhexue?* (Whose Globalisation? Which Legal Science?) (Beijing: Shangwu chubanshe).

Deng, Zhenglai, 2009b. "Academic Inquiries into the 'Chinese Success Story'," in Zhenglai Deng (ed.) *China's Economy: Rural Reform and Agricultural Development*, pp. 1–20 (Singapore: World Scientific).

Deng, Zhenglai, 2009c. *Hayek shehui lilun* (*Hayek on Social Theories*) (Shanghai: Fudan daxue chubanshe).

Denoon, David, B. H., 2007. *The Economic and Strategic Rise of China and India: Asian Realignments after the 1997 Financial Crisis* (London: Palgrave Macmillan).

Derrida, Jacques, 1977. "Limited Inc abc," *Glyph* 1977 (2): pp. 162–254.

Deshingkar, Priya and Edward Anderson, 2004. "People on the Move: New Policy Challenges for Increasingly Mobile Populations," in John Farrington (ed.) *Natural Resource Perspectives* (London: Overseas Development Institute).

Deutsche Bank, 2009. "China," *Asia Economics Monthly*, 13 March.

DHE (Department of Higher Education), 2010. *Government of India Ministry of Human Resource Development,* 1986. *National Policy on Education 1986.* Accessed on 3 September at http://www.education.nic.in/natpol.asp.

Diamond, Jared, M., 2005. *Collapse: How Societies Choose to Fail or Succeed* (New York: Viking).

Domar, Evsey, D., 1946. "Capital Expansion, Rate of Growth and Employment," *Econometrica*, 14 (2): pp. 137–47.

Dore, Ronald, 2000. *Stock Market Capitalism: Welfare Capitalism: Japan and Germany versus the Anglo-Saxons* (Oxford University Press).

Dore, Ronald, 2000a. "Will Global Capitalism be Anglo-Saxon Capitalism," *New Left Review*, 6 (Nov/Dec): pp. 101–19.

DPES (Department of Population and Employment Statistics, National Bureau of Statistics of China). 2008. *Zhongguo Renkou He Jiuye Tongji Nianjian 2008 (2008 China Population and Employment Statistics Yearbook)* (Beijing: zhanggou tongji chubanshe).

DPES (Department of Population and Employment Statistics, National Bureau of Statistics of China). 2006. *2005 Zhongguo Renkou (2005 China Population)* (Beijing: Zhongguo tongji chubanshe).

Dreze, Jean and Mamta Murthi, 2001. "Fertility, Education, and Development: Evidence from India," *Population and Development Review*, 27 (1): pp. 33–63.

Durkheim, Emile, 1893. *De la Division du Travail Social* (Paris: F. Alcan).

Dwivedi, O. P. and R. B. Jain, 1988. "Bureaucratic Morality in India," *International Political Science Review*, 9 (3): pp. 205–14.

Economist, 2007. "The Capitalist Communist: How a Poetic Marxist has Transformed Business Prospects in West Bengal," 385 (September 22): p. 74.

Economy, Elizabeth, C., 2004. *The River Runs Black: The Environmental Challenge to China's Future* (Ithaca: Cornell University Press).

Eichengreen, Barry, Poonam Gupta and Rajiv Kumar, 2010. *Emerging Giants: China and India in the World Economy* (Oxford: Oxford University Press).

EIU (Economist Intelligence Unit), 2009. *China: Country Profile 2009* (London: EIU).

EIU (Economist Intelligence Unit), 2010. *India: Country Report 2010* (London: EIU).

EIU (The Economist Intelligence Unit), 2004. *Country Report: China*, December.

Election Commission of India. 2010. "FAQs – Electoral Rolls," Election Commission of India. Accessed on 19 April 2010 at http://eci.nic.in/eci_main/index.asp.

Enderwick, Peter, 2007. *Understanding Emerging Markets: China and India* (London: Routledge).

EPW *Economic and Political Weekly.*

Euromoney, 2010. "Country Risk Indicators", September 30, 2010. Available at: http://www.euromoney.com/Article/2675660/Country-risk-Full-results.html.

Fallows, James, 2007. "China Makes, the World Takes," *The Atlantic Monthly*, 300 (1): pp. 48–72.

Fan, C., Cindy, 1994. "Urbanization from Below: The Growth of Towns in Jiangsu, China," *Urban Studies*, 31 (10): pp. 1625–45.

Fan, Gang, 2003. "China's Nonperforming Loans and National Comprehensive Liability," *Asian Economic Papers*, 2 (1): pp. 145–52.

Fan, Guang, 1996. *Jianjin gaige de zhengzhixue fengxin* (Political Economics of Gradual Reform) (Shanghai: yuandong chubanshe).

Fatemi, Khosrow, 2002. *Globalization and East Asia: Opportunities and Challenges* (Bangkok: International Trade and Finance Association).

Feenstra, Robert, C. and Gordon H. Hanson, 1996. "Globalization, Outsourcing, and Wage Inequality," *American Economic Review*, 86 (2): pp. 240–5.

Fei, Xiaotong, 1998. *Xiangtu zhongguo shengyu zhidu* (Earthbound China Reproductive Institutions) (Beijing: Beijing daxue chubanshe).

Findlay, Ronald, 1990. "The New Political Economy: Its Explanatory Power for LDCs," *Economics and Politics*, 2 (2): pp. 193–221.

Frank, Andre Gunder, 1998. *ReOrient: Global Economy in the Asian Age* (Berkeley: University of California Press).

Freeman, Richard, 2004. "Doubling the Global Work Force: The Challenge of Integrating China, India, and the former Soviet Bloc into the World Economy," Harvard University, manuscript, 8 November.

French, Howard, W., 2005. "Protesters Say Police in China Killed up to 20," *New York Times*, 10 December, at A1.

Friedman, Edward and Bruce Gilley, 2005. *Asia's Giants: Comparing China and India* (New York: Palgrave Macmillan).

Friedman, Edward, 2009. "Measure for Measure: China and India: A Longue Duree Perspective," *India International Centre Quarterly*, 36 (3/4): pp. 80–93.

Friedman, Thomas, 2005. *The World is Flat: A Brief History of the Twentieth-first Century* (New York: Farrar, Straus and Giroux).

FT *Financial Times*.

Fu, Jun, 2000. *Institutions and Investments: Foreign Direct Investment in China during an Era of Reforms* (Ann Arbor: University of Michigan Press).

Fu, Jun, 2009. *Guofu Zhidao* (The Dao of the Wealth of Nations) (Beijing: Beijingdaxue chubanshe).

Gajwani, Kiran, Ravi Kanbur, Xiaobo Zhang, 2006. "Patterns of Spatial Convergence and Divergence in India and China," Paper prepared for the Annual Bank Conference on Development Economics (ABCDE), St Petersburg, 18–19 January.

Galenson, Walter, 1959. *Labor and Economic Development* (New York: Wiley).

Gan, Yang, 2008. "Dierci sixiang jiefang shi baituo meiguo moshi de mixin(The Second Thought Liberation is to Break Away from the Superstition in the American Model)" *Ershiyi Shiji jingji Daobao* (Economic Report of the 21st Century) 17 December.

Geertz, Clifford, 1983. *Local Knowledge* (New York: Basic Books).

German Watch, 2010. *Global Climate Risk Index*, 9 December 2010, available at: http://www.germanwatch.org/.

Ghosh, Suresh Chandra, 2000. *The History of Education in Modern India* (New Delhi: Orient Longman).

Gilley, Bruce, 2011. "China and India: Assessing Sustainability," in *Berkshire Encyclopedia of Sustainability*, edited by Chris Laszlo (Great Barrington: Berkshire).

Ginsburg, Tom, 2000. "Does Law Matter for Economic Development? Evidence from East Asia," *Law & Society Review*, 43 (3): pp. 829–56.

Goldman Sachs, 2003. "Dreaming with BRICs: The Path to 2050," *Global Economics Paper* No. 99. (New York: Goldman Sachs Global Research Centres).

Goldman Sachs, 2004. "The BRICs and Global Markets: Crude, Cars and Capital," *Global Economics Paper* No. 118. (New York: Goldman Sachs Global Research Centres).

Gordon, James and Poonam Gupta, 2003. "Understanding India's Service Revolution," Paper prepared for the IMF-NCAER Conference, *A Tale of Two Giants: India's and China's Experience with Reform*, 14–16 November, (New Delhi: India).

Gruzalski, Bart, 2002. "Gandhi's Contributions to Environmental Thought and Action," *Environmental Ethics*, 24 (3): pp. 227–42.

Guest, Ross, S. and Ian Martin McDonald, 2007. "Global GDP Shares in the 21st Century – an Equilibrium Approach," *Economic Modeling*, 24 (6): pp. 859–77.

Guha, A., 2007. "Peasant Resistance in West Bengal a Decade before Singur and Nandigram," *Economic and Political Weekly*, 42 (37): pp. 3706–11.

Guo, Xiaolin, 2001. "Land Expropriation and Rural Conflicts in China," *The China Quarterly*, 166 (June): pp. 422–39.

Gwartney, James and Robert Lawson, 2009. *Economic Freedom Dataset*, published in Economic Freedom of the World: 2009 Annual Report. Economic Freedom Network.

Habermas, Jürgen, 1993. *Justification and Application: Remarks on Discourse Ethics* (Cambridge: MIT Press).

Habermas, Jürgen, 1984. *The Theory of Communicative Action Vol 1: Reason and the Rationalization of Society*. Translated by Thomas McCarthy (Boston: Beacon).

Habermas, Jürgen, 1998. *The Inclusion of the Other: Studies in Political Theory* (Cambridge: MIT Press).

Habermas, Jürgen 1994a *Postmetaphysical Thinking: Philosophical Essays* (Cambridge: The MIT Press).

Hall, Peter, A. and David Soskice, 2001. *Varieties of Capitalism: the Institutional Foundations of Comparative Advantage* (Oxford: Oxford University Press).

Hameiri, S., 2007. "Failed States or a Failed Paradigm? State Capacity and the Limits of Institutionalism," *Journal of International Relations and Development*, 10 (3): pp. 122–49.

Hamilton, Gary, 1991. *Business Networks and Economic Development in East and Southeast Asia* (Hong Kong: Centre of Asian Studies, University of Hong Kong).

Hannum, Emily, 1999. "Political Change and the Urban-rural Gap in Basic Education in China, 1949–90," *Comparative Education Review*, 43 (2): pp. 193–211.

Hanushek, Eric, A. and Ludger Woessmann, 2010. "Education and Economic Growth," in Penelope Peterson, Eva Baker and Barry McGaw (eds) *The International Encyclopedia of Education*, pp. 60–7 (Amsterdam: Elsevier Science).

Harrod, Roy, F. 1939. "An Essay on Dynamic Theory," *Economic Journal*, 49 (193): pp. 14–33.

Hayek, Friedrich von, 1952. *The Sensory Order* (London: Kegan & Paul).

Hayek, Friedrich von, 1967. *Studies in Philosophy, Politics and Economics* (London: Routledge & Kegan Paul).

Herd, R. and S. Dougherty, 2007. "Growth Prospects in China and India Compared," *The European Journal of Comparative Economics*, 6 (1): pp. 65–89.

Heston, Alan, Robert Summers and Bettina Aten, 2011. *Penn World Table Version 7.0*, Center for International Comparisons of Production, Income and Prices at the University of Pennsylvania, March 2011.

Hobsbawm, Eric, 1997. *On History* (New York: The New Press).

Hollingsworth, J. Rogers and Robert Boyer, 1997. *Contemporary Capitalism: The Embeddedness of Institutions* (Cambridge: Cambridge University Press).

Homer-Dixon, Thomas F., 2000. *The Ingenuity Gap* (New York: Knopf).

Homer-Dixon, Thomas F., 2006. *The Upside of Down: Catastrophe, Creativity, and the Renewal of Civilization* (Washington: Island Press).

Hong, Shen, 2010. "The Mystery of China's Labor Shortage," *The Wall Street Journal*, China Real Time Report, 22 February.

Hong, Wontack and Lawrence B. Krause, 1981. *Trade and Growth of the Advanced Developing Countries in the Pacific Rim* (Seoul: Korea Development Institute).

Howlett, Michael and M. Ramesh, 1995. *Studying Public Policy: Policy Cycles and Policy Subsystems* (Oxford: Oxford University Press).

Hsieh, C. T. and P. J. Klenow, 2009. "Misallocation and Manufacturing TFP in China and India," *The Quarterly Journal of Economics*, 124 (4): pp. 1403–48.

Hu, Angang and Shaoguang Wang, 1993. *Zhongguo guojia nengli baogao* (report on China's State Capacity) (Shenyang: Liaoning renmin chubanshe).

Hu, Angang, Shaoguang Wang and Xiaoguang Kang, 1995. *Zhongguo diqu chaju baogao*(China Regional Inequality Report) (Shenyang: Liaoning renmin chubanshe).

Hu, Angang, 1989. *Renkou yu fazhan: zhongguo renkou jingji wenti de xitong yanjiu* (Population and Development: A Systematic Analysis of China's Population and Economy Problem) (Hangzhou: Zheijiang renmin chubanshe).

Hu, Angang, 1997. *Zhongguo ziran zaihai yu jingji fazhan* (China's Environmental Disaster and Economic Development) (Wuhan: Hubei keji chubanshe).

Hu, Angang, 2001. *Zhongguo tiaozhan fuBai* (China Fighting against Corruption) (Hangzhou: Zhejiang renmin chubanshe).

Hu, Angang, 2002. *Quanqiuhua tiaozhan zhongguo* (Globalization challenging China). (Beijing: Beijingdaxue chubanshe).

Hu, Biliang, 2005. "*Guanxi gongtongti* (Guanxi Community)," *Zhongguo shehui kexue pinglun* (China Social Sciences Review) 4 (Beijing: Falu chubanshe).

Huang, Rende and Zheng, Wenfa, 1997. Zhonggong gaige kaifang hou de caizheng tiaokong (*Financial Control by Chinese Communist Party after Reform and Opening-Up*) (Taipei: Huatai shuju).

Huang, Xiaoming, 2010. *The Institutional Dynamics of China's Great Transformation* (London: Routledge).

Huang, Xiaoming, 2005. *The Rise and Fall of the East Asian Growth System 1951–2000: Institutional Competitiveness and Rapid Economic Growth* (London: Routledge).

Huang, Yasheng and Tarun Khanna, 2003. "Can India Overtake China?" *Foreign Policy*, 137 (July/August): pp. 74–81.

Huang, Yasheng, 2006. "China Could Learn from India's Slow and Quiet Rise," *Financial Times*, 23 January.

Huang, Yasheng, 2008. *Capitalism with Chinese Characteristics: Entrepreneurship and the State* (Cambridge: Cambridge University Press).

Huang, Yiping, 2008. "Will China Fall into Stagflation," in Ligang Song and Wing Thye Woo (eds) *China's Dilemma: Economic Growth, the Environment, and Climate Change* (Washington, DC: Brookings Institute Press).

Huntington, Samuel, P., 1965. "Political Development and Political Decay," *World Politics*, 17 (3): pp. 386–430.

Huntington, Samuel, P., 1968. *Political Order in Changing Societies* (New Haven, CT: Yale University Press).

Huntington, Samuel, P. and Jorge I. Dominguez, 1975. "Political Development," in F. I. Greenstein and N. W. Polsby (eds) *Macropolitical Theory Reading*, pp. 1–114 (Massachusetts: Addison-Wesley).

Hutchfroft, Paul, 1991. "Oligarchs and Cronies in the Philippine State: The Politics of Patrimonial Plunder," *World Politics*, 43 (2): pp. 414–50.

Ikenberry, John, 2001. *After Victory: Institutions, Strategic Restraint, and the Rebuilding of Order after Major Wars* (Princeton: Princeton University Press).

ILO (International Labor Organization), 2010. *Labor Statistics Database* (Geneva: ILO). Accessed on 3 September 2010 at http://laborsta.ilo.org/.

IMF (International Monetary Fund), 2011. *World Economic Outlook* (Washington, DC: World Bank).

IMF (International Monetary Fund), various years. *World Economic Outlook*, http://www.imf.org/external/pubs/ft/weo.

Jayasuriya, Kanishka, 1999. *Law, Capitalism, and Power in Asia* (London: Routledge).

Jefferson, Gary, H., Albert G. Z. Hu and Jian Su, 2006. "The Sources and Sustainability of China's Economic Growth," *Brookings Papers on Economic Activity*, 2006 (2): pp. 1–61.

Jha, Praveen and Mario Negre, 2007. "Indian Economy in the Era of Contemporary Globalization: Some Core Elements of the Balance Sheet," Centre for Economic Studies and Planning (New Delhi: Jawaharlal Nehru University).

Jha, Raghbendra, 2007. "The Indian Economy: Current Performance and Short-term Prospects," *Working Paper* 2007/04 (Canberra: Australia South Asia Research Centre).

Jiang, Ziqiang, et al., 1997. "*Yizhe xuyan* (Translators' Introduction)," in *A Moral Sentiment: Adam Smith* (Beijing: Shangwu chubanshe).

Johnson, Chalmers, 1982. *MITI and the Japanese Miracle: The Growth of Industrial Policy, 1925–1975* (Stanford: Stanford University Press).

Jorgenson, Dale, W. and Khuong Vu, 2005. "Information Technology and World Economy," *Scandinavian Journal of Economics*, 107 (4): pp. 631–50.

Joshi, Seema, 2004. "Tertiary Sector-driven Growth in India: Impact on Employment and Poverty," *Economic and Political Weekly*, 39 (37): pp. 4175–8.

Jürgen Habermas, 1993a. *The Postmetaphisical Thinking: Philosophical Essays*, trans. William Mark Hohengarten (Cambridge: MIT Press).

Kahn, Joseph, 2004. "China Crushes Protest, Turning 3 Friends into Enemies," *New York Times*, at A1.

Kalish, Ira, 2006. *China and India: The Reality beyond the Hype* (New York. Deloitte Research), May.

Kang, David, 2002. *Crony Capitalism: Corruption and Development in South Korea and the Philippines* (Cambridge: Cambridge University Press).

Kang, Myung Hun, 1996. *The Korean Business Conglomerates: Chaebol Then and Now* (Berkeley, CA: Center for Korean Studies, Institute of East Asian Studies).

Kaufmann, Daniel, Aart Kraay and Massimo Mastruzzi, 2010. *Worldwide Governance Indicators 2010* (World Bank).

Keidel, Albert, 2006. "China's Social Unrest: The Story behind the Stories," *Policy Brief* no. 48, Carnegie Endowment for International Peace, September.

Kennedy, John, F., 1959. "The Basis of US Interest in India: Its New Dimensions," Paper presented at the Conference on India and the United States, Committee for International Economic Growth,, Washington, DC, 4–5 May.

Kennedy, Scott, Richard Suttmeier and Su Jun, 2008. "Standards, Stakeholders, and Innovation: China's Evolving Role in the Global Knowledge Economy," *Draft NBR Project Report* (Seattle: National Bureau of Asian Research).

Keynes, John, M., 1936. *The General Theory of Employment, Interest, and Money* (London: Palgrave Macmillan).

Khemani, Stuti, 2004. "Political Cycles in a Developing Economy: Effect of Elections in the Indian States," *Journal of Development Economics*, 73 (1): pp. 125–54.

Khoshoo, T. N. and M. S. John, 2009. *Mahatma Gandhi and the Environment: Analysis of Gandhian Environmental Thought* (New Delhi: TERI Press).

Kidd, John, B. and Frank Jurgen Richter, 2003. *Corruption and Governance in Asia* (Houndmills: Palgrave Macmillan).

Kim, Eun Mee, 1987. *From Dominance to Symbiosis: State and the Chaebol in the Korean Economy*, Ph.D. dissertation, Brown University, Providence, RI.

Kingdon, Geeta Gandhi, 2007. *The Progress of School Education in India* (Oxford: Global Poverty Research Group, Oxford University).

Kohr, Leopold, 1957. *The Breakdown of Nations* (New York: Rinehart).

Kornai, Janos, 2010. "There is no 'China Model'," accessed 10 August 2010 at http://www.caijing.com.cn/2010-04-12/110414752.html.

Kowalski, Przemyslaw, 2008. *China and India: A Comparison of Two Trade Integration Approaches* (Paris: Organization for Economic Cooperation and Development).

Krishnan, A., 2009. "China Adopts Law on Rural Land Dispute," *The Hindu*, 29 June.

Krueger, Anne, O., 2002. "Introduction," in Anne O. Krueger (ed.) *Economic Policy Reforms and the Indian Economy* (Chicago: University of Chicago Press).

Kumar, A., 2006. 2009 "Headline Singur," accessed 7 December 2009 at http://www.countercurrents.org/ind-kumar301206.htm.

Kumar, Rajiv and Abhijit Sen Gupta, 2008. "Towards a Competitive Manufacturing Sector," *Indian Council for Research on International Relations Working Paper* no. 203.

Kumara, Kranti, 2007. "West Bengal Stalinist Regime Perpetrates Peasant Massacre," Accessed 16 March 2007 at www.wsws.org.

Kuznets, Simon, 1955. "Economic Growth and Income Inequality," *American Economic Review*, 65 (1): pp. 1–28.

Lal, Vinay, 2000. "Gandhi and the Ecological Vision of Life: Thinking beyond Deep Ecology," *Environmental Ethics*, 22 (2): pp. 149–69.

Lam, Peng, Er and Tai-Wei Lim, 2009. *The Rise of China and India: A New Asian Drama* (Singapore, Hackensack, NJ: World Scientific).

Lardy, Nicholas R., 1998. *China's Unfinished Economic Revolution* (Washington, DC: Brookings Institution).

Laszlo, Chris, 2011. *China and India: Assessing Sustainability*, Berkshire Encyclopedia of Sustainability vol. 7 (Great Barrington, MA: Berkshire).

Lau, Lawrence J., Yingyi Qian and Gérard Roland, 2000. "Reform Without Losers: An Interpretation of China's Dual-track Approach to Transition," *Journal of Political Economy*, 108 (1): pp. 120–43.

Lee, Boon, L., D. S. Prasada Rao and William Shepherd, 2007. "Comparison of Real Output and Productivity of Chinese and Indian Manufacturing," *Journal of Development Economics*, 84 (2): pp. 378–416.

Lee, Ronald and Andrew Mason, 2006. "What is the Demographic Dividend?" *Finance and Development* (Washington, DC: IMF).

Levine, Ross and David Renelt, 1992. "A Sensitivity Analysis of Cross-country Growth Regressions," *The American Economic Review*, 82 (4): pp. 942–63.

Lewis, W. Arthur, 1954. "Economic Development with Unlimited Supplies of Labor," *The Manchester School*, 22 (May): pp. 139–91.

Lewis, W. Arthur, 1955. *The Theory of Economic Growth* (London: Allen and Unwen).

Li, David D., 1996. "A Theory of Ambiguous Property Rights in Transition Economies: The Case of the Chinese Non-state Sector," *Journal of Comparative Economics* 23 (1): pp. 1–19.

Li, Lianjiang, 2004. "Political Trust in Rural China," *Modern China*, 30 (2): pp. 228–58.

Li, Yuefen and Bin Zhang, 2008. "Development Path of China and India and the Challenges for their Sustainable Growth," *World Economy*, 31 (10): pp. 1277–91.

Liang, Shumin, 1990. *Liangshumin quanji* (The Complete Collection of Works of Liang Shumin) vol. 3 (Jinan: Shandong renmin chubanshe).

Lin, Yifu Justin and Yang Yao, 2006. *Zhongguo qiji: huigu yu zhanwang* (China Miracle: Retrospect and Prospect) (Beijing: Beijingdaxue chubanshe).

Lindsey, Tim and Howard Dick, 2002. *Corruption in Asia: Rethinking the Governance Paradigm* (Sydney: The Federation Press).

Lingle, Christopher, 1998. *The Rise and Decline of the Asian Century: False Starts on the Path to the Global Millennium* (Hong Kong: Asia 2000).

Liu, Gensheng, 2008. "*Qiye renji guanxi chengben you duo gao* (How High Is the Cost of Socialisation for Enterprises)," *Dongshihui* (Board) 9.

Liu, Liang-Yn and Wing Thye Woo, 1994. "Saving Behavior under Imperfect Financial Markets and the Current Account Consequences," *Economic Journal*, 104 (424): pp. 512–27.

Liu, Yanxun, 2010. "Huaxi cun de jiacun gongrongti (The Family-Village Co-Prosperity Union of Huaxi Village," Zhongguo xinwen zhoukan (China Newsweek) 4.

Lo, Bobo, 2010. *China and the Global Financial Crisis* (London: Center for European Reform).

Lu, Yi-long, 2002. "*1949 Nianhoude Zhongguo Huji Zhidu: Jiegou Yu Bianqian* (Structure and Transition: The Household Registration System in China after 1949)," *Beijingdaxue xuebao* (Journal of Peking University) 39 (2).

Lu, Yi-long, 2003. *Huji zhidu: kongzhi yu shihui chabie* (The Huji System: Control & Social Disparity) (Beijing: Shangwu chubanshe).

Lucas, Robert, 1988. "On the Mechanics of Economic Development," *Journal of Monetary Economics*, 22 (1): pp. 2–42.

Ma, Guonan and Yi Wang, 2010. "China's High Savings Rate: Myth and Reality," *BIS Working Papers*, no. 312.

Maddison, Angus, 1998. *Chinese Economic Performance in the Long Run* (Paris: OECD Development, Development Center).

Maddison, Angus, 2001. *The World Economy: A Millennial Perspective* (Paris: OECD Development Center).

Mahtaney, Piya, 2007. *India, China, and Globalization: The Emerging Superpowers and the Future of Economic Development* (Basingstoke: Palgrave Macmillan).

Marshall, Julian and Michael Toffel, 2005. "Framing the Elusive Concept of Sustainability: A Sustainability Hierarchy," *Environmental Science & Technology*, 39 (3): pp. 673–82.

Mattoo, Aaditya, Deepak Mishra and Anirudh Shingal, 2004. *Sustaining India's Services Revolution: Access to Foreign Markets, Domestic Reform and International Negotiation* (Washington, DC: World Bank).

Mauro, Paolo, 1997. "Why Worry about Corruption?" *IMF Economic Issues*, no. 6.

McCraw, Thomas, 1984. *Prophets of Regulation* (Harvard University Press).

McKibbin, Warwick, J. and Wing Thye Woo, 2003. "The Consequences of China's WTO Accession on its Neighbours," *Asian Economic Papers*, 2 (2): pp. 1–38.

McKibbin, Warwick, Peter Wilcoxeu and Wing Thye Woo, 2008. "China Can Grow and Still Help Prevent the Tragedy of CO_2 Commons," in Ligang Song and Wing Thye Woo (eds) *China's Dilemma: Economic Growth, the Environment, and Climate Change* (Brookings Institute Press).

Menon, Surabi, James Hansen, Larissa Nazarenko and Yunfeng Luo, 2002. "Climate Effects of Black Carbon in China and India," *Science*, 297 (5590): pp. 2250–3.

Meredith, Robyn, 2007. *The Elephant and the Dragon: The Rise of India and China and What it Means for All of Us* (New York: Norton).

Meri, Tomas, 2009. "Science and Technology," *Eurostat: Statics in Focus*, no. 25 (Luxembourg: European Commission).

Merrill, Stephen, David Taylor and Robert Poole, 2010. *The Dragon and the Elephant: Understanding the Development of Innovation Capacity in China and India* (Washington, DC: National Academies Press).

Miller, Max, 2005. *Worlds of Capitalism: Institutions, Governance, and Economic Change in the Era of Globalization* (New York: Routledge).

Minzner, Carl, 2006. "Social Instability in China: Causes, Consequences, and Implications," Center for Strategic and International Studies, December 2006, available at http://csis.org/files/attachments/061205_Minzner.pdf.

Mishra, Ankita and Ranjan Ray, 2010. "Multi Dimensional Deprivation in the Awakening Giants: A Comparative Study on Micro Data," *Discussion Paper* 53/10, (Melbourne: Department of Economics, Monash University), www.buseco.monash.edu.au/researchpapers/2010/5310dimensionalmishraray.pdf.

Mitra, Siddhartha, 2007. "Special Economic Zones in India: White Elephants or Race Horses," *SSRN Working Paper Series*, accessed at: http://ssrn.com/abstract=969274.

Miyazaki, Ichisada, 1976. *China's Examination Hell: The Civil Service Examination of Imperial China* (New Haven: Yale University Press).

MLJ (Ministry of Law and Justice, India), 2007. *The Constitution of India* (New Delhi: Government of India).

MOF (Ministry of Finance, India), various issues. *The Economic Survey* (New Delhi: Government of India).

Mohanty, Manoranjan, 2007. *Grass-roots Democracy in India and China: The Right to Participate* (New Delhi: Sage).

Morrison, Wayne, M. and Marc Labonte, 2009. "China's Currency: A Summary of the Economic Issues," *Congressional Research Service*, 7–5700. RS21625. Accessed 15 September at www.crs.gov.

Morse, Stephen, 2008. "The Use of Headline Indices to Link Environmental Quality and Income at the Level of the Nation State," *Applied Geography*, 28 (2): pp. 77–150.

Munshi, Kaivan and Mark Rosenzweig, 2009. "Why is Mobility in India so Low? Social Insurance, Inequality, and Growth," *National Bureau of Economic Research Working Paper Series No. 14850.*

Myrdal, Gunnar, 1968. *Asian Drama: An Inquiry into the Poverty of Nations* (New York: Pantheon).

NBSC (National Bureau of Statistics of China), 2005. *China Compendium of Statistics 1949–2004* (Beijing: Zhongguo tongji chubanshe).

NDRB (Nandou ribao), 2010. "*Qing Linag Hui Daibia Weiyuan Guanzhu bing Duncu Hujizhidu Gaige* (Requesting Representatives in Congress Pay Attention to and Press for Reform of the Huji System)," in *Nandushelun* (NDDAILY) 1 March: Nanduwang (Southern Capital Online) www.nddaily.com.

NDRC (National Development and Reform Commission), 2007. *China's National Climate Change Programme*, June.

NEP (New Economics Foundation), 2005. *Life Satisfaction: Happy Planet Index 2.0*: available at: http://www.happyplanetindex.org/explore/global/life-sat.html.

North, Douglas, 2005. *Understanding the Process of Economic Change* (Princeton University Press).

North, Douglass, C. and Robert Paul Thomas, 1973. *The Rise of the Western World* (Cambridge: Cambridge University Press).

Nussbaum, Martha, C., 2008. "Violence on the Left: Nandigram and the Communists of West Bengal," *Dissent*, 2008 (Spring): pp. 27–33.

NYT New York Times.

O'Brien, Kevin, J. and Lianjiang Li, 2006. *Rightful Resistance in Rural China* (Cambridge: Cambridge University Press).

O'Neill, Jim, Dominic Wilson, Roopa Purushothaman and Anna Stupnytska, 2005. "How Solid are the BRICs?" *Global Economics Paper* 134, 15 December, (New York: Goldman Sachs Global Research Centre).

Oakeshott, Michael, 1991. *Rationalism in Politics and Other Essays* (Indianapolis: Liberty Fund).

O'Connor, James, 1973. *The Fiscal Crisis of the State* (New York: St Martin's Press).

OECD, 1995. *Monitoring the World Economy 1820–1992* (Paris: OECD).

OECD, 2001. *The World Economy: A Millennial Perspective* (Paris: OECD Development Centre).

OECD, 2003. *The World Economy: Historical Statistics* (Paris: OECD Development Centre).

OECD, 2006. *Challenges for China's Public Spending: Toward Greater Effectiveness and Equity* (Paris: OECD).

OECD, 2006. "Public Debt and State Revenue Data," accessed at http://stats.oecd.org/wbos/viewhtml.aspx? QueryName=2&QueryType=View&Lang=en.

Ohara, Moriki and Koichiro Kimura, 2009. *Comparative Study on Industrial Development Process in China and India: Interim Report* (Chiba, Japan: Institute of Developing Economies).

Olson, Mancur, 1991. "Autocracy, Democracy, and Prosperity," in R. J. Zeckhauser (ed.) *Strategy and Choice*, pp. 131–57 (Cambridge, MA: MIT Press).

Ottaviano, Gianmarco, I. P. and Giovanni Peri, 2005. "Rethinking the Gains from Immigration: Theory and Evidence from the US," *NBER Working Paper* No. 11672. (Cambridge, MA: National Bureau of Economic Research).

Pan, Wei, 2009. *Dangdai zhonghua tizhi: Zhongguo moshi de jingji, zhengzhi, shehui jiexi* (Contemporary Chinese System: An Economic, Political and Social Analysis of the Chinese Model) (Beijing: Zhongyang bianyiju chubanshe).

Panayotou, Theodore, 1997. "Demystifying the Environmental Kuznets Curve: Turning a Black Box into a Policy Tool," *Environmental and Development Economics*, 2 (4): pp. 465–84.

Parris, Thomas, M. and Robert W. Kates, 2003. "Characterizing and Measuring Sustainable Development," *Annual Review of Environment & Resources*, 28 (1): pp. 559–86.

Patnaik, P., 2007. "In the Aftermath of Nandigram," *Economic and Political Weekly*, 42 (21): pp. 1893–5.

Peerenboom, Randall, 2004. *Asian Discourses of Rule of Law* (London: Routledge).

Pei, Minxin, 2005. "China is Paying the Price of Rising Social Unrest," *Financial Times*, 7 November.

Pei, Minxin, 2006a. *China's Trapped Transition* (Harvard University Press).

Pei, Minxin, 2006b. "China is Stagnating in its 'Trapped Transition,'" *Financial Times*, 24 February.

Pepper, Suzanne, 2000. *Radicalism and Education in 20th-Century China* (Hong Kong: Cambridge University Press).

Perry, Elizabeth, J. 2008. "Chinese Conceptions of 'Rights': From Mencius to Mao," *Perspectives on Politics* 6 (1): pp. 37–50.

Pistor, Katharina and Philip A. Wellons, 1999. *The Rule of Law and Legal Institutions in Asian Economic Development, 1960–1995* (New York: Oxford University Press).

Poddar, Tushar and Eva Yi, 2007. "India's Rising Growth Potential," *Global Economic Paper* 152, 22 January (New York: Goldman Sachs).

Polanyi, Karl, 1944. *The Great Transformation: The Political and Economic Origins of Our Time* (Boston: Beacon Press).

Polanyi, Michael, 1967. *The Tacit Dimension* (New York: Anchor Books).

Posner, Richard, A., 2004. *Catastrophe: Risk and Response* (Oxford and New York: Oxford University Press).

Posner, Richard, 1970. "A Statistical Study of Anti-trust Enforcement," *Journal of Law and Economics*, 13 (2): p. 366.

Prater, Edmund, Patricia M. Swafford and Srikanth Yellepeddi, 2009. "Operational Issues in China and India," *Journal of Marketing Channels*, 16 (2): pp. 169–87.

Prime, Penelope, B., 2009. "China and India Enter Global Markets: A Review of Comparative Economic Development and Future Prospects," *Eurasian Geography & Economics*, 50 (6): pp. 621–42.

Prosterman, Roy, Keliang Zhu, Jianping Ye, Jeffrey Riedinger, Ping Li and Vandana Yadav, 2009. "Secure Land Rights as a Foundation for Broad-based Rural Development in China," *NBAR special report #18* (The Seattle: National Bureau of Asian Research).

Przeworski, Adam, Michael E. Alvarez, Jose Antonio Cheibub and Fernando Limongi, 2000. *Democracy and Development: Political Institutions and Well-Being in the World, 1950–1990* (New York: Cambridge University Press).

Przeworski, Adam, 1990. *The State and the Economy under Capitalism* (Chur, Switzerland: Harwood Academic Publishers).

Psacharopoulos, George, 1985. "Returns to Education: A Further International Update and Implications," *The Journal of Human Resources*, 20 (4): pp. 583–604.

Pye, Lucian, W., 1966. *Aspects of Political Development* (Boston: Little Brown).

Qin, Hui, 2010. "*Youmeiyou zhongguo moshi* (Is There a China Model)," *Nanfang Duoshi Bao (Southern City Newspaper)* April 6.

Rai, Saritha, 2006. "India's Outsourcing Industry is Facing a Labor Shortage," *The New York Times*, 16 February.

Railey, Jimmy, A. and Richard Martin Reycraft, 2008. *Global Perspectives on the Collapse of Complex Systems* (Albuquerque: Maxwell Museum of Anthropology).

Raj, Baldev and M. Rajan, 2007. "India's Fast Reactor Program in the context of Environment Sustainability," *International Journal of Environmental Studies*, 64 (6): pp. 729–47.

Ramachandran, Sudha, 2007. "Indian Villagers Resist Corporate Land Grab," *Asian Times Online*, accessed 7 November 2009, at http://www.atimes.com/atimes/South_Asia/IK17Df07.html.

Ramakrishnan, Venkitesh, 2006. "Conflict zones," *Frontline*, 23 (20).

Ramesh, Jairam, 2005. *Making Sense of Chindia: Reflections on China and India* (New Delhi: India Research Press).

Rao, Nirmala, Kai-Ming Cheng and Kirti Narain, 2003. "Primary Schooling in China and India: Understanding How Socio-contextual Factors Moderate the Role of the State," *International Review of Education*, 49 (1–2): pp. 153–76.

Rao, Vaman, 1984. "Democracy and Economic Development," *Studies in Comparative International Development*, 19 (4): pp. 67–81.

Ravallion, Martin, 2009. "A Comparative Perspective on Poverty Reduction in Brazil, China and India," *Policy Research Working Paper No. 5080*, October (Washington, DC: The World Bank).

Rawski, Thomas, G. and Perkins Dwight, 2008. "Forecasting China's Economic Growth to 2025," in Loren Brandt and Thomas G. Rawski (eds) *China's Great Economic Transformation* (Cambridge: Cambridge University Press).

RBI (Reserve Bank of India), various issues. *The Handbook of Statistics of the Indian Economy* (Mumbai, India: Reserve Bank of India).

RDI (Rural Development Institute), 2003. Memo on "Land Takings in China: Policy Recommendations", 5 June.

Rein, Shaun, 2010. "China's Growing Labour Shortage: Low-end Factories Are no Longer the Future, and the Cost of Doing Business is Rising," *Forbes*, 15 March, online at http://www.forbes.com/2010/03/15/china-labor-shortage-leadership-managing-rein.html. Accessed on 3 September 2010.

Rice, Susan E. and Stewart Patrick, 2008. *Index of State Weakness in the Developing World* (Washington, DC: Brookings Institution).

Rice, Susan, E. and Stewart Patrick, 2008. *Index of State Weakness in the Developing World* (Washington, DC: Brookings Institution).

Robinson, James, 1998. "Theories of 'Bad Policy'," *Journal of Policy Reform*, 2 (1): pp. 1–46.

Rodrik, Dani, 2007. *One Economics, Many Recipes: Globalization, Institutions, and Economic Growth* (Princeton University Press).

Romer, Paul, M., 1990. "Endogenous Technological Change," *Journal of Political Economy*, 98 (5): pp. S71–S102.

Rosett, Arthur, Lucie Cheng and Margaret Y. K. Woo, 2002. *East Asian Law: Universal Norms and Local Cultures* (London: RoutledgeCurzon).

Ross, John, 2010. "Key Determinants of the Different Growth Rates in China and India," accessed 15 April 2011, at http://www.istockanalyst.com/article/viewarticlepaged/articleid/4079906/pageid/1.

Rostow, W. W., 1960. *The Stages of Economic Growth: A Non-Communist Manifesto* (Cambridge: Cambridge University).

Rowthorn, Robert, 2006 *The Renaissance of China and India: Implications for the Advanced Economies*, United Nations Conference on Trade and Development Discussion papers no. 182 (Geneva: UNTP).

Rural Development Institute, 2007. "Compensation and Valuation in Resettlement: Cambodia, People's Republic of China, and India," *Asian Development Bank Report*. See http://www.rdiland.org/RESEARCH/Research_Publications.html.

Sachs, Jeffrey, D. and Howard J. Shatz, 1994. "Trade and Jobs in US Manufacturing," *Brookings Papers on Economic Activity*, 1: pp. 1–84 (Washington, DC: Brookings Institution).

Sachs, Jeffrey, D. and Wing Thye Woo, 2000. "Understanding China's Economic Performance," *Journal of Policy Reform*, 4 (1): pp. 1–50.

Samuelson, Paul, 2004. "Where Ricardo and Mill Rebut and Confirm Arguments of Mainstream Economists Supporting Globalization," *Journal of Economic Perspectives* 18 (3): pp. 135–46.

Santos-Paulino, Amelia U. and Guanghua Wan, 2010. *The Rise of China and India: Impacts, Prospects and Implications* (Basingstoke: Palgrave Macmillan).

Sanyal, Saptak and Aditya Shankar, 2009. "Property Rights and Sustainable Development in India," *Columbia Journal of Asian Law*, 22 (2): pp. 235–57.

Schumpeter, Joseph, 1942. *Capitalism, Socialism, and Democracy* (New York: Harper and Brothers).

Schweinitz, Karl de, Jr, 1959. "Industrialization, Labor Controls, and Democracy," *Economic Development and Cultural Change*, 7 (4): pp. 385–404.

SCMP South China Morning Post.

Seema, Joshi, 2004. "Tertiary Sector-Driven Growth in India: Impact on Employment and Poverty," *Economic and Political Weekly*, 39 (37): pp. 4175–8.

SFT (State Fragility Taskforce), 2008. *Global Report 2009, Table 2.* Political Instability Taskforce, Center for Global Policy, George Mason University, 9 December 2010. available at: http://www.systemicpeace.org/Global%20Report%202009.pdf.

Sheth, Jagdish, N., 2008. *Chindia Rising: How China and India will Benefit Your Business* (New Delhi: Tata McGraw-Hill).

Shonfield, Andrew, 1965. *Modern Capitalism: The Changing Balance of Public and Private Power* (London: Oxford University Press).

Singh, Arvinder, 2005. "Comparisons between China and India," *China & World Economy*, 12 (3): pp. 72–5.

Sinocast, 2004. "First Power Generator in Dingzhou Power Plant Starts Generation," *Business Daily News*. Accessed 22 April 2010, at http://www.sinocast.com.

Skeldon, Ronald, 2010. "Migration and Development: Contested Consequences," in Monique Kremer, Peter van Lieshout and Robert Went (eds) *Doing Good or Doing Better: Development Policies in a Globalizing World*, pp. 321–39 (The Hague: Amsterdam University Press).

Smith, David, 2007. *The Dragon and the Elephant: China, India and the New World Order* (London: Profile Books).

Solinger, Dorothy J., 1999. *Contesting Citizenship in Urban China: Peasant Migrants, the State, and the Logic of the Market* (Berkley: University of California Press).

Solow, Robert, 1956. "A Contribution to the Theory of Economic Growth," *Quarterly Journal of Economics*, 70 (1): pp. 65–94.

Solow, Robert, 1970. *Growth Theory: An Exposition* (Oxford: Clarendon Press).

Solow, Robert, 1991. "Sustainability: An Economist's Perspective," the 18th J. Seward Johnson Lecture to the Marine Policy Center, Woods Hole Oceanographic Institution; in Robert N. Stavins (ed.) 2000, *Economics of the Environment: Selected Readings*, pp. 131–8 (New York: Norton).

Speak, Suzanne and Graham Tipple, 2006. "Perceptions, Persecution and Pity: The Limitations of Interventions for Homelessness in Developing Countries," *International Journal of Urban and Regional Research*, 30 (1): pp. 172–88.

Srinivasan, S., 2005. "Skilled-labour Shortage Hits India," *The Associated Press*, 8 June.

Srinivasan, T. N., 2005. "Productivity and Economic Growth in South Asia and China," paper presented at the *Annual Conference of the Pakistan Society Development Economics*, Islamabad, Pakistan, 19–21 December 2005.

Srinivasan, T. N., 2006. "China, India and the World Economy," *Working Paper No. 286*, Stanford Center for International Development, Stanford University.

Srinivasan, T. N., 2009. "China and India in the Global Economy: Development Strategies, Economic Reforms and Responses to the Global Economic Crisis and Recession," paper delivered at the *Conference on Institutions and Economic Development, China Center for Economic Studies*, Fudan University, Economic Growth Center, Yale University, 11–12 August, Shanghai, China.

Standard & Poor's, 2010. *Sovereign Risk: Country Profiles and Ratings*, 9 December 2010, available at: http://www.standardandpoors.com/ratings/.

State Council (China), 2008. *China's Policies and Actions on Climate Change* (Beijing: Information Office of the State Council).

State Development and Reform Commission (China), 2009. *Zhongguo Yingdui Qihou Bianhuade Zhengce Yu Xingdong: 2009 Niadu Baogao* (China's Policies and Actions in Response to Climate Change: 2009 Annual Report) (Beijing: State Development and Reform Commission).

Stiglitz, Joseph E., 1996. "Some Lessons from the East Asian Miracle," *The World Bank Research Observer*, 11 (2): pp. 151–77.

Streeck, Wolfgang and Kozo Yamamura, 2001. *The Origins of Nonliberal Capitalism: Germany and Japan in Comparison* (Ithaca: Cornell University Press).

Streets, David, 2005. "Black Smoke in China and its Climate Effects," *Asian Economic Papers*, 4 (2): pp. 1–23.

Sufian, Abu Jafar Mohammad, 1989. "Socio-economic Correlates of Life Expectancy at Birth – The Case of Developing Countries," *Journal of Population and Health Studies*, 9 (2): pp. 214–26.

Sun, Liying, Jinren Ni and Alistair Borthwick, 2010."Rapid Assessment of Sustainability in Mainland China," *Journal of Environmental Management*, 91 (4): pp. 1021–31.

Swan, Trevor, W., 1956. "Economic Growth and Capital Accumulation," *Economic Record*, 36 (73): pp. 55–6.

Tai, Hung-chao, 1989. *Confucianism and Economic Development: An Oriental Alternative* (Washington, DC: Washington Institute Press).

Tainter, Joseph, A., 1988. *The Collapse of Complex Societies*, New Studies in Archaeology (Cambridge and New York: Cambridge University Press).

Tanzi, Vito and Hamid Davoodi, 1998 "Roads to Nowhere: How Corruption in Public Investment Hurts Growth," *IMF Economic Issues* no. 12.

TFHES (Task Force on Higher Education and Society), 2000. "Higher Education in Developing Countries: Peril and Promise," database available through the Harvard University Center for International Development. Accessed on 3 September 2010 at http://www.cid.harvard.edu/ciddata/ciddata.html.

Thirlwell, Mark, 2007. *Second Thoughts on Globalisation: Can the Developed World Cope with the Rise of China and India?* (Double Bay: Longueville Media).

Thompson, Warren Simpson, 1930. *Population Problems* (New York: McGraw-Hill).

Tian, Bingxin, 2003. *Zhongguo diyi zhengjian: Zhongguo huji zhidu diaocha shougao* (China's First Credential: China's Huji System Research Manuscript) (Guangzhou: Guangdong renmin chubanshe).

Tilak, Jandhyala B. G., 2005. *Post-Elementary Education, Poverty and Development in India* (University of Edinburgh Centre of African Studies Working Paper).

Todaro, Michael P., 1976. *Internal Migration in Developing Countries: A Review of Theory, Evidence, Methodology and Research Priorities* (Geneva: International Labor Organization).

UNCTAD (United Nations Conference on Trade and Development), 2009. *UNCTAD Online Databases*. Accessed 3 September 2010 at http://www.unctad.org.

UNDP (United Nations Development Programme), 2006. *2006 Human Development Report* (New York: UNDP).

UNDP (United Nations Development Programme), 2008. *Gender Inequality Index*, 9 December 2010, available at http://hdr.undp.org/en/statistics/gii/.

UNDP (United Nations Development Programme), 2009. *Human Development Report 2009: Overcoming Barriers – Human Mobility and Development* (New York: UNDP).

UNDP (United Nations Development Programme), 2010. *Multidimentional Poverty Index*, 9 December 2010, available at: http://hdr.undp.org/en/statistics/mpi/.

UNESCO, 2004. *"India: National Report on the Development of Education,"* Presented at the 47th Session of the International Conference of Education, Geneva, September. Accessed on 3 September 2010. http://www.ibe.unesco.org/International/ICE47/English/Natreps/reports/india.pdf.

UNESCO, 2007. *Education for All Global Monitoring Report 2007*. Accessed 3 September 2010 at http://www.unesco.org/education/GMR/2007/EDI.pdf.

UNESCO, 2008. "Education Statistics," accessed at http://www.uis.unesco.org on 3 September 2010.

Ungson, Gerardo R., Richard M. Steers and Seung-Ho Park, 1997. *Korean Enterprise: The Quest for Globalization* (Cambridge, MA: Harvard Business School Press).

United Nations, 2008. *World Population Policies 2007* (Department of Economic and Social Affairs/Population Division: United Nations).

UNSD (United Nations Statistics Division), 2010. "UNdata, A World of Information," United Nations Statistics Division. Accessed 28 January 2010, at http://data.un.org/.

Urban, Frauke, 2009. "Climate-change Mitigation Revisited: Low-carbon Energy Transitions for China and India," *Development Policy Review*, 27 (6): pp. 693–715.

Valli, Vittorio and Donatella Saccone, 2009. "Structural Change and Economic Development in China and India," *The European Journal of Comparative Economics*. 6 (1): pp. 101–29.

Virmani, Arvind, 2004a. "India's Economic Growth: From Socialist Rate of Growth to Bharatiya Rate of Growth," *Working Paper No. 122*, Indian Council for Research on International Relations.

Virmani, Arvind, 2004b. "Sources of India's Economic Growth: Trends in Total Factor Productivity," *Working Paper no. 131* (New Delhi: Indian Council for Research on International Economic Relations), 3 March 2011, www.icrier.org.

Wade, Robert, 1992. *Governing the Market: Economic Theory and the Role of Government in East Asian Industrialization* (Princeton: Princeton University Press).

Wallerstein, Immanuel M., 1996. *Open the Social Sciences: Report of the Gulbenkian Commission on the Restructuring of the Social Sciences* (Stanford: Stanford University Press).

Wang, Chaohua, 2010. *"Lishi zhongjie zai zhongguo* (The End of History in China)," *Sixiang* (Thoughts) 14.

Wang, Fei and Wenhai Liu, 2006. "*Bufen difang huji zhidu gaige qingkuang diaocha baogao* (Research Report on the Conditions of Reform of the Huji Institution in Selected Areas)" in Liqun Wei and Changfu Han, *Zhongguo nongmingong diaoyan baogao: guowuyuan yanjiushi ketizu (China's Nongmingong Research Report: Discussion Group of the Research Department of the State Council)* (Beijing: China yanshi cbubanshe).

Wang, Fei-Ling, 2005. *Organizing Through Division and Exclusion: China's Hukou System* (Stanford: Stanford University Press).

Wang, Keqing, and Guodong Qiao, 2005. "Hebei dingzhou chunmin zaoxi shijian diaocha (Ingestigation of Attacks on villagers in Dingzhou, Hebei," *Zhonguo jingji shibao* (China Economic Times) 20 June 2005.

Wang, Shaoguang, 1997. *Zhongguo guojia caizheng nengli de xiajiang jiqi houguo* (Decline of State Fiscal Capacity in China and Its Consequence) in Yang Gan and Zhiyuan Cui, *Zhogguo gaige de zhengzhi jingji xue* (The Political Economy of China's Reform) (Hong Kong: Oxford University Press).

Wang, Shaoguang and Angang Hu, 1993. *Zhongguo Guo Jia Neng Li Bao Gao* (Report on China's State Capacity) (Shenyang: Liaoning renmin chubanshe).

Weber, Max, 1994. *Weber: Political Writings*, Peter Lassman and Ronald Speirs (eds) (Cambridge University Press).

Weingast, Barry, 2010. "Why Developing Countries Prove so Resistant to the Rule of Law," in James Heckman, Robert Helson and Lee Cabatingan (eds) *Global Perspectives on the Rule of Law*, pp. 28–51 (London: Routledge).

WGSSD (Working Group on Statistics for Sustainable Development), 2008. *Measuring Sustainable Development* (New York: United Nations Economic Commission for Europe, Organization for Economic Cooperation and Development, and Eurostat).

Whalley, John and Xin Xian, 2006. "China's FDI and Non-FDI Economies and the Sustainability of Future High Chinese Growth" (Cambridge: National Bureau of Economic Research), accessed 20 September 2010 at www.nber.org/papers/w12249.

Willems, Emilio, 1958. "Brazil," in Arnold M. Rose (ed.) *The Institutions of Advanced Societies*, pp. 525–91 (Minneapolis: University of Minnesota Press).

Wilson, Dominic and Anna Stupnytska, 2007. "The N-11: More than an Acronym," *Global Economics Paper No: 153* (New York: Goldman and Sachs).

Winters, L. Alan and Shahid Yusuf, 2007. *Dancing with Giants: China, India and World Economy* (Washington, DC: The World Bank).

Wolf, Martin, 2005. "Asia's Giants on the Move," *The Financial Times*, 23 February.

Woo, Wing Thye, 2008. "Understanding the Sources of Friction in US–China trade relations: The Exchange Rate Debate Diverts Attention away from Optimum Adjustment," *Asian Economic Papers*, 7 (3): pp. 65–99.

Woo, Wing Thye and Liang-Yn Liu, 1995. "Investment-motivated Saving and Current Account Malaise," *Asia-Pacific Economic Review*, 1 (2): pp. 55–68.

Woo, Wing Thye and Wei Zhang, 2010. "Monetary Policy: Same Medicine, Different Outcomes in China, UK and USA," University of California, manuscript.

Woo, Wing Thye and Wei Zhang, 2010. "Time for China to Move from Macro-stability to Macro-sustainability: Making Macro-stimulus Work and Maintaining its Effects," *Journal of the Asia Pacific Economy*, 15 (4): pp. 349–68.

Woo, Wing Thye, 2001. "Recent Claims of China's Economic Exceptionalism: Reflections Inspired by WTO Accession," *China Economic Review*, 12 (2/3): pp. 107–36.

Woo, Wing Thye, Shi Li, Ximing Yue, Harry Xiaoying Wu and Xinpeng Xu, 2004. "The Poverty Challenge for China in the New Millennium," *Report to the Poverty Reduction Taskforce of the Millennium Development Goals*, Project of the United Nations. Combating: The Global Financial Crisis with Aggressive Expansionary.

Woo, Wing Thye, Wen Hai, Yibiao Jin and Gang Fan, 1994. "How Successful has Chinese Enterprise Reform Been? Pitfalls in Opposite Biases and Focus," *Journal of Comparative Economics*, 18 (3): pp. 410–37.

Woo-Cumings, Meredith, 1999. *The Developmental State* (New York: Cornell University Press).

World Bank, 1993. *The East Asian Miracle: Economic Growth and Public Policy* (Oxford: Oxford University Press).

World Bank, 2001. *China: Overcoming Rural Poverty* (Washington, DC: World Bank).

World Bank, 2011. *World Development Index (WDI) Database* accessed 3 September 2010 at http://data.worldbank.org/indicator.

Wright, Ronald, 2004. *A Short History of Progress* (Toronto: House of Anansi Press).

WSJ The Wall Street Journal.

WTO (World Trade Organization), 2009. *International Trade Statistics 2009*, Geneva. October.

WVS (World Values Survey), 2006. *World Values Survey*, Wave Four, Question V.23, 9 December 2010, available at: http://www.wvsevsdb.com/wvs/WVSAnalizeIndex.jsp.

Xiong, Wenzhao, 2005. *Daguo defang* (Great Country The Local) (Beijing: Beijing daxue chubanshe).

Yang, Rui, 2004. "Towards Massification: Higher Education Development in the People's Republic of China since 1949," in J. C. Smart (ed.) *Higher Education: Handbook of Theory and Research* XIX, pp. 311–74 (Kluwer Academic Publishers).

Yardley, Jim, 2004. "Farmers Being Moved Aside by China's Real Estate Boom," *New York Times*, 8 December, A1.

YCWLP (Yale Center for Environmental Law & Policy), 2010. *Environmental Performance Index*, Yale Center for Environmental Law & Policy, Yale University, 9 December 2010, available at: www.epi.yale.edu.

Yin, Pumin, 2005. "Sands of Time Running Out: Desertification Continues to Swallow up 'Healthy' Land at an Alarming Rate," *Beijing Review*, 16 June.

Yu, Jianrong, *2006. Nongmin weiquan kangzhen jizhaong tudi joufen, chudi chenwei nongchun shuoyao wenti* (Farmers defending their rights, land rights become a primary issue for rural areas), accessed at http://rdi.cass.cn/show_News.asp?id=6168.

Yu, Jianxing, 2008. "*Fazhan zhuyi yishi xingtai de fansi yu pipan* (Developmentalism: Reflections and Critique)." *Makesi zhuyi yanjiu* (Studies of Marxism), 11.

Yu, Yongding, 2009. "China's Policy Response to the Global Financial Crisis," *Richard Snape Lecture*, sponsored by the Productivity Commission, the Government of Australia, delivered in Melbourne, Australia, on 25 November.

ZGZZ (Zhonggong Zhongyang Zuzhibu, Zhonggong Zhongyang Dangshi Yanjiushi and Zhongyang Dang'an Ju) 2000. *Zhongguo Gongchandang Zuzhishi Ziliao* (Materials on the Organization History of the Chinese Communist Party) vols 5, 6, 7. (Beijing: Zhonggong Dangshi Chubanshe).

Zhang, Jingping, 2003. *Shishen wurenbao he tade jiebanren* (Wu Renbao the Gentleman and His Successors *Nanfeng chuang* (16).

Zhang, Jun, 2005. "*Dingzhou shijian sanbian* (Dingzhou incident and its evolution)," *Minzhu yu fazhi* (Democracy and Rule of Law) 16.

Zhang, Longxi, 2006. *Dao yu luogesi* (*Dao and Logos*) (Nanjing: Jiangsu jiaoyu chubanshe).

Zhang, Shuguang, 2008. "*Ruhe pojie zhongyang yu defang 'tudi boyi' kuanju* (How to resolve the dalimma of the central and local government on land bargaining), accessed 8 December 2009, at http://www.infzm.com/content/12915/1.

Zhang, Tingguo, 2004. "*Dao yu luogesi: zhongxi zhexue duihua de kenengxing* (Dao and Logos: the Possible Dialogue between Chinese and Western Philosophies)." *zhongguo shehui kexue* (China Social Sciences) 1.

Zhang, Wanli, 2000. "*Zhongguo shehui jieji jieceng yanjiu ershi nian* (*Two Decades of Social Class* Studies in China)," *Shehuixue yanjiu* (Sociological Studies) 1.

Zheng, Ge, 2006. *Falu yu xiandairen de mingyun* (Law and the Fate of Modern Man) (Beijing: falu chubanshe).

Zheng, Yongnian, 2010. *Zhongguo moshi: jingnian yu kunjue: zhongguo moshi* (*Chinese Model:* Experiences and Dilemmas) (Hangzhou: Zhejiang renmin chubanshe).

Zhongguo Dangshi, 2000. *Zhongguo Gongchandang Zuzhishi Ziliao* vol. 5 (Beijing: Zhongguo Dangshi Chubanshe).

Zhu, Keliang and Roy Prosterman, 2007. "Securing Land Rights for Chinese Farmers: A Leap Forward for Stability and Growth," *CATO Development Policy Analysis*, 15 October, no. 3.

Zhu, Keliang, Roy Prosterman, Jianping Ye, Ping Li, Jeffrey Riedinger and Ouyang Yiwen, 2006. "The Rural Land Question in China: Analysis and Recommendations Based on a Seventeen-province Survey," *NYU Journal of International Law & Politics*, 38 (4): pp. 761–839.

Zhu, Yunhan, 2009. *Zhongguo moshi yu quanqiu zhixu chonggou* (China Model and A Reconstruction of World Order) in Pan Wei, *zhongguo moshi* (The China Model) (Beijing: Zhongyang bianyiju).

Zweig, David, 2003. "To the Courts or to the Barricades: Can New Political Institutions Manage Rural Conflict?" in E. J. Perry and M. Selden (eds) *Chinese Society: Change, Conflict and Resistance* (New York: RoutledgeCurzon).

Index